To Daniella, Hagit, Osnat, and David

Spinoza and the Case for Philosophy

ELHANAN YAKIRA
The Hebrew University of Jerusalem

CAMBRIDGE
UNIVERSITY PRESS

32 Avenue of the Americas, New York, NY 10013-2473, USA

Cambridge University Press is part of the University of Cambridge.

It furthers the University's mission by disseminating knowledge in the pursuit of education, learning, and research at the highest international levels of excellence.

www.cambridge.org
Information on this title: www.cambridge.org/9781107069985

© Elhanan Yakira 2015

This publication is in copyright. Subject to statutory exception and to the provisions of relevant collective licensing agreements, no reproduction of any part may take place without the written permission of Cambridge University Press.

First published 2015

Printed in the United States of America

A catalog record for this publication is available from the British Library.

Library of Congress Cataloging in Publication data
Yakira, Elhanan.
Spinoza and the case for philosophy / Elhanan Yakira, The Hebrew University of Jerusalem.
  pages cm
Includes bibliographical references and index.
ISBN 978-1-107-06998-5 (hardback)
1. Spinoza, Benedictus de, 1632–1677. Ethica. 2. Ethics. I. Title.
B3974.Y35   2014
199'.492–dc23   2014020953

ISBN 978-1-107-06998-5 Hardback

Cambridge University Press has no responsibility for the persistence or accuracy of URLs for external or third-party Internet Web sites referred to in this publication and does not guarantee that any content on such Web sites is, or will remain, accurate or appropriate.

Contents

Preface	*page* vii
Acknowledgments	xiii

PART I

1. Spinoza and the Question of Religion ... 3
   1.1. *The Polemics* ... 3
   1.2. *The* Tractatus Theologico-Politicus ... 16
      1.2.a. From the *Tractatus Politicus* Back to the *Tractatus Theologico-Politicus* ... 17
      1.2.b. The *Tractatus Theologico-Politicus*: From the Refusal of Judaism to the Critique of Religion ... 23
   1.3. *Spinoza's Religiosity* ... 39
   1.4. *Spinoza as a Philosopher of Seriousness* ... 42
   1.5. *The Question of Normativity* ... 45

PART II

2. Mind and Body I: The Exegetic Inadequacy of Parallelism ... 53
   2.1. *Preliminary Remarks* ... 53
   2.2. *The Anachronism of Parallelism* ... 59
3. Mind and Body II: The Context ... 72
   3.1. *What Is It That Some Hebrews Saw as if Through the Clouds?* ... 72
      3.1.a. Contextualizing Spinoza's Mind-Body Theory ... 75
      3.1.b. A Remark on Spinoza and the Averroist Tradition ... 78
   3.2. *Spinoza's Non-Traditional Traditionalism: The* Noétique ... 83
4. Mind and Body III: *Ethics* II, Propositions 1–13 ... 93
   4.1. *The Centrality of Propositions 11 and 13* ... 93
   4.2. Ordo and Connectio *of Ideas* ... 106
      4.2.a. The Logic of Involving ... 111

    4.3. *Souls and Bodies*   116
        4.3.a. Ideas and Ideate: Primordiality and Uniqueness   118
        4.3.b. *Idea Corporis*: The Text   121
    4.4. Quis sit Idea, Quid sit Corporis   126
        4.4.a. Objective and Formal Being: The Cartesian Moment   130
        4.4.b. Objective and Formal Being in Spinoza   137
    4.5. *The Concept of Immanent Intelligibility*   151
        4.5.a. The Body   155
        4.5.b. *Idea Corporis*: What Does It Sense Like to Be a Body?   158
    4.6. *Intelligibility and Episteme*   160

PART III

5. Bodies and Ideas: A Few General Remarks   167
    5.1. *The "External" World*   167
    5.2. *The* Idea Ideae: *Consciousness, Evidence, and Method*   170
    5.3. *The Body as Being in the World*   175
    5.4. *Representation and Intentionality Problematized*   180

PART IV

6. The Norm of Reason: Adequacy, Truth, Knowledge, and Comprehension   189
    6.1. *Adequacy*   193
    6.2. *The Genetic Definition*   200
    6.3. Index sui: *The Norm of Truth*   202
    6.4. *Explaining Error and Truth*   209
    6.5. *Adequate Ideas in God and in Man*   213

7. Man, a Mode of the Substance   219
    7.1. *The Eternity of the Soul*   219
    7.2. *The Third Kind of Knowledge*   224
        7.2.a. Perfection I   232
    7.3. *Necessity, Reason, Wisdom, and Philosophy*   240
    7.4. *Perfection II (or: The Mouse and the Angel)*   249
    7.5. *The Body and Its Eternal Idea*   254
    7.6. *The Doctrine of Value*   261

    Instead of a Conclusion: *Salus sive Beatitude sive Libertas*   265

Works Cited   269
Index   281

Preface

This book is neither a general introduction to the philosophy of Spinoza nor a guide for its perplexed reader. My aim in writing was not a consistent reformulation of Spinoza's philosophy, and it is not based on the assumption that the philosophical value of a system of thought such as Spinoza's resides in its inner coherence. I did not conceive my role as a commentator to consist in uncovering an ever-eluding coherence or in overcoming real or apparent contradictions.[1] It is sometimes profitable to remain attentive to the paradoxical, counterintuitive, or even bizarre nature of some philosophical doctrines; there are cases in which one can get in this way a deeper perception of the underlying motivations beneath the surface of a philosophical discourse. Arguably, Spinoza's *Ethics* is one of these cases. As is often the case with the inner tensions or other difficulties of this kind, it is worth probing deeper into them not because we may find real or imaginary solutions to them, but rather because through the difficulties we may achieve a better understanding of the thought behind them, the philosophical discontent that led to formulating them or the stakes involved. This study of Spinoza's *Ethics* thus centers on two of its main and, undoubtedly, more difficult – even paradoxical – doctrines, offering a close reading of them; it also contains an attempt to insert theses doctrines within a larger framework. This gives it what might seem a somewhat unusual structure. One reason for

---

[1] The great historian of philosophy, Marital Gueroult, is the author of one of the most authoritative studies of Spinoza; in two large volumes he offered a comprehensive interpretation of the first two parts of the *Ethics*, still unavoidable for any serious reading of Spinoza (there is a third, posthumous volume containing his unfinished study of the rest of the *Ethics*). In a number of other works (among them studies of Descartes, Leibniz, Shlomo Maimon, and more) he applied a general conception of the nature of philosophical writing and, based on it, of the work of the interpreter. He called this conception *Dianoématique*, and a number of posthumous volumes (see the Works Cited section) contain his hermeneutical theory, based on the idea that what makes a work or thought into a philosophy is mostly its inner coherence.

this is the following: I have been writing this book, intermittently, over a long period of time. Leaving it periodically to do other things, I kept coming back to it, always changing, revising, and rewriting large portions. A few core positions and ideas remained more or less stable, but much of the rest – structure, scope, content, style, and so on – evolved and changed continually. As the material was accumulating, threatening to get out of hand, I made two, as it were, strategic decisions: to keep the book within reasonable size, and to limit myself to those matters on which I thought I had something to add to the abundant and often learned and insightful literature on Spinoza.

There is, however, more to it. Specifically, the book concentrates on two sections of the *Ethics*: the first thirteen propositions of the second part and the last twenty propositions of the fifth part. These are, respectively, the epicenter of Spinoza's so-called mind-body doctrine and the doctrine of salvation. I chose to concentrate on these rather short texts because I believe that the question of *salvation*, or of what Spinoza calls by this name (but also by the names *beatitude* and *freedom*), is what everything leads to and what his philosophy was in the last analysis all about; and obviously, the *soul* or mind (*mens*) is where the stakes of the search for freedom and salvation are played. The *Ethics*, and the entire Spinozistic corpus, contain of course various other things, many of which have been studied for their own sake, often with great philosophical gain. The doctrine of salvation and freedom, of salvation as freedom, and of freedom as salvation, however, has not always been one of them and is often seen as Spinoza's most enigmatic doctrine, at least by his more strictly philosophical readers. It may become perhaps less so if one takes into account the fact that these two groups of propositions – EIIp1–13 and EVp21–42 – are profoundly connected in many ways; in fact, they remain largely incomprehensible if the links – explicit or semi-implicit – that connect them are not analyzed in a systemic way. I would even venture to say that they add up to a kind of thematic axis, a theoretical scaffolding supporting the whole edifice of Spinoza's philosophy. Their conjoint study would thus hopefully afford a point of entry into the Spinozistic world and a clue to the Spinozistic conundrum.

Hence the decision to concentrate on these two sections of the *Ethics*. But there was a price to pay for this decision and for the wish not to exceed the limits I set for myself regarding the book's eventual volume: I had to neglect almost everything else. I had to assume that what I did not address in this book is of secondary importance for my main purposes, but also that it was well known to most students of Spinoza and sufficiently studied in the secondary literature. I addressed these matters only to the extent that it seemed to me indispensable for making sense of what I considered essential.

Yet this book was not conceived as a monographic study of one or two local themes. It was meant to offer a more general outlook. Many of the students of Spinoza's philosophy share a strong sense that the *Ethics* in particular, and his *oeuvre* in general, revolve around a central and fundamental interest, some elusive and hard-to-define thematic *core*, that there is in it something that can be described as a *project*. Insofar as this study of the *Ethics* is, as has just been said, the outcome of long years of reading and reflecting on Spinoza's philosophy, indeed of struggling with it, it also expresses an attempt to come to terms with this philosophy in its entirety, to get to its core, to assess Spinoza's philosophy as a philosophical project. This core, or project, would be best described, I believe, as a fundamental grappling with religion, and its significance can be assessed only by contextualizing it, both thematically and historically, within the horizon of what Leo Strauss for one called the "Critique of Religion."

In itself, of course, there is nothing original in this observation.[2] Spinoza's place in the history of the *question of religion* has been very largely studied, and more so nowadays than ever before. But it is usually dealt with from historical or theological-political perspectives – that is, either from the perspective of the study of the advent of modernity and of secularism, or from that of philosophical discussion of the claims of religion (or of what is taken to be the claims of religion) for having a moral, and even more so political, saying. My perspective is different. The *Ethics*, unlike the *Tractatus Theologico-Politicus*, is not concerned directly with the question of religion as a historical, civilizational, or theological-political question. It can be said, however, that it presupposes the critique of religion consummate and the religious prejudice demolished, and that this had been the condition permitting the free philosophical inquiry, reflection, and search for salvation that the *Ethics* now purports to conduct. It begins thus where the *Tractatus Theologico-Politicus* ends. But the critique of religion and, consequently, the question of religion, and even religion itself, remain very much present in the *Ethics*, not always above the surface, but in a real and very pertinent manner all the same. What Spinoza was doing in it can perhaps be described as the transformation of the historical facticity of the *problem of religion* into a trans-historical philosophical reflection that can, and should, be discussed on its own philosophical and argumentative terms.

All these different and somewhat conflicting considerations – the wish to avoid excessive length, to concentrate on what is both central and less satisfactorily dealt with in the secondary literature, to read very closely only two relatively short sections of the *Ethics* but to use them in order to offer a general assessment of the project, to read them philosophically but to understand them within the context and historicity of the *critique of religion* – result in the perhaps somewhat unusual structure of this book. It comprises four parts, the two longer ones of exegetical nature, the other two more general. Although hope-

---

[2] Only when I was already applying the finishing touches to the manuscript of this book did I read Steven B. Smith's latest book on Spinoza. Although very different in approach and in understanding many of Spinoza's central doctrines, Smith's book has some similar aspects to the present study of Spinoza – it is also an attempt to give a kind of general assessment of Spinoza's philosophy (more political and less metaphysical than mine), and it is based on a similar assumption – more directly Straussian than mine again – about the place of the critique of religion in shaping Spinoza's fundamental philosophical worldview; see especially Smith (2003), chapter 7.

fully adding up to one coherent whole, each of the four parts can be considered as a relatively independent essay and even read without the others.

Part I contains an attempt, more thematic than historical, to inscribe the ensuing reading of Spinoza within the context of the critique of religion. It deals, in a rather general way, with the essentially polemic nature of Spinoza's philosophy, with the *Tractatus Theologico-Politicus*, and with Spinoza's position vis-à-vis his Jewish background, notably Maimonides. It then raises, again in a general way, the question of Spinoza's religiosity and discusses it in relation to two famous attempts to define the specific nature of "the religious," namely Rudolf Otto's and William James's.

Part II is a study of Spinoza's conception of the unity that holds between the body and its soul (or mind). It comprises three chapters. The first (Chapter 2) is an attempt to refute the famous parallelism interpretative paradigm; the second (Chapter 3) examines the thematic, and to some extent historical, background against which the discussion contained in the first thirteen propositions of *Ethics* II has to be read; in the third (Chapter 4) I offer my interpretation of Spinoza's mind-body doctrine. It is not based on the parallelism paradigm but on the double contention that the soul is an idea (EIIp11) and that its object is the body (EIIp13).

Part III (Chapter 5) tries to put Spinoza's mind-body doctrine, discussed in Part II, in the perspective of a few later-day philosophical discussions of questions related to this topic, thus hopefully gaining better understanding both of Spinoza's stance and of the larger philosophical stakes involved in his positions.[3]

Part IV (Chapters 6 and 7) is a discussion of the doctrine of *salus, sive beatitude, sive libertas* as it is expounded in the second half of EV. At its center is the contention, which can also be regarded as the conclusion of this study of Spinoza's *Ethics*, that this final moment of the *Ethics* is incomprehensible if it is not understood as fundamentally a theory of the irreducible value of being and of human existence in general and of philosophical life in particular.

An anonymous early reviewer of this book for Cambridge University Press suspected that it was written in an overly emphasized "French scholarly idiom." Following the reviewer's remarks, I made a few adjustments in the original manuscript. I hope it is now more comfortably situated in an English idiom. But the question of the book's French background merits perhaps a few words of explanation. I spent, in fact, many years in France, and one of the main things I was doing there was studying Spinoza. This took place largely at a

---

[3] The discipline called "The History of Philosophy" is a peculiar occupation. It is not exactly history, and whether it is philosophy or not – and if it is, in what way – is a matter of much controversy. Leibniz once said that the best way to gain philosophical understanding is to use the comparative method. Following his advice, and in order to transcend the philological attitude, I thus tried to put my reading of Spinoza's text in perspective and "compare" it, in some Leibnizian way, to a few later-day philosophical enquiries. This was the rationale behind adding Chapter 5 immediately after the section devoted to an analysis of Spinoza's mind-body doctrine.

Preface xi

time when Paris was the undisputed capital of Spinoza scholarship, and when in the English-speaking philosophical world there was only a trickle of writings continuing an always-present but relatively marginal Spinozistic tradition. Like their colleagues from other places, some of the few American – there were even fewer British – scholars who were interested in those years in Spinoza were much involved with French Spinoza scholarship. In later years the trickle has turned, as someone has put it to me, into a tsunami, and nowadays there are probably more publications on Spinoza in English than in any other language, perhaps in all languages combined. Becoming more self-sufficient and self-confident, the young American community of Spinoza scholars has perhaps become also less open to French – or other – idioms than it used to be.

It is indeed undeniable that my own writing on Spinoza echoes the years I spent in France and my ongoing interest in what has been written and done there since. But this is only part of the story. In the 1970s and 1980s, there was not only a vibrant community of older and younger scholars united by a common interest in the philosophy of Spinoza, a common philosophical culture, and – as is often the case in France – a great deal of first-rate erudition (all this is still the case today), but also a sense of breaking new ground: discovering the importance of Spinoza as a political thinker.[4] There had been a widespread and philosophically significant presence of Spinoza in French thought and scholarship beforehand and indeed from the time of Spinoza himself, but now a *New Spinoza* would have emerged, as announces the title of a book published in the late 1990s[5] that purports to introduce the new French Spinoza scholarship to the English-speaking audience. The "New" here refers, however, not just to a new theoretical or historical-philosophical understanding of Spinoza himself, but rather to an allegedly new general materialist philosophy, or ideological-political understanding of human reality as essentially carnal, political, and social, and of which Spinoza would be a quasi-prophetic announcer.

It looks sometimes – in any case, it looked so to me in those years in Paris – that with the decline of Marxism and the fading of the figure of Marx,[6] a new

---

[4] As Moreau (2005, p. 5) notes, citing Alexandre Matheron – both, belonging to two different generations, important contributors to this discovery – before the 1960s, Spinoza's political thought was more or less ignored in France.

[5] See Montag and Stolze (1997). For the history of the earlier reception of Spinoza in France, see Vernière (1954); see also Montag for the ideological stakes involved in the kind of scholarship he expounds both in his own book on Spinoza (1999) and in the collection of essays he edited with T. Stolze (1997).

[6] Much has been written on this chapter of the cultural-political-intellectual French history. A captivating and compelling story of a philosophical and political itinerary, from the École Normale Supèrieure, via the resistance, to the Communist Party and to an eventual disenchantment, is told in Desanti (2001). Jean-Tossaint Desanti was my instructor during the years I studied in Paris, and I have nothing but good things to say about him, both as a person and as a philosopher. He wrote a number of things on Spinoza, some of them very interesting. Among other things, he wrote a "materialistic" book when he was regarded as the "official intellectual" of the Communist Party, which he wished, as he once told me many years later, he had never written.

figure – Spinoza – appeared as a surrogate materialist prophet. With it, however, emerged also a robust and authentically philosophical interest in Spinoza as a political and social thinker. Although often ideologically motivated, it is beyond doubt that some first-rate scholarly work has been done during those years and by the New Spinoza Spinozists. Some were good and some less so, but some fresh insights into the nature of Spinoza's philosophy were offered, and some previously largely neglected aspects of his thought were vigorously studied. I was a witness to these developments; I had the chance to know most of its protagonists, and quite a few of them became personal friends. But I was never completely absorbed by this scholarship, even less so by the dogmatics underlying it, and I never felt either the will or the ability to immerse myself fully in the French idiom.[7] I never thought, for example, that Spinoza was a materialist any more than he was a mystic, and I have never had much sympathy for the attempts to appropriate an alleged Spinozism, savage or not, by one ideological school or another.

That all this echoes in my own writing on Spinoza is unavoidable. Being, however, partially inside and partially outside the French idiom – in fact, in the English idiom too – is not necessarily such a bad thing. I would add here, however, that what follows is imbued with yet another idiom: the Hebrew idiom. It may be less conspicuous to many readers, but it is perhaps more important than all the others. For despite being written in English, and despite the resonance of the French idiom in it, the vantage point from which it was written is that of Hebrew-speaking reader of and writer about Spinoza, and of the acute and special form the problem of religion assumes in Jerusalem, Tel Aviv, or Haifa.[8]

---

[7] The very instructive, and sometimes hilarious, Cusset (2008) depicts the emergence in America of at least partially fictional "French Theory." A kind of suspicion of things French, mainly philosophical, that is not rare among English-speaking writers and readers is arguably just as exaggerated as the admiration of "French Theory," "Critical Theory," "New Materialism," and so on that one finds in other quarters of American and British academe (and elsewhere).

[8] I take this opportunity to pay tribute to a teacher and scholar practically unknown outside Israel, but who had been very instrumental in making Spinoza a central figure in the study and teaching of philosophy in Israel. He was also the teacher who first awakened my own interest in Spinoza. Yossef Ben Shlomo (1930–2007) was a professor of philosophy and later of Jewish thought at the Hebrew University and at Tel Aviv University. A charismatic teacher and a connoisseur of Spinoza, but also of the Jewish tradition, Jewish philosophy, and the Kabbalah, Ben Shlomo wrote relatively little, almost exclusively in Hebrew. Noteworthy are the very detailed notes – in fact comprehensive commentaries – he added to the Hebrew translations of the TIE and the *Short Treatise*. Shortly after the current book was ready to go to the Press, there appeared a posthumous volume containing, under the title *The Challenge of Spinozism* (in Hebrew), a number of studies on Spinoza and on the reception of his philosophy. Ben Shlomo, like me, saw this "challenge" as mainly a challenge to religious thought; unlike myself, however, he considered Spinoza's work as the expression of deep religiosity, which he interpreted as a kind of quasi-mystical sentiment of union with the "whole."

Acknowledgments

As this book has been written over a long period of time, I have had the opportunity to discuss it on many occasions – in class, at conferences, in more or less formal settings – and with many people. Quite a few friends and colleagues read parts of it or the whole manuscript or heard me talking about it – not always knowing that what they heard was parts of, as it is sometimes called, a "work in progress." Many of them often made useful comments or raised pertinent, sometimes difficult and challenging questions. I would like to thank, in a general way, the diverse audiences that listened to me talking about Spinoza over the years, and in particular the many students who attended my classes, in Israel and elsewhere, which were often used by me as sounding boards for the ideas I had been trying to develop. In the course of these dialogues with friends, colleagues, unknown critics, and students, I discovered more than once that I was heading toward dead ends. I hope I avoided many traps thanks to these exchanges, although probably not all of them.

There are, however, a few people I would like to thank here in a more direct way. I have cooperated for many years with Yirmiyahu Yovel, first as his student at the Hebrew University, then assisting him in establishing and running the Spinoza Institute in Jerusalem, and finally as his colleague in the department of philosophy. Eli Zilbepfening, Yoash Meisler, and, in particular, Emily Grosholz with real friendship and in a very helpful way read the manuscript and discussed it with me. Yoram Navon was a demanding and challenging editor. His help in turning writing that was not always clear and coherent into a more respectable text was invaluable.

I was carrying this manuscript with me to many places. I worked on it in the gorgeous Rockefeller Foundation Bellagio Center, during visits to the École Normale Supérieure in Paris and to the one in Lyon, to the École des Hautes Études en Sciences Sociales, also in Paris, and, more recently, at the Institute for the Study of Contemporary Antisemitism of Indiana University in

Bloomington, where I spent two long, pleasant, and fruitful sabbatical leaves and where I finished writing this book. I made many friends there, and I would like to thank all of them here, in particular my hosts, Professor Alvin Rosenfeld and his wife Erna.

This book was published with the support of the Israel Science Foundation as well as the Research Committee of the Faculty of Humanities, the Hebrew University of Jerusalem.

PART I

1

Spinoza and the Question of Religion

1.1. The Polemics

Spinoza's philosophy is thoroughly polemical. It is no less polemical than inventive of a positive philosophical content, and even when it does not appear as a straightforward polemic, his thought unfolds as a movement of constant defiance, of an incessant questioning of fundamental conventions and of universally accepted truths, a shaking of the supposedly firm foundation of the Christian civilization within which his otherwise most radical contemporaries – Hobbes, for instance – were living and thinking. Unlike most of his contemporaries, he had to carve a niche for himself – philosophically but also existentially – in a world in which he could take nothing for granted. He was a marginal member of the *République des lettres*, a somewhat outlandish figure – he is often called "the Jew" – and modest contributor to the so-called scientific revolution, but a definitely well-informed interlocutor of some of its more illustrious leaders. A renegade Jew living in relative comfort and acceptance by his non-confessional Christian neighbors, he had basically four main traditions within which he could shape his life and thought: the emerging new science and the new scientific ethos; the Cartesian school of philosophy; the religious tradition, both Jewish and Christian, mainly Calvinist and reformist; and the tradition of thinking about the state in republican terms. His thought grew as a complex dialogue with these traditions, without ever fully belonging to any of them. Needless to say, if we are still studying Spinoza so intensively, there must be something in his thought that transcends the immediacy of the concrete discussions, debates, and quarrels in which his thought was inscribed; but it cannot be fully understood and its universal or timeless value, as one may call it, assessed outside the context of its emergence. The complex stance he took vis-à-vis his cultural, political, social, spiritual, and intellectual surroundings, the partial acceptance and radical criticism, the marginality and awkward participation, the notoriety and suspicion – all added up to a very unusual mode of life and philosophical enterprise. Within this complex and multifaceted experience, the critique, even revolt, was necessarily part of the positive life and thought project. Spinoza's critique of religion, of the theologico-political or of Jewish theology and of Jewish tradition and ways of life in a more general way, of Cartesianism as well, has a generally acknowledged historical importance; but it is also very important for any attempt to understand the positive content of his philosophy. The polemics is a constitutive element of his philosophy, not, however, only in its *negativity*, or as a critical stance vis-à-vis some fundamental aspects of the theologico-political-philosophical reality in which he was living, but also from the point of view of the positive content of his philosophy.

Is there something that can be described as the core of the Spinozistic philosophical project? Whereas Descartes was imbued with enthusiasm upon having discovered his vocation as looking for the foundations of an *inventi mirabilis*,[1] an enthusiasm lurking in the background of his entire scientific-philosophical enterprise, Spinoza – at least if one takes seriously his own presentation of his philosophy – was looking all his life for a "permanent and lasting joy."[2] This engages religion in a much more intimate way than, say, the question of whether the sun revolves around Earth or vice versa. For Spinoza may well have had some other things on his mind (scientific issues, technical matters concerning lens grinding, or, more importantly, questions about the desirable form of government), but above all, his thinking was about what he usually called by such terms as "salvation," "beatitude," and "freedom." This was the core of his philosophy and its deepest motivation, at least as I understand his philosophical enterprise. This means that he had a complex attitude toward the Cartesian conception of what philosophy is all about. It also follows that he had a very singular attitude toward religion.

Is it correct to say that Spinoza's philosophy is "religious" in any way? Is there in it some form of religiosity that it shares with the established religions? Does it perhaps articulate the very essence of religion? This is the question I raise in this preliminary chapter.

That Spinoza was a radical critic, indeed an unyielding and determined opponent, of organized religion, of the role it covets for itself in the state, of what to him was the usurpation of political power, is well known. That he was a trenchant critic of superstitious, irrational, and simple-minded religion or of theology is, again, inseparable from his fame. Whether, however, he should be ranged on the side of deism, or as an advocate of some kind of universal, natural, or rational religion, is another matter.

---

[1] As he calls it in the *Olympiques*, where he recounts the semi-mystical experience he had during the night between November 10 and 11 of 1619, AT, X, 216. Baillet calls it "les fondements de la science admirable," which are, roughly, the metaphysical foundation of the new mathematical physics.

[2] TIE, §§ 1–14.

1.1. The Polemics

The question about Spinoza and religion is, of course, not new. It has been a permanent theme in the diverse reactions to his thought. This has been the case ever since, and even before, he began to write and to be read by others. The dramatic event of his breach with the Jewish-Portuguese community of Amsterdam, the famous *Herem* or excommunication (literally, ban), clearly concerned religion, although we know very little about the exact accusations leveled at him. Yet in the particular way religion was practiced and thought about by the Jews of Amsterdam, it was more a matter of identity or way of life and, above all, of allegiance (to the congregation, to a tradition, to a certain historical community) than a matter of profession of faith and doctrine.[3] I shall add a few remarks on the thorny question of Spinoza and Judaism in the section on the *Tractatus Theologico-Politicus* later in this chapter. Whatever the exact nature of Spinoza's intercourse with the Jews and Judaism, and whatever the exact case against him in the *herem* affair, it is certain that already during his short lifetime Spinoza became known as an enemy of religion, and his reputation as an atheist – later, due mainly to Pierre Bayle as the "virtuous atheist" – had spread rapidly far beyond his city of birth. The famous *pantheismus Streit* was again about religion, or more accurately, about God;[4] and if we are to believe Jonathan Israel and a growing number of other writers on the question of "modernity,"[5] Spinoza was the major, or at least a major, figure in the advent of secularity in Europe. For Leo Strauss Spinoza was, alongside Epicure, Averroes, Hobbes, and a few others, an archetypal critic of religion.

In our time the debate over the religious character of Spinozism continues. Some think he was an atheist; others maintain that his thought, non-confessional as it may be,[6] is nevertheless suffused with deep and authentic religiosity, that his metaphysics of God articulates a religious point of view on Nature and on man, that it expresses even a kind of mystical experience. The constant use of religious language, of doctrines such as that of the eternity of the soul or of the intellectual love of God, seem to some readers of the *Ethics* to allow for

---

[3] A permanent theme in the Jewish anti-Spinoza writings is that of betrayal. Most known among these accusations are Herman Cohen's and Emanuel Levinas's. Recapitulating the same kind of claims, in an extremely severe, provocative, and even violent way, obliquely directed toward contemporary discourses about the Jews, about Zionism, and about the State of Israel, by some allegedly *compagnons de route* of Spinoza's, is Milner (2013). Not less harsh critique of Spinoza's attitude towards the Jews and their traditions can be found in a number of Henry Méchoulan's works (e.g., 1985 and, in particular, 2013). For presentations of the circumstances and roots of Spinoza's breach with the Jewish community of Amsterdam, see, among others, Kaplan (1989); Yovel (1992), Méchoulan (1991), and Meinsma (1983); Lagrée's and Moreau's introduction to their French translation of the TTP (1990) has a comprehensive bibliography; Nadler (2001) is an inquiry into the possible reasons of the *herem* and its unusual severity.
[4] See, among others, Beiser (1987). Goetschel (2004) is particularly valuable for the emphasis it puts on Spinoza's Jewishness.
[5] See Israel, (2002), (2006), (2010).
[6] After leaving Amsterdam Spinoza was living mainly among what is sometimes referred to as "church-less Christians"; on these sects, see Kolakowsky (1969).

a reading of this text as a quasi-mystical one, comparable to some allegedly similar Kabalistic attitudes.[7] Others, again, opine that there could not be a more radical opposition to the mystical spirit and to the religious attitude than his alleged rationalism.

This continual questioning is the general framework of the present study of the *Ethics* of Spinoza, and the historical and philosophical "question of religion," as I shall refer to it here, is the general backdrop against which, I believe, it was written and against which it should be read. Thus, a central assumption guiding the present study is that Spinoza's philosophy is shaped by a fundamental struggle with religion. Even when he deals with matters that are not usually considered religious, the full sense of Spinoza's often-idiosyncratic positions can be appreciated only if his grappling with religion is taken into consideration. As explained in the Preface, the first part of this book is devoted to a close reading of Spinoza's so-called mind-body doctrine. The mind-body question is usually not regarded, especially in contemporary philosophical literature, as part of the question of religion. But the full significance of Spinoza's particular mind-body doctrine can be, I think, understood only in the context of the discussion that closes the *Ethics*, namely the doctrine of "salvation, beatitude and freedom," the culmination of both the polemic against religion and of his attempt to describe finally the permanent and lasting joy he had long been seeking. That Spinoza's theory of the human soul can be read today with such great interest as a significant contribution to the discussion of the so-called mind-body question is a tribute to his great philosophical acumen; its success threatens, however, to obscure its deeper philosophical significance.

How, then, should one describe Spinoza's attitude toward religion, his philosophical, fundamental position vis-à-vis religion? Is it religious, anti-religious, or religiously neutral? Opinions vary considerably as to how to understand Spinoza's attitude to religion, faith, or God. For instance, there is Novalis's famous "God intoxicated man." Or Ernest Renan's no less famous exclamation (in his address at The Hague on the occasion of the unveiling of the Spinoza monument in February 1877) that from his granite pedestal the philosopher "shall teach everyman the way to happiness he himself had found; and for ages to come the cultivated man who passes along the Pavilioengragt will inwardly say, 'It is here, perhaps, that God has been seen most near!'" But some find his "abstractions" cold as the snow on the top of an icy mountain,[8] while others think Spinoza is the main forerunner of the modern materialist vision of society or of man, of the Freudian deconstruction of religious consciousness, of neo-atheism, not to speak of secularism in its more political or theologico-political

---

[7] While others dismiss it as incomprehensible or at least incompatible with Spinoza's rationalistic philosophy, most famously by Jonathan Bennett but also, albeit with more moderation, by others, for example, Edwin Curley.
[8] Hessing (1977).

1.1. The Polemics

manifestations. Bayle, as we have just mentioned, thought that Spinoza was an atheist. He actually regarded him as a prototypical atheist and even modeled his definition of atheism on Spinoza as he understood him. Atheism, he says in his *Thoughts on the Comet*, boils down "to this general doctrine, that nature is the cause of all things; that she exists eternally, and by herself, and that she acts according to the whole extent of her powers and according to immutable laws which she does not know."[9] A more curious, but nevertheless typical, description is attributable to Tony Negri, who sees in Spinoza a "religious atheist."[10]

Was Spinoza indeed an atheist? Was he religious? Can one be both religious *and* an atheist? These terms, and many others like them, are notoriously difficult to define, and any discussion of them often deteriorates into what Spinoza described as arguing about words, not things. He himself denied being an atheist on several occasions, for example in a letter from the end of 1665 to Oldenburg, where he explained that one of the three reasons for writing the *Tractatus Theologico-Politicus* was "[t]he opinion of me held by the common people, who constantly accuse me of atheism. I am driven to avert this accusation, too, as far as I can."[11] Was he honest in writing these words? Being accused of atheism could be rather dangerous in those days, especially if his place in society was that of "the Jew." But there is also no real reason to suppose any deception on Spinoza's part. Rather than question Spinoza's frankness, one should ask what he might have meant by denying that he was an atheist.

If "atheism" means arguing that the term "god" is empty, then Spinoza, of course, was no atheist; but if it means something along the lines of Bayle's description, then he certainly was. The meaning of the term changes with time, even if it is taken in a very general sense as the outright denial of the existence of God.[12] An illuminating attempt to bring some conceptual order to the question of atheism can be found in an uncompleted early essay by the Russian-French philosopher Alexandre Kojève, which bears the simple title *L'athéism*. Kojève remarks there that a person can significantly be said to be a *theist* only if God is for him something that is religiously effective.[13] Inversely, one can

---

[9] Cited according to Bayle (2004), "Présentation," 28. The longest entry in Bayle's dictionary is on Spinoza; for an English translation and general presentation, see Van Bunge et al. (2011), 85–106.

[10] See Negri (1997). One could just as well say of Spinoza that he was an "anti-religious theist (or a deist, or a God-ist)." Negri's full unorthodox views of Spinoza are expounded in his (1991).

[11] Letter 30, Shirley 844.

[12] Is atheism the lack of a belief in God, or the positive belief that there is no God? In the latter case, is atheism after all a belief? See, for example, the "General Introduction" as well as some of the contributions in Martin (2007). The last decade or so has seen the emergence of a very wide new, or renewed, interest in the question of religion, both in the form of a "New Atheism," of what can be considered as a "New Apologetic," and under the purportedly more theoretical study, much of this done under the title of the "theologico-political." See, among others, Amarasingam (2010), De Vries and Sullivan (2006), and Bellah and Tipton (2006).

[13] Kojève (1998), 82–83. This work was published posthumously, and it constitutes a kind of blueprint for the philosophical outlook he would develop later.

say that at least in modern times, an *atheist* is someone who has an effectively *anti*-religious concept of the *non*-existence of God; or, which is more pertinent to the question of Spinoza and religion, that an *atheist* is also someone who has a non-religious, or a religiously ineffective, or counter-effective, concept of God. As has been said by many students of the question of religion, the modern question of God is more about religion than about God, and the question of faith has become a question of belief in belief.[14] In this sense, if one grants, at least for the sake of argument, that Spinoza has settled, or believed he had settled, the *philosophical* question of God, what remains completely open is the question of religion.

Some neo-atheists find in Spinoza a venerable forerunner.[15] There is some truth in this self-assigned pedigree, but also a good deal of typical misappropriation. Atheism – taken in its vague, but useful, sense – has in fact always accompanied religion and already the Psalmist (53, 2) talks of the "fool who hath said in his heart, there is no God."[16] But it becomes a significant social, cultural, and intellectual phenomenon only around Spinoza's times, and the problem was indeed religion not less than God. Blaise Pascal – to take just one, very significant example – wrote his *Pensées* as a comprehensive defense of the Christian religion against the indifference or positive opposition of the atheist, incarnated in the figure of the *libertin*.[17] But the God on whose existence he invited the atheist to wager was a *Deus absconditus*, an unseen and unknowable God leaving man to a solitary and tragic existence; more than a belief in belief, he was talking on the *need* to believe, and what he was trying mainly to do was to convince the *libertin* to become Christian, not to prove the existence of God.

If we take seriously what Spinoza tells us at the beginning of his *Treatise on the Emendation of the Intellect*, then one can affirm that for both Pascal and Spinoza the question of eternity – of eternal joy or of the eternal life of the soul – was the most urgent question; and yet, one can hardly think of two more far apart answers to this question than theirs. But is this question necessarily a

---

[14] Mark Lila has recently expressed this idea by saying that the "crisis" of modernity consists, in the context of what concerns us here, in that "political philosophy would no longer concern itself with God ... [but] with man as a believer in God" – see Lila (2007), pp. 297–298. Lila sees in Hobbes the main and practically the sole initiator of this change, and hardly mentions Spinoza. "Belief in belief" is a phrase used by A. Macintyre who says, in Macintyre (1969), similar things. This explains also why from Durkheim and Weber until our own days, religion has become a sociological problem as much as a theological one.

[15] Among the numerous recent publications advocating the cause of atheism, I shall mention here only Hitchens (2007) and Dawkins (2008); less partisan and more scholarly is Minois (1998).

[16] According to the King James Version. The Hebrew text says נבל, which should perhaps be translated not as "fool," but as "scoundrel" or something like it. It means in Hebrew a morally evil person.

[17] Macintyre, op. cit., p. 12 suspects that Pascal "treated atheism as a serious option for the first time in theistic history."

1.1. The Polemics

religious question? I would venture to say that this is where the most important stakes of a philosophical understanding of Spinozism are played. The great complexity of these stakes arises from the fact that Spinoza, in fact, envisages philosophy – his own philosophy in the first place, but also "philosophy" as a name of a general attitude or way of life, a "love of wisdom" – as what should replace religion as a comprehensive doctrine of the good life; not however – and this is important – as a form of life shared by all, but as a philosophical life, open to the few who are capable of serious theoretical thinking along the lines he traced in his *Ethics*. This, however, means something more than offering a surrogate dogma to the dogmas advocated by the religions existing around him; it means, in the first place, a radical and complex criticism of the most fundamental presuppositions of what he must have conceived as a religious conception of God, world, and man.

I believe, contrary to what is sometimes said or implied, that Spinoza did not see himself as, and to an even lesser degree was, in the foremost a kind of social and political critic or reformer, let alone a revolutionary, or that Spinozism can be conceived as a blueprint for a post-religious state and society or even human existence in some general sense. What was the impact, influence, or historical role of his philosophy in the advent of modernity is one question; what is the core of his philosophy as a written corpus is another. The salvation, beatitude, and freedom he spoke about should not be interpreted, I believe, in other than a very personal, elitist manner, but also as what was, from his own philosophical point of view, the most important, the only *really* important, thing in the sense, at least, that everything else derives its sense and value from it. He was, of course, among the early modern advocates of liberal democracy or, more accurately, of democratic republicanism, but this was not necessarily what he conceived as most important. His attempt to formulate a positive theory of democracy (in the unfinished third part of the *Tractatus Politicus*) was aborted by his early death, and his main remaining political work, the *Tractatus Theologico-Politicus*, is a critique of theocracy more than a positive political theory. This applies also to the later chapters of this work, where some central themes of political theory are addressed as well as to the first chapters where theocracy is directly criticized. Spinoza expresses here a great suspicion of the role religion fulfills in the state, and this suspicion indeed extends to almost everything else that usually falls under the heading "religion," including, in particular, its claim to be the bearer of a special understanding of the ultimate structure of reality and the meaning of Being. But his philosophical attitude toward religion expresses some kind of inverted respect that is completely absent from his political theory. Consequently, there is a permanent tension between the political and the more largely philosophical dealings with religion in his work. Politically, he was one of the most astute and trenchant advocates of the full submission of religion to the authority of the state, a major voice – alongside, notably, Machiavelli and Hobbes – in the emerging discourse about the *practical* need to "tame religion"[18] and the *theoretical* doctrine of the superiority of the "political" over the "theological." But unlike Hobbes and Machiavelli, political philosophy never occupied for him the place of *philosophia prima* and, as I have just suggested, he was, in the last analysis, much closer to Pascal in seeing salvation and the eternity of the soul as the most important question of intellectual labor than to any of them.

Historically speaking, secularization, or a deep mutation in the status of religion – in the public sphere, the private sphere, and the intellectual and theoretical domains – can undoubtedly be considered an essential element of what we call "modernity." It is not a matter of much controversy, moreover, that the seventeenth century was a pivotal moment in the history of Western civilization in general and the historical epicenter of the momentous secularizing transformation it went through in particular. Whether conceived as the "disenchantment" of the world (Max Weber), the *sortie de la religion* being a trans-historical beginning with the first crystallization of public ritual; whether one considers the history of religion (and of secularization) a part of a comprehensive evolution of humankind;[19] whether modernity is seen as a radical novelty, a "crisis of civilization" as it was described by Paul Hazard and many others;[20] whether its legitimacy, or the irreducibility of what was new in it, is defended or questioned;[21] whether seen as surpassed by a welcome or an unwelcome, real or imagined "return of the religious" or not, religion and its negation by secularization and secularism are almost universally seen as essential for any attempt at self-understanding by modern man. Are there atheist religions like, perhaps, Buddhism (Alexandre Kojève)? Can one talk of divinities outside organized, institutionalized, traditional religions (Deism)? Does it make sense to talk of "civil religion" (Rousseau, Robert Bella, lately Ronald Beiner)? Or of "secular religions" (Raymond Aron, Eric Voegelin)? These and many more similar questions can be studied from the point of view of political history and theory,[22] from sociological, economic, and psychological points of view, from that of the theologian, or in any other way, but few of the very big number of scholars and writers of all kinds who invoke it seem to question either the importance of the seventeenth century for any interrogation of the nature and role of religion in modern times or, more importantly from our present point of view, the centrality of the question of religion for the upheavals – political, theologico-political, social, intellectual, philosophical – that added up to what has come to be known as "early modernity."

---

[18] See, e.g., Beiner (2011): "What to do with religion? This is an inescapable problem of politics" (p. 2). Spinoza was undoubtedly one of those who asked this question with a great sense of urgency.

[19] See Gauchet (1999) and Bellah (2011).

[20] See Hazard (1990). Hazard's book was first published in French almost a century ago and only recently translated into English. It has not lost its importance. See also Macintyre and Lila, op. cit.

[21] See, among others, Blumenberg (1983) and Taylor (2007).

[22] Bourdin (2010) is particularly illuminating.

1.1. The Polemics

The period during which Baruch-Bento, becoming Benedictus, Spinoza came to age and then produced what is acknowledged almost universally as a paramount philosophical work was a period dominated by theologico-political and philosophical-theological and even scientific-theological – in short, religious – fundamental questioning. This questioning, in fact, occupied the public space almost in its entirety. This was the reality into which Spinoza was born, as a Jew in Amsterdam, as a citizen in the Dutch United Provinces, as a European, and as a member of the *République des lettres*. The Jewish-Sephardic community of Amsterdam had been founded only a few decades before his birth, Jews being allowed to settle in the city only under many restrictions. The Thirty Years' War ended in the Peace of Munster in 1646, and with it began the consolidation of the Modern European system of states, when Spinoza was fourteen years old. This was also the year the Spanish-Dutch war ended. Descartes was working during these years not only on developing his "magnificent science" but also on trying to surmount the opposition of a number of powerful Calvinist theologians who sought to censure his writings. Galileo was condemned by the Inquisition in 1633, one year after Spinoza's birth. Pascal died in 1662, some three years before Spinoza began working on the TTP.[23] In 1670 Pierre Bayle had to flee France after having reconverted to Protestantism, and in the years before Spinoza's death the young and restless Leibniz was already trying in diverse ways to enhance the ecumenical case.

Boyle – one of Spinoza earliest correspondents (via the good services of Oldenburg)[24] – Hobbes, Pascal, Bayle, Leibniz, Locke, even Newton, and dozens of others more or less well-remembered men, a few women as well, in fact almost the entire *République des lettres*, were all preoccupied with the question of religion. In diverse, even opposing, ways, they all considered this question crucial and dealt with it with a great sense of urgency. Each of the foregoing names represents a prototypical response to this question, but also a concrete, often dramatic experience. I would suggest that among them, Spinoza and Pascal, the polar opposites regarding the question of religion, had the most radical answers to it.

For all of these men – to a lesser degree, perhaps, for Boyle and Newton – the question of religion was essentially and immediately an acute political, or theologico-political, problem. For all of them, however, it was also, albeit in varying degrees (least of all probably for Hobbes), more than a purely political, or even theologico-political, question. There was more than just a "surface," in it, and it had for them, as for most of their contemporaries, a certain thickness

---

[23] According to Piet Steenbakkers, "The Text of Spinoza's *Tractatus Theologico-Politicus*," in Melamed and Rosenthal (2010), pp. 29–40. See also the two recent biographies of Spinoza, Nadler (1999) and Gullan-Whur (1998); both give detailed descriptions of the historical and political background of Spinoza's life.

[24] Boyle is largely considered of the most significance precursor of modern chemistry and of experimental science in general; on his preoccupation with the religious question, see MacIntosh (2005).

that can be referred to, for the sake of convenience and brevity, as the thickness of "faith." The lines separating the two kinds of interrogation – the political and the, say, philosophical – are of course very hard to trace. In Spinoza's case they can be said to have the contours of the separation between the political treatises on one hand, the *Ethics, The Short Treatise,* the TIE, and many of the letters on the other. There is obvious overlapping among all these writings, but looked at from a certain distance, it becomes quite obvious that there were in fact two main, but different, fields of questioning for him: philosophy as a doctrine of salvation and theory of the state.

The notion of faith has conceptual, epistemological, psychological, and phenomenological, as well as ontological and soteriological, aspects through which it can be said to capture the sense in which the question of religion can be conceived as a philosophical, and not merely political, question. In chapter 14 of the TTP Spinoza tries to undermine the religious specificity of this basically religious category by what can be described as radical deconstruction: the only rationally acceptable meaning of the Biblical notion of faith is obedience to the authorities that govern the state (see *infra*). This is Spinoza's most straightforward discussion of this notion, but the *problem* of faith may be said to be all-pervasive in his philosophy and even, in a sense, the source from which it sprang. If, as one commentator has recently put it, it was quasi-impossible for Spinoza to deal with the state without addressing the question of religion,[25] it can be maintained that this was also the case concerning philosophy. Most philosophical matters, or the question of philosophy in general, were, for Spinoza practically coextensive with the question of religious faith (or, simply, religion). What the use of terms such as "faith" here can help show is that it was the full range of religiosity, not just the important, but nevertheless limited, theologico-political, social, and even ethical that he confronted.

There is consequently a great complexity in Spinoza's attitude toward religion. It is due, in part, to its double-faced nature and to the different forms it assumes in his two main realms of theorizing, the theory of the state (or of the "political") and philosophy proper. A rational understanding of the nature of political reality shows that a political "taming" of religion meant not only rejecting the legitimacy of its claim to political "say," but also acknowledging a pragmatic need to come to terms with it, that is, with the superstitious or, more benevolently put, the non-philosophical nature of man, or of most men. The best way to achieve a peaceful political order is to let people go to churches or synagogues and see to it that they are preached to in ways that enhance – not

---

[25] Moreau (2005), p. 5. This claim is not altogether accurate, since the question of religion is not discussed directly, or as a specific political problem in either the *Ethics* or the TP; in a less trivial way, it is however a correct observation: the all-pervasiveness of the question of religion in the *Ethics* – which is my main point here – applies also to the discussion of the state in part IV of the *Ethics*; and the relative disappearance of the question of theology from the TP in a historical moment when political theory was practically always about theology is very telling as well.

1.1. The Polemics

jeopardize – obedience. Tamed and subdued religion provides the state with the most efficient and least violent way to ensure obedience to the political authorities.

But when we enter the realm of *philosophy*, when we seriously read the *Ethics*, everything changes. It changes, however, in two seemingly opposing ways. Here, firstly there is no room for any compromise with religion, and any pragmatic accommodation with it would amount to a philosophical outrage. One can be a Cartesian and still go to church or to the synagogue; it is much harder to do so if one is a Spinozist. For here it is not a question of taming religion, even less so assigning it a domain outside the jurisdiction of philosophical reason, but of replacing it with something else. The notion of *replacing*, however, is neither innocent nor simple. For philosophically Spinoza was, so to speak, playing on the same playground as religion. The purpose of Spinozism can be reconstructed as a will to take over the whole ground, to expel religion from the philosophical playground, to relegate it to a secondary, merely social, and politically subservient role but to philosophical irrelevancy – and yet remain on this very same playground.

It is here that, secondly, the inverted respect for religion I referred to above enters. The militant atheist would usually dismiss faith as illusory and the content of religion as nothing but superstition and prejudice. He does not have much use, respect, or patience for what his adversary has to say; religious language is empty and does not deserve serious consideration. It usually undergoes reduction or is explained away in one way or another, derided, and ridiculed. It is rarely, if ever, taken as carrying any intelligible content. But it is also, one may add, a kind of mirror picture of the ways religion often treats the atheist: he is the emblem of corruption and his arguments do not merit much more than apologetics. The latter is a form of discourse based on the presumption that the adversary's arguments are fundamentally wrong and do not deserve consideration in themselves, not even serious refutation. In the endless quarrels between faith and its atheistic counterpart, the two rivals speak incommensurable languages.

This, however, is not altogether the case with Spinoza, who does speak the language of religion. It is here that everything becomes difficult. One may assume that by insisting on keeping the language of religion, Spinoza took it to be an indispensable means of philosophical expression; if this were the case, the use of this language by him necessarily expresses a certain acknowledgment of its pertinence and value. Spinoza indeed constantly uses the language of religion. This is conspicuous in particular in the *Short Treatise*, but also in the *Ethics* and the letters, and it complicates considerably any attempt to describe him as a radical critic of religion, so much so that his philosophy appears sometimes as a strange hybrid of antireligious religious philosophy. No wonder that the attempt to understand its nature has given rise to diverse and even contradictory views. Philosophy had often conceived itself as the handmaid of religion and sometimes as its master. On other occasions it acknowledges, implicitly or explicitly, in earnest or just as lip service, the legitimacy of a sphere extending beyond its own jurisdiction and that it surrenders to revelation. In yet other cases it may announce the death of God and deny the pertinence not only of what religion seems to be saying but also of the basic motivations allegedly giving rise to it. Spinoza seems to be walking a different, perhaps unique, path. He appears to be at once a radical opponent of religion and also more religious than the devout, to both conserve and also radically undermine the fundamental claims of religion, indeed of religiosity as such.

Unlike the typical atheist, then, Spinoza does not deny the pertinence of his religious adversary's language; on the contrary, he uses it extensively. But paradoxically – a paradox that explains much of the misunderstandings and disagreement surrounding the fundamental character of Spinoza's philosophy in its relation to religion – his critique of religion is more radical than that of the standard atheist. Spinoza claims to know better, better than the original owners of the language of the sacred. This, arguably, is why his stance on religion was considered such an outrage and greeted with such anger by so many defenders of religion, Christian or Jewish. Although it is hard to tell with accuracy where Spinoza's use of this language is ironic, where it is subversive, or where it is straightforward and candid, it is still true that at least in some cases Spinoza means what he says and can be seen to manifest unexpected respect for religion.

But Spinoza's use of the language of religion was not at all innocent. Rather than borrowing, it can be better described as appropriation and taking over, even usurpation. For he seems to be saying to an imaginary religious adversary something like the following: "Since my own use of the language you think belongs to you expresses its true, real, full, and only rationally, or philosophically, justifiable sense, it is also the only legitimate one. What you, the adversary, that is, the man of the multitude, but also the theologian and the moralist, attribute to the words you use in your prayers or sermons or theological tracts is false, inadequate, and even contradictory and unintelligible, eventually dangerous. The state will see to it that it will not have any bearing outside the churches and be used only to induce obedience among the churchgoers. Philosophically, however – that is, from the point of view of truth – it is not only false but also morally wrong. These words are taken over now by philosophy; you are no longer free to use them as you please."

I have been using a number of metaphors: appropriation, taking over, playing on the same playground, replacement. They all lead to yet another metaphor, this one well known in the context of the debates about the closely related questions of religion and of secularization. One could thus suggest that for Spinoza, philosophy had to "reoccupy" the place of religion. The metaphor of *reoccupation* emerged indeed in the context of the last century's debates on the nature of secularism and secularization and on the legitimacy of modernity. It appeared in the debate between Carl Schmitt and Hans Blumenberg, and the latter elaborated on it further in his book *Legitimacy*

1.1. The Polemics

of the Modern Age.[26] Blumenberg uses this metaphor in order to account for the alleged persistence of certain questions, as he calls it, that modernity found itself in need to answer. The questions, or questionings, he has in mind are mainly religious and moral-religious questions, and although Spinoza does not figure greatly in his writings, one could say that this idea applies to him perfectly. I would only add here one more remark: Blumenberg describes the appearance of void positions, which characterizes what he calls the "threshold" of modernity, as a condition of modernity but in itself more or less independent of it. Differently put, in most cases, the evacuation of the positions now in need of reoccupation had not been the result of a direct attack on the previous holders of these positions. In the case of Spinoza, however, the reoccupation is preceded by an active attempt of occupation – the emptiness and the need to reoccupy is the result of a conscious attempt to dismiss and chase away, as it were, the previous holder of the position. Spinoza is certainly neither the first nor the only one to have mounted such an attack on the pre-modern position holders, but he can be said to be one of the more radical among them, certainly one of the more systematic and philosophically effective as well, and perhaps unique in his ambition to preserve the position and to take it over completely.

The continuous existence of the positions that have to be taken over and reoccupied means that Spinozism is also an acknowledgment, tacit to some extent, of the irreducible importance, indeed absoluteness, of certain elements of religious motivations and aspirations, traditions, experiences, forms of life, or attitudes toward the world, toward one's fellow man, and, in particular, toward one's own self. Spinoza, to use Max Weber's famous metaphor, was not musically deaf to religion. He had, in fact, a very good ear for things religious, even, one is tempted to say, an absolute pitch. But, at the same time, his philosophy in its entirety – not just the *Theological-Political Treatise* – amounts also to a radical critique, even a negation – certainly one of the most radical in the history of Western philosophical tradition – of religion. Paradoxically, the proximity to religion adds force to the critique, and it is no accident that Spinoza was conceived by religious thinkers as a deadly enemy of all orthodoxies.

So much for the question of religion as the general matrix, or horizon, within which, I believe, Spinoza's thought constantly moves. That Spinoza was a central and highly influential figure in the process of secularization – however one understands it – is generally conceded. In what follows I shall not address this question. I shall also not address the question of religion as such, nor the question of religion and philosophy, or reason, as a general question. Instead of dealing with any of these questions *in abstracto*, I wish to look closely at one particular case, at the way the general problematic manifests itself concretely at the core of Spinoza's philosophy. I shall not try to draw general conclusions from the "Spinoza case," and I am not sure there are any such lessons to be

---

[26] See Blumenberg, op. cit., notably part I, chapter 6.

drawn from it. But I do think that the problematic referred to by terms such as "religion" and "secularization" is the one that any serious study of the philosophy of Spinoza has to take into consideration as the main context within which it has to be read.

The rest of this preliminary Chapter 1 first explores briefly the radically critical side of Spinoza's grappling with religion as it appears in the TTP and where its concrete terrain of its inception – the Jewish religious tradition – is most evident. Then I say a few words about the "positive" side, as it were, of this grappling, of the difficult and problematic "respectfulness" towards religion that informs Spinoza's philosophy from the beginning to the end; in other words, I try to draw a portrait of a Spinozistic religiosity, to pinpoint the sense in which the religious language used by Spinoza makes sense and can be taken as more than sheer rhetoric, more than lip service aimed at appeasing a potentially hostile and non-understanding audience.

1.2. The *Tractatus Theologico-Politicus*

Part of the difficulty in resolving the enigma of Spinoza's religiosity is due to the opaqueness of the *Theological-Political Treatise*. Its notoriously complex structure and message, or messages, or perhaps strategic purposes, gave rise to diverse interpretations, often expressing contradictory ideological and even emotional reactions to this work that only attests to its extraordinary force.[27] The TTP was famously born, at least partially, out of a wish to intervene in the political-theological conflicts that raged in Holland in the mid-century. It purports to defend the freedom of thought in a general way, but its immediate purpose was to lend theoretical backing to the more liberal forces in Holland in their struggle against the Calvinist orthodoxy. Besides its declared purpose to defend freedom, however, it does a number of other things and also seems to be an occasion for settling older accounts and maybe even discharging still-live resentment toward the Jews. Some probably not fully healed scars, or not entirely resolved inner conflicts, crystallize in the TTP in the form of a systematic refutation of traditional Jewish theology. But the particular critique of the Jewish tradition is meant to be transcended into a general exposure of the prejudice and superstition that are inseparable from religion. Hence, understandably, polemics play an essential role in the TTP. On the more, as it were, affirmative side, apart from the defense of the freedom of philosophical thought, the book purports to advocate a separation of philosophy and theology, which is sometimes understood, perhaps too hastily, as a liberal-like separation of Church and State, but it certainly does prefigure a modern theory of democracy. It also offers what is considered as the inauguration of Biblical criticism. It contains a few different *dissertations*, as its elaborate subtitle puts it, that were apparently collated

---

[27] For a long – but still partial – list of differing attitudes towards the TTP, see Verbeek (2003), p. 1.

together;²⁸ it may be based in part on an older *apologia* written in reaction to the ban imposed on him by the Amsterdam Jewish congregation, and there are certainly many more things that can be said of it. But more than anything, it is the polemics – the critique of theocracy and of organized religion in general, as well as of what Spinoza refers to as "theology" – that give this book its special flavor, a sense of subversiveness, defiance, and revolt that is undoubtedly an important part of its great attractiveness.

Spinoza's image and reputation derive to a large degree from the constant reading and rereading of the TTP;²⁹ if the *Ethics* contains a philosopher's philosophy, the TTP seems more accessible and attractive, and it speaks to a larger and a varied audience. In fact, it has often served – and still does – as the main source of the discourse on Spinoza. so much so that the views he expressed in it about religion; state and church; and Scripture and its interpretation and Judaism have sometimes eclipsed other aspects of his thought and in particular the deeper sense of his attitude to religion as it transpires in the *Ethics*. Thus, clearly, any serious discussion of the question of Spinoza and religion must consider Spinoza's political theory and, of course, especially the critique of theocracy as it is formulated in the *Tractatus Theologico-Politicus*. A few general remarks are thus in order.

1.2.a. *From the* Tractatus Politicus *Back to the* Tractatus Theologico-Politicus

My first remark on the *Theological-Political Treatise* actually concerns the later *Political Treatise*. The TP has attracted much less attention than the TTP. In fact, the TP is very largely ignored, which is perhaps understandable – it remained unfinished, it does not manifest the passion and intensity of the TTP, and it is sometimes pedantic and even somewhat tedious – but its neglect is nevertheless unfortunate, as it sheds new light on a number of issues that had remained more or less obscure, or not fully explicit, in Spinoza's previous works. Moreover, it contains a number of original theses that should have given Spinoza more visibility in the history of political theory. The TP is also the least polemic of Spinoza's writings, and reading it gives the impression that its author is no longer haunted by his old demons. The tone is less passionate, and the work, although not abstractly or purely philosophical, is also much less imbued with the sense of immediacy and urgency than is the TTP. It is noteworthy that theocracy, and indeed the question of religion in general, is largely left out of its main theoretical exposition. The tripartite typology of regimes in the TTP – monarchy, aristocracy, and theocracy³⁰ – disappears, and

---

²⁸ See Verbeek, op. cit., passim; Steenbakkers (2010); James (2012), p. 234.

²⁹ For a few recent works on the TTP, besides those cited in the previous note, see Preus (2001); Melamed and Rosenthal, op. cit.

³⁰ "Theocracy" was coined by Flavius Josephus, in *Contra Apionem*, pp. ii, 16, as a term describing the biblical Hebrew state. On the widespread Christian, mainly protestant, interest in

the traditional classification of monarchy, aristocracy, and democracy returns. Together with theocracy, the theologico-political question also disappears and, indeed, a whole century's worth of thought on the state. The reduction of the political to, or its identification with, the theologico-political is now seen by Spinoza – perhaps prematurely and too optimistically – as at least exaggerated.[31] Sure enough, Spinoza acknowledges, in the TP too, the need to find a place for religion in the state, but here religion is not very different from other sociological, cultural, or psychological facts of human life that the statesman or the theoretician have to reckon with; thus the political question of religion seems to have lost the urgency and distinctiveness it had for Spinoza when he was writing the TTP. In retrospect, the theologico-political question seems to have been of special importance in the particular – political, cultural, and perhaps even personal – circumstances of the late 1660s and early 1670s, to be later conceived by Spinoza as just part of the more general question of the political as such. This, I believe, only emphasizes, on the one hand, the importance of the *philosophical* confrontation with religion that remains essential, although not always in a direct and explicit way, in the *Ethics* and, on the other, the need to put the TTP in perspective, at least insofar as Spinoza's own thought, rather than its historical reception is concerned.

What distinguishes Spinoza's two political treatises should not, however, be interpreted as a *Kehre* or a change of mind. On many of the main topics and doctrines, there is an unmistakable, although not always immediately conspicuous, continuity between the earlier and the later works. From the point of view of political theory, in a more precise sense, however, the TP advances a general theory of the state that is of considerable originality and that is in many ways more interesting, or at least more mature and elaborate, than what he says on the question of the state in the TTP or in the *Ethics*. It can be interpreted, or reconstructed, as a theory of the *sui generis* nature of the political, or of the inner logic of power, of what Spinoza calls *imperium*, or of the particular

---

the Hebrew – biblical and rabbinic – political thought, see Nelson (2010). According to this remarkable study "the Hebrew Revival" and political Hebraism in the seventeenth century were the real origin of modern political theory. The Netherlands was an important center for this scholarship, and the TTP is certainly a critical reaction to it. The TP can be thus seen as a first manifestation of, and a sign of its author's role in, the change of heart in the eighteenth century when, for the *philosophes* already, the Bible and the Jewish tradition in general have become, in Voltaire's words (quoted ibid., p. 139) "the tiresome history of the forgotten chiefs of an unhappy barbarous land."

[31] There has been lately a remarkable upsurge of writings dealing with political theology or with the political-theological. The notion is ancient, and in the seventeenth century is appears on several occasions, but it has been linked in particular to Spinoza until Carl Schmitt used it as a central concept in his critique of liberal democracy. It now signifies myriad questions and issues that make it sometimes hard to see what is common to them besides the title, under which one finds discussions of the "essence of the political," the "return of the religious," the alleged emergence of a "post-secular era," and more. See, e.g., De Vries and Sullivan, op. cit.; in the almost 800 pages of this volume, there is only one article on Spinoza (in fact, on Levinas on Spinoza).

1.2. The Tractatus Theologico-Politicus

mode of being we know as the State.[32] If the TTP can be seen as a gesture of liberation – as the liberation of political theory from theology as a source of theoretical understanding and legitimation – the TP would be an attempt to elaborate what has been only foreshadowed in the TTP, namely the positive content of the *political* as a quasi-*sui generis* or irreducible theoretical sphere.

In a very curious way, the TP also implies a heterodox, or rather skeptical, attitude toward philosophy as a source of political understanding. It is true that Spinoza purports to incorporate the theory of the state into his philosophical enterprise as a whole, and both in the opening chapters of the TP and in the *Ethics* he pretends to deduce it from his general metaphysical, anthropological, and psychological principles. But it is still the case that the state, or the imperium, is a special kind of self-contained entity operating by its own laws. Although natural laws, they have their own configuration, which is different from that of the laws of reality in the, say, physical and metaphysical senses, and their logic is different from the logic of philosophical reason. This is what the whole exposition in the TP is meant to show. But the laws of "the political" are thus a source of specific, even *sui generis*, normative principles warranting a special form of rationalization.[33] The very peculiar, heavily ironic opening of the TP is a plea to the philosophers to keep off the grounds of the state. This makes full sense only in light of the general theory of the state that follows. Spinoza, of course, does not have much confidence in the politicians as well, and this double suspicion is the opening for a kind of constitutionalism, or rather institutionalism, or a doctrine of the need of some kind of built-in mechanism, as it were, in the body politic – of checks and balances if you will – that may assure, independently of the good will or the virtues of either citizens or politicians, that a commonwealth becomes and remains salutary and sane.

Spinoza, however, seems to have a greater respect for the politician than for the philosopher. Insofar as the matters of state are concerned, experience has made the first a more reliable or at least more competent figure than the philosopher. If the aim of the *Tractatus Theologico-Politicus* had been to counter theocracy, the *Tractatus Politicus* is now opposed to what can be called *Ratio-cracy* or *Sophia-cracy*: listening to what the philosophers have to say about running the state may be hazardous. By "philosophers" Spinoza refers here, at the beginning of the TP, to the moralizing breed, and since Spinoza's philosophy is, generally speaking, an uncompromising attack on moralizing, one is tempted to see in these philosophers a kind of semi-theologians, a crowd to which Spinoza would not want to belong. But there also may very well be here a kind of ironic self-reference. Having gained a better conception of political reality, and having realized that his own fear of an imminent

---

[32] See Goetschell, op. cit., chapter 5.
[33] There is an obvious dialogue here with the classical and, in particular, Stoic doctrines of practical reason. I shall not discuss this issue in the context of this general remark on the TTP, where I wish to emphasize Spinoza's own theory, which, I believe, is quite original.

theologico-political catastrophe that had led to his writing the TTP was in the last analysis unfounded, Spinoza now writes in a more detached and objective, but also less philosophical, way on the political question.

The deduction of the theory of the state from general principles does not necessarily diminish the specificity of the doctrine of the political. But it opens two parallel avenues of non-philosophical rationality. The state can be rationalized – this is the main message of the TP – but not in the way in which individual life can become rational, that is, philosophical. Political theory, the discourse on the political as it is formulated in the TP for example, is not strictly philosophical, but it is certainly rational; political action can lead to a possible rationalization of the state that, however, is always not only relative but also usually not the result of real theoretical understanding. It is true that the (always relatively) rational state can be constituted only to the extent that it respects the inner logic of the political, supposedly explicated in the TP, but the people who can accomplish such an exploit would usually not do it from a fully rational, or philosophical, understanding either of the nature of the political or of human nature. These two activities – that of the political theorist and that of the man of action – are not rational in the way of philosophy because both of them obey a logic of *experience*, more precisely of *historical* experience, not the logic of the *more geometrico* a priori deduction of philosophical truth.[34]

Consequently, the realm of reason appears to be not completely homogeneous or, more accurately, to bifurcate into two sub-spheres of somewhat different rationalities. The very fact of writing the *Political Treatise* after having finished the *Ethics* means that political theory has not been completely incorporated into the philosophical, supposedly comprehensive opus. The doctrine it contains makes this even clearer. The gesture of writing the TP amounts to a systematic positioning of a relatively independent sphere of rationality: the political. The point, however, is not only that political praxis is not the same as philosophy – there isn't much originality in this – but that the political evolves according to a semi-*sui-generis* logic. Both praxis and theory can go astray, but each has its own way to become pathological. The political may turn into one form or another of tyranny or chaos; philosophy can become, for example, moralistic or prejudicial; and political theory may turn into political theology. But insofar as reason itself is concerned, there are two main ways in which it manifests itself: in philosophy and in the political.

Seen from a modern vantage point, the irony at the beginning of the TP can be read as a double movement of demystification: of the political and

---

[34] In fact, there is a particular sense in which *experience* is pertinent in philosophy too. See discussion later in the book and in particular the comprehensive study of the place of experience in the philosophy of Spinoza, in Moreau (1994). As remarked by numerous commentators, history plays an important, even revolutionary (see, notably, Preus, op. cit.) role in Spinoza's hermeneutics of Scripture. More however than a philosophy of history, there is here a view of history as a paradigmatic experience.

1.2. *The* Tractatus Theologico-Politicus

of philosophy. The demystification of the political in the TP goes beyond the mere non-utopian, down-to-earth, or realistic – to some extent pessimistic – conception of the political Spinoza obviously has. It is a peculiarly modern, even post-modern, kind of demystification. In order to prevent any misunderstanding about what had nevertheless been quite clear in his earlier work, Spinoza opens the TP by reiterating in particularly strong terms his deep suspicion of the "multitude." That he was not inclined toward a Rousseau-like democratic idealization of the "people," and that this was said at the very beginning of what was most certainly destined to be a treatise in favor of democracy, is highly significant. But in reversing or redoubling the anachronism of Julian Benda's famous metaphor, Spinoza makes it now clear that he had no particular sympathy for the "clerks" as well. He apparently had no illusion about the role philosopher-kings or Panglossian instructors of princes could fulfill in the state. His scornful depiction of the moralizing philosopher that comes immediately after the denunciation of the *vulgus* can be interpreted as a rejection, or deconstruction *avant la lettre*, of the modern figure of "the intellectual," the revolutionary mystique, or other forms of secular clericalism. The man of political action or the statesman do not need the aid of philosophy; the prerogative of the state is not to decide about "truth," and it cannot incarnate truth, morality, or other high ideals. The state of the TP is not even altogether concerned with "freedom" – as it had seemed to have been the case in the TTP – but with something that is both more ambiguous, more plebeian, and less exhilarating than freedom. Spinoza is concerned with that which he calls "peace," which is best understood as a kind of specifically political virtue, not so much, however, of the individual citizen, minister, or statesman, but of the state as such. The political, the state, or "praxis" are all the elements of one large sphere of the reasonable, of what experience teaches, of the more or less; a monarchy can be salutary and democracy corrupt;[35] there are no absolutes in the realm of the political.

Although he can be said to be a philosopher of freedom, Spinoza is not really one of those political philosophers who, especially in modern times, set freedom or political liberty as the highest political, indeed human, value. Again, this can be seen only from the perspective of the TP. The full title of TTP reads as follows: *Theological-Political Treatise Containing Several Different Studies Showing that the Freedom to Philosophize may not only be Given without any Harm to Piety and to the Peace of the Republic, but on the Contrary it cannot be Withheld without Destroying the Peace of the Republic and Piety Itself*. It thus presents itself as an essay on political freedom and is often perceived as such. But the truth is that Spinoza did not share the typically modern mystique

---

[35] Although Spinoza wrote only a couple of pages on democracy before he died, his dealing with monarchy and aristocracy shows that there is one logic of power, which is built on a principled distinction between the sane and the corrupt and which is applicable, *mutatis mutandis*, to all forms of government.

of political freedom.[36] The political is the place of neither full and real freedom nor salvation, and neither the political nor any form of anti-political can be a liberating agent. Although Spinoza was no conservative, let alone reactionary (as opposed to Hobbes or Leibniz for example), there was also no room in his political theory for anarchistic or libertarian idealizations of political freedom. Nor was he prefiguring political messianism or anything that would be much later referred to as political (or secular) religions. Given the tendency of so much modern thought – from Hobbes to Fichte, Hegel, and Marx, and all the way to their more recent heirs on the right and on the left – to turn political theory – the theory of the state or, more subtly, of the political – into *philosophia prima*, Spinoza's actual position, as described here, and especially given his unique status in this tradition, becomes quite striking.

But there is no symmetry or full analogy between the two spheres of rationality. Thus, for example, if political freedom is relativized, Spinozism's most important and most valuable aspiration remains philosophical, personal freedom, which Spinoza insists on calling "salvation" and which is essentially a kind of freedom. There is nothing in his political theory that resembles the metaphysical doctrine of freedom of the *Ethics* in depth, complexity, conceptual subtlety, and, in particular, subversive originality. The demystification of the role and figure of the clerk, or even a self-directed irony, do not undermine or relativize philosophy. Theoretical wisdom, philosophy, or salvaging understanding, or "saving knowledge," is what counts most, and the critique of "sophia-cracy" – the appeal to the philosophers or theoreticians to keep off the political – is very different from the struggle against the theologians in the TTP. There is no real analogy between theology and philosophy, as the TTP seems to suggest. If keeping the theologians, preachers, priests, ministers, or other spiritual leaders in their churches does not mean much more than politically taming them, the warning addressed to the philosophers to stay out of the political arena is itself a philosophical position. It expresses the sage's self-restraint, something that I suspect Spinoza did not consider the theologians inclined to do. There is thus nothing in the irony of the TP that amounts to a disavowal of, say, the *Ethics* or, more importantly, that is comparable to the repudiation of theology in the TTP.

The TTP, however, had seemingly sought to defend a mutual independence of philosophy and theology. The title of chapter 15 of the TTP is as clear as can be: it declares the intention to show "that Theology is not the Handmaid of Reason, nor Reason of Theology; and also Why the Authority of Scripture

---

[36] See, for example, Arendt (1977), who forcefully argues in this article that freedom makes sense only as a political concept. Arendt is interesting in this context because as a partially estranged Jewish public intellectual, she embodied much of what Spinoza had prefigured but also denounced. What is most striking perhaps is the very ambiguous and equivocal attitude both have toward their Jewish origin, the centrality of the idea of freedom in their respective world-views, and – against this background – the very different understanding of what freedom is all about.

is Evident to Us." In truth, however, Spinoza does nothing of the sort, neither in this chapter nor anywhere else. One suspects that despite the conciliatory title, the real, although not always fully straightforwardly formulated, message of the TTP is that intellectually, theology is not a match for philosophy and has to be put, as it were, under the jurisdiction of philosophical reason. In political terms this or the handmaid metaphor cannot mean much more than a reiteration of the principle that the church has to be put under the authority of the state, serve it by inducing obedience, and be controlled by it. What could be the practical ramifications of this principle is, of course, an open question, but the principle is clear enough, and a careful reading of chapter 15 shows that this indeed is what it says.[37] What Spinoza pretends to acknowledge as theology's prerogative is, on the most generous reading, very meager: by "theology," explains Spinoza, he means "revelation, insofar as it shows the purpose of Scripture" (184), which, as was shown in the TTP's previous chapter, is nothing but obedience. To this Spinoza adds that he confirms "absolutely that this fundamental principle of theology cannot be studied by the natural light, or at least no one has demonstrated it, and for this reason revelation was very necessary" (185; my translation). But the experience-based theorization of the state as it is elaborated in the TP purports to do just this – rationally show how an obedient or law-abiding citizenry can be envisaged; and of course, the theory of the TP can hardly be considered as "revelation." Unless, that is, one recalls that in chapter 1 of the TTP Spinoza had stated, after defining prophecy or revelation as "an evident knowledge revealed to men by God," that actually this definition means that one can call "natural knowledge" by the name of "prophecy" (15). Despite appearances, neither revelation nor prophecy is accorded any independent conceptual standing or specificity.

1.2.b. *The* Tractatus Theologico-Politicus: *From the Refusal of Judaism to the Critique of Religion*

Much of Spinoza's struggle against theology was cast, in the *Tractatus Theologico-politicus*, as a quarrel over the correct method of interpreting Scripture. Keeping with the language of Hermeneutics, one can suggest that for him this was a struggle over who occupies a "hermeneutical instance" or is the arbiter in matters of hermeneutics. This means that the quarrel he was waging was about who had a better understanding of his rival – he himself speaking in the name of reason or philosophy, or the theologian speaking in the name of revelation – not less than over who can better read Scripture. Spinoza's struggle against the theologians can thus be reconstructed as a quarrel over the question

---

[37] See James, op. cit., in particular chapter 12, which gives such a careful reading of Spinoza's text and shows indeed how narrow the space is that Spinoza actually leaves for "theology." Read in light of the *Ethics* and especially of the TP, this space seems to completely disappear from the sphere of truth, remaining only as a form of political toleration in its original meaning (i.e., as acquiescing in the existence of untruth).

of who was in a position to interpret whom or who had the power to define his rival as to whom and what he was. In more general terms it was a quarrel over what – theology or philosophy – has hermeneutical jurisdiction over the other, over who has the right to deconstruct whom. Obviously, deconstruction cannot work both ways, and there is no reciprocity here. One either deconstructs or is deconstructed. Between Spinoza and the theologian it is a zero-sum game: if one is right, the other is wrong. If reason or philosophy has the right and ability to understand religion from outside religion, then it *ipso facto* refutes theology's claim that it has access to a higher understanding of the nature of human reason. Theology is thus not only refuted but also denied the position it covets, which is the position of final judge or hermeneut who understands better and, consequently, has the authority to judge philosophy's shortcomings.[38]

But philosophy – Spinoza's philosophy – and theology all speak the same language, which is the language of salvation. This means that the Spinozist philosopher is convinced that he, or she, understands better than the preachers, the clerics, and the theologians – or, for that matter, the rabbis – not only what they are and why they say what they say, but also what is the true meaning of the words they use. With this, the latter's right to use them is put in question, circumscribed, and even, from the point of view of the real economy of salvation and freedom, altogether denied. It is this hardy but complex position that explains why Spinozism constitutes such a scandal for religious consciousness and for faith. It is the attempt to appropriate the language of religion, to criticize religion in order to open the way for the possibility to be at one and same time religion's most radical critic and more religious than religion.

The way things are presented in the TTP is ambiguous enough to permit different readings. But seen from the perspective of the *Ethics* and the TP, it seems that Spinoza did not consider seriously the possibility of letting theology enjoy some "independence," that is, theoretical or cognitive legitimacy and relevance, vis-à-vis philosophy or reason. In fact, even in the political sphere he restricts the prerogatives of the ecclesiasts and gives the political authorities full jurisdiction over them (chapter 19 in particular). Seen from the vantage point of the twentieth-first century, Spinoza can be said to have succeeded in pinpointing a central theme of the obstinately recurring debate between religion and non-religion. There has been lately – at the beginning of the third millennium – much talk of a "return of the religious," the emergence of "new atheism," and a rival "new orthodoxy" or "radical" and even "secular theology." After what had been seen by many as a victory of secularism, the appropriation of its language by theology and religion can be seen as a revival of a struggle for hermeneutical supremacy, for the stance from which the atheist claims to be able to say, in the name of reason or science, that the theological discourse is

---

[38] This is precisely the question that is debated between Spinoza and Albert Burgh; see Curley (2010), who claims, rightly I believe, that there was much more in this correspondence than just the question of miracles, as J. Israel had claimed in his (2002).

nonsense, and the theologian to "assert the urgency, in the late stages of secular reason's reign, of reclaiming theology's supremacy as a discourse."[39] The theologian, in other words, still insists on his right to tell a secular world that it is a religious or theological phenomenon after all; the secular critique of religion tries to do the same and tell religion that it is, as it were, a non-religious phenomenon – political, sociological, psychological, and so on – and they seem all to find themselves anew in a Spinozistic predicament of a hermeneutical struggle.

The metaphor of "hermeneutical struggle," or of Spinoza's "hermeneutical offensive" against orthodoxy and theology, is obviously brought to mind by his discussion of the right method of reading and understanding scripture. This is a central issue in the TTP, and it has always attracted a lot of attention.[40] With a few others, notably Hobbes and Richard Simon, Spinoza is very often considered a pioneer founder of the critical study of the Bible or "high criticism." Usually attributed to the rise of modern scientific rationalism and of critical-historical consciousness, but also to the upheavals inside Christianity such as the reformation or the Wars of Religion, the use of critical methods in the study of the biblical text is not necessarily an endeavor aimed at undermining its religious authority and privileged or canonical status. Much modern biblical theology assumes critical methods of reading Scripture and regards as a positively religious achievement the "critical breakthrough" in biblical studies to which Spinoza would have thus been a major contributor. The notion of "critical breakthrough" is taken from Preus's study of Spinoza's hermeneutical struggle: according to a "standard account" in the field of biblical theology, this breakthrough was a "breakthrough of a new theological perspective."[41] Insofar as Spinoza's approach to Scripture is concerned, however, the "standard account" misses its main point, for he, claims Preus, was not part of the traditional debates about how to read the Bible. A more radical alteration was happening, and Spinoza was the first to accomplish it: "the Bible's uniquely privileged (i.e. canonical) status had to be set aside entirely in order to open the way for comparing the Bible with other ancient texts, and the biblical religion with other religions" (ibid.). The stakes of Spinoza's debate against the theologians, at least as he himself saw it, were not the best way to decipher and expose the message of Scripture – based on the belief that it contained a revealed or divine message – but to understand its *essence*. Looking for a better, basically naturalist understanding of Scripture, Spinoza *ipso facto* refused to accord to the biblical text any special status and denied its claim to contain a supernatural message. All traditional, pre-Spinoza (again according to Preus) quarreling biblical interpreters and exegetes shared one main presupposition: the meaning

---

[39] Klassen (2011), p. 9. This is an example chosen in a haphazard way, but it captures nicely the idea of a hermeneutical struggle.
[40] See, among others, Zac (1965); Chalier (2006).
[41] Preus, op. cit., p. ix; Preus alludes here to H. K. Kraus.

of the words of Scripture is a special truth – revealed, divine, prophetic, and so on – that has to be understood properly. Opinions may differ in the most extreme ways and even become literally violent as to everything else, but that there was a revealed message in the Bible was beyond question. Even, as Preus shows in detail, Spinoza's heterodox Dutch contemporaries such as, notably, his friend and close collaborator, the hyper-rationalist Ludwig Meyer, did not put in question this presupposition.[42]

As remarked already, Hebrew studies in general, and erudite discussions of the biblical text, of its adequate interpretation, of the Rabbinical literature, and of the lessons it contained for contemporary political theory in particular, were an important element of the context into which Spinoza lanced his *Tractatus Theologico-Politicus*, "perhaps the most famous seventeenth-century text on the *respublica Hebraeorum* – and the only one to have been written by a Jew."[43] But Spinoza, the only Jew, then, who followed the Hebraic Erastrians in using the Bible and the biblical story of the Mosaic state for political-theoretical purposes, had a "radical vision of the Hebrew Bible [that] places him outside this tradition."[44] Indeed, more than participating in the process, as Nelson describes it, Spinoza actually contributed to undermining its theological presuppositions and, by it, the whole project. The great novelty of Spinoza's discussion of the biblical text did not reside in providing a better method for the study of the biblical text but in showing its pointlessness for any theoretical, or philosophical, endeavor.

The perspective opened by studies such as Preus's or Nelson's is very important for any attempt to understand the nature, origin, and message, or messages, of the TTP, which was presumably addressed mainly to a non-Jewish audience. But the dialogue with, or rather the accusation leveled against, Judaism is no less important. Given the attention accorded to Spinoza's breakthrough in Biblical hermeneutics, it is noteworthy that he did not really have any radically new insights into the content of the biblical text. The novelty of Spinoza's approach to the study of the Bible is not a scholarly achievement, and it does not reside in his great erudition or in new insights into the content or structure of Scripture. Most if not all of the biblical allusions, citations, and examples he brings in order to prove the historicity, or naturalness, or human origin, of the biblical text were well known to his Jewish predecessors and to many of his contemporaries, Jews and non-Jews.[45] What was new was the boldness with which these contradictions and incoherencies were presented and, in particular, the use to which they were put. If seen from the perspective of the Christian Hebraists one could conclude, as we have just seen, that Spinoza was trying to

---

[42] Preus, op. cit., pp. 34–67 and passim. On Ludwig Meyer, see also Lagrée (1988, 2001, 2004) and Nadler (1990), passim.

[43] Nelson, op. cit., p. 21.

[44] Ibid., p. 133; see also note 30 to this chapter.

[45] See, for example, Harvey (2010), who discusses one famous case of a mediaeval Jewish biblical exegete who hints toward seemingly unresolvable difficulties in the biblical text.

1.2. The Tractatus Theologico-Politicus

undermine the theological authority of the Bible rather than reform it, yet from the Jewish perspective the significance of his gesture was even more radical. On the one hand, Jewish religion traditionally evolved on the basis on a constant reading of its canon, of which the Bible is supposed to be the source;[46] on the other hand, theology has traditionally had a relatively small role for Jews, and Jewish thought (notably during the Middle Ages), when it has not been Halakhic, has been more philosophical than theological. In her recent book on Spinoza and Maimonides, Catherine Chalier[47] suggests, rightly I believe, that Spinoza's attempt to prove the Bible's philosophical vacuity and its pointlessness for the philosophical quest for truth emancipates, as she puts it, philosophy from the Bible; the result of this emancipation is that the very idea of Jewish, Christian, or Muslim philosophy is undermined. Philosophy, just like geometry, was meant to be a universal enterprise. Philosophy emancipated from the Bible – and from its Jewishness – also meant philosophy emancipated from theology in general and under all its manifestations. But Spinoza's quarrel with the Dutch Reformed theologians was theological-political. Its stakes were mainly political, and this, as I suggested above, was not altogether a philosophical matter for Spinoza. His quarrel with the Jewish philosophers was philosophical or theological-philosophical and, as such, more fundamental.

Chapter 15 of the TTP closes the "critique of theology" part, a critique supposedly aimed at opening the way for a universally valid non-theological theory of the foundations of the state, which is also, *ipso facto*, its justification. There are numerous allusions to and remarks on the New Testament and Christian theology in the TTP, as well as one relatively long and the more elaborate discussion in chapter 11,[48] but the first fifteen chapters of the TTP deal mostly with Jewish sources, biblical and mediaeval. Most of the theological themes, principles, and doctrines Spinoza addresses in the TTP are presented in the forms they have assumed in the Jewish tradition, especially in the Maimonidean corpus, and although the argumentative thrust of this discussion is obviously strategic – it was safer to attack Jewish theology, but the real rival was Calvinist orthodoxy – not everything he was saying against the Jews, their traditions, and their sages can be explained as mere strategy or rhetoric.

In chapter 14 Spinoza proposes a list of seven principles of what he calls "universal religion" (*religio catholica*). There is a certain ambiguity in this doctrine of Spinoza's: the universal religion is presented by him both as the essence of the biblical political-theology and as a projected foundation for a universal

---

[46] Jewish – and sometimes non-Jewish – attempts to capture the essence of Judaism, or the fundamental trait of its history, are many. One such attempt is Halbertal (1997), who emphasizes the constitutive role of the canon (biblical and post-biblical) and of its incessant reading and re-reading in this history.
[47] Chalier, op. cit., p. 9.
[48] Chapter 11 deals with the question "whether the Apostles wrote their Epistles as Apostles and Prophets or rather as Scholars [doctors]."

religion yet to come.⁴⁹ As Jacquline Lagrée remarks (op. cit., p. 80), the expression "universal religion" usually designates in the seventeenth century "natural religion," or that which is common to all religions and is also the essence of revealed religion. And the question one can ask is whether the universal project of philosophy has to recognize another form of universality, which is also natural and, as such, common to all men.

It is not altogether certain if everything Spinoza says about universal religion should be taken with full seriousness. There is in it a subtle play of explicit reference to Jewish sources – essentially negative and critical – and an implicit use of Jewish modes of thinking as an ironic means for a parallel, albeit more or less dissimulated, critique of Calvinist orthodoxy, Christianity, and, in particular, religion in general. After rejecting the religious specificity and intellectual pertinence of *belief* – the Bible is about inducing obedience, not teaching truth – Spinoza famously offers a list of seven *dogmata* or basic principles of faith, sometimes referred to as a "minimal credo," that are apparently supposed to crystalize under propositional form the psychological or cognitive foundation of obedience or, more benevolently put, civil morality. It is frequently read against the background of Christian doctrine and the debates between Protestants and Catholics and between different reformed confessions about, for example, the relative weight of "faith" and "works" in the economy of salvation.⁵⁰ But there are also very good reasons for reading it against the Jewish background of some similar ideas about universal morality.

Spinoza evokes twice in chapter 14 what he presents as, as it were, a moral meta-principle: "love thy neighbor." On page 176 (Gebhardt edition, Vol. 3), he affirms, citing from chapter 4 of the First Epistle of John, that "he who loves God loves his brother too," and two pages earlier he says that Scripture teaches in the clearest way what should be considered as obedience to God, so that we can learn from it that the whole of the Law consists in one precept, which is love thy neighbor as thyself. The Hebrew translation of this difficult-to-translate Latin phrase⁵¹ clearly alludes to a famous Talmudic story about Hillel the Elder, who, asked by a gentile to teach him the entire Torah "[standing] on one leg," answered that "that which is hateful to you, do not

---

⁴⁹ See Donagan (1996) for a similar observation. The notion *religio catholica* appears several times in the TTP and almost never elsewhere (but see Ep. 43, G. IV, 225). The doctrine of universal religion has triggered many controversies among commentators. See in particular Matheron (1971). See also Lagrée (2004), pp. 79–82, 128–130; Curley, op. cit., pp. 24–26; James, op. cit., pp. 207–213 (in particular n. 72, p. 213, which contains extensive references to the differing opinions on this issue); Verbeek, op. cit., pp. 28–34.
⁵⁰ See James, op. cit., for a concise elaboration of this matter.
⁵¹ The TTP was translated into Hebrew by the historian and Latinist Haim Wirshubsky (Jerusalem: Magnes, 1961). The Latin reads: "Deinde quidnam unusquisque exequi debeat, ut Deo obsequatur, ipsa etiam Scriptura plurimis in locis quam clarisime docet, nempe totam legem in hoc solo consistere in amore scilicet erga proximum, quare nemo etiam negare potest, quod is, qui ex Dei mandato proximum tanquam se ipsum diligit, revera est obediems et secundum legem beatus."

1.2. *The* Tractatus Theologico-Politicus

do to your fellow. That is the whole Torah; the rest is interpretation. Go and study" (*Shabbat* 31a). The exegetic tradition often links this phrase to Leviticus 19:18, which is the earliest biblical source of "love thy neighbor." It is, of course, impossible to know with certainty if Spinoza was thinking about this Talmudic story when he wrote these words. But the association of the story for an educated Hebrew speaking reader is probably not gratuitous.

Another half dissimulated allusion to the Jewish tradition of universal morality is the seemingly innocent and trivial fact that Spinoza lists seven *dogmatas* or principles of faith in his so-called minimal credo. The Hebrew tradition knows a number of lists of principles of faith, morals, and religious commandments. Most famous among them are, of course, the Ten Commandments, but there are also Maimonides's Thirteen Principles and Yosef Albo's Three *Iqarim*, as well as many more. One of these lists is what is known as the שבע מצוות בני-נוח or "Seven Noachite Commandments." With allegedly Biblical roots, the Talmud (Sanhedrin 9:1) lists seven *mitzvoth* (roughly, laws, commandments, or moral exigencies) that bind all humans (unlike the 613 *mitzvoth* that obligate only the Jews) and that have an immediate linkage to Hillel's teaching.[52]

The feeling that the Hebrew translator was right in rendering Spinoza's words about the moral meta-principle the way he did is further supported by an explicit reference to the Noachite Laws that occurs before and that is also the occasion for a sharp rebuke of Maimonides and of "the Jews" in general. Chapter 5 (pp. 79–80) is an elaborate explanation of the educational and psychological value of the biblical ceremonies, stories, histories, and myths: they are not depositories of philosophical truth, but are useful for inducing morally, socially, and politically correct forms of behavior – what Spinoza calls "obedience and observance" (*obedientiam et devotionem*). The end of the chapter puts the previous discussion in perspective: whatever name we give to the mode of existence of the obedient and observant, it is attainable also by the "natural light" and without the aid of the edifying stories of the Bible.

So much for the universality of the biblical moral teaching. It is not entirely clear how this strengthens his argument, but Spinoza then adds that the Jews are of a contrary opinion.[53] They acknowledge as salutary ways of life or beliefs solely those that are chosen because they were prophetically revealed to Moses. This sweeping – and, one may add, quite inaccurate – generalization is supported by a reference to Maimonides's canonic formulation and discussion of this issue in *Mishne Torah*. Maimonides states there that gentiles who observe the seven Noachite Laws on the basis of the natural light, and not because

---

[52] Wikipedia has a fairly good entry on the topic "Seven Laws of Noah." For an interpretation of the *dogmata* outside its historical context, see Rosenthal (2001).

[53] The question of whether salvation is possible outside Christianity is also a central issue, of course, of Christian traditional theology, and it is conceivable that here, too, the allusion to Maimonides and to the Jews has strategic reasons. But the violence of Spinoza's words and the very specifically Jewish formulation of the problem show that he must have had Maimonides in mind at least as much as he had Calvinist theologians.

they accept the Torah's commandments as prophetically revealed, do not have a share in the world to come (or are not saved); this applies also to those who are among the sages of the "nations of the world." Spinoza then quotes from fifteenth-century commentator of Maimonides Yosef Ben Shem Tov, who draws the hard-to-accept conclusion from these words of Maimonides that even Aristotle, whom Maimonides considered to be almost of the status of a biblical prophet and who knew and kept all the moral precepts, would not be saved. Such opinions, concludes Spinoza, are pure figments of the imagination without any foundation whatsoever, their futility is so obvious that there is no need to refute them, and it is enough to watch the ways of life of those who claim to possess something higher than reason – the Jews? – in order to realize that what they have is actually much below it.

The words of Maimonides cited by Spinoza have been subject to much discussion and debate that continues well into our times.[54] For Moses Mendelssohn, Herman Cohen, and other Jews trying to present Judaism in the age of the Enlightenment to the non-Jewish, always suspicious audience, they were a source of embarrassment. Attempts to come to terms with and interpret what may seem as an excessive affirmation of Jewish particularism can be still found in the literature on Maimonides. The image of Jewish exclusivism that emerges from Spinoza's presentation of Maimonides's words (supposedly the highest religious authority in Jewish tradition and thus an authentic representative of Judaism), as well as numerous other matters in the TTP, famously infuriated Cohen, who attacked Spinoza on a number of occasions. In the particular context of the Noachite Laws, he blamed Spinoza for distorting Maimonides's text (which he did not) and for falsely presenting Judaism as exclusivist and xenophobic (in which Cohen was arguably right).[55]

Cohen's allegations notwithstanding, it is noteworthy that there are exactly seven *dogmata* and that they are the very general principles of a moral and political religion destined to be accepted by all the "nations of the world." Here is one of the many places in the TTP – besides the explicit uses of Jewish sources – where there is a strong Jewish resonance. Layer upon layer of irony add up in the subtext to a complex play of overt and covert messages of rejection and criticism, but also of what looks like a paradoxical nostalgic love-hate attitude toward the religion of his ancestors and at the same time a somewhat condescending view of the gentile readers of the book.

The traditional seven Noachite *mitzvoth* are essentially moral or moral-religious rules: they prohibit idolatry, murder, theft, incest, blasphemy, and eating flesh taken from live animals, and they enjoin the establishment of

---

[54] See Schwarzschild (1990), which is a comprehensive study of the debates about this Maimonidean principle and its ramification in Spinoza and in the anti-Spinoza literature (notably Herman Cohen's), as well as its philosophical significance. Nieöhner (1984) adds to it some clarification about the links between Spinoza and Uriel da Costa on this matter.
[55] Schwarzschild, op. cit., pp. 46–49.

1.2. *The* Tractatus Theologico-Politicus

courts of justice. They thus differ from Spinoza's seven principles in two fundamental ways: the content of the items in the two lists is different;[56] and Spinoza's principles have the form of *theses* and not of moral, legal, or religious *rules* or *commandments*. They are supposed to lead to certain moral forms of behavior, as seen from the short developments in the second parts of the formulation of each *dogma*,[57] but the principles of faith themselves are items of propositional, not normative or prescriptive, structure and content. One way or another, the very fact of choosing precisely seven items in this particular context and in this particular form makes one, once again, think of the Jewish tradition as a semi-hidden source, if obviously not of the exact content of the list, then of the idea of formulating such a list altogether. If our assumption that Spinoza's list of seven principles of universal religion has to be read also in light of the traditional Noachite discussion, then what transpires here is the curious nature of an apparent "universalistic" moral religion that emerges from a specific religion with a strong particularistic configuration and that becomes, through a curious, dialectical move, the very negation of its own origin.

Spinoza's first principle states that God exists. His second principle states that God is one and unique. At first glance, what can be more universally acceptable and ecumenical than this, that there is a God, and He is one? Looking more attentively, however, it appears to be not so innocent. *Deum, hoc est ens supremum, summe iustum et misericordem, sive verae vitae exemplar existere* is the opening of the statement of the first principle. God, it says, exists. God is a sovereign being, most just and forgiving and compassionate, *that is* (*sive*) a model or an *exemplar* of truthful life. The idea that God is a moral *exemplar* occurs on a number of occasions in the TTP, but besides the more general and vaguer possible allusion to ideas such as the creation of man in the image of God or the tradition of human morality as a kind of *imitatio dei*, the notion of *exemplar* brings to mind a few other issues. It reminds one of Uriel da Costa's autobiographical *Exemplar humanae vitae*, written in 1640; of Spinoza's uses of it in the *Ethics*; and of the role of Moses and Christ in the TTP itself as two archetypal models. We remarked earlier (see note 53) about the relevance of da Costa to the general question of universal morality, and I shall not further elaborate on it here. In the *Ethics* Spinoza refers to the idea of an *exemplar* or *model* at least twice, and both cases seem to allude ironically to the discussion in the TTP: the long scholium II after EIp33 (the very important affirmation of Spinoza's necessitarianism – things could not have been different from what they actually are) contains a critique of views supporting one kind or another of God's free will. It ends

---

[56] Spinoza's list includes there is a God; he is one and unique; he is omnipresent; he has sovereign right for everything; worship is justice and love to one's neighbor; those, and only those, who obey God in this manner are saved; sinners are forgiven if they repent.

[57] See Rosenthal, op. cit., p. 67.

by what amounts to a general refutation of the pertinence of the concept of *exemplar* in the context of the doctrine of God:

> I admit that the opinion which subjects everything to some indifferent will of God,... is less far from the truth than that of those who maintain that God operates in everything in view of the good [*sub ratione boni*]. The latter seem to pose outside God something, which does not depend on God, to which God looks, as a model [*exemplar*], in acting.

Contending that God (or Nature) act *sub ratione boni* is, then, a grave philosophical blunder. But in the present context the real lesson is that the pure necessity, which is God, cannot become a "model" for human morality: if God is an *exemplar* of human morality, and if God does not act according to a model, then, of course, man's true morality is also not based on looking at an "external" model. In the preface to EIV, however, Spinoza affirms that despite his general rejection of teleological considerations, he still thinks that terms such as "perfection" and "imperfection" and "good" and "bad" should be retained, to the extent that we wish "to form an idea of man as a model of human nature [*naturae humanae exemplar*] that we can look at."[58] An idea of a man – not God – can serve as an *exemplar*.[59]

The second dogma states that God is not only unique but also *one*. This can be, and has been, interpreted as an endorsement of a Socinian-like rejection of the Trinity or, more specifically, of Christ's divinity. It can also be read as an opening toward the philosophical one infinite *Deus sive natura* of the *Ethics*.[60] But insofar as it is a *principle of faith* and not a theoretical truth deduced *more geometrico*, it also should perhaps call to mind Judaism's fundamental belief in the oneness and unity of God, and, even more so, its thorough rejection of the Trinitarian conception of God as a kind of idolatry. One suspects that in Spinoza's words about the oneness of God resonate a kind of disdain with which the idea of the Trinity was typically looked at by many Jews.

The question whether, and how, the TTP was Jewish has indeed been asked many times. Chapters 1–10 and 12 of the TTP deal directly and for their greater part with themes taken from the Jewish tradition. More specifically, Spinoza's discussion of such issues as prophecy, miracles, the right ways of understanding Scriptures, the election of the Hebrews, and the nature and origin of the law in general and of ceremonial law in particular is based to a very large extent on Maimonides's *Guide of the Perplexed*. Since Jöel's mid-nineteenth-century classical study of Spinoza's Jewish sources, the question of the nature and significance of Spinoza's relation to Maimonides is discussed repeatedly. Lately, however, this question has gained prominence, largely due to an influential article by Zeev Harvey, who advanced in it (as in a number of other writings)

---

[58] Last two quotes are translated by me; the question of perfection is at the center of the discussion of Part IV of this study.
[59] See Frankel (2001).
[60] See James, op. cit., p. 209.

1.2. *The* Tractatus Theologico-Politicus

the thesis that Spinoza was essentially a "Maimonidean" philosopher.[61] Some contest this position,[62] but no one doubts the omnipresence of Maimonides in the TTP. As the great scholar Shlomo Pines remarked in an older article on the TTP and Maimonides that the first chapters of Spinoza's book are a sort of tribute to Maimonides. It is unusual that an author bases his own doctrines on such a close and detailed reading of another author, especially, one may add, if this reading is as critical as Spinoza's reading of Maimonides is. Pines, however, apparently thought that more than Spinoza was a Maimonidean, Maimonides was a Spinozist.[63] More recently Chalier (op. cit.) enumerates several central doctrines of the TTP that Spinoza borrows almost entirely from Maimonides, but what she finds even more remarkable is the way in which Spinoza turned the Maimonidean ideas on their heads and constantly used them against him.

Alluding to Strauss's ideas about the esoteric messages within works that are potentially subversive, such as the *Guide*, Pines playfully remarks that Maimonides did not find in Spinoza the reader for whom he had been hoping. The detection of contradictions did not follow the principle of charity in interpretation, and did not lead to a search for a deeper comprehension of the message but, on the contrary, served a bitter antagonism. The rise of the new science and philosophy with their constant tendency to discard much of mediaeval Aristotelism partially explains Spinoza's attitude. More important, according to Pines, is the fact that Spinoza was unresponsive and indifferent to the political obligations and constraints that motivated the great tradition of coded writing.[64] Strauss suggests that one regards the TTP as belonging to this tradition, but as he himself conceded in his classic essay "How to Read Spinoza *Theologico-Political Treatise?*,"[65] the kind of caution and restraint Spinoza displayed in this work is very different from Maimonides's. Spinoza was addressing a non-Jewish audience, and he had of course to beware of the ecclesiastics whose authority he was trying to undermine. But his attitude toward Jewish thought and traditions was the exact opposite of Maimonides's. The latter was addressing a Jewish audience, and the Jewishness of his whole venture was its obvious and unquestionable presupposition, in a sense the thing that mattered most. The caution he had to display in his philosophical

---

[61] See Jöel (1870) and Harvey (1982 and 1994); one has to mention here also Wolfson and Roth, and see Nadler (2009) for a review of the studies, mainly recent, that deal with this question. I shall discuss later on (Chapter 3) the more generally philosophical question of Spinoza's alleged traditionalism; here it is a question of his rapport to Maimonides as an emblematic thinker of Judaism. However, I would suggest, already at this point, that despite some obvious similarities and analogies, Jewish mediaeval philosophy is a source for Spinoza in a particular way; not less than being influenced by it, it is for him also an occasional cause for the elaboration of a systematic criticism of both theology and religious philosophy in general, but also, more specifically, of the Jewish tradition as such.

[62] See in particular Parnes (2012), who gives in the introduction a useful review of the debate.

[63] Pines (1968), p. 4.

[64] Ibid., pp. 4–5.

[65] Strauss (1988).

work – which was not the case with his enormous Halakhic corpus – was a manifestation of a sense of responsibility toward the community from which he came; of which he had always been part and, indeed, one of its main leaders; and whose existence and thriving, both material and spiritual, was what gave its ultimate meaning to his lifework. Maimonides was well aware of the risks involved in the kind of philosophical reflection he was presenting in his *Guide*; it could undermine the authority of Scripture and shake the basis on which Jewish life was set. Still, he also thought that the truth involved in his philosophical-rationalistic enterprise was, in many ways, indispensable. What he was worried about when he was supposedly trying to hide the fully rationalistic message of his *Guide* was not his own personal safety but the cohesion and inner solidity of the Jewish world. Although very critical of some important aspects of orthodox discourse, he was also aware of the subversive potential of philosophical thinking and apprehensive of its dangers. There was nothing he was afraid of more than jeopardizing Jewish religious life; after all, he invested much more time, effort, and intellectual energy in his Halakhic work and in attending to the welfare of the Jews than to his philosophic work. Spinoza apparently did not care much about this anymore. That he retained much of the critical aspects of the Jewish attitude toward Christian theology and political theology adds complexity to his stance, but it does not mean that he retained a Maimonidean-like fidelity to his Jewishness. This difference between Spinoza and Maimonides is not trivial. It concerns the very nature of their respective enterprises, and it touches upon the most profound motivations from which they sprang. Maimonides plays a significant, but also paradoxical, role in the TTP: he serves Spinoza both as a starting point for his critique of religion but also as the main target of his attack. There are two connected but different aspects to Spinoza's critique of Maimonides. First of all, the latter is the emblematic Jewish theologian and philosopher. This is explainable by the fact that he is usually considered as the greatest figure of the tradition of Jewish mediaeval philosophy (and, most probably, a preferable subject of reading and study of Spinoza during his youth) as well as the greatest codifier of the *Halakha*.

But Maimonides was also a radical adversary and critic of religious simplemindedness and irrationality. What is at issue between Spinoza and Maimonides is thus not the value (or, actually, lack of it) of prejudice and superstition in religious life. Maimonides opposes them, and the fundamentalism that arises from them, as vehemently as Spinoza does; as a defender of rational religion, in a certain sense he is even a greater enemy of religious irrationality than Spinoza is. Just as Spinoza would do more than five centuries later, Maimonides too offers a rational explanation – often not to the liking of orthodoxy – of both miracles and prophecy, and also ways of accommodating Scripture to the teachings of scientific reason. But when Spinoza sets out on his assault on Maimonides's "method" of reading Scripture, he does it from a point of view that is not only incommensurable but also radically opposed to

1.2. The Tractatus Theologico-Politicus

Maimonides's most fundamental presuppositions that are not methodological or even philosophical, but religious.

Maimonides appears in the TTP as the chief adversary, indeed as an archetypal enemy of philosophy. But this is so because behind the prejudice, credulity, and naïve religiousness looms the real enemy: religious rationalism. Maimonides is, in the last analysis, more dangerous, and much more difficult to refute than orthodoxy. And this is so precisely because of the great proximity to Spinoza, or because Spinoza was so close to be, as Harvey claimed, a Maimonidean. He makes it possible to pretend that the essence of religion is not superstition and that it can be overcome within religion itself, but also to hide the danger it poses to the state – to the freedom of philosophy, and, in particular, to philosophy as an enterprise of pure reason and rational salvation – behind an appearance of rationality. The fact that Spinoza is willing to accommodate some kind of universal, rather commonsensical if not simple-minded religiosity, but not rational religion, arguably also politically moderate – and Maimonides was precisely this kind of rationalist – is far from being trivial. This is why the attack on Maimonides's doctrine of the Noachite Laws in chapter 5 is so telling: what Spinoza could tolerate least of all was the kind of universal wisdom Maimonides incarnated and his attempt to incorporate it into an undaunted and non-compromising defense of the specific and irreducible value of Jewish religiosity.

Much of the difference between Spinoza and Maimonides turns on the difference of attitude – loyalty or lack of it – toward a tradition. This is far from being a trivial question. Through it takes shape the deeper philosophical question of the ultimate pertinence, legitimacy, and justifiability of certain fundamental religious categories, in the last analysis of the category of religiosity itself. Behind the similarities and dissimilarities, the continuities and discontinuities that exist – or not – between Spinoza and Maimonides, at the bottom of their interpretation of Jewishness and of the Jewish phenomenon there stands something even more fundamental and of universal significance. Theirs are opposing answers to the fundamental question whether such concepts as *miracles*, *prophecy*, or *Scripture* retain for the philosopher an irreducible, original religious meaning – of the sacred, enchanted, supernatural, awe-inspiring, moral, and so on – or not. Maimonides answers in the affirmative, Spinoza in the negative.

According to Jonathan Israel, for example, "no other element of Spinoza's philosophy provoked as much consternation and outrage in his own time as his sweeping denial of miracles and the supernatural."[66] According to another recent scholar, Maimonides's views on miracles evolved from a rejection to an

---

[66] Israel (2001), p. 218. Chapter 12 of this seminal work discusses Spinoza's doctrine of miracles. See chapter 5 of Nadler (2011), which contains a comparison with Maimonides's doctrine. Lagrée, op. cit., discusses Spinoza in the context of Christian theological discussion of the miraculous, such as Calvin's rejection of the cult of relics – but not of miracles as such.

acceptance. According to his mature doctrine – so goes this reading – those events that are to be considered as miracles do not put in question the overall rationalistic conception of the universe; they show, however, that the natural order is *insufficient* to explain everything that happens. There is a higher order, that of Divine will and providence.[67] Without risking here any controversial interpretation of Maimonides, I would retain from what has just been said the following: Maimonidean religiosity does not require the suspension of the rationalistic attitude. The Maimonidean philosopher would agree with the Spinozistic rationalist that miracles are not an intervention in, and suspension of, the natural order, which does not mean that he would reject the pertinence of the *concept* of miracle as Spinoza did. The *miraculous* signifies a rationally acceptable concept of a higher order that does not contradict – or "suspend" – the natural order, but somehow contains it, and that is specifically *religious*: nature itself is miraculous or, differently said, created,[68] which is not to be equated with, say, magic, sorcery, or the like. For Spinoza, on the other hand, nature, since not created, is natural. Just as for Kant the priority of practical reason does not imply the suspension of theoretical reason, so for the Maimonideans the priority of the religious interest was not intended as a compromise with irrationality. Rather than a *reduction* of the religious meaning of the concept of the *miraculous*, which is arguably what Spinoza will envisage, Maimonides effects its rationalist rehabilitation. Not succumbing to the claims of orthodoxy, Maimonidean thought expresses, I believe, an authentically religious need to incorporate the specifically religious within a larger concept of reason, an attempt not to forsake reason despite the demands, even onslaught, of theocracy.

That Spinoza's criticism of miracles was indeed seen by his readers as such a scandal was not necessarily, at least not always, because they disliked his interpretation of the stories about miracles as because they sensed that what was implied in his interpretation was a radical undermining of the legitimacy of the category of the *miraculous* as such. Leibniz was one of these readers. For him, just as for Maimonides, it was not the irregularity seen in nature, neither the extraordinary nor the unexplainable, that justified holding a positive concept of the miraculous, but the religious (yet fully rationalistic, at least as he saw it) recognition of the need to acknowledge a higher order of reasons, as much under the jurisdiction of the *principle of reason* as the natural order, but distinct and irreducible to it. Just as for Maimonides, for him too this was part of a philosophical project of justifying loyalty toward a whole tradition, of

---

[67] See Langermann (2004), which contains also references to the main studies of Maimonides's attitudes toward miracles.
[68] The "belief in eternity as Aristotle sees it ... destroys the Law in its principle, necessarily gives the lie to every miracle, and reduces to inanity all the hopes and threats that the Law has held out." On the other hand, "with a belief in the creation of the world in time, all the miracles become possible and the Law becomes possible, and all questions that may be asked on this subject, vanish." *Guide of the Perplexed*, II, pp. 25.

1.2. *The* Tractatus Theologico-Politicus

retaining its vocabulary and reinterpreting it so that the stance of *faith* can become rationally acceptable. Apparently, then, "loyalty" and "faith" are not easily separable; at least they were not in Spinoza's times, and his critique of Maimonides and of religion in general has to be seen within this context.

Chapter 14 – *Quid sit fides*, or "What is Faith"[69] – sums up the critique of theology. As suggested earlier in the chapter, the notion of faith can be seen as expressing the more fundamental feature of a religious attitude. Just a couple of pages before presenting his seven *fidei universalis dogmata*, Spinoza defines faith: it is "the holding of certain beliefs about God such that without these beliefs there cannot be obedience to God" (Ch. 14, G III, p. 175). To be a man of faith just means holding some opinions that induce obedience – apparently to God, but in reality to the civil authorities. The key term here is "obedience." In Spinoza's language, obedience always presupposes constraint. Since the essence of obedience, he says earlier in the TTP, is compliance with the precepts only because of the authority of those who command, in democracy respecting the laws is not obedience strictly speaking (Ch. 5, G III, p. 74). Originating always from without, it is the antithesis of freedom and, consequently, does not have any intrinsic value. The philosopher does not *obey*, reason does not *command*, and philosophy is a form of freedom, not of obedience or compliance with precepts, rules, or laws. If the pious man, mainly due to the fear and hope that religion instills, obeys, it is plain that the geometrician cannot be said to "obey" the rules that he "follows" when demonstrating – and hence affirming, or, as it were, agreeing with – the truth of, say, the Pythagorean Theorem; the philosopher too does not "obey" reason when he understands – and, thus, accepts – the truth about himself and the world and, in particular, renders it his way of life. What is referred to by the term "faith" does not constitute a *sui generis* human experience. The justification of faith is purely conditional and is based wholly on considerations of expediency. Whatever cognitive content there is in faith, it is not conceived as a theoretical, rational, or true content, for the distinction between true or false does not apply to it. It has to be assessed only functionally, in terms of its utility and efficacy as a means of solidifying political peace, the cohesion and stability of the state and, in particular, the right of the political authorities to rule.

Given that Spinoza did not fool anybody as to the real nature of the book he wrote, and that the radical subversiveness of its attitude toward theology, or of its conception of the non-religious nature of the state in general, was pretty transparent – the immediate scandal it provoked being evidence enough – the question that many of its later-day readers understandably ask is: for whom was it written?[70] I shall not venture a full answer to this old question, but suggest one possible such reader – Spinoza himself. Leo Strauss said somewhere

---

[69] The full title is "What is Faith, and who are the Faithful (*fideles*); The Foundations of Faith are Determined and Separated from Philosophy."

[70] See Frankel (1999), who reviews much of the debate on this question.

that the TTP, or Spinoza's critique of religion, had been a kind of philosophical propaedeutic, a preparation for philosophy in the sense of overcoming prejudice and superstition together with the force of religious tradition, authority, and communal identity. In this sense the TTP is an oblique record of a personal journey of liberation (used here in a morally neutral key), of a freedom from religion achieved through great effort. The fruit of generalization, the TTP thus can be presented as a plea to secure freedom of thought in two different domains, political and philosophical. The state's withdrawal from the realm of truth is a condition for free thinking, but political freedom does not ensure freedom from superstition. These two forms of freedom are tacitly assumed in the *Ethics*. If there had not been an open road to philosophy, there would have been no point in writing the *Ethics*. But full personal freedom, which is a philosophical and not a political virtue, can apparently be attained only at the end of the philosophical journey; the relative lack of freedom at the outset is not an insurmountable obstacle on the road to free philosophizing, provided enough freedom to set out is assured in advance. Assuming that the state, or the theologians do not jeopardize one's relative freedom of thought, what remains to be done – and this is the most arduous and important of all human enterprises – is to get liberated from all remaining superstition and, by the same token, positively build oneself as a free man. Since superstition and religion are coextensive (in the TTP; not anymore in the TP), in the realm of *truth* theology and religion have no say. In a *more geometrico* philosophy, just as in geometry itself, there is no room for untruth. It is simply banished as non-being. Truth or true philosophy does not tolerate untruth. It may take time to accomplish the task, and one has to begin with lower forms of knowledge, but once true understanding is achieved, there is no more room for error. Toleration presupposes an authority that is neutral on the questions debated. The liberal state can be said to be such an authority, which provides a space where all opinions, true and untrue, are tolerated. Hence, toleration is a political and not a philosophical virtue. In fact, in the Spinozistic state, theology and religion enjoy only relative toleration.[71] But in the realm of truth, theology is not tolerated. As a non-truth pretending to be truth, religion's object is a non-object, its pronouncements signify nothing (unless it can be shown, sometimes, that a real object had been seen, by some philosophers-theologians, apparently mainly Jewish, as if through the clouds).[72] Outside philosophy, however, religion is an insurmountable reality. But what occupies the vacant place of its non-existent object is a "will to power;" religion is thus a political fact. To the extent that theology and religion in general are interpreted as essentially political, toleration and religious freedom in the state are limited so that the religious will to

---

[71] TTP chapter 19. See James, op. cit., p. 14: superstition is a "deformation of religion, a pathology that arises when religion goes wrong." But religion cannot *but* go wrong; when it does not, it is either sane politic, or sane reason, that is, Spinozism.

[72] As Spinoza says in the scholium to EIIp7; see discussion later in the book.

power serves the only legitimate power – the state, which, for Spinoza, was a secular, anticlerical republic rather than liberal. In any other form, religion is, by definition, harmful and dangerous.

1.3. Spinoza's Religiosity

These are then crucial questions: What is the nature of the TTP? What is the significance of Spinoza's use of a language with such heavy religious or even mystical resonance? Although these are real questions – perhaps even the most important – from the hermeneutical, historical, and philosophical points of view, the debates about them are often more verbal than substantive. Whether Spinoza's philosophy is religious or atheistic, whether he was the first secular Jew (or otherwise) or a non-confessional religious rationalist, whether his concept of God or the constant use of religious language has positive religious content or is subversive, perhaps radically so, depends, before the hermeneutical question can be seriously addressed, on what meaning is given to words such as "religious," "mystical experience," or, for that matter, "secular," "atheist," and so on – all notoriously ambiguous and imprecise notions.

There is no need to elaborate here on the difficulty and inherent ambiguity of the question of religion or on the great difficulty of offering a coherent and historically, biographically, and, in particular, philosophically interesting answer to the question of Spinoza's religiosity. There are a few points, though, about which a kind of consensus can perhaps be assumed. That Spinoza was a critic of theocracy, or of what he saw as the characteristic attempt to usurp political power by the ecclesiastics of all creeds, seems to be beyond any serious contention. The same can be said about the claim that his critique of theocracy was also a systematic critique of theology, that is, of what he conceived to be mostly a justification of theocracy. Although here and there one can hear some doubts about it, it seems also quite safe to say that with what can be described as a rejection of the very intelligibility of the notion of the "supernatural" – or, positively put, Spinoza's philosophy of "immanence" – he also rejected, or at least radically deconstructed, a number of the most fundamental elements of the great theistic traditions of Jewish, Christian, and Islamic civilizations. Notably, the notions of "personal," "legislator," or "transcendent God;" of "creation," "miracles," "revelation," "prophecy," "providence," "afterlife," and – more problematically – "reward and punishment" and, eventually, (moral) "good and bad" but also absolute "authority" and especially the authority of tradition and of any ecclesiastic institutions, instances, or – to use a modern word – establishment, are radically criticized, relativized, undermined, subverted, and, eventually, refuted.

But, it is sometimes said, there is also another dimension. There is also a trans-political, non-confessional, extra-institutional, and subtraditional religiosity, and Spinoza, as a person, apparently lived this religiosity, and his philosophy is the result of this life, a life of a "God intoxicated" man. The idea that a religiosity can exist outside any concrete historical or communitarian crystallization is highly questionable. In fact many, perhaps most, historians let alone sociologists or anthropologists of religion would deny it. But this only adds urgency to the need to understand the sense of the religious language used by the recluse from Pavilioengragt. Even if, in any case, religiosity does not exist outside some concrete crystallization, it is still apparently legitimate to speak of such an inner, more or less universal content of all, or at least many, such crystallizations. Attempting a general definition of the concept religiosity or even seriously justifying the use of it are, of course, completely outside the confines of the present study. In order to try to give, however, some general indication of the basic orientation of what follows, two classical attempts to define, or rather describe, religiosity can be of some help: one is William James's *The Varieties of Religious Experience* and the other is Rudolf Otto's *The Idea of the Holy*.[73]

As the subtitle of Rudolf Otto's book explains, *The Idea of the Holy* is "An inquiry into the non-rational factor in the idea of the divine and its relation to the rational." The book begins with an attempt to define a category of the "non-rational," to distinguish between it and the simple "irrational," and, in particular, to justify not only its theoretical use but also its applicability to what Otto regards as a sound and fundamentally sane human mode of existence. It would be vain, it seems, to look in Spinoza for anything that can be described as the non-rational. There is certainly for him a lot of irrationality around, and the enterprise of philosophy is a plaidoyer for the cause of reason and of rationality; but the idea that there is a category of legitimate human experiences that lies outside the rational-irrational continuum and that, in particular, without being rational would nevertheless be immune to the critique Spinoza directs against all forms of the irrational, would certainly be completely unacceptable for him. In fact, his critique of religion – blatantly in the TTP, and in a more subtle way in his other works – may very well be interpreted as considering religion as the paradigm of irrationality.

Besides this, and briefly– very briefly – put, it would certainly be wrong to look in Spinoza's philosophy for anything that can be construed as an authentic expression of what Otto calls the "consciousness of *der Heilige*" (the "sacred" or "holy"). It seems absurd to suggest that Spinoza's substance or god or nature could be described as "numinous," and the awe a "numinous object" inspires in the religious consciousness is arguably what Spinoza describes – alongside hope – as one of the most pernicious "bad affects." Calling it "fear" – notably fear of death – he may be assumed to deny implicitly any specificity of the experience of an allegedly *religious* "awe." The attitude of the Spinozistic philosopher toward what he calls God does not seem to be anywhere in the phenomenological or psychological vicinity of what Otto calls the *mysterium*

---

[73] Another such an attempt that comes readily to mind is, of course, Kierkegaard's, but it is quite obvious that is there is nothing in Spinoza's radical rationalism that would permit anything like Kierkegaard's "leap."

tremendum, and the infinitely infinite of the Spinozistic God, although not known to the finite soul, is nevertheless not describable as "wholly other."

But it is perhaps in the context of the inherently ethical nature of the experience of the numinous (as Otto sees it) that the complex relation of Spinoza's thought to religion can be better appreciated. In the later parts of the present study the concepts of *value* and *valuableness* will play a central role. I shall try to show, notably in the last two chapters, that, among other things, for all its radical rejection of the legitimacy of deontological considerations, and for all its undaunted critique of "moralism," Spinoza's ethical theory can all the same be interpreted on the basis of a certain concept of the irreducible *value* of existence.[74]

Now, an important aspect of Otto's phenomenology of "The Holy" is the claim that one important element of the idea of the "Divine" is that it is, in an immediate and original way, "a category of Value." Chapter VIII of *The Idea of the Holy* (pp. 50–59) is titled "The Holy as a Category of Value: Sin and Atonement." Assuming for the moment the as-yet-unproven hermeneutical legitimacy, in the context of the *Ethics*, of the concept of *value*, it would seem very hard to deny that the religious-moral categories of "sin" and "atonement" *cannot* be a part of it. Otto, however, goes much farther. The idea of "sin," he thinks, and just like the category of "the holy" in general, is *sui generis*. It should not be confused with that of lawlessness, transgression of the moral law, or failing to comply with one's duty. Its origin is in a specifically religious experience of the radical self-depreciation, of "absolute 'profaneness'" (p. 51), which is a judgment passed, by the religious person, "not upon his character, because of individual 'profane' actions of his, but upon his own very existence as a creature before that which is supreme of all creatures." This is when and how one

> passes upon the numen a judgment of *appreciation* of a unique kind by the category diametrically contrary to "the profane", the category "holy", which is proper to the numen alone, but to it in an absolute degree; he says: *Tu solus sanctus* (ibid.).

The "*Tu solus sanctus*" is a "paean of praise," and it is the place where *prayer* begins. Despite the religious language he uses so frequently, it seems safe to say that there is no room in Spinoza's conception of the world and of man for any of these. On the other hand – and this will be the core of the hermeneutical attitude proposed in the present study – not only Spinoza's conception of the world and of man is authentically and essentially an ethics, but it can be said also to be a particular kind of ethics; it can even be said to be based essentially on a peculiar – in some sense *sui generis* as well – doctrine of the absolute *value* and *valuableness* of existence. This concept of *value* is metaphysical and, I would suggest, irreducible to more conventional forms of theorizing about values; it is also very different from, if not altogether opposed

---

[74] See Bidney (1940), last chapter.

to, Otto's concept of the valuableness of the numinous. Among other things – and this is perhaps its most peculiar feature – this is because it purports to be a doctrine of the value of existence insofar as existence is conceived as a radically and solely *hic et nunc*, which is, paradigmatically, the *hic et nunc* of the private body. Needless to say, this is a very paradoxical – some would certainly say oxymoronic – doctrine.

1.4. Spinoza as a Philosopher of Seriousness

Similar observations can be made apropos of William James's *Varieties of Religious Experience*. Most of the elements that James ascribes to this experience are wholly alien to Spinoza's famous model of the free and wise man, or even to the third kind of knowledge, the intellectual love of God, or the final achievement of the philosophical enterprise, which Spinoza calls "salvation, beatitude and freedom," as it is exposed in the second half of EV. However, as James remarks already in the Second Lecture, "There must be something solemn, serious, and tender about any attitude which we denominate religious."[75]

Notwithstanding the tenderness manifested by some contemporary religious movements, it seems safe to say that in Spinoza's "attitude," if one may so call it, or rather, of that of an imaginable Spinozist personality or type (in his *exemplar* of human nature, or as it has innumerable times been depicted by poets, playwrights, or authors, not to speak of philosophers and commentators), there would be very little, if at all, of solemnity or tenderness. On the other hand, there is in it much that can be referred to as seriousness; not gravity nor severity nor somberness nor anything that can be interpreted as *tristitia* or a bad affect of any kind, but something that is perhaps best rendered in the Hebrew כובד ראש (literary, "a weighty head," which is the opposite of frivolousness).

James nowhere explains the exact meaning of seriousness. Like many notions of this kind, it is rather vague and ambiguous. It has its everyday uses, which are quite often either simply factual or pejorative. We say of someone that "he is seriously ill;" and Oscar Wilde, for example, famously said that "life is too important to be taken seriously." Umberto Eco's *The Name of the Rose* turns around the idea of Christianity's, or perhaps religion's in general, seriousness as a fear of laughter. Not only literary people but philosophers as well have had deep reservations vis-à-vis what they considered to be an excess of seriousness. Nietzsche was one of them, as was Kierkegaard and Sartre, who said that seriousness was a form of *mauvaise foi*, typical of materialists and revolutionaries. He certainly had in mind some comrades from his immediate *milieu*.

---

[75] William James (2004), p. 44. Another element of the religious attitude that is pertinent in the context of the present study of Spinoza is what James calls "acceptance": "'I accept the universe' is reported to have been a favorite utterance of our New England transcendentalist, Margaret Fuller; and when someone repeated this phrase to Thomas Carlyle, his sardonic comment is said to have been: 'gad! She'd better!'" (pp. 46–47).

1.4. *Spinoza as a Philosopher of Seriousness*

A famous cliché says that "humor is a serious thing;" one can say that seriousness too is a serious thing. Pascal and Kant are two particularly significant examples of thinkers who took seriousness seriously. Pascal's wager is a justly famous expression of a doctrine – a strictly religious one – of seriousness. The stakes involved in the way one lives one's life are so high, it says, that it is worthwhile – indeed rational, even necessary – to bet everything one possesses on one's choice. Pascal is basically saying one's entire life depends on it. Whether one calls it "salvation" or "eternal life," what is to be gained is so important that the risks cannot be too high to take. Spinoza says something quite similar to this in the opening paragraphs of the TIE. For him too life, in a way, depends on it. In the TIE he calls it "lasting joy," and in the *Ethics* it would become a question of the eternity of the soul, of salvation, beatitude, and freedom. It is so important and so much more valuable than everything else one can find that it is indeed worthwhile to risk everything else for the slim chance one has to achieve it. Needless to say, it is hard to think a deeper gap than the one that separates Pascal's and Spinoza's salvation and eternal life.[76]

Despite some similarities between Spinoza and Kant, a similar gap separates these two philosophers. Their philosophies constitute parallel enterprises of philosophical liberation, and in both cases it is liberation from theology and religion. For both the ultimate justification of the truthfulness, or of the binding force, of the precepts or principles (in Kant's terminology, the "imperatives") of ethics is not to be looked for in revelation and is not to be grounded in an *extramundane* principle. Not the will of God, but "reason" is the source of morality and the guarantee of what is conceived to be its absolute validity. The weight of the exigency imposed by practical reason is, however, similar to the weight of the religious commandments, and Kant's "respect for the Law" expresses the kind of seriousness James was discussing. It was meant, by Kant, to solidify or, so to speak, thicken an abstract sense of duty with concrete affectivity. Spinoza too makes the psychological, or existential, effectiveness of reason depend on its affectivity; but unlike Kant, theoretical truth is conceived by him to be as "categorical" as is Kant's moral imperative. One might even risk saying that Kant and Spinoza are the most radical ethicists of modern times: both conceive reason as the final arbiter of ethical judgment that has an absolute validity as truth and is absolutely compelling as morality. It is in this sense that they both can be considered as philosophers of the seriousness of the moral attitude and as proposing to replace the seriousness of the religious attitude with that of philosophy.

---

[76] Bove, Bras & Méchoulan (2007) is the result of what has probably been the only attempt of a systematic confronting Spinoza and Pascal. As the editors of this collection of articles note, the TTP and the *Pensées* appeared on the same year, 1670. They also cite Léon Brunschvicg, a passionate reader of both Pascal and Spinoza, who (1951, pp. 198–9) reminds us the two had on their desks both the Bible and the *Discours de la Méthode*. The articles grouped in this volume discuss different aspects, mostly limited, of the *oeures* of the two thinkers. Curiously, though, none of them deal with the two "wagers."

But this is where the similarities end. Completely alien to any Kantian-like deontological theory of the nature of the moral point of view or of ethics, Spinoza's philosophy implies a radical rejection, from the perspective of a definitive theory of reason, of the very pertinence of such notions as "moral duty" or "imperative," but also of "good and bad," let alone of "evil," radical or not, or guilt and even moral responsibility, which express all the kinds of absoluteness Kant attributed to the demands of the ethical point of view. Yet, it is an ethics *ordine geometrico demonstrata* and, hence, absolute.

All writers about Spinoza are aware, of course, of the importance of the moral dimension of his philosophy; quite a few of them even consider Spinoza as first and foremost an ethicist or as a moral theorist.[77] But precisely the similarities and profound differences between, for example, Spinoza and Kant on the one hand, and Spinoza and Pascal on the other, raise the question of what the seriousness of the *Ethics* can mean. The full significance of this will – hopefully – become clearer only as we proceed, but a few words of explanation seem to be in order. By its refusal to allow a primordial role to concepts such as duty, obligation, guilt, and so on, Spinoza's ethical theory is positively anti-moralistic. It is nevertheless a *moral* theory, and its particular nature as a moral theory can be best understood as an attempt to conceptualize, systematize, and justify a normative stance based on the recognition in the irreducible seriousness, importance, and valuableness of existence and of human existence. This means that the ultimate and highest achievement of the philosophical journey Spinoza offers his reader to embark on, what he calls the "soul's intellectual love which is God's love in which he loves himself" (EVp36), is not only happiness or joy the Spinozistic sage possess as a personal assess, but also, and in particular, a fulfillment and realization of the intrinsic and objective importance and valuableness of being.

The notions of "value," "norms," or "normativity" are not absent from the literature on Spinoza. Rejecting, as has just been said, the ultimate pertinence of "obedience," "good and bad," "duty," or the like, neither value nor normativity can belong, if they are to make sense in the context of the *Ethics*, to the realm of what habitually falls under the "ought" way of relating to the world, to one's fellow-men, or even to one's own self. Philosophical reason, as we have just seen, does not command and does not impose obligations or demands. Philosophy as a moral theory is the locus of truth about existence, and human existence as a part of it, and not the source of *rules*, let alone of commandments, of good behavior, of wise conduct, or of a "healthy" life.

The "health'" in the last paragraph refers to the quasi-omnipresence of a medical metaphor in the *Ethics*: the moral good is useful and profitable in the way medicine is, and philosophy is a kind of *medicina mentis*. Gilles Deleuze,

---

[77] See notably Duff (1903), Delbos (1988), Bidney (1940), Deleuze (1981), and, very recently, LeBuff (2010); there is an issue of the *Studia Spinozana* under the title of *The Ethics in the Ethics* (7: 1991) that brings several articles on Spinoza's ethical theory.

1.5. The Question of Normativity

for one, made much use of this medical metaphor. A philosopher and a great reader of Spinoza, he utilized the interesting but relatively neglected exchange of letters between Spinoza and Blyenbergh and their dispute of the sense to be given to the Biblical story of the "forbidden fruit" to give sense to, and illustrate, an important hermeneutical claim: Spinoza's "practical philosophy" is "ethics," not "morality," and Spinoza's *medicina mentis* is anything but "moralism."[78] God's forbidding of eating the fruit of the tree of knowledge has to be interpreted, says Spinoza, as a warning or a prescription: it is poisonous and harmful. Pure, as it were, "forbidding" has no rational meaning; the interdiction to eat it is actually knowledge of the body and of the effect the eating of the fruit will necessarily have upon it. The common man calls it "divine law," but the philosopher knows that it is an "eternal truth." An absolute "forbidden," just like "sin," is a chimera. Respect of interdictions has to be understood in terms of knowledge, and transgression is ignorance.

1.5. The Question of Normativity

One thing that probably resonates in Deleuze's use of the medical metaphor, and that may explain to some degree his fascination with it, is a fundamental philosophical-historical discussion that has been going on mainly in France in the aftermath of the work done first by George Canguilhem and then by (mainly the early) Foucault and that in different forms revolved around the question of the nature of "normality" and "normativity": how to account, for example, for the distinction between "the normal" and "the pathological," "health" and "disease," "normality" and "madness." Those were the questions that preoccupied these two thinkers and still preoccupy many of their followers. A more explicit connection between Canguilhem and Foucault on the one hand and Spinoza on the other has been made more recently by Pierre Macherey, another French scholar.[79]

Canguilhem's investigation of the nature of normativity can be helpful in formulating some indications as to how to understand the "seriousness" of Spinoza's ethics. The core of Canguilhem's theory of normativity is the idea that living beings produce the norms according to which they – and in a derivative sense the practitioners of the medical professions – judge their health and illness. There is an immanent logic of life and an original dynamics that connects the "normal" and the "pathologic" and that constitutes, in a sense, life

---

[78] See Deleuze (1981); Letters 18–24, 28 and TTP (ch. 4).
[79] In an autobiographical preface he added to the collection of articles (2009), Macherey tells about his attachment to both Canguilhem and Foucault and of his many years of work on Spinoza. See also Canguilhem (1966); Foucault, notably (1963) and (1972). A great deal has been written in the last years on Canguilhem, who is much less known in the English-speaking world than Foucault; e.g., Braunstein (2007); Bing (1998); Giroux (2010). The question of "normativity" has gained lately considerable interest in the English-speaking philosophical world as well.

itself. Life is a polarity, and it is in the course of the movement between the two poles, which is the movement of the living organism itself and, to that extent, subjective – that is, understood and conceived only by taking into account the experience of life – that emerges what Canguilhem diversely calls "biological value," "a norm immanent to life," "biological normativity," and more:[80] living things *prefer* life to death and *value* health over disease or well-being over suffering, and there is in life – not as the result of haphazard process of blind evolution, but as the fundamental characteristic of the *sui generis* phenomenon of life – an auto-evaluation.[81]

This sense of "normativity" is usefully, albeit partially, applicable to the philosophy of Spinoza. At its basis is a sense of the *non-indifference* of things, of the *valuableness* of being, of the absolute relevancy and validity of *preferences*, of the need to make distinctions, of insistence on the idea that things *do matter*, that it does make a difference what kind of life one lives, that philosophical truth is important, that it is all, precisely, a very serious matter.

But a few fundamental distinctions still have to be made. Canguilhem's concept of "normativity" is grounded in his medical and scientific thinking and is essentially descriptive and, in some sense, phenomenological. Spinoza's doctrine of normativity and of the seriousness of being – not just of life – is metaphysical, which means that it is neither descriptive nor phenomenological. The preferability or desirability of Spinozistic philosophical life is different from the biological normativity of the French physician-philosopher. More precisely, Canguilhem's concept of normativity is more usefully applicable to what I will refer to in what follows as the "stoic-medical moment" of Spinoza's philosophy (see further discussion later in the book); but there is also a "final moment" in this philosophy,[82] and it is less useful in this context. The reason is

---

[80] Canguilhem, op. cit., p. 148 and passim; see Giroux, op. cit., p. 23.

[81] There is, of course, nothing "vitalistic" nor any mystification of life in all this, just insistence on the irreducibility of life to biology or, from the point of view of the physician that Canguilhem was, on the priority of the "clinic" over the objectifying view of the physiologist. In a particularly illuminating article, Jean-François Braunstein shows that the motivation behind Canguilhem's life-long *scientific*-philosophical critique of behaviorism, of scientific psychology, and, later in his life, of neuroscience, which add all up to a coherent anti-reductionist and anti-mechanistic project, had always been deeply *moral*. Noteworthy are the references to Spinoza in Canguilhem's writings on his friend Jean Cavaillès, a Spinozist and a hero of the anti-Nazi resistance who was killed by the Gestapo: "It is because Spinoza's philosophy represents the most radical attempt at a philosophy without *cogito*, that it was so close to Cavaillès, so present to his mind when he had to explain either the idea of his combat of a *resistant* or his idea of the construction of mathematics." See Braunstein, "Psychologie et milieu. Ethique et histoire des sciences chez Georges Canguilhem," in Braunstein, op. cit., p. 89.

[82] I borrow the expression "stoic moment" from an article by Alexandre Matheron bearing it for title (Matheron, 1999), although I use it in a slightly different way. A lot has been recently written about the relation of Spinoza to the Stoic philosophy, especially to Seneca. See, among other things, Lagrée (2004), esp. pp. 82–95; James, op. cit., deals at some length with Cicero's possible influence on Spinoza; a book-length study of this topic is DeBrabander (2007). The "final moment" refers to Rousset (1968). Written during the times when the "new Spinoza" (see Montag

1.5. The Question of Normativity

that Spinoza's normativity is based on an objective, or ontologically positive, concept of value. To put it somewhat blatantly, the living organism's "normal" and "pathological," or the concepts of "health" and "disease," make very little sense, if at all, *sub specie aeternitatis*. They also do not make much sense from the point of view of the biological sphere as a whole: the disease of one organism may be the well-being or survival of another, big fish eat small fish, and nature is indifferent to either the calamity of the one or the thriving of the other. Decay is the general rule, or the "normal," from the point of view of the organic realm as such. At this level, it seems, the notion of "norms" does not make much sense. Spinoza's theory of the good, or philosophical, life is thoroughly and at one and the same time ontological and normative. Philosophical life, unlike "health," makes a difference that is valid *sub specie aeternitatis* and not only from the subjective point of view of the individual organism. Disease, decay, and the inevitable eventual defeat of individual existence is the rule of Spinoza's theory of the life of reason as well; but the inner value of this kind of life – of philosophy – is not said from the exclusive point of view of the individual, and the normativity involved in the Spinozistic view of himself is both more personal and objective than the view Canguilhem's medical practitioner has of his patient. The latter would not as much as dream call the state of health or well-being "eternity". Spinoza did and, as I shall try to show, he was very serious about it.

Spinoza's theory of the affects, the description of human "pathology" (or "bondage"), the figure of the "wise man" who is the master of his emotions, and the doctrine of "wisdom" constitute indeed a sort of "medical," stoic, or eudemonic moment of his philosophy. The elaboration of this theory of man, of "anthropology" in its original sense,[83] occupies the central part of the *Ethics* (roughly, from the scholium after EIIIp9 until EVp13), and there are in it obvious traces of stoic influence. Although the theory of the affects itself has as a main, perhaps even more important, point of reference – Descartes – as well, and in particular in *Les Passions de l'âme*, the fact that it is grounded in a radically anti-Cartesian mind-body doctrine, justifies referring to this central part of the *Ethics* with an explicit allusion to the Stoic tradition.

Already in this "Stoic-medical" part of the *Ethics*, the deontological, or "ought," meaning of either normativity or valuableness would not do as an adequate hermeneutic key. Founding the ethical view of man on the deployment

---

and Stolz, 1997) was the main figure of Spinoza studies in France, and off the beaten track, the book has been relatively ignored, which is a pity, since it contains not only many valuable insights, but also, and mainly, because it addresses directly what constitutes after all Spinoza's main concern, namely the question of beatitude.

[83] The word "anthropology" (or rather "anthroplogie") was first introduced in the 1629, in the French translation of the physician Jean Riolan the Son, *Anthropographia*. See A. Bitbole-Hespériès (2009), who also cites the following phrase: "Man is composed of two natures greatly different, of the soul and of the body, the first being joined to the body is the principle of life and of all the actions, and hence the form and perfection of the body" (my translation).

of a concrete effort of self-perseverance, what Spinoza calls *conatus*, amounts to a radical rejection of any abstract, a priori, or transcendentally anchored discourse of the "ought," or of values that have their source outside the being of things. The medical metaphor, on the other hand, is hermeneutically useful for conveying the concept of immanent normativity, and for a Stoic-like concept of "wisdom," which allows ethical life to be based on a dispassionate rational, even scientific, understanding of the workings of the self, of society, and of the world.

Spinoza seems to be aware of the limitations of the medical metaphor and, by implication, of the notion of "biological value." The scholium after EVp20, which sums up the discussion up to it, concludes with the affirmation that "with this, I have covered all the remedies for the affects [*affectum remedia*]." This can be taken as the closure of a certain stage in the development of the main theses of the *Ethics* and the opening of the final, concluding, part of it (specifically, propositions 21–40 of EV; propositions 41 and 42 are again a sort of step back; see discussion later in the book).

This brief excursion into the realm of the philosophy of religion and the philosophy of medicine is not meant to be more than a schematic sketch preparing the way for the following study of the *Ethics* of Spinoza. The decision to embark on it was not completely arbitrary. The few notions that have emerged here – *norms* and *normativity*, *value* and *valuableness*, and *seriousness* – seem to me to provide adequate means to express something important about the overall – metaphilosophical, if one prefers – nature of Spinoza's philosophical venture. It is a radical ethics, but an essential and constitutive element of it is a radical negation of religion and of what Spinoza must have conceived to be the core of the religious and theological tradition – Jewish and Christian – of which he was a scion – a rebellious one, but a scion all the same. This applies to the doctrinal aspects of religions – theology, cosmogony, theosophy and so on – to theistic moral theory, and, finally and very importantly, to the political theory based on divine authority as well. By implication, it also applies to all deontological ethical theories, which Spinoza would have most probably considered as avatars of religion.

The positive and the polemic are intimately interlaced in Spinoza's philosophy. The polemic side is articulated mainly around a doctrine of the body, which means the concrete, here and now, private body. Thus, to take just one – important – example, the very last moment of the *Ethics*, the proof of the "eternity of the soul" culminates in the statement "He who has a body capable of a great many things has a mind whose greatest part is eternal" (EVp39). It is through this role that the body plays in his metaphysical-ethical doctrine of human existence that his theory acquires its iconoclastic and, indeed, original character. Although formulated, and often read, as a mind-body doctrine, it does not in fact belong with the more standard history of doctrines we range under this epithet. At its center stands the extremely counterintuitive claim

1.5. The Question of Normativity

that, first, the mind, or rather soul, is an idea (EIIp11); and second, that this idea is the idea of the body (EIIp13). The next part of the present study consists in an attempt to understand this doctrine and to draw some philosophical consequences from it. It is based mainly on a very close reading of the first thirteen propositions of the second part of the *Ethics*.

It is noteworthy that after the elaboration of his alleged answer to the mind-body question in the first part of EII, Spinoza returns to it in a substantive way in two main places: at the beginning of the theory of the affects (notably in EIIIp2 and the scholium after it) and then in the preface to EV. That the theory of the affects is informed by the doctrine of the unity of soul and body is not surprising, and it is in this context that Spinoza is the closest to anything that can be reasonably qualified as a prallelistic theory.[84] It is also not surprising that the contemporary scientists, cognitivists, or philosophy of mind practitioners who return to Spinoza for some illumination or inspiration concentrate mainly on this chapter of Spinoza's philosophy. Less obvious and more intriguing is the fact that Spinoza's very particular mind-body doctrine, namely the doctrine that the soul is the idea of the body, is also the foundation of his theory of *salus, sive beatitudo, sive libertas*. The latter, which is often considered enigmatic to the point of being incomprehensible, is the ultimate moment of Spinoza's philosophy. It appears in the last half of EV. The last part of this study is again a close reading, this time of propositions 21–40 of EV. It is there that the ultimate significance of Spinoza's moral theory, of his *Ethics* as ethics, can possibly be found.

I thus concentrate in what follows on two rather restricted sections of the *Ethics* – the beginning of the second part and the end of the fifth. All the rest is referred to only insofar as it is needed for the sake of its main argument. The first part (Chapters 2–4) constitutes an inquiry into the meaning of Spinoza's doctrine of the human soul and of its relation to the body, as it is developed in the first thirteen propositions of EII. And Chapters 6 and 7 contain an attempt to understand Spinoza's doctrine of salvation, beatitude, and freedom as he formulates it in propositions 21–40 of EV. Chapter 5 is a digression where a few ramifications of Spinoza's so-called mind-body doctrine, viewed from a more general perspective, are discussed.

---

[84] A number of commentators of Spinoza have lately become quite skeptical as to the exegetic utility of the notion of "parallelism." See in particular Jaquet (2004). Concentrating almost exclusively on the theory of the affects, and despite the undeniable value and audacity of her book, Jaquet does not liberate Spinoza completely from the "parallelism paradigm." Deleuze, though retaining the term, suggests a more adequate interpretation of it than the usual ones. Macherey too has expressed some reservations about the pertinence of the parallelism thesis.

PART II

2

Mind and Body I
The Exegetic Inadequacy of Parallelism

2.1. Preliminary Remarks

I begin this study of the *Ethics* with an analysis of the first thirteen propositions of the second part. The scholium after the last of these propositions, EIIp13, resumes thus the main lesson they contain: "From these [propositions] we understand not only *that* the human mind is united to the body, but also *what* should be understood by the union of mind and body" (italics added). One major theme of EI had been the unity of extension and thought as two attributes of the one substance. But the nature of this unity remained unclear. We now understand that the first part established, in a formal and, as it were, nominal way, only the metaphysical fact that extension and thought are one. It did not specify the concrete content of this abstract unity in general – for when what is conceived to be disparate is said to be one, the nature of this oneness has to be specified – and, in particular in the context that interests us most, namely in man and insofar as it is the unity of soul and body. The understanding of the *quid* of the thought-matter (or thought-extension) unity is accomplished in the development occurring in the first thirteen propositions of EII. It thematizes the thought-matter unity as a concrete mind-body unity. This, however, is still too abstract, and Spinoza adds now a decisive supplementary thesis. The *concrete content* now given to the nominal metaphysical principle is gnoseological: the mind *knows* the body; or rather, the mind, or soul, *is* the knowledge of the body.[1] This happens in a multi-staged move that contains

---

[1] The corollary to EIIp13 states that the body "exists as we *feel* [*sentimus*] it" to exist. Some interpreters give to this "feeling" (of the body) its modern, non-intellectualist sense. A typical case is Damasio's book on Spinoza, which is a reading of Spinoza based on the idea that the mind is the "sensing" or "feeling" of the true state of the body. However, the Latin term *sentire* is used by Spinoza often to designate *knowledge* or *thought* in a more intellectualist sense. As Vinciguerra (2005), pp. 26–28 remarks, the term *sensatio* is very rare in classical and mediaeval Latin as well as in early modern times. Spinoza's use of this term, occurring mainly in the TIE and the *Ethics*,

notably the famous parallelism proposition (EIIp7) but also the puzzling claims that the soul is an idea (proposition 11) and that its "object" is the body, or that the soul is the idea of the body (proposition 13). These propositions, however, still belong to the domain of what was the subject matter of EI. I shall refer to this kind of discourse as "ontology." The soul is thus treated in the first thirteen propositions of EII as a kind of being that has to be understood by theoretical means lying beyond the theory of man strictly speaking. The theory of man will appear only after a doctrine of the nature of corporeal individuality is formulated in the group of lemmas after EIIp13.

The *Ethics* invites its reader to follow a certain order – to begin in general metaphysics (the First Part); to continue with the particular metaphysics of the soul (formulated especially in the first thirteen propositions of EII); then to move to a theory of knowledge gradually exposed in the rest of EII then to progress in parts three, four, and the beginning of part five to a philosophical theory of man; and to end in a theory of beatitude. But there is nonetheless some justification for a certain reversal of the order of reading. The general metaphysics of EI renders intelligible the kind of local ontology exposed in EII by leading to it and supplying grounds for the developments it contains. This means that the Second Part of the *Ethics* (and the rest of it) has to be read in light of the First Part. Not less than that, however, the general metaphysics of EI has to be read in light of the Second Part and particularly of EIIp1–13. This means that there is perhaps a second, silent beginning of the *Ethics*. Just as EII is unintelligible without the foundations laid in EI so the general metaphysics remains abstract and, in the end, unintelligible as well without EII.

This "second beginning" of the *Ethics* does not reproduce a Cartesian-like reflexive act wherein of the *cogito* is posited as the unavoidable beginning of philosophy. The theory of the soul is still an ontological doctrine, and the subject or the theme of the thinking and knowing "I" will appear only in the course of later developments. It establishes nevertheless a special point of view, a kind of metaphysical and methodological decision that the first part does not altogether justifies: it implies that the metaphysician has certain theoretical interests that are not immediately explicable by the general considerations in the EI or from the necessitarian theory of the one infinite substance.

The first thirteen propositions of EII form a sort of an axis of the whole work, a passage from the theory of substance to that of human modal existence. The notorious problem of "particularization," as it is sometimes called, is often considered to be a main stumbling block of Spinozism. Allegedly, Spinoza does not have the systematic or theoretic means to proceed from the doctrine of the one infinite substance to a positive and coherent conception of the finite mode or to justify the notion of a finite individual. The question of particularization

is thus an originality. In the *Ethics* it refers mainly to perception the soul has of its proper body (while *percipere* designates the rapport to external bodies). In both cases, it is a kind of cognition. In TIE § 78 the *idea* is said to be "nothing else but a *sensation*."

2.1. Preliminary Remarks

is usually treated as a difficulty concerning the efficacy of some conceptual or ontological mechanism of a "passage" or "descent" from the theory of substance to that of human modal existence. I suggest that it would be more fruitful to consider the issue as a textual question concerning the passage from the First to the Second Part of the *Ethics*. Put in this way, the passage from the First Part of the *Ethics* to the rest of the book appears to be a passage from the position of general and abstract theoretical principles to an effective and operative use of these principles in a theory of the concrete. Rather than trying to reconstruct first and in the abstract the meaning of Spinoza's metaphysical principles, beginning, as it were, in the middle will hopefully make it easier to see how they function *in concreto* and thus to understand their metaphysical meaning as well. Expositions of Spinoza's philosophy usually try to reproduce the systematic order in which the *Ethics* was written. Attempting a different approach may have a liberating effect and shed some light on some of the more obscure points of his philosophy.

It is remarkable that the thematic core of this axis of the system, or the systematic place where the notorious passage – from metaphysics to science, from a theory of the substance to a theory of the soul, or described in whatever way – is actually effected, is not formulated as a mechanism of particularization, but as a doctrine of what has become to be known as the "mind-body question." The actual move from the level of abstract and general metaphysics to that of the concrete is made through a discussion of what is often presented as a Cartesian question, or as a special contribution within the field of philosophical and scientific reflection determined by the Cartesian thought-extension and mind-body dualisms. This, as we shall see, does not tell the whole story, although it is undoubtedly true that Cartesian dualism is the immediate context of Spinoza's reflection on the mind-body question and its occasional cause.

But there is more to it. The mind-body problem is the axis of Spinoza's system both horizontally and vertically. It mediates the crucial move from general metaphysics to the theory of man; but it is also present throughout the *Ethics*, and always as an essential element in the development of its central issues. From the First Part and the theory of the attributes; through the Second Part's theory of the soul and its relation to the body and to the world, which is the foundation of a theory of knowledge; to the Third and Fourth Parts and the theory of the affects; down to the Fifth Part and its doctrine of freedom and beatitude, it is always through the mind-body thematic that Spinoza addresses central issues. It is certainly not without intention that the Preface to the Fifth Part of the *Ethics* contains a relatively long and elaborate criticism of Descartes's theory of the pineal gland.

The mind-body problem seems to be coextensive with the field of philosophical reflection of the *Ethics*. One could even say, as in fact it has been said by some philosophers, that the mind-body question is the question of philosophy itself. It is also as old as philosophy itself. Again, it typically goes under deep transformations in modern times. There are specifically modern, Cartesian and post-Cartesian versions of raising the question – it is now asked as a question about the kind of relation that permits understanding the *influence* body and mind exercise – or not – on each other and not, as it had been conceived in pre-modern times, either as that which *informs* the body, render intelligible the difference between lifeless and live matter, or is the site of the superior – spiritual or rational – side of man. It has then to be taken historically. Understood, as is implied in much of the recent literature on the mind-body question, as a well-defined, delineated, and rather local question, it risks blurring the fact that, at least within the context of the seventeenth century, behind what we call the mind-body question stands not a single question but a complex field of diverse problems, differentiated both historically and thematically. There are both unity and continuity in philosophical reflection on the nature of thought, mind, or the mental, and on the ways it is related to matter, to the body, and to the world in general. But there is also great diversity of philosophical, theological, sometimes ideological, and also scientific motivations that develop by using the same, or similar, terms. There is a subtle play here, diachronically, of continuity and diversity as well as, synchronically, of overlapping and diversity. "Soul," "body," "spirit," "matter," and so on mean different things at different times and in different contexts. The deciphering of this complex undoubtedly depends also on the historian's or commentator's own point of view, but we can at least say that the terminological continuity attests perhaps of some underlying unity, of a common horizon, that constitutes around some semantic core the unity and horizon of a fundamental and universal mute experience.

The very rich literature on Spinoza's philosophy deals extensively with the mind-body question. It is true, of course, that at different times and according to the differing philosophical or other interests that characterize writers on Spinoza, the exegetic and hermeneutical emphases differ. Again, it is also true that what is understood under the common title of "the mind-body question" changes. But since Leibniz and then the *lumières*, with the French *Philosophes*'s reading of Spinoza as a "naturalist" and "materialist," Spinoza's thought-extension and mind-body monism has been a main theme in the complex and continual attempt to make sense of his philosophy as a whole.

Although iconoclastic in many ways, and although echoing diverse sources, it was within the Cartesian universe of thought and mainly as an immediate reaction to Descartes's dualism that Spinoza's mind-body and extension-thought monism was conceived. According to a rather customary presentation of the major difficulty involved in Cartesian dualism, the latter is a theory about the fundamental furniture of the world, or about the entities that constitute reality: there are two separate kinds of thing in the world, two "stuffs," as it is sometimes paradoxically called.[2] It is difficult, if not impossible, to give an intelligible and satisfactory theoretic account of the ways in which

---

[2] Paradoxically, because "stuff" is just a more general and less determinate word for "matter."

2.1. Preliminary Remarks

these stuffs are related. The difficulty results from two contradictory claims that impose themselves on the Cartesian dualist: there is a radical difference of nature between these two stuffs, and they are somehow connected or related to each other. The first claim is conceptual and although based on some basic experience is a priori in the sense that no further experience can refute it; the second is a fact known through undeniable experience. But every relation – causal or otherwise – that may link these two stuffs presupposes some elementary common denominator or shared qualities, a condition rendered impossible by the first assumption. Cartesian metaphysics is thus – this is the meaning of the *Cogito* – an assertion of the absolute unavoidability of concepts such as "spirit," "thought," or "consciousness" in any serious attempt to give a scientific and philosophical account of the essence of man.[3] It is also an assertion of the existence of a counterpart of thought – matter or extension – as well as of the union in man of thought and extension. It is, thus, admitting two (created) substances – mind and matter or thought and extension – where "substantiality" means that these are real entities that are ontologically independent and conceptually irreducible to one another, but that are also somehow connected, in fact unified, in man. So much for the standard presentation of the problem.

This is a rather general, schematic, and simplistic view, though it permits describing the contours of a general mind-body question. The two stuffs thesis seems thus to raise a paradigmatic difficulty. A possible way of presenting it is the following. There are two essentially different realms of being, and there are thus two fundamentally different and mutually exclusive principles, or methodologies, of rational explanation. In slightly different terms, Cartesian dualism means that there are two different causal chains, each of them operate according to its own laws, the two sets of laws being incommensurable. A cause in one chain cannot become a cause in the other. In a more radical way, one could suggest the existence of two independent fields of rationality, alluding to a well-known distinction, of two "cultures" of intellectual dealing with the world. Within each of these realms, causal relations, or causal explanations, remain the main manifestation of rationality and the condition of possibility of science – either of matter or of the psychic. They also express the allegedly specific ontological structure and, indeed, of what, so to speak, they are made. Affirming something like causal interaction between these two different fields, or kinds of entity, such as the determination of bodily (physical) motion by the will, is unintelligible according each of these possible descriptions of Cartesian dualism. But there are relations between mind and body. This seems to be an undeniable fact of immediate experience. The Cartesian mind-body theory is thus at one and the same time the formulation of a problem and an attempt to offer a solution to it. It is a paradigmatic acknowledgment of a fact unexplainable by modern mechanistic physical theory.

---

[3] Descartes thought that this was his chief philosophical achievement; at least this is what he wrote in the dedicatory letter and the preface of the *Meditations*.

Spinoza's so-called mind-body theory is customarily read as a particular contribution to the long debate that this dualism initiated among Descartes's successors and that is still alive in our own times. There is some truth in this presentation. It is undoubtedly true that Cartesian metaphysics, especially the thought-extension dualism, is the framework within which the modern mind-body question was framed. This had been so already in the second half of the seventeenth century, and insofar as the Cartesian and modern discussions of this problem depend to a large degree on what we call the "scientific revolution," it does indeed enjoy an irreducible specificity vis-à-vis the pre-modern discussions of it. As the new science was rapidly gaining the status of the one true science of nature, the nature of the body had to be understood in terms determined by the mechanistic theory of matter. This was also the background for Spinoza's discussion of man in general and of the mind-body problem in particular. But this was not the whole story. In many ways – and this was true for Descartes too, and certainly for Spinoza, Malebranche, and Leibniz (just to mention a few names) – the full context of this discussion was much more complex, rich, and multi-layered than what has come to be known as Descartes's dualism and his theory of the union of soul and body. Because the full context of the early modern discussions is not always fully taken into consideration, contemporary presentations of Descartes's dualism and of the debates about and around it are sometimes limited and even distorted. This is presumably also one of the reasons for the ease with which the parallelism exegetic thesis has become so universally accepted as adequately presenting Spinoza's alleged solution to this problem: interactionism is impossible because no causal influence between the attributes or between soul and body is conceivable. The relation we conceive as a unity of mind and body is actually a relation of parallelism between two (in fact infinite) independent series of causes and effects. There are exceptions, of course, and a few commentators – such as Hallett, Gueroult, or Deleuze, or more recently Pierre Macherey, Genevieve Lloyd, or Chantal Jacquet – have proposed more sophisticated and nuanced positions and expressed misgivings about the pertinence of the parallelistic reading of Spinoza. But by and large it seems that there is a quasi-unanimous agreement that Spinoza's doctrine is a doctrine of mind-body and thought-extension parallelism.

What follows is a relatively elaborate and detailed attempt to refute the parallelism thesis. It is, in other words, an attempt to show that its value as an exegetic key to Spinoza's philosophy is, at best, limited and that it actually misses what is most important about it. Such a refutation is needed, I believe, in order to open the way for another understanding of Spinoza's doctrine about the nature of the union of soul[4] and body. According to the reading suggested here, this

---

[4] I shall as a rule prefer to use *soul* to *mind*. The reason is mainly that *mind* has become too general and too common a term. By using *soul* it will hopefully be easier not to lose the specificity of Spinoza's doctrine. However, when citing existing translations into English – Curley's or Shirley's – I shall keep to the way they render the Latin terms in question.

doctrine is not only original and iconoclastic, but also highly counterintuitive. Although conceived within the Cartesian tradition and cast in Cartesian terminology, it can be said to undermine the very pertinence of the difficulties that Descartes's dualism allegedly set afloat and that have become, under one form or another, the main conceptual frame within which the mind-body is, to a large extent, still thought nowadays. But at the same time it is also a refusal of the pre-Cartesian theories – philosophical and theological – of the soul as the seat of the spiritual and opposed to the charnel.

The importance of a this reading resides, moreover, not just in its hopefully greater interpretative adequacy insofar as Spinoza's mind-body doctrine is concerned, but also, and mainly, in the key it provides to the most enigmatic and problematic part of Spinoza's philosophy, namely the doctrine of salvation, beatitude, and freedom in the Second Part of EV. The basic coherence and intelligibility of this last chapter of the *Ethics* is conditioned upon – this is the central claim of the final chapters of this study – the coherence and intelligibility of the radically non-parallelistic mind-body doctrine Spinoza, I believe, proposes notably in the first thirteen propositions of EII.

The so-called mind-body parallelism's long career in Spinozistic scholarship began very early and its success is, of course, not accidental. Although it signifies different things to different writers and at different times, it has a basic thematic and conceptual coherence. There are also good reasons why it has become so deeply rooted in the literature about Spinoza; foremost among them are Spinoza's own pronouncements. There are many places in the *Ethics* where it seems that Spinoza does not break the conceptual framework of the Cartesian mind-body problem and that indeed his "solution" to it is a kind of parallelism. This is the case, for example, in the Preface to EV where he criticizes Descartes's dualism in terms very close to those that appear in the modern depictions of the difficulties involved in it referred to before. This is also the case at the beginning of EIII, and especially in the second proposition and the scholium following it. The proposition says that the body and the mind cannot determine each other in whatever way, and the scholium repeats what appears in EIIp7, which is known as the "parallelism proposition" and which affirms, very famously, that the order and connection of things is the same as the order and connection of things. But enough support for a more critical approach can be gathered, both from the text and from the context. The parallelism paradigm, based on a more or less customary reading of proposition 7 of EII as containing a claim that the union of mind and body is actually a relation of isomorphism, does not exhaust the matter and even blurs its full philosophical significance.

2.2. The Anachronism of Parallelism

Treating the mind-body question, or any other major philosophical question for that matter, outside its historical context is anachronistic. It conceals, for example, the fact that the mind-body question as it is understood in our times, and as it is often read back into the seventeenth century, is conditioned by the appearance of new fields of scientific conceptualization and effective research (one of the aforementioned spheres of causal laws or "nomological fields"); the institutionalization of scientific, medical, and social practices; the professionalization of diverse forms of taking care of human beings; and so on. It is notably the emergence of the fields of psychology and experimental psychology and, more recently, of what is known as neuroscience and cognitive science, as well as the need to coordinate between different scientific disciplines and their typical ways of theorization, that affect current attempts to understand seventeenth-century discussions of mind and body. The ways in which the mind-body question is raised in contemporary discussions often take for granted the existence of a certain scientific culture and ignore the latter's historicity. The fact that the "mental" has become the subject of theorization and that a science of the "mental" has been institutionalized is relatively recent. Although it had been anticipated in Descartes and his successors, the real terms of the question have been deeply transformed: from a philosophical attempt to understand the fundamental nature of man – of man as a thinking thing, of thought and of reason, of man as a moral agent or as an agent *tout court* – it has become a question about the possibility to coordinate different, allegedly parallel, scientific discourses, therapeutic practices, and scientific, academic, and medical types of institution. The anachronistic discussion on classical philosophy masks the real stakes of its grand debates as well as the full significance of the changes that have taken place since. In particular, it prevents us from extricating from it its sense as a living philosophical concern, namely its emergence as a whole body of problems, a whole "problematique," with its own inner logic. Indeed, rather than an interrogation about the relation that holds, or should hold, between different scientific disciplines and practices, its thematic core was supplied by the rapidly changing relations between science and philosophy. The emergence of the "new science" as an autonomous field of intellectual work raises the question of the pertinence of the notion of different, sometimes competing, or at least not compatible, rationalities – philosophical and scientific – and of the *sui generis* nature of philosophical knowledge and the possibility of a properly philosophical theorizing. One can see in it an even wider question: Merleau-Ponty, for example, in his lectures on Malebranche's theory of mind-body, says that this is a question about the relation of being and thought, which is in fact the true sense of the question of reason. As on many other issues, here too Merleau-Ponty shows himself to be one of the keenest and most insightful students of seventeenth-century philosophy.

This mostly anachronistic reading of Spinoza (and to a large extent of the seventeenth-century mind-body debates in general) is the framework within which the so-called parallelism thesis gained such a prominence in Spinozistic scholarship. The parallelism exegetic paradigm is based on the famous EIIp7, which states that the same order and connection that hold among ideas hold also among things. It seems to offer a solution to the difficulty that emerges

2.2. *The Anachronism of Parallelism*

in the footsteps of Descartes's dualism and the alleged impossibility to explain rationally, or to think philosophically, within its framework, what Descartes himself presents as the *fact* of the relation that holds together bodies and minds or, more accurately, of the *union* of mind and body. Spinoza's solution to this difficulty, according to this approach, would thus be the parallelism doctrine, which apparently states that this unity is a unity of *order* (or, in more modern jargon, of structure or of form – the kind of relation we call "isomorphism").

According to a recent presentation that seems to typically accept its allegedly unproblematic exegetic value, the parallelism thesis means "that for each thing there is a corresponding idea, and for each idea there is a corresponding thing ... [and] in each case, the idea enters into causal relations with other ideas that match the causal relations the corresponding thing enters into with other things. The networks of ideas and of things are causally isomorphic."[5] Despite its quasi-universal presence in the literature on Spinoza, and despite a number of Spinoza's own pronouncements that seem to give credibility to this interpretation, it in fact conceals the full significance of Spinoza's doctrine rather than explains it.

Spinoza never uses term *parallelism*. As is well known, it was coined by Leibniz; more importantly, it was used by him in the context of his critical discussion of Spinozism. It was not used by Leibniz, however, as a convenient representation of Spinoza's doctrine of the unity of mind and body, but, on the contrary, as a title of his own, opposite to Spinoza's, doctrine.[6] In fact, Leibniz conceived the term "parallelism" as expressing a principle that is radically opposed to Spinozism, both in the field of ontology and in that of the theory of rationality. The term itself appears first in several more technical – mathematical and logical – writings, and in the sense that interests us here, in a famous phrase in *Considérations sur la doctrine d'un esprit universel unique* (1702). Leibniz criticizes in this writing what would become known as "pantheism" or, more precisely, different versions, ancient and modern, of alleged Averroist negations of the existence of particular, or "separate," souls. He portrays Spinoza as belonging to this tradition, and then explains his own, opposite, position: "I have established a perfect parallelism between what happens in the soul and

---

[5] Della Rocca (1996), p. 18. One of the more curious aspects of this presentation is the way in which it takes as apparently unproblematic the notion of causality, or "causal relations," allegedly holding among ideas. But no one has ever really explained what a "causal relation" between ideas is. Another typical formulation is to be found in Bennett (1984), a classic of Spinoza scholarship, p. 127: the parallelism doctrine "seems to be the doctrine that there is a one-one relation correlating mental items with physical ones, mapping similarities onto similarities and causal chains onto causal chains." Again, the term "mental items" is now widely used, although I am not sure anyone really knows what it exactly means. About what is, to my mind, the core of Spinoza's doctrine, namely that the mind-body relation is an idea-object relation, Bennett says (ibid.) that "this is not a doctrine ... but merely terminology." The widely used metaphor of "mapping" is strictly Leibnizian.
[6] Deleuze, Macherey, and many others are well aware of the fact that the term is Leibniz's invention. Few of them, however, note that it was used by Leibniz as an anti-Spinozist concept.

what happens in matter." This parallelism, which is just another name for the general principle of harmony, is meant to permit a systematic defense of the substantiality of the particular, or individual, soul, a position diametrically opposed to Spinoza's, at least according to Leibniz's portrayal of him.

On other occasions, directed explicitly and exclusively against Spinoza, Leibniz exposes his radical opposition to Spinoza on this matter:

> Spinoza says (EIIIp2s) that spirit and body are the same thing, only expressed in two different manners, and (EIIp7s [i.e., the parallelism proposition]) that the thinking substance and the extended substance are one and the same substance, that one conceives either under the attribute of thought or under the attribute of extension.... I contest this. Spirit and body is not the same thing, not more than the principle of action and that of passion.

And a little later, in confronting the core (as we shall soon see) of the matter, the claim (EIIp13) that "all things are animated"[7] is based on the following bizarre reason:

> It is completely unreasonable to say that the soul is an idea; ideas are something completely abstract, like numbers or figures, and they cannot act. The ideas are abstract and universal. The idea of some animal is a possibility, and it is misleading to say that souls are immortal, because the ideas are immortal, as if one said that the soul of a sphere is eternal because the idea of a spherical body is indeed [immortal]. The soul is not at all an idea, but the source of numerous ideas.[8]

There is indeed a real irony in the fate of parallelism. Not only has a Leibnizian term expressing a radical opposition to Spinoza come to designate Spinoza's doctrine but, moreover, this very use of the term risks reversing the whole sense of the controversy. Although he too transcends it, Leibniz can still be said to think within the framework of the Cartesian and occasionalist problematique: he tries to show that *order* alone, or *structure*, are enough to rationally explain a relation (conceivable even as a kind of unity) between what is metaphysically separate. This idea transcends the more restrained nature of Descartes's dualism, let alone of what has become of it in contemporary literature on the question, as it is conceived by Leibniz as a general principle of rational thinking: it is true of mind and body relations as a special case of other theological, ethical, and political seemingly disparate entities, or realms of reality, that can thus be rationally related.[9] For Spinoza the terms of the difficulty

---

[7] Leibniz is not completely fair here toward Spinoza. According to the exact wording of the phrase cited, not only man, but all the rest of *individuals* as well, are animated. This is a small, but significant, nuance.

[8] Leibniz, *Réfutation inédite de Spinoza*, pp. 25 and 30, respectively; cited according to the edition of this text by M. de Gaudemar, Arles: Actes Sud, 1999.

[9] Actually parallelism in its strict sense exists among substances (monads or simple substances), and bodies are not substances. Insofar however as bodies, or matter in general, are "well founded phenomena," there is still an orderly relation between the foundation and these phenomena that may permit seeing in it a kind of parallelism. Leibniz, however, on a few famous occasions,

2.2. The Anachronism of Parallelism

are completely different: the sameness of order or structure – parallelism – is an obvious and trivial element of unity or, indeed, oneness. Spinoza reverses, in fact, the order of the argument. He did not want to give a better solution to the difficulty Descartes raised – he wanted to show that it was a pseudo-difficulty and that it was based on completely wrong presuppositions. What had been for Descartes a fact one needs to explain – the union of the body and the soul – became with Spinoza the first principle, both metaphysically and as the *non plus ultra* of rational explanation, the ultimate condition of the intelligibility of everything else: the absolute unity and uniqueness of reality and, hence, of mind and body. For Descartes this *non plus ultra* had been the *Cogito*, namely the metaphysical *experience* in which the I as a *thinking* substance is discovered. The union of soul and body was a *fact* we should accept and trust as truth on the basis of the demonstrated veracity of God, but without fully understanding its nature, or without attaining full intelligibility of this fact. As Merleau-Ponty astutely remarks at the opening of his lectures on Malebranche's doctrine of the mind-body union, Descartes never affirmed that this union can be fully conceptualized.[10] The nature of this fact, of the experience of the union of mind and body, remains opaque. As we shall soon see, experience plays an important role in Spinoza's theory as well, but it is opposite in some fundamental ways to the role it had for Descartes: the experience of the body, of one's own body, is, in the last analysis, a metaphysical experience. In it being experiences itself, and the supposed distance between the agent of experience and its object is completely obliterated. This experience is thus not only fully transparent but also rational and, indeed, the origin of reason.

What makes the Leibnizian notion of parallelism seem applicable to EIIp7 is the use of the words *ordo et connexio*. The concept of order and particularly its function as a foundation of scientific rationality, however, is not less Leibnizian than the notion of parallelism. For Leibniz, indeed, the former is a generalization of the latter. Spinoza, on the other hand, expresses often by order the idea of the contingent and rather arbitrary givenness or factuality of natural things that from the philosophical point of view constitute rather disorder. On other occasions he underplays the philosophical pertinence of the concept of order, depicting it as an anthropomorphic construct imposed by man on reality.

Isomorphism, or identity of structure existing between two disparate entities or realms of entities, is the basis of Leibniz's doctrine of *expression*, or of the *pre-established Harmony*. It was basically an attempt to generalize the essential role *structure* and *order* have in the work of reason. This has to be seen also against the background of his general formalistic conception of logic and of truth. Spinoza did not have a similar predilection for formalisms, and he considered order neither as the foundation or configuration of rationality nor

---

notably in the clocks parable, speaks as if the general principle of harmony-parallelism solves straightforwardly also the conundrum of the union of soul and body.

[10] Merleau-Ponty (1978), p. 15.

as a source of intelligibility. Leibniz's doctrine of expression is close in many regards to doctrines of scientific rationality as they evolve in modern times, much closer than Spinoza's. Appropriating a Leibnizian-like concept of rationality by scientists looking for some philosophical inspiration or corroboration of their theories would be more appropriate than the frequent, perhaps more symbolic than authentically conceptual, looking for Spinoza.[11]

What isomorphism basically gives is, according to Leibniz's often-repeated metaphor, the possibility to "map" one realm (i.e., the body) to another (i.e., the soul) in a systematic and unequivocal way. A city's map is its representation, and, under conditions properly defined, the act of mapping can be said to satisfy basic demands of scientific rationality. There is knowledge and explanation in mapping or, in more general and modern jargon, in modeling. This was in fact a central part of Leibniz's theory of rationality, and from such point of view parallelism is indeed a form of union, so that the relation between thought and extension, or mind and body, insofar as it is conceived as a relation of parallelism, can be said to be rationally understood. From the point of view of Spinoza, on the other hand, a relation of parallelism cannot satisfy the claims of philosophical reason. Even if one ignores the assumption of the disparateness of thought and extension, implicit – but necessary – in the concept of parallelism, a theory like Leibniz's would amount to a statement of a fact and, hence, to an acknowledgment of incomprehensibility and lack of understanding of the relations concretely existing between thought and extension and, more specifically, between mind and body. The monads did not have windows, and the two clocks parallelly showing the same hour were mutually opaque, lacking the transparency of the Spinozistic ideal of intuitive knowledge. The suppressed incompatibility between these two points of view – the Spinozistic and the Leibnizian – results in such hybrid notions that one finds in the secondary literature, as "representational parallelism" that is both transparent and parallel, while simple parallelism is blind. The relation between mind and body in Spinoza's *Ethics* is indeed not at all blind: the corollary of EIIp13 states that "man consists of a mind and a body, and that the human body exists, *as we sense [sentimus] it*" (Curley's translation, slightly altered; italics added). But this is so precisely because there is no parallelism there, either transparent or blind. From a Spinozistic point of view, parallelism, if not an incomprehensible fact, can at best be the trivial truth that one complex thing has two, or even many, parallel sides.

The ways in which parallelism has become a Spinozistic term is not less significant. It surfaces again, after its first formulation by Leibniz, at the second

[11] "Looking for Spinoza" is, of course, the title of Damasio's famous book, which is the testimony of a modern man of science in search of some philosophical inspiration and corroboration of his scientific work. See Damasio (2003). Damasio is just one in a long list of modern and contemporary men of science who take Spinoza as an incarnation of scientific rationality. A far more interesting attempt to use Spinoza in an attempt to contextualize the founding of present-day life sciences and put them in some perspective can be found in Henri Atlan's numerous works.

2.2. The Anachronism of Parallelism 65

half of the nineteenth century as a name of an allegedly Spinozistic kind of mind-body theories, and soon of Spinoza's own theory as well. It appears first in the writings of Gustav Theodor Fechner (1801–1887), who more or less inaugurated, around the mid-century,[12] the new discipline of psychophysics.[13] It was conceived as an empirical science, which meant for Fechner, roughly, a theory based on experimentation, its findings expressed in a mathematical form. A main presupposition of this enterprise was the existence of systematic relations between the physical and the mental, or psychological, phenomena. It was to this relation that Fechner referred as a parallelism between the kinds of phenomenon he was measuring. Fechner also thought that these different phenomena were manifestations of one and the same unitary entity – an individual organism.[14] He borrowed the term "parallelism" from Leibniz and was very explicit about his debt to him, but thought that his presuppositions were in fact closer to Spinoza's philosophy and that the parallelism he was investigating could be better understood in Spinozistic terms. Referring to Leibniz's famous clocks parable,[15] he adds that in it Leibniz disregarded a fourth option besides the three he counts, which is in fact the simplest and most reasonable one. To the three doctrines Leibniz talks about in his parable – causal interactionist (as it is called nowadays) dualism that he attributes, somewhat hastily, to Descartes; occasionalism; and his own theory of the pre-established harmony – Fechner suggested adding Spinoza's doctrine as well. According to the latter, the two clocks would be in fact only one. And, of course, if it is only one clock, no wonder that it/they always show(s) the same hour; or, more accurately (one may suggest), that it always shows the hour it shows.

As suggested above, Spinoza's mind-body theory is meant to undermine the very basis of the Cartesian thematics Leibniz refers to in his parable. In fact, Fechner commits here a number of faults. The most obvious one is the forcing of Spinoza's mind-body theory into Leibniz's clock-work maintenance shop. By this move both the parable and Spinoza's doctrine lose their specific significance. Although with Leibniz it is always difficult to know for sure, one may assume that in this case at least he sincerely thought he had good philosophical

---

[12] Exactly, on October 22, 1850. According to his own testimony, he had suddenly, on that day, an insight about the way to measure the intensity of a sensation and its relation with the energy of the corresponding stimulus. What is known as the "Fechner's law" states that there is a logarithmique functional correspondence between the two: when the energy of the stimulus increases according to geometric augmentation, the sensation increases – in parallel – algebraically.

[13] *Elemente der Psychophysik* appears, in 2 volumes, in Leipzig, in 1860. There is an English translation of the first volume (Fechner 1966). Cf. also Dupéron (2000); Heidelberger (2004).

[14] Fechner was a very prolific writer and during his long and rich career went through stages. Although he never gave up a certain metaphysical vision of reality, his conception of psychophysics, and within it of the nature of the organic entities, is non-metaphysical. There are a few studies of Fechner's work; two of the more recent ones are Heidelberger (1993) (English translation 2004) and the shorter Dupéron (2000).

[15] From the third *Eclaircissement* on the *Système nouveau de la nature*. This reference appears at the very beginning of *Elements of Psychophysics*; cf. Dupéron, op. cit., pp. 29–30.

reasons for not including Spinoza in his parable. Indeed, Spinoza does not fit in here, and the whole point of Leibniz's criticism of Spinoza as we have just seen it is to affirm precisely this. The possibility of representing Spinoza's position by the image of two clocks is discarded at the outset, and the fact of the correspondence between them is explained away, rather than explained, by his theory of the unity of mind and body: the whole point of the parable is that the two clocks are fully distinct, this distinction representing the substantiality of the individual souls, affirmed by Descartes, Malebranche, and Leibniz, but rejected by Spinoza. Leibniz, unlike many modern readers of both his own and Spinoza's theories, understood perfectly well that Spinoza's mind-body theory was not a direct contribution, in the last analysis, to the kind of question that he was referring to in his parable and that was considered by him, as well as by Malebranche and the other occasionalists, as emerging out of Descartes's mysterious "union of body and soul." Union and unity are two different things, union the result of an act, unity a pre-given original property of a thing. As we shall soon see – and Leibniz, as attested by the quotation just given, was well aware – the difficulty with Spinoza's doctrine is not necessarily limited to the field of abstract ontology, but belongs rather to the metaphysics of knowledge and of thought and, in a more general way, not less, and perhaps more, importantly to a general ethical-theological theory of man.

Although obviously a blunder, Fechner's suggestion was very effective. It is apparently here – with the imposition of Spinoza's conception into the framework of Leibnizianism and with the tendency to consider the two doctrines as two competing, albeit commensurable, theories about the mind-body correspondence, which can even be combined to some degree – that a tradition of using of the term "parallelism" to represent Spinoza's doctrine of mind and body commences. It is also here that a typical and hard-to-get-rid-of misrepresentation of Spinoza begins. It might seem that Fechner, as he himself thought, was indeed closer to Spinoza than to Leibniz. The two allegedly share the view that there is one original unity that is the common source of two different manifestations ("attributes" in Spinoza's language, "phenomena" in Fechner's) conceived by us as mind and body or spirit and matter. It might seem then, as indeed many subsequent experimental psychologists but also commentators of Spinoza thought, that a similar notion of parallelism is applicable both to Fechner's study of the nature of the correspondence that allegedly exists between physical, physiological, and psychological phenomena, and to Spinoza's theory as it is expressed notably in EIIp7, but also in his theory of the affects, which are undeniably psychological phenomena that seem to have bodily parallels.

This, however, is not the case. Fechner's phenomena are not the same as Spinoza's attributes (since attributes are irreducible "objective" realities), and Spinoza's original substantial unity is not the same as Fechner's unity of the individual organism. Obviously, "organism" and, in particular, "phenomena," do not carry the metaphysical import of Spinoza's "substance" and "attribute."

2.2. The Anachronism of Parallelism   67

Fechner did not think otherwise, but he did think that his psychophysics brings the mind-body parallelism from metaphysical skies to the firm ground of empirical science and of measurement. What his case shows, perhaps, is that the relations between science and metaphysics are not always as simple as that.

Fechner's is a particularly revelatory case that can help illuminate the nature and causes of the ease with which the Leibnizian term "parallelism" has become so common in Spinozistic literature. Fechner was, on the one hand, the main founder of a new scientific discipline or, as it has been said, the author of an important research program. The latter is still pertinent in the present, incredibly richer, and more sophisticated scientific research. It is not rare to find commentators who claim that the roots of experimental psychology and even of quite recent developments such as cognitive science as well as neuroscience can be traced back to his pioneering work. It is also not rare to find contemporary psychologists, neurologists, and practitioners of other experimental or therapeutic disciplines who find in Spinoza, just as Fechner did, both an ancestor and a source of inspiration for a reflection that, they think, can give sense to their own scientific work.

Fechner conceived his new science of psychophysics as part of a much larger program, philosophical and ethical in nature, perhaps religious in some sense, or even proto-mystical. In his youth he had been deeply influenced by German *Naturphilosophie* (notably Schelling's philosophy of nature), and he had always been opposed to what he called later in his life the "Night View" (in contradistinction to his own "Day View"), by which he meant the reductionist mechanism and materialism of much of his day's scientific worldview. This is significant because the fascination with Spinoza is typically associated with some kind or another of philosophical interest in science, of scientific interest in philosophy, or, more specifically, with a certain desire to transcend the boundaries of experimental work in its strict sense. It often expresses attempts to acknowledge some aspects of a scientific worldview while looking for a reassurance of its philosophical, even ethical, soundness and validity. But, and this is also typical, by this reference to Spinoza Fechner, in the last analysis, missed much of Spinoza's original intention. Fechner's own attribution of the thesis of parallelism to Spinoza did not necessarily hamper with his own scientific work; but when this has become a commonplace of Spinozistic literature, the hastiness, or even a certain philosophical clumsiness, that characterizes his attitude to Spinoza is more problematic.

There is no question of giving here a full, or even partial, account of Fechner's rich and complex work.[16] It seems, however, not unimportant to emphasize a point or two. The three orders of phenomena Fechner investigated were conceived by him as different manifestations of one underlying unity. He did not

---

[16] There are a few recent works on Fechner: Dupéron (2000) is a short and useful presentation; Heidelberger (1993) is a more elaborate to show the relevance of Fechner's work for contemporary concerns.

think that the unity behind the parallel phenomenal manifestations was an unattainable thing in itself, but a real and scientifically accessible reality – that of the living organism and of the natural world in general. Although it has been argued that one can interpret some of Spinoza's main insights in light of the concept of organism,[17] it would be wrong to push the rapprochement with Fechner too far. Spinoza's is a metaphysical theory of man, while Fechner's psychophysics is a scientific theory. It is, of course, impossible to draw a rigid and clear-cut line of separation between science and philosophy in general; yet, there are deep and irreducible differences between Spinoza and Fechner, differences that can be considered as paradigmatic and that also give Fechner's misunderstanding of Spinoza paradigmatic significance.

These differences are not about the accessibility or non-accessibility of the original unity supposed to lie at the bottom of phenomena. Spinoza too did not think in Kantian-like terms of phenomena and things in themselves. The fundamental unity was, for him, neither a heuristic principle nor the accomplishment or result of empirical or experimental work. It was not only fully attainable, but indeed, and in its full and original intelligibility, the very foundation and condition of any further rational work. The difference between the two is also not that much about ontology, if one understands in this word, as is often done in contemporary literature about Spinoza's (and others') mind-body theory, some conception about the constitution of the entities in question (e.g., "matter" or "spirit,") or about the nature of the main manifestations of the underlying unity; it is rather about the *modes* of access to them, or the kinds of intelligibility they possess. Although Fechner's three orders of phenomena are not particular beings but three domains of characteristic natural lawfulness, and in this respect might have seemed to be not that different from Spinoza's attributes, the differences are in fact far more important than the similarities. Sphere of characteristic lawfulness is not the same as "that which the intellect conceives as constituting the essence of a substance" (EIdef4). Moreover, "thought" in Spinoza's rationalistic philosophy is much closer to what we would rather call perhaps "reason" or "rationality" than it is to Fechner's sphere of inwardness and privacy, or to what is often referred to as the "mental."

Fechner gives a typically modern, non-metaphysical characterization of the mind, or soul, as a special phenomenon, or sphere, defined essentially as "private" and "internal." For Spinoza – and we shall see it in more detail later on – thought, insofar as it is one of the infinite attributes of the substance, constitutes the essence of the singular soul as well as that of an "infinite intellect;" as such, it is not *essentially* private, and the internal-external distinction, which is so central to the Cartesian conception of thought or of the mental, is seen as, at best, a metaphor that does not do justice to the real, metaphysical reality of mind and body, and even falsifies it. If at all, the internal-external

---

[17] See for example H. Jonas (1965).

2.2. The Anachronism of Parallelism

distinction is applicable to the relations that hold between human beings considered wholly – mind and body – and that which is alien to their personal being, namely, the world and the things that are in it and that Spinoza in fact often refers to as "external." But the body as such, one's own body, is *not*, according to the present reading of Spinoza, external to the soul.

The importance given to the "privacy" and "internality" of the mental is characteristic not only of Fechner's work, but also of the emerging science of psychology in general. This characterization of the soul is quite different from the absolute self-presence of the Cartesian subject. Not less than the subjectivist nature of psychology as a theory of the psychic, it expresses its ideal of scientificity, among other things because it is said and defined as "private" and "internal," from the point of view of the scientific observer and experimentalist. More shall be said about this later. Suffice it to say for the moment that precisely because it defines the mind on the basis of what is conceived to be opposite to science's self-conception as being essentially public, it expresses in fact the search of the new science for acceptable and legitimate methods that could be considered "empirical" or "observational" and non-metaphysical. It is against this background that one has to consider Wundt's method of "introspection," the fact that it has become after him, and for a very short while, the preferable method of access to psychological reality, only to be rejected shortly afterwards and give way to behaviorism.[18]

Fechner conceived his new science of psychophysics on the model of mathematical physics (as it was developing then notably in France), understood as a program of mathematization of experimentally gathered data. In fact, of course, he was doing nothing of the sort. He developed ingenious strategies of experimentation, methods of measurement, and formulated – in what has become to be known as Fechner's law – what is basically a heuristic rule, formally expressed, for a research strategy based on the idea that since there is a correspondence between mind and body, a correlation can be established between measurable phenomena such as external stimuli, the excitation of the sensing apparatus and sensation.[19]

---

[18] See, e.g., Danziger (1994), chapter 3; Boring (1929), passim. It is not uninteresting to note that Wilhelm Wundt, the main protagonist in the emergence of the new discipline and its institutionalization, writes in a programmatic article from 1896 that psychology and the different natural sciences are irreducible to one another; they have to be coordinated "and the perspectives of both complement each other in such a way that only together do they exhaust the empirical knowledge open to us" (cited by Kusch [1995], p. 133).

[19] Fechner distinguished between "external" and "internal" parallelism: the first applies to the correspondence between the physical stimulus (e.g., the intensity of light) and the excitation of the nervous system (to the extent that it could be measured by him), the second to the correspondence between the nervous system activity and the feeling (conscious or unconscious). As Fechner says at the beginning of his *Elements of Psychophysics*, this science is an "exact science of the relations of functional dependence existing between the body and the soul or, more generally, between the material and the mental worlds, the physical and the psychological" (cited by Dupéron, op. cit., p. 46, who also gives a concise but illuminating summary of this matter).

The presupposed correspondence between different spheres of being, which is also, perhaps even more, a presupposition about the possibility to correlate different strategies of scientific research,[20] seems to be a fundamental presupposition of the emerging science of the psychic, and an essential guarantee of its scientificity. As Boring says, already at the end of eighteenth and the beginning of the nineteenth centuries, the phrenologists, the founders of what was to be proven to be pseudoscience, built their theories "upon the central problem of correlation" – in their case, the alleged correlation between the form of the skull and the nature of the mind or of its functioning.[21] This correlation is a correlation conceived from the point of view of the scientific "external" observer: it is a correlation between what is hidden from him on the one hand, and the measurable and public on the other. And it is precisely as such that it can be said to express an ideal of scientificity, constitutive to the new science of psychology.

Scientific or academic psychology emerged out of philosophy. The first psychologists, notably Wundt, thought of their work as a continuation of traditional philosophy. This was certainly true insofar as the sociological and institutional aspects of this history are concerned. Thematically, however, it is a somewhat more complicated an issue. Although traditionally the "soul" or, more precisely, the attempt to talk rationally about it, had been largely an affair of philosophers, there is no simple continuity between the philosophical dealing with it and the new science of psychology or, for that matter, of psychophysics. It is often said that modern science, or at least some of its important disciplines, emerged out of philosophy and gradually proved itself to be its legitimate heir and the real executor its program. It is thus often claimed that it is "science" that can deal rationally with, and perhaps solve, the questions philosophy had asked before. Bacon and Comte, to cite just two older cases, gave two of the better-known, explicit, and systematic formulations of this widely held view. Although this is certainly the case sometimes, the course that thought follows is often more complex. Sometimes much of the sense of the original concerns is lost in the course of the emergence of new scientific disciplines. Sometimes a new and more profound understanding of a properly and irreducible philosophical significance of old questions emerges as science solves, or deals with in its own way, other aspects of these old questions.

---

[20] Whether science is a kind of ontology, positivist construction of theories, pragmatic methods of prediction, or strategies of rational work (and there are more possibilities, skeptical, relativistic, or not) is not a question that has to occupy us here. It is not without interest, however, to note that Fechner also misses the true sense of Leibniz's theory of the preestablished harmony. The latter expresses not so much a theory about the constitution of the world as a conception about the nature of scientific rationality – structure, order, and regularity of relations are the sources of intelligibility, not causality of imaginary mechanisms, nor suppositions of supernatural intervention. Ironically, Fechner, in a sense, executes Leibniz's program of rational (or scientific) work rather than Spinoza's.

[21] Boring, op. cit., p. 51.

2.2. The Anachronism of Parallelism

Germany of the second half of the nineteenth century was the main scene of experimental psychology becoming an autonomous discipline. It is no wonder that it was there and then that the notion of parallelism becomes central for a whole scientific culture struggling for recognition, trying to delineate its proper field of research and to justify its positing of the feeling and sensing human being as its legitimate subject matter. It is through this notion that a relation was supposed to hold between diverse research fields and thus, as has just been suggested, guarantee its scientificity. In this context, Fechner's blunder (in talking of a Spinozistic-like parallelism) is perhaps only one manifestation of a more general phenomenon, and it characterizes not only the self-conception of experimental psychology and of psychology as they have been becoming autonomous disciplines (or one general autonomous discipline with a few sub-disciplines), but also, more generally and, admittedly, vaguely, the positivistic spirit of modern science and of much of scientific philosophy. It also expresses a certain tendency to lose the ability to see the *sui generis* nature of certain philosophical issues. Fechner's use of the term "parallelism" as an adequate representation of Spinoza's mind-body theory is symptomatic to a general difficulty to capture truly what was at stake – philosophically, ethically, theologically, and even politically – in Spinoza's mind-body theory and in his particular contribution to the debates about this question in his time. This is where the charge of an "anachronistic" reading of Spinoza becomes pertinent.[22]

It is thus apparently here that the term "parallelism" makes its appearance as a central element in Spinoza's exegesis. It is here that not only the irony of using a Leibnizian anti-Spinozistic term turned into an allegedly adequate representation of Spinoza becomes apparent, but also that a whole tradition of Spinozistic scholarship begins that uses the parallelism thesis without suspecting that this might distort the original teaching and the fundamental motivations of Spinozism as well as, in particular, the stakes of the original debates in which the term first appears. Although the use of a term such as "parallelism" is not necessarily detrimental for sound and adequate interpretation of Spinoza's philosophy in general, the fact is that Fechner's blunder provided subsequent generations of Spinoza scholars with an allegedly key term for a sound understanding of his mind-body theory, but in fact perpetuated the blunder.

---

[22] The emergence of psychology provoked a general criticism of "psychologism," which is the context where two of the main philosophical traditions of contemporary philosophy were born, notably in the work of Husserl and Frege. Both were trying to reclaim, and redefine, the *sui generis* nature of philosophical reflection. There is an interesting dialectics here: these attempts follow the – partial but real – loss of the ability to see the sense of classical philosophy, a loss exemplified also in Fechner's use of the notion of parallelism.

3

Mind and Body II

The Context

3.1. What Is It That Some Hebrews Saw as if Through the Clouds?

Anachronistic and even misleading as it may be, the parallelism thesis has nevertheless come to play a central role in Spinoza scholarship. Although, and notwithstanding the kind of conformism academic writers often display and the ways terminology and interpretative habits are perpetuated in scholarly literature, this is not completely gratuitous. The parallelism thesis – whether in the simplistic (anti) "two stuffs" version or under some subtler or softer form – misses Spinoza's deeper philosophical motivations. The use of the parallelism thesis is anachronistic not only because it obscures the difference between Spinoza and Leibniz or because it ignores the fact that the notion has undergone deep changes since it first appeared in Leibniz's writings, so that the kinds of question almost instinctively understood nowadays under this term are rather different from what Leibniz understood by it, but also because it more or less ignores what is referred to sometimes as Spinoza's "traditionalism." This side of Spinoza's philosophy is often either not taken seriously enough or taken too seriously: either one reads Spinoza (specifically his mind-body theory) as if he was our contemporary, or one reads him as taking part in a pre-modern, even medieval, discussion. Both these attitudes have to be overcome.

It has been often said that Spinoza is less modern and that his thought is still much more part of pre-modern philosophy than his Cartesian contemporaries. Put in this way, this claim is certainly wrong. It expresses, however, the deep iconoclastic nature of Spinoza's philosophy in general, and in relation to the Cartesian legacy in particular. The classical formulation of the claim about Spinoza's traditionalism is, most probably, Wolfson's. His book on Spinoza is also the most fully documented attempt to sustain it. As he puts it, Spinoza, or rather a hidden author who "lurks behind" the explicit text of the *Ethics*, was "the last of the mediaevals," meaning by this term mainly Jewish mediaeval

3.1. What Is It That Some Hebrews Saw as if Through the Clouds? 73

philosophers.[1] As it stands, it appears to be a rather simplistic and even dogmatic thesis. All the same, Wolfson's book is a particularly rich, indeed invaluable, inventory of all possible analogies, similarities, and rapprochements between Spinoza and the Jewish mediaeval philosophers. Wolfson undoubtedly points to some real sources of Spinoza's philosophy. He was not the first to advance claims about Spinoza's Jewish mediaeval sources, and a number of scholars, mainly specialists of Jewish thought, keep looking for more evidence and fresh insights on this matter.[2]

In the scholium after EIIp7, the parallelism proposition, appears a famous phrase: from the proposition and from what precedes it, says the scholium, it should be clear that the extended substance and the thinking substance are one and the same substance, which is sometimes conceived as thought, sometimes as extension. "Some of the Hebrews," adds Spinoza, "seem to have seen this, as if through a cloud, when they maintained that God, God's intellect and the things understood [or rather, thought] by Him are one and the same thing." Wolfson thinks that this phrase is a reference to Maimonides. Chapter 68 of the first part of *More Nebukhim* (*The Guide of the Perplexed*), opens with an allusion to "this famous saying of the philosophers about God, that He is the *intellectus*, the *intelligens* and the *intelligibile*."[3] As Wolfson notes (vol. 2, p. 24), similar pronouncements are found both in Maimonides's Halakhic great work *Mishne Torah* (in *Yesode ha-Torah*, II, 10) as well as in Ibn Ezra and in Yehudah Ha'Levi's *Ha'Kuzari*. There are more references to this thesis in the writings of mediaeval Jewish philosophers, some, such as Maimonides, or even more so Gersonides, favorable, others critical.

Spinoza's commentators do mention usually the phrase about the Hebrews who saw something as if through the clouds, they know that Spinoza refers here mainly to Maimonides, and they even cite the right places where Maimonides refers to this Aristotelian doctrine. Some of them, usually those who are better acquainted with, and are more interested in, Jewish mediaeval philosophy – and with Spinoza's relation to it – gloss to some extent on the ways this issue was discussed by other mediaeval Jewish philosophers. However, more often than not, scholars who are better acquainted with Spinoza's Jewish sources are interested mainly in the theologico-political, or the general ontological-cosmological, questions or in the different aspects of Spinoza's criticism of traditional Judaism, and less with the mind-body question. Consequently, they generally do not pay much attention to the fact that this remark occurs precisely in the framework of what is supposed to be a comment on, or a clarification of, the parallelism thesis, namely at the very core of a systematic exposition,

---

[1] Wolfson (1969), vol. 1, p. vii.
[2] See Section 1.2.b in Chapter 1. Besides the authors referred to there, one could add here the older Dunin-Borkowski (1912) as well as the more recent Dobbs-Weinstein, Boldoc (2009), Atlan (1999, 2003), and others (see Works Cited).
[3] According to Wolfson's translation. Pines translates: "He is the intellect as well as the intellectually cognizing subject and the intellectually cognized object."

or deduction, of the mind-body theory. But this is less innocent a detail than is suggested by the ways it is usually referred to. The decision to allude here, of all places, to this traditional thesis is a decision that invites some attention on the part of the commentator. For there are few things that are more alien to anything a contemporary reader is bound to understand by parallelism than this mediaeval, maybe Aristotelian, doctrine.

Wolfson does not address this difficulty, and he tries to explain neither Spinoza's decision to talk of this highly problematic doctrine in this particular place nor how it relates to his mind-body theory. He merely points to some similarities and dissimilarities between Spinoza and his Jewish mediaeval predecessors concerning the use of the terms that appear in this place, without probing into the philosophical significance that these similarities and dissimilarities may or may not have. He points notably to what he considers to be a significant difference between Spinoza and Maimonides on that matter: while Maimonides distinguishes four elements – God, the intellect, the intellect in act, and the intelligible – Spinoza mentions only three – God, God's intellect, and the things cognized by God.[4] It is not clear how significant this difference is, if at all, because the allusion to these "Hebrews" appears to be rather casual. Wolfson sees the difference as resulting from Spinoza's "removing the distinction between *intellectus potentia* and *intellectus actu* not only in God but in all beings," in which he is undoubtedly right. He also remarks about Spinoza's use of the "term *intellectus* in the sense of *intelligens*, i.e., *intellectus actu*" (vol. 2, p. 25), and again he is in the right. However, it is doubtful whether Spinoza intended to make here any determinate statement. He was just mentioning *en passant* something that had been seen as if through a cloud, while trying to formulate a fully accurate doctrine, presented *more geometrico* of that which had been seen in this way.

But the question ignored by Wolfson, and by most other commentators for that matter, deserves some attention. Indeed, why did Spinoza, certainly a meticulous writer, choose to incorporate here, as a part of a clarification of the parallelism thesis, a remark, surprisingly positive, on Maimonides? The text is undoubtedly too brief to permit a full answer. But it does seem to show, or at least suggest, that what was at stake in Spinoza's so-called mind-body theory was not exactly what the notion of parallelism usually conveys. Leibniz's critical remark quoted before thus probably manifests, despite its typically dubious nature, a greater philosophical acumen than that of many of Spinoza's more recent readers. It seems thus worthwhile to consider the possibility that the main *philosophical* (and, in a radically critical and subversive manner, *theological*) motivation behind Spinoza's discussion of the mind-body question belongs to the thematic field and the philosophical tradition to which belong the Maimonidean and Averroist doctrines of the identity of the intellect, the

---

[4] "Quod qûidam Hebraeorum quasi per nebulam vidisse videntur, qui scilicet statuunt, Deum, Dei intellectum, resque ab ipso intellectas unum."

3.1. What Is It That Some Hebrews Saw as if Through the Clouds?

knower (or thinker), and the known (or thought). Bracketing its theological ramifications, the philosophical thematic this tradition (or the aspect of it that is important to us here) revolves around is sometimes called *the noetic*.[5] This term, derived from the Greek *nous* – intellect – refers to what can be described as the age-long philosophical interrogation about the *being* of thinking, understanding, reason, and rationality. It is, in other words, an ontology of that faculty that is the locus of thought and thinking or, more specifically, of rational thought. Spinoza's allusion to those ancient Hebrews is one indication that the core, origin, and real philosophical significance of what is usually referred to as his mind-body theory fall within this field of an interrogation about the nature of *the noetic*. This, in any case, will be the guideline for what follows.

Descartes's "invention," as it is sometimes called, of subjectivity – or, differently recounted, his "discovery" that he, the self-reflecting thinker, was a thinking substance (*res cogitans*) – is a metaphysical or ontological – more than psychological, anthropological, or phenomenological – doctrine. Due mainly to Etienne Gilson's pioneering work, continued and transformed in many ways more recently by other scholars, it has become clear that the Cartesian doctrine of the thinking "ego" has many roots in the scholastic and late-scholastic philosophical-theological tradition. The Cartesian substantiation of the thinking self, however, is more Augustinian than Averroist, and, more importantly, it paves the way to the transcendentalist perspective on thinking. In this sense it can be seen as announcing the end of the *noétique* as a central philosophical theme. The traditional notion of *noétique* may give us the means to sketch the broader lines of the thematic horizon within which Spinoza's mind-body doctrine has to be read: a general – or ontological – interrogation about the meaning of *thought* as a mode of being. It is also an indication of Spinoza's deeply iconoclastic and critical Cartesianism (or post-Cartesianism).

3.1.a. Contextualizing Spinoza's Mind-Body Theory

The little phrase about "some Hebrews" is Spinoza's sole explicit allusion to the mediaeval debates on the unity of the intellect and the intelligible. Leibniz used his newly formed term "parallelism" in his long quarrel against Spinoza's monism (as well as, of course, as the name of his own contribution to the debate about Cartesian dualism and "interactionism"). By presenting Spinoza's doctrine, as he sometimes did, as "panpsychism," Leibniz explicitly inscribed his anti-Spinoza discourse on the still-alive theological-philosophical debate against Averroism.[6] As usual, he was right in a sense and manipulative in

---

[5] In contemporary philosophical French, the term *noétique* is used as noun, while *noetic* in English is usually used as an adjective. I shall use in what follows either the French or the substantivizing form *the noetic*.

[6] On December 10, 1270, Etienne Templier, bishop of Paris, condemned ten propositions attributed to Averroes; the first said that there was numerically one intellect, shared by all humans. This event marks the great debate against Averroism. Renan's classic study has not lost its value as a comprehensive work on Averroism.

another. Spinoza's doctrine of the nature of the human soul does indeed echo the Averroist themes. However – and although much of what Spinoza says, for instance about God's loving himself through the human intellectual love of God or about the eternity of the soul, might seem as a denial of both the unity and separateness of the human intellect – Leibniz was, in the last analysis, wrong. It is not unlikely that he knew it himself. It would be indeed wrong to present Spinoza's *noétique*, as Leibniz implies and as some modern commentators do, as yet another version of the allegedly Averroist theory of the non-existence of separate particular intellects or of what is known as the "conjunction"[7] or "union" of the (human) "acquired intellect" and the "agent intellect." But even if he was not altogether fair to Spinoza, and even if his amalgamation of Spinoza and Averroism had political and polemical motivations no less than philosophical, he was right insofar as the larger context of Spinoza's theory is in question, a context that has to be made explicit in order to see its full significance.

Spinoza's alleged traditionalism was a kind of radical, if iconoclastic, modernity. He was no *panpsychist*. The parallelist language he uses as well as the quasi-universal tendency to read parallelism, in one form or another, into the *Ethics* and into his philosophy in general attest to his modernity. More precisely, it attests to the fact that it has been conceived in Cartesian – hence modern – terms. That there is one substance and not two, that extension and thought are attributes and not substances, and in particular the extension-thought monism and the mind-body unity, are all doctrines cast in Cartesian language. Opposed to Descartes's own answers, they are all the same answers to questions Descartes raised. Yet – and whether fully or partially, directly or indirectly, explicitly formulated or implicitly assumed – the philosophical horizon within which Spinoza's so-called mind-body doctrine evolved, and against which it has to be read, is not the one we tend to think of when we use of the term "parallelism." This is true of Descartes and the other Cartesians as well, but it is particularly important to emphasize when Spinoza is concerned because of his deep opposition to Descartes and his radically unorthodox Cartesianism.

If the remark about those Hebrews, who did and did not see, does allude to something real, it is to a fundamental and long discussion, of which Spinoza most certainly had only a very partial knowledge. Notwithstanding Spinoza's supposed limited acquaintance with this tradition outside its manifestations in the writings of a few Jewish mediaeval philosophers and, of course, its scantiness, this remark is nonetheless revelatory. Seeing as if through a cloud means that something was seen, although, apparently, the seeing person did not fully, or exactly, know what he was seeing. However harsh as is usually his judgment

---

[7] "Conjunction" is the common translation of the Hebrew דבקות (*dvekut*), which is basically a religious concept meaning, roughly, a close attachment to God, in general or during prayer or religious ceremonies. See, e.g., Dobbs-Weinstein (1999) and (2003) and references there.

about the ancient Hebrews (especially on Maimonides, apparently a kind of an emblematic Hebrew), Spinoza seems to imply that they had had some rudimentary understanding of certain philosophical truths. The little metaphor thus deserves more attention than it usually gets, and a more serious attempt to understand what was meant, or at least suggested, by this half-playful, half-ironic phrase, may be worthwhile.

Spinoza speaks in a very general and elusive way about those "Hebrews." As was said before, it is customary to read this as an allusion to Maimonides, and there is, in fact, no way to know whom exactly he had in mind. He rarely alludes to non-Jewish mediaeval philosophers, although he apparently had some knowledge of scholastic philosophy, mainly late-Dutch scholasticism but also, in a less direct way, other scholastic schools.[8] But he might have had some other Jewish philosophers in mind, since the doctrine of the unity of the intellect and the intelligible appears not only in the writings of Maimonides but also in those of a few Jewish Averroists, such as Gersonides (whom Spinoza mentions) and Yitzhak Albalag (whom he never mentions).[9]

It is sufficient for our present purposes to assume that although Spinoza thought that what Maimonides or Gersonides were saying was, sure enough, distorted and partial, it was not a mere figment of the imagination. There was a real philosophical object behind the clouds. Spinoza's momentary and very relative indulgence toward Maimonides points to the permanence of certain fundamental philosophical interests, problems, and interrogations, which appear in a long and multifaceted philosophical-theological discussion that lasted several centuries, assumed many forms, comprised of many controversies, occasioned much ingenuity and philosophical inventiveness, and may have constituted an essential *thematic* element of the context of Spinoza's thought. It evolved around the question of the nature of thinking – of the "mental" in general and of rational thought in particular; of the agent, or subject, of thought; of the object of rational thought; and so on. As a philosophical *tradition*, it had its roots in the Greek notion of *Logos* in Plato's doctrine of the *Intelligible*; more specifically, it originates in Aristotle's theory of the soul, and it evolves within the genre of commentary, in the form of incessant debates about the correct interpretation of "the philosopher." In this tradition, Averroism is of a special interest. Spinoza was neither a panpsychist nor an Averroist. But to the

---

[8] Although Spinoza's rapports to mediaeval Jewish thinkers have been quite extensively studied, his rapports to the non-Jewish scholastic have been quite neglected in the 20th century. This lacuna has been recently largely filled up by the collection of studies in Manzini (2011).

[9] There is ambiguity in the traditional terminology. Spinoza speaks of the doctrine of the unity of the intellect, the intelligible, and the intellecting (agent); the result of this seems to be that the intellect is not fully a part of the human individual soul. When Thomas (see below) speaks of the "unity of the soul," he argues precisely against this, defending the existence of a "separate" human intellect as part of the one unified human soul. On Jewish Averroism, in particular about Gersonides, cf. Davidson (1992) and Dobbs-Weinstein (1998). Averroes (1126–1198) and Maimonides (1135 or 1204, who is considered often as the most important Jewish philosopher

extent that Averroism is a historically and thematically pivotal element in an ongoing philosophical interrogation about the nature of reason as at one and the same time an ontological fact and a mode of human existence, it is important not to neglect it in any attempt to understand the deeper motivations of Spinoza's philosophy.

3.1.b. A Remark on Spinoza and the Averroist Tradition

Around the time Maimonides was busy formulating the ideas to which Spinoza was alluding, another great son of the city of Cordova, Averroes, or Ibn Rushd in his Arabic name, was advancing very similar ideas. Although the Muslim philosopher preceded Maimonides by a few years, scholars usually think that the latter developed his ideas independently of the former. Both belong to the mediaeval, both Latin and Arab, neo-Platonic and Aristotelian traditions that, on this particular issue, originate in an obscure but well-known few phrases of *De Anima*. This Aristotelian text contains a complex inquiry about the nature of rational thinking and of the intellect, about the relations of the higher faculty of rational thinking to the other faculties of the soul, notably the sensitive, and about the relations of the knowing rational faculty with its specific object of knowledge, which is the intelligible, or form. It is also here that the problematic notion of *active* (or *agent*) *intellect* appears as well as notions such as *passive* or *potential* intellect (third book, chapters IV and V, respectively), which were still – and we shall presently come to it – used, or rather mentioned, by Spinoza.

More specifically, the question of panpsychism, or of the union or conjunction of the rational soul with the non-personal agent intellect has its origin in a few enigmatic phrases of *De Anima* – book III, chapter 4, pp. 429b, 30–31 and book III, chapter 5, pp. 430a20 – where Aristotle had raised the possibility that the intellect, or the faculty of the soul capable of rational thinking, is, when it is not just potentially such a capability but when it is "in act," or actually thinks, an (intelligible) object, the same as its object.

Two of Aristotle's commentators in particular, Alexander of Aphrodisias in the second century and Themistius in the third century, offered extensive, albeit divergent, interpretations of these matters that determined much of the subsequent discussions of the subjects falling under the title of *noétique*.[10] But over and above this or that particular, however complex doctrine, the real importance of the Aristotelian theory of the intellect resides in the role it played in the history of Western philosophy and in its ongoing reflection on reason, on

---

and Halakhik codifier), were both born in Cordova. According to Shlomo Pines (e.g., in his introduction to his English translation of the *Guide*), Maimonides did not know Averroes's writing when he was conceiving his own philosophical doctrines. Despite important differences, there is also deep affinity between the two philosophers on some fundamental issues falling in the field of *noétique*.

[10] For a concise description of this history, cf., e.g., Seymor Feldman (1978); see also Dobbs-Weinstein, op. cit. Particularly important is Merlan (1963).

3.1. What Is It That Some Hebrews Saw as if Through the Clouds?

rational thought, on itself as a paradigmatic rational activity.[11] A long and multifarious tradition of commenting and interpreting this passage ensued, culminating in the Averroist scandal, caused to a large degree by the doctrine of the transcendent, non-personal nature of rational thought.

Many of the issues involved in this history are addressed in often very illuminating and pertinent ways in a number of recent attempts to consider anew the relationships between philosophical modernity and pre-modernity. Among the authors involved in this discussion, the work of the French scholar Alain de Libera is of a special relevancy for our concern here. This is so both for its undoubtedly exceptional erudition, the vast historical panorama it portrays, and its analytical acumen; and for the methodological and historiosophic presuppositions on which it is based. In numerous books and articles published in the last thirty years or so, de Libera has been trying to describe and analyze what he has lately come to call "The Archeology of the Subject." This is the title of an announced series of studies, of which, at the time these lines are being written, only the first and the second, titled, respectively "The birth of the Subject" and "In Search of the Identity," have appeared.[12] It is, of course, out of question to enter here in any detail either into the vast field of scholarship and reflection contained in de Libera's numerous publications or in the controversies that this work has already sparked and will certainly continue to do in the years to come. A few brief remarks seem, however, to be in order here.

De Libera's is a remarkable work of scholarship; it also purports to contribute to some contemporary philosophical discussions and debates. As the general title of his project – *Archeology of the Subject* – suggests, its general approach is inspired by Foucault;[13] it also constitutes a critical standpoint on the Heiddegerian thesis of the Cartesian origin of the "modern subject."[14] The

---

[11] As says E. Barbotin in his introduction to Hamelin's (1953) classical study. Similarly in Davidson (1992), p. 8: "The most intensely studied sentences in the history of philosophy are probably those in Aristotle's *De Anima* that undertake to explain how the human intellect passes from its original state, in which it does not think, to a subsequent state, in which it does."

[12] Alain de Libera, *Archéologie du sujet. I: Naissance du sujet; II. La quête de l'identité*, Paris: Vrin (2007 and 2008, respectively).

[13] And, as he explains in an interview, by a number of historians and historians of philosophy such as, notably, Gueroult, Hyppolite, or Collingwood. What is common to all three is a methodological attitude that can be described as genealogical-structuralist. See H. Monvallier, "Entretien avec Alain de Libera: autour de l'Archéologie du sujet," at www.actu-philosophia.com. As he explains on a number of occasions, what he means by "archeology" is that instead of the more habitual history of the philosophies of the philosophers, what he set to investigate is the long history of changes and transformations a number of central concepts and interrogations went through during the long history of European philosophy.

[14] Heidegger and his theses about the "modern theory of the subject" are omnipresent in de Libera's works. It seems safe to suggest that, although defining his original motivations as historical, De Libera's *oeuvre*, as it gradually takes shape in these years, constitutes a critical position within Heideggerianism, this all-important *episteme*, if one may say so, shared by many second-half of the twentieth-century so-called continental philosophers in general, and of French philosophers in particular, but also by psychologists, sociologists, political or literary theorists, and so on.

subject(s) – or rather the discursive practice(s) or form(s) expressed by this term – were born (or maybe conceived), says de Libera, slowly, painstakingly, more or less silently, non-linearly, and haphazardly, sometimes in contradictory manner, long before Descartes, in fact all along the history of European philosophy and theological philosophy.

Yet, the archeology de Libera offers his readers seems, in the last analysis, to unearth if not a teleological genealogy of a concept then a relatively coherent history. Although perhaps not given a priori, it can be seen in retrospect that in the *longue durée* emerges a non-arbitrary intelligibility. De Libera explicitly borrowed from Foucault a number of concepts; it is not so clear, though, if, and to what extent, he embraces Foucault's radical skepticism as well. In the transpositions (*déplacements*) of sense, the inventiveness, and contingency of the doctrines and theses he studies, there is, at the end, a *history*, not just archeology; down the road appear some constant and continuous philosophical and theological interrogations, not completely reducible to the events of the appearance of their concrete expressions.

Averroism plays a central role in the vast panorama de Libera draws. He invested great efforts in studying the debates against Averroism by such central figures as Albert the Great (from a more theological point of view) and, in particular, Thomas Aquinas, to whose anti-Averroist struggle de Libera had already devoted two independent studies.[15] He also sees a direct line linking Aquinas and Leibniz; this claim is based on the latter's use of the scholastic principle (going back to Boece) according to which *actiones sunt suppositorun*, which means that actions presuppose a substrate, (ontological) support, or, so to speak, a "carrier" or, simply, agent.[16] If thought is an action, or activity, the principle seems to imply, then there must be a subject or an agent, in the sense of some entity, of something, or of someone, that would be the source and the locus of thought, a subsisting underlying active reality. The alleged inseparateness of the intellect seems to be incompatible with the exigency of a substrate or an agent or, in more general terms, of an individuality and substantiality of the personal soul.

Another main line of development leads de Libera from Augustinian neo-Platonism through Ibn Rushd and the Jewish and Latin Averroists, to Franz Brentano. One theme that gives unity and coherence to the Augustine-Brentano continuum is the identity of the intellect, the intelligible, and act of thinking (or "intellecting").[17] This ancient way of putting things, thinks de Libera, appears later as the scholastic principle of *in-existence* (or *inesse* as Leibniz

---

[15] ; See de Libera (1994) and (2004).
[16] See de Libera (2007), e.g., pp. 72, 225, 445.
[17] What to call this specific kind of action that is the characteristic activity of the intellect, or *nous*, and in the latter does what it characteristically does with the *ineligible*, is not a simple question. "Thinking" is too general and does not connote the specificity its agent, the intellect; hence, "intellecting" is sometimes used. Merlan (op.cit, p. 4) translates *nous* as "intelligence" and its action, *noein*, as "intelligizing."

3.1. What Is It That Some Hebrews Saw as if Through the Clouds? 81

called it) that is famously resuscitated by Brentano, to become later, mainly in the hands of Husserl, the principle of *intentionality* and the founding moment of phenomenology. Averroism can thus be portrayed as being the center – both diachronically and thematically – of a series of interrogations built around (among other things) two main motivations, one more theological in nature, the other more philosophical. A fundamental tension, perhaps contradiction, seems to emerge here. The theological doctrine of the immortality of the human soul on the one hand, and the crystallization of the philosophical theory of rationality as a doctrine of the identity of the intellect and its object on the other, seem to contradict one another. Trying, on several occasions, to offer some indications as to what may define the thematic core of the controversies, or give the sense of the questions debated during the long period (practically the whole history of Western philosophy) that, he thinks, constitutes the real birthplace – or accidentally intersecting birthplaces, pedigrees, histories, and traditions – of the "subject" (or "subjects"), de Libera formulates a number of questions that are supposed to delineate together the field within which unfolds the archeology of the subject: What is thought? Who is the subject of thought/thinking? Or: *Qui pense? Quel est le sujet de la pensée? Qui sommes-nous? Qu'est-ce que l'homme?* (Who thinks? What is the subject of thought? Who are we? What is man?)

The purpose of this long digression is to suggest that it is in the historic-thematic field studied by de Libera's archeology that one has to contextualize Spinoza's mind-body doctrine. It is not about mind-body parallelism but about the nature of reason, about thought and its *locus*, and about the nature of he who thinks or what is it that thinks. It is, of course, unavoidable that some lacunas exist in such an ambitious project as de Libera's. Two of them seem to be particularly relevant from the point of view of Spinoza's place in the archeology of the subject. The first is of a general nature: de Libera conceives his archeology as a study of the internal genealogy of certain concepts, themes, and doctrines. He explicitly rejects the pertinence of "external" influences. This may be acceptable in most cases but is less so when the emergence of what was called in the seventeenth century "the new science" is concerned. Typically[18] absent from de Libera's work, there seem to be good reasons to think that

---

[18] Perhaps due to Heidegger's critique of modernity and of the place in it of science, and probably sometimes expressing some philosophical, theological-philosophical and even ideological agendas, a whole scholarly work on the origins of modernity has evolved in which the scientific revolution and the appearance of modern science is more or less ignored. Not less typical is the fact that different "legitimation" projects of modernity deal extensively with the new science. De Libera's work, as well as that of some other mediaevalists or post-Heideggerians students of modernity, is apparently motivated, among other things, by the will to counteract such ideas as the "invention" (of the subject in this case) and with it, again probably, the ideological agendas made possible by such an idea. But that there were particularly "happy moments" in intellectual history, like the emergence of the new science in Galileo, Descartes and a few others does not necessarily lead to reductionist, historicist, or other relativist conclusions. Neglecting these moments may constitute indeed a lacuna.

any adequate evaluation of, notably, Descartes's doctrine of the subject and of subjectivity have to take into consideration the so-called scientific revolution. More specifically, the emergence of the new mechanical and mathematical science of matter, to which Descartes was a major contributor, conceivably played a double role in the history of the subject: it imposed new forms of rationality, modeled on the new science; and it also provided a paradigmatic new object for the thinking and knowing subject, namely matter as conceived or imagined by the new science. There is here, among other things, a deep displacement – to use one of de Libera's concepts – of the sense of such terms as "matter," "body," "movement," and notably "causality," "cause," and so on, and of their role in forming concepts such as "self" and "consciousness" and, most importantly, "concept" and "object" of knowledge.

The second lacuna concerns us more directly: de Libra is relatively silent about Spinoza. He deals extensively, besides Leibniz and Descartes, with many other early modern philosophers, such as Hobbes, Locke, Bayle, and more. He has, however, very little to say about Spinoza.[19] Spinoza's absence (so far at least) from de Libera's work is not without significance. Although the range of topics he covers, or intends to cover, is vast enough to include what he calls the "anti-subject" tradition, that of the *Es dankt* (it, or this, thinks) of Nietzsche or Wittgenstein, among others,[20] Spinoza seems somehow to elude any localization even within de Libera's generous classification. As essentially modern, or even postmodern, the anti-subject tradition is also anti-metaphysical; in this sense, and precisely by his alleged traditionalism, Spinoza is not part of the anti-subject tradition. On the other hand – and this is a commonplace – he is also not a theorist of the "subject" as substrate, as substance, or as the condition or source of agency. His demystification of the subject, as ontological as it is, is also as radical as that of the anti-subject philosophers. Spinoza, it seems, is indeed not classifiable in any simple way within de Libera's historical-conceptual schemes.

Two main lessons can be drawn from this long digression. The first is that if the concept of parallelism does not demarcate the context within which

---

[19] In the index of de Libera (2007), Spinoza has two entries (pp. 113 and 429); the second refers to the bibliography, and the first concerns, in fact, Descartes more than Spinoza. In the second volume Spinoza is already mentioned four or five times, but again just mentioned, never discussed. It is obviously too early to judge, as we dispose, by the time these words are being written, only of the first two volumes of a series of four or five announced. However, insofar as the first volume contains the outline of the whole venture, it seems that Spinoza will occupy in it, at best, a very secondary place. Silence about Spinoza characterizes phenomenology in general and is in particular notable in Heidegger and in much of the philosophical discourse that has been influenced by his ontology. In a recent study that has some vague parallelism with the post-Heideggerian study of the rapports between modernity and mediaeval ontology, Hight (2008), purporting to tell the "tale" of the so-called early modern ontology of ideas, explicitly chooses to disregard Spinoza. The explanations he gives for this choice are illuminating as symptoms more than for the philosophical insights they contain.

[20] See the interview by H. Monvallier, op. cit.

Spinoza's mind-body doctrine has to be understood, then, conceivably, de Libera's archeological site does. The second is that unclassifiable, Spinoza participates in this history as a sort of alien, embracing critical and ironic attitude toward all the competing traditions that constitute it. What Spinoza's "Hebrews" had seen as if through a cloud had apparently been what de Libera describes as the thematic core around which he conducts his research: a major philosophical interrogation about the nature of thought, of rationality and reason, and about the nature of the human agent of thinking. Spinoza thus seems to suggest that this interrogation is the right subject of philosophy; it has, however, to be explored under an altogether different conception of the nature of rationality and of scientific work.

Averroism is particularly important in this context since this term connotes an apparent incompatibility, or at least a deep tension, between theological and philosophical motivations. The immortality seen from the point of view of theology is quite different from, and in some ways even the opposite of, the eternity of the rational soul seen from the point of view of the philosophical theory of reason. These two themes – the eternity of reason and the immortality of the personal soul – constitute an axis around which much of Spinoza's doctrine of *salus, seu beatitude, seu Libertas* evolves. This doctrine is the topic of the second half of the fifth part of the *Ethics*, and it is cast, to a large degree, in the terminology of mediaeval theological philosophy. The doctrine of the eternity of the soul, the intellectual love of God, or even the third kind of knowledge are a permanent source of embarrassment to readers of Spinoza, especially to those who are less inclined to religious or semi-mystical interpretations of his philosophy. I shall come back to the doctrine of salvation and freedom in the last part of this study; but I would add already at this point that the second part of EV is incomprehensible if Spinoza's iconoclastic traditionalism and deep, but idiosyncratic, modernity are not taken together into consideration. Traditional, first, is the theory of the human mind that is an ontology of thought or a *noétique*; it is iconoclastic because it is anti-theological by its fundamental motivations. Its modernity is conspicuous in its so-called mind-body theory, which evolves on the basis of a Cartesian, or fully modern, conception of the nature of matter and of the body.

3.2. Spinoza's Non-Traditional Traditionalism: The *Noétique*

Whether or not one can profitably use the term *noétique* to describe the first thirteen propositions of EII, or consider Spinoza's mind-body theory as an ontology of thinking, it is in any case clear that this doctrine is deeply unorthodox. Spinoza's *noétique* has undoubtedly to be read against the background of what he, like the Cartesians in general, saw, or at least presented, as a general collapse of the mediaeval paradigm. Among many other things, this implied the rejection of final causes and the entire legitimacy of teleological considerations. Spinoza's own famous and radical version of this rejection is expounded mainly in the appendix to EI. The critique of teleology is particularly important because it has deep repercussions on the foundations of a common theological and moral outlook. This was exactly what Spinoza was targeting in his rejection of final causes.

In a more restricted sense, the collapse of the mediaeval paradigm meant a profound change in the metaphysical image of the structure of physical reality. The related concepts of *causality*, *causal relations*, and *causal laws* and, with them, that of scientific explanation, all become very different from what they had been before. Also very relevant in this context is the transformation of the concepts of *matter* and *body* implied by the new science and concretely effected in the Cartesian doctrine of *extension*. Extension for Descartes – and for Spinoza as well – was no longer the formless and unqualified matter, but the semi-idealized object of mathematicized science.

One fundamental traditional distinction that lost much of its pertinence with the advent of modern science is the distinction between what is "potential" and what is "actual" or "in act." This is evident in regard to physics, or the science of matter and movement, but it is also important from the point of view of the doctrine of thought, since much of the mediaeval conception of thought turns on the fundamental Aristotelian distinction between the potential and the actual intellect. Wolfson has a few remarks on this matter that can serve as a convenient starting point for our discussion. As already remarked, he thought that one thing that differentiated Spinoza from his mediaeval predecessors was that he removed the distinction between *intellectus potentia* and *intellectus actu* not only in God but in all beings. The term *intellectus actu* appears in propositions 30 and 31 of EI. As Wolfson indicates, Spinoza immediately (EIp31s) explains that his use does not mean that he accepts the existence of any potential intellect. Obviously, this remark is meant to demarcate, immediately and explicitly, his own thinking from the mediaeval tradition.

Wolfson, consistent with his policy of always reading Spinoza as participating in the mediaeval debate, interprets this remark as of relatively minor significance, more or less technical, and not exceeding the confines of mediaeval philosophy. In fact, however, Spinoza's explicit denial of the theoretical efficacy of the concept of "potential intellect" amounts to more than just a loss of interest in a concept that has somehow become obsolete. There are good reasons to suppose that with the rejection of the potential intellect, the original meaning of *intellect in act* is lost too. This may even suggest that a fundamental way of considering the relations between being and thought has lost its pertinence. Yet, the fact that Spinoza was using these traditional terms of *intellectus actu* and *intellectu potentia* is not without significance. The loss of the original sense of what used to be expressed by these terms does not necessarily mean that they do not have any bearing on the interpretation of Spinoza's philosophy in general and of his mind-body theory in particular. The preservation of the traditional terminology may hint to the fact that the question of the relations between being and thought remains for Spinoza a fundamental question.

3.2. Spinoza's Non-Traditional Traditionalism: The Noétique

This question can be formulated as "what is thinking being?"; this can mean any one of the following questions, or all at once: "What is a thinking thing?" "What does it mean to think being?" "What kind of being is thought?" Spinoza asks all these questions as belonging to one thematic field unified under the title of the unity of mind and body. It can thus be maintained that his so-called mind-body doctrine belongs to the field of *the noetic*.

A careful reading of the propositions 29–32 of EI is needed in order to better understand the meaning the traditional term *intellectus actu* assumes in Spinoza's text or the theoretical functions it fulfills in his doctrine. Generally speaking, Spinoza effectuates through his use of this term a typically complex gesture of preservation and transformation. The notion of "actual intellect" appears in propositions 30 and 31, which constitute a semi-parenthetical clause within the larger argument for the inadequacy of the notion of free will and of the proof of the validity of necessitarian determinism (respectively EIp32 and p33). The main lesson of this move seems to become apparent in the second corollary of proposition 32, which states that will and intellect relate to God just like motion and rest. Intellect and will are "natural" entities and do not enjoy any ontological privilege over all natural things.

The main systematic function propositions 30 and 31 fulfill is to delineate an *ontological* space where the concept of *intellect* rightfully belongs and against the background of which its "naturalistic" interpretation has to be read. Specifically, "intellect," whether considered as finite or as infinite, is something that belongs with the ordinary things of the world and is subject, as such, to the necessity of the laws governing the world. Propositions 30 and 31 are enclosed between two scholia. The first follows EIp29, which contains one of Spinoza's boldest claims: "In nature there is nothing contingent." Without clear connection to the denial of contingency, the scholium introduces the (traditional) distinction between *Natura naturata* and *Natura naturans*, and the main point of these two propositions is that "intellect" belongs to "natured nature."

EIp30 affirms that "An actual intellect, whether finite or infinite, must comprehend [*comprehendere*] God's attributes and God's affections, and nothing more." This affirmation can be interpreted as a demystifying gesture: the conditions of possibility of thought are the same as the conditions of nature in general, and the intellect – finite or infinite – or the capacity to think, understand, and know do not exceed the range of nature, or of what actually exists. EIp31 adds that "The actual intellect, whether finite or infinite, like will, desire, love, and the like, must be referred to *Natura naturata*, not to *Natura naturans*." The beginning of the demonstration of p31 specifies "By intellect ... we understand *not absolute thought*, but only *a certain mode of thinking*" that "must be conceived through absolute thought," that is, through "an attribute of God, which expresses the eternal and infinite essence of thought" (italics added). If not an *absolute*, this particular mode of thought, the intellect – whether infinite or finite – is, evidently, a *conditioned* being or thing. What is called "God's intellect" is also not an absolute; it is thus neither a *cause* nor a *reason* nor the *ground* of existence, and it too does not have any surplus of being over whatever else there is.[21]

The intellect's specific condition, or condition of possibility – both ontologically and conceptually – is the attribute of thought. In other words, the concept of *intellect* is conceivable only if "absolute thought," or the attribute of thought, which is an "eternal and infinite essence," is presupposed. As "essence," however, it is not an *existent*.[22] By defining the attribute as that which "the intellect perceives" and not as that which "is" (either in itself or in another), Spinoza certainly (and notwithstanding some other interpretations) does not intend a subjectivist or idealist interpretation of it. An attribute should perhaps be understood as both an ultimate condition of *intelligibility* and a fundamental and *sui generis* ontological possibility; *possibility* being said here not in its strictly modal (or formal) sense (i.e., as that which is simply not impossible, or may be or not be), but rather in the more complex sense of the *thinkable*. In the noetic realm – the ontology of intellecting – or in the specific context of thinking, absoluteness belongs to the eternal essence, or attribute, of thought. The absolute becomes here something of a peculiar ontological status – it is a *principle* (and not a thing or an existent). While "intellect" can be understood as referring to some kind of an entity, either finite or infinite, thought, on the other hand, in the absolute sense of the word – that is, as one of the substance's attributes – does not designate an entity, or an existent, but rather something else. It conditions the intelligibility of the concept of intellect; ontologically, and as a condition-of-possibility of intellect, either finite or infinite, it is a general and fundamental possibility of being, but, again, not an entity.[23] Perhaps it can in fact be best described as a *principle*. This, or something similar to this, is probably what Spinoza means by using the notion of "infinite essence."

---

[21] According to the famous remark in scholium to EIp17, those who attribute intellect (and will) to the nature of God can do it only homonymously: such a divine intellect would differ from human intellect like "the dog that is a heavenly constellation [differs from] the dog that is a barking animal." The difference as Spinoza defines it here is very similar to Averroes's injunction, according to which human knowledge is caused by its object, while Divine knowledge is the cause of its object, a position rejected by Spinoza. See, e.g., A. de Libera, Introduction to Averroès, *Le livre du discours decisive*, tr. Marc Geoffroy, Paris: GF-Flammarion, 1996, p. 33. See also Koyré (1950). As Wolfson, op. cit., I, pp. 316–317 remarks, this illustration is found already in Philo and also in Maimonides.

[22] Spinoza's use of the notion of *essence* is notoriously ambiguous and complex. It is true that "*Dei existentia, eujs'que essentia unum et idem sunt*" (EIp20), but it is also true "*atqui praeter substantias, et modos nil datur*" (EIp15dem). "Substance" and "mode" are defined as modes of being (in itself versus in another) and of being conceived (through itself versus through another). "Attribute" is defined as that which the intellect perceives as the essence of a substance. Clearly what can be described perhaps as the respective "ontological species" of substance and modes on the one hand, and of attribute on the other, are not the same. In this sense the attribute can indeed be said not to be an *existent* but something else.

[23] "Except for substances and modes there is nothing," says EIp15dem.

3.2. Spinoza's Non-Traditional Traditionalism: The Noétique

Defining thought as an attribute and the intellect as an entity belonging to *natura naturata* amounts to a double-faced demystifying or naturalizing gesture: intellect is a natural entity, and thought, as an attribute, is also part of being or nature. As an "eternal essence," however, thought is also fully transparent. This means that there is nothing mysterious about it, but also that it is natural in a very special sense. Insofar as it is a fundamental and irreducible ontological possibility or principle and, in particular, a concept (or essence), thinking cannot be conceived as an accident of any kind or as a purely given factuality. It is not miraculous, but it also cannot be conceived, for example, as a happy, unexpected, and unexplainable "emerging" property, an outcome of a more or less blind process of "evolution." But, of course, it cannot also be said to be the result of intelligent design of any kind or be explained on the basis of final causes or the work of a *supra mundana* intelligence. Just as matter or physical existence are accepted as "natural" and do not provoke the feeling that a special explanation for their existence is needed,[24] or that it involves any special mystery, so thought and thinking belong to the original armature of being. Or, since as Spinoza famously puts it, no one yet knows what the body (or matter) can do, if some kind of wonder is justified, it is justified when matter is concerned not less than when we talk about thought. Both thought and extension are principles in this sense: they are the fundamental possibilities of being or, precisely, the attributes of the one and infinite "substance." There is no wonder in the fact that whatever there is, is also *thinkable*, at least not more than the fact that there is something.

The scholium after EIp31 contains the reservation about the use of the traditional term of *intellectus actu* referred to by Wolfson. Spinoza also explains here why he chose nevertheless to use this notion. His explanation is very illuminating:

> The reason why I speak here of actual intellect is not because I concede that there is any potential intellect, but because, wishing to avoid all confusion, I wanted to speak only of *what we perceive the most clearly, that is the intellection itself* [ipsa scilicet intellectione]. We perceive nothing more clearly than that. For everything we understand leads to more perfect knowledge of intellection [Nihil enim intelligere possumus, quod ad perfectionem intellectionis cognitionem non conducat] (italics added; translation modified).

Intellection itself – the act of thinking an object, conceiving an intelligible content, understanding something – is what "we perceive most clearly." In the TIE Spinoza had said already, and in greater detail, similar things. The fact that Spinoza reduces the rather long and elaborate discussion contained in the earlier work to a few condensed lines in the *Ethics* has to be seen against

---

[24] What do sometimes provoke such feelings are the "design," structure, or order that we find, as either physicists or biologists, for example, in nature. But these often lead to one form or another of the concept of "thought."

the background of the more general abandonment of the project of writing a treatise on how to conduct the intellect in the search for truth. The TIE was conceived on the model of Descartes's *On Method*. But already in this work one senses the ambiguity of Spinoza's initial pursuit of the "good method" as well as his awareness of the difficulties involved in the project of a special science of "method" or theory of knowledge. The same holds for Spinoza's other early works. Understanding what understanding, thinking, or intellecting are, and developing an effective normative conception of truth on the basis of this understanding, depends on having effected already that which truth characterizes, namely thinking and knowing. In order to recommend how to look for truth, or to have a theory of true knowledge, one has to have already adequately known something (e.g., a mathematical theorem) to be true. There is no systematic knowledge prior to actual, active knowledge, so the idea of a *sui generis* science of "method" or, more generally, a theory of knowledge, is inadequate.

Descartes's "method" had also been a reflective enterprise. The incomplete and unpublished *Regulae* was based on Descartes's early mathematical inventions, and the *Discourse de la méthode* was added as a preface to three scientific essays – *La Géométrie*, *La Dioptrique*, and *Les Météores* – previously conceived and written. Cast in less technical language, and condensing the richer and much more elaborate earlier work to a few principles, the *Discourse* purports to explain the kind of method operative in them but also, and in particular, to outline a universal method. Like light, which equally and indifferently illuminates all things, so the method too should be applicable to all fields of knowledge and be indifferent to the kind of object to which it is applied. Light and method, being universal and indifferent to the particular objects they illuminate or lead one to know, are made of a different stuff, so to speak, from that of these objects. *Method* was thus conceived by Descartes as a kind of knowledge both independent of and prior to what was positively known. It was also conceived as a normative kind of knowledge and its principles as rules to be followed if true knowledge is to be achieved.[25]

Spinoza eventually abandoned what was initially conceived as a "method" à la Descartes. He now saw the idea of a set of normative rules, in effect abstracted from actual knowledge yet claiming priority over it, as a chimera. *Habemus ideam veram* – we have a true idea – is the quite remarkable, and problematic, opening of § 33 of the TIE.[26] A few lines later comes another extraordinary claim: method is nothing but the *idea ideae* or the reflexive idea. This amounts, in the first place, to placing a human experience as the necessary

---

[25] See Grosholz (1991), p. 2: Descartes conceived his method as a "cannon," prior even to logic. This is an "intuitionist" attitude, "intuitionism" understood in a rather general way and applied to a number of philosophical positions (e.g., Epicurus and Kant) that base a systematic critique of dogmatic metaphysics on theorizing "canonical procedures" of the construction of representations.

[26] See discussion later in the book.

3.2. Spinoza's Non-Traditional Traditionalism: The Noétique

point of departure of "method,"[27] only the "experience" in question here is of a very special nature: it is the experience of truthful thinking. But this constitutes a rejection of Descartes's idea of *method* as an independent kind of knowledge. Already in the TIE, improving the understanding is part of positive knowledge and of the process of acquiring positive knowledge. We improve our ability of understanding and of knowing as we proceed. In the TIE, it still seems to be assumed – which is no longer the case in the *Ethics* – that we can interrupt the process of thinking, abstract from what we actually understand or know, and formulate a relatively independent theory about how to "improve the understanding." But a major point of divergence from Descartes is already conspicuous: self-reflection and methodology do not enjoy any epistemological privilege or autonomy. They do not constitute a beginning. The improvement of the understanding is comparable to the way in which material instruments are built. Man began his long ascent to technical know-how by using natural instruments, with the aid of which he forged simple artificial instruments, which then enabled him to produce ever more sophisticated ones (ibid. § 26). Positive, rational knowledge does not depend on a special, or a previously posited, set of rules or an absolute instrument of knowledge. That "method" is nothing but the "reflexive idea" means that actual knowledge and truth – "the idea" – is an effective part of "method," or of the theory of the way to achieve truth, and not just the basis for a process of abstraction from which an independent set of normative rules can be extracted. This is, in itself, a radical breach with Descartes.

The breach with Descartes is, however, deeper than the rejection of the idea of method. It means also a rejection of the very idea of a theory of knowledge as an independent enterprise, as the starting point of a rational science of being, of man, and of the world. It is a rejection of all that made Descartes devote the first part of his *Principles of Philosophy* to expounding "The Principles of Human Knowledge."[28] But it goes even further and amounts to a rejection of the Cartesian ideal of *prima philosophia*. There is an intimate connection between the following: the enterprise of "method" is abandoned, the idea of a prior-to-philosophy theory of knowledge is rejected as well, and the *Cogito* no longer serves as the beginning of philosophy. Spinoza, it would seem, is abandoning the ideal of an absolute beginning of philosophy, free of all presuppositions and of all previously acquired knowledge, conceived also as the founding moment of science. In the TIE we have, as we have just seen, the "we have a true idea"; in the *Ethics* a "man thinks" appears (in the second axiom of EII; see discussion later in the book) as an absolute affirmation of what appears to be sheer factuality. A certain original rationality, already operative, is not only the concrete starting point for the search for

---

[27] For an analysis of the role of *experience* in Spinoza's philosophy, which goes against many well-rooted exegetical habits, see Moreau (1994).

[28] Grosholz, op. cit., p. 1.

truth (a claim that a Cartesian might concede) but also, and in particular, a theoretical element in the construction of an adequate theory of reason; for, as the scholium of EIp31, just quoted, says, "we can understand nothing that does not lead to more perfect knowledge of the intellection." Consequently, "method" cannot be conceived otherwise than as a gradual elaboration of forms of fuller rationality – of positive knowledge, of the understanding of what knowledge is, and of the subsequent use of this knowledge of knowledge in order to achieve higher and better – that is, philosophical – understanding. Just as Pascal had said in a different context, *nous sommes embarqués*. We always are already *en route*.

But the full sense of the scholium after EIp31 is still not exhausted by these considerations, and the recycling the old term *intellectu actu* arguably implies something even more important. The claim that what we perceive in the clearest way of all is intellection itself is not trivial. Spinoza interprets this experience as pointing to what surpasses the confines of the phenomenology of thinking. It shows that the factuality of thought and of understanding stands on metaphysical foundations. The immediacy and superiority of evident thought has deep causes and is an indication of the metaphysical nature of the human soul. The experience of thought, the fact that "we have a true idea" is not Spinoza's *non plus ultra*. His doctrine of method leads, beyond the theory of truth and of knowledge, to the theory of being or more accurately, to an ontology of thought. The TIE leads to the *Ethics*. As Léon Brunschvicg has put it, method has become in Spinoza's hand suspended on being. Separating logic and metaphysics is possible only if "thought" is considered as devoid of profundity and ontological "thickness" of its own, if it is thought just capable to reflect reality, transparent – like Descartes' light – to all kinds of reality.[29]

Spinoza's theory of thought is an ontology. This claim is supported not only by the presence of the traditional *intellectus actu*, but also by the fact that the question of the *potential intellect* has not disappeared altogether. It reappears, in a rather curious way, in EII, immediately after the parallelism proposition. Proposition EIIp8 and its corollary and scholium introduce the peculiar notion of "ideas of modes which do not exist." The wording of this semi-parenthetical half page conducts a complex dialogue with the mediaeval ontologies of thought. It echoes, albeit in a radically iconoclastic way, the question one historian of Jewish mediaeval philosophy described as the question with which a whole tradition was occupied: how do you explain the difference between an intellect that knows and its state when it does not know (or think).[30] Obviously Spinoza cannot account for the difference between the two states of the intellect – knowledge and lack of knowledge – in terms of the passage from potential to actual knowledge or, in traditional terminology, from "material" to "actual" intellect (or, in a psychologistic vein,

---

[29] Brunschvicg (1951), p. 31.
[30] Davidson, op. cit., pp. 7–8.

3.2. *Spinoza's Non-Traditional Traditionalism: The* Noétique

from dispositions to their realization). He thus inverts the question and from a question about the agent or the locus of thought and of *knowledge*, it becomes for him a question concerning the status of truth when it is not actually conceived or known. All the same, Spinoza implicitly conducts a critical dialogue with the Hebrews (and with the Averroist tradition as a whole) he referred to in the previous scholium. As the example given in the scholium shows, the non-existence Spinoza is concerned with is rather relative: it applies to the non-existence of modes that *do* exist when certain conditions are fulfilled. Spinoza does not raise the question of ideas of that which does not have any kind of being, for his necessitarism implies that one cannot talk about it at all. The logically impossible is coextensive with non-being, and the self-contradictory that is radically inconceivable or non-thinkable has no being. The notion of modes that do not *ever* exist, so to speak, or that cannot exist, would amount, in Spinozistic terms, to an utter contradiction; differently put, these non-modes do not have ideas. Judging by the later appearances of this issue in the *Ethics* (almost exclusively in EV), it seems that what Spinoza has really in mind here is not so much the mode of being of deducible or constructible geometrical properties as the question of the immortality of the soul (which he radically rejects: the soul does not exist after the death of the body) on the one hand, and of its eternity on the other (to which he seeks to give a positive interpretation; see Chapter 7).

The discussion is conducted from an ontological perspective. Mediaeval *noétique* provides an adequate key to understanding it much more than modern or contemporary mind-body theories. The full significance of all this will hopefully become clearer as we proceed; but if we needed additional proof that the real thematic space in which the discussion at the beginning of *Ethics II* is being held is very different from what is usually understood under the title of "mind-body parallelism," then proposition EIIp8, its corollary, and its scholium provides it. It is in this context (the scholium after EIIp7) that the allusion to the ancient Hebrews who saw something apparently important as if through the clouds is made, and it is in light of the previous remarks that its sudden appearance in this place would hopefully not be seen as out of place.

It is worth noting here that the example given by Spinoza for illustrating the real significance of what was seen as if through the clouds by the Hebrews is that of "a circle existing in Nature and the idea of the existing circle, which is also in God"; both are "one and the same thing, which is explained [*explicatur*] through different attributes" (EIIp7S). This is certainly a curious example if it has to explicate a mind-body parallelism in the prevailing sense. Does it mean that our mind and body are "parallel" in the same way in which the circle and its eternal concept are? It is, however, a reasonable example to give if the issue under examination is not the relations of the mental and the corporeal, or physiological, but those that hold between thought in the strict and literal – namely intellectualist – sense of the word on the one hand, and extension, understood not as deaf matter but primarily as that which thought thinks or the intellect intellects – namely as that which is given to the intellect to be *understood* or, precisely, intellected – on the other hand. Simply put, the question dealt with here is that of the relations between *ideas* and their *ideate*, which are the intelligible objects of ideas, not consciousness and brain; and the answers given to this question are meant to be the theoretical foundation for further answering the mind-body question.

4

Mind and Body III

Ethics *II, Propositions 1–13*

4.1. The Centrality of Propositions 11 and 13

The great complexity of the issues discussed under the title of the "mind-body question" manifests itself in some special characteristics of the discussion in the first thirteen propositions of EII. One of these is Spinoza's recurrent warnings and reservations about the adequacy, clarity, or sufficiency of the arguments or examples given in it. Spinoza often remarks on his arguments and deductions. In the first part of the *Ethics* for example, where some of his more difficult doctrines are expounded, he often remarks, precisely at these difficult points, that "it is easy" to see; that what he says is "obvious," clear as the sun in the middle of a bright day; that enough has been said to make the issue sufficiently understood, and so on.[1] It is thus remarkable that the beginning of the second part contains quite a number of pronouncements expressing reserve. He admits the insufficiency of an example to explicate a point, warns us of the difficulty of an issue he discusses, or implores his reader to be patient, explaining that an argument cannot yet be fully understood at this point. One example, particularly interesting from our point of view, is the scholium to EIIp7, which ends with a modest concession that for the present he cannot explain these matters more clearly. Yet many readers of Spinoza do not find the notion of parallelism particularly difficult.

It is also not without interest that this is one of the few places that flatly clashes with the earlier works, and in particular with the TIE. That there are important differences between Spinoza's earlier writings and the *Ethics* is a well-known and widely discussed fact. But a complete reversal of opinion is rare. A particularly

---

[1] For example, in the very difficult scholium of EIp15, where Spinoza discusses the indivisibility of extension, based on his theory of the infinite (see also letter 12), he expresses several times his assurance that what he says here is sufficient to solve this question, and that one has only to get rid of some prejudices to see its truth. There are numerous other examples in EI.

significant such case is the discussion in paragraphs 33 and 34 of the TIE. The same issue reappears, with exactly the same examples, but with diametrically opposed conclusions, in the scholium of EIIp7, the parallelism proposition, and EIIp17. I discuss this matter at some length later on in this chapter, but already at this point one can say that this is certainly an indication of ceaseless deliberation on a question that must have seemed both difficult and important.

EIIp8, its corollary, and its scholium, constitute together one of the most enigmatic doctrines of the *Ethics*. One indication of it is the fact that it plays almost no role in the argumentation until the fifth part. Spinoza talks here of "ideas of non-existent modes," and he tries to clarify this notion with the aid of one of his geometric examples, which, at least in this case, he warns his reader, "obviously" cannot fully explicate this "unique matter." The short scholium of EIIp11 is simply a plea addressed to the reader to be patient and to withhold judgment until the author has the opportunity to complete his argumentation. The scholium of EIIp13 also contains a similar reservation. All these examples show that something rather special is happening at this place, and should indeed raise the suspicion that those thirteen propositions are to be treated with extra care and attention.

Another exceptional feature of the beginning of EII is the fact that the normal course of deduction is broken off after the first thirteen propositions for the sake of a curious "little physics" (as I shall refer to it) or, better, physical biology. I refer, of course, to the group of definitions, axioms, and lemmas that come after proposition 13 and that deal with what makes a complex body into one body. This is the only occasion where we find such a breach in the systematic order of exposition; it is, moreover, very loosely connected to the previous, metaphysical, discussion. The basic notions of motion and rest, of degrees of velocity, and even of physical causality, are *sui generis*. They are not defined, and Spinoza incorporates here, somewhat *ex nihilo*, a number of axioms that are supposed to be self-evident and that seem to establish a new "order of reasons." Most curious is the fact that at the very core of what is promised to be a doctrine of "The Nature and Origins of the *Soul*," appears a doctrine of the nature and origins of corporeal individuality.

Up to this point – the little physics of EII – Spinoza has been discussing either general metaphysics – or a theory of the real as such and of its fundamental nature – whose main conclusions are supposed to apply to all forms of reality or, in the language of the *Ethics*, to all "attributes" (part 1), or "special metaphysics," which is a general theory of the nature of things, or modes, considered under the attribute of thought. As a matter of fact, and seen from a more general perspective, the first propositions of EII can be said to be a general theory, or rather an ontology, of thought or of the intellect. After it, Spinoza talks mainly about the human "soul," dealing with questions that are specific to this particular kind of existence, such as, notably, truth and error, rational knowledge, and the nature of the will; and then, in the subsequent parts of the *Ethics*, the nature of affects and the portrait of the free-and-wise

4.1. The Centrality of Propositions 11 and 13

man. It is true that the question of *man* is explicitly introduced in proposition 10 (it also appears in the short introductory remark at the beginning of EII and in the axioms, but these do not form an immediate part of the development contained in the first thirteen propositions), which states that man is not a substance, but until proposition 14, after the little physics, the context of the discussion remains essentially metaphysical, namely fundamental and general: "for the things shown so far," says the scholium to EIIp13, "are completely general and do not pertain more to man than to other individuals."

EIIp7 stands at the center of the development in the beginning of EII. Its alleged parallelism is usually taken to be the core of Spinoza's mind-body doctrine. The full significance of EIIp7 can only be understood by taking into consideration the real context in which it appears, both historically and thematically. To recapitulate briefly the preceding discussion, historically, this context is that of the constant philosophical inquiry into the nature of reason, of a theoretic *noetic*, of an ontology of what we call "thinking" in general and "rational thinking" in particular, of understanding, or of the metaphysical status of thought and of the human thinking agency, be it soul or mind. A careful reading of the first thirteen propositions of EII will show, I believe, that what Spinoza says in them shares with the pre-modern thinkers, both Jewish and non-Jewish, a general philosophical concern for these questions, and that in this sense his mind-body doctrine belongs to the same fundamental inquiry. However, it does so, as will hopefully soon transpire, in a thoroughly unorthodox and original way, both radically secular (hence modern) and deeply anti-Cartesian. The great iconoclastic significance of Spinoza's doctrine lies in the fact that his *noétique* is launched by immediately turning to the *body*, and by positing it as the foundation of the theory of rational thinking. This gesture determines Spinoza's philosophy as a thoroughly iconoclastic venture vis-à-vis both the pre-Cartesian and the Cartesian traditions.

The scholium after EIIp13 sums up the special ontology of the first thirteen propositions of EII and leads to the little physics and the "anthropological" parts of the *Ethics*, the concrete theory of man. From the previous propositions, it says, "we understand not only *that* the human mind is united to the body, but also *what* should be understood by the union of mind and body" (italics added). The previous discussion is thus supposed to have demonstrated not only that what may seem disparate, namely the body and the soul, are in truth united; but also, and in particular, what the nature of this union is. There is a specific content to the claim that body and soul are one thing; and the content of this claim, or the concrete nature of the union of the body and the soul, is arguably better elucidated by propositions 11 and 13 more than by proposition 7.

To say, as EIIp11 says, that the soul is fundamentally[2] an idea or, indeed, a *concept*, means that the agent of the act of thinking, the act of thinking itself, and the thought are all ontologically homogeneous. There is neither ontological

---

[2] "The first which constitutes the actual being of the human mind ... "

difference nor hierarchy between the soul (or mind), the act of thinking, and its content. The thinking agent and its/his acts – namely the particular thoughts, ideas, concepts, and so on, as well as the latter's intentional objects – are collapsed into one overall entity that is built by Spinoza around the concept of *idea*. The soul is a mode and not a substance; but it is a mode of exactly the same kind as what we call sometimes "particular" or "singular" thoughts and, more significantly, attribute to the idea-soul as "its" thoughts or ideas.[3] Alongside the rejection of the teleological conception of the intellect (or the *potential-actual intellect* distinction), Spinoza also rejects the notion of a *substrate* of the act of thinking, a *subject* in the ontological sense of the word or, more generally, the ontological distinction between the *locus* of thinking and thinking itself. The soul is not that which, as it were, *carries* its predicates, and, more significantly, it does not constitute a space of interiority wherein the act of thinking occurs; it is also not an agent that is the origin of its action – thinking – and it does not transcend either the act of thinking itself or its content in any way.

This is just one moment of the elucidation of the identity – the very same identity that some Hebrews saw as if through a cloud – of intellect, intellection, and content of thought. The second aspect of this identity is even more significant and constitutes, according to the reading of the *Ethics* proposed here, the kernel of Spinoza's mind-body doctrine. It is also more difficult to make sense of. For, as EIIp13 affirms, the "object" of the soul is the body. Paradoxical to the point of being unintelligible, this means, if taken to the letter, that the body is the content of the soul and that the mind-body unity, or union, is the unity in which an intellected content is united to the act of its intellection and to the intellect intellecting it. The fundamental noetic identity, then, is the real sense of what we conceive as the union of mind-body. The relation between soul and body is a relation between an idea and its object. If "union," however, means bringing together, cementing or mechanically juxtapositioning, that which is not originally one, then there is no mind-body union for Spinoza.

Obviously then, the attempt to delineate a specific theoretical field within which one may give sense and coherence to the first part of EII leads to difficulties. As we have seen, Spinoza himself was not unaware of that. The hesitations apparent at the beginning of the second part of the *Ethics* express, in all probability, some very real and fundamental difficulties that, essentially, are not merely exegetical. The questions that emerge here are properly philosophical questions. As suggested above, the first thirteen propositions of EII can be considered as a "special metaphysics." It is, in other words, a first – but essential – step in a systematic attempt to give concrete meaning to the general, and more or less formal, metaphysical principles of EI. It thus mediates the elaboration of a theory of the concrete man. The latter can be described as "philosophical anthropology" or even psychology. As a foundation of such a theory, the beginning of EII is not intended, primarily, to warrant its truth, but

---

[3] Or what is called in contemporary literature "mental items."

4.1. The Centrality of Propositions 11 and 13

rather to set it in a context, to put it inside a conceptual horizon that renders it intelligible. If read from the perspective of the second part, the sense of the first part (and of the fifth part as well) of Spinoza's *Ethics* is that the question of man cannot be considered a purely scientific question. The full significance of anthropological, psychological, socio-political, or even ethical theories of man cannot be grasped outside the metaphysical context. More specifically, the metaphysical question is concretized at the beginning of EII as essentially an ontology of man's fundamental characteristic activity, which is thinking. This means an attempt to locate *thinking, understanding, intellecting*, and *knowing* as well in the general economy of being. To the extent that, as we have already suggested, *intellecting* and *intellect*, or *thinking* and even *mind*, are more or less equivalent concepts for Spinoza, this part of the *Ethics* can, in fact, be said to constitute a noetic, or an (ontological) theory of *nous*, or the intellect. Once again, it is remarkable that this is done in the form of a mind-body theory.

Trying to summarize EI in a few lines would be futile and pretentious. Nonetheless, some general remarks are in order here. The first part of the *Ethics, De Deo*, contains not only general metaphysics or general ontology, but also a theory of God. The latter is profoundly polemical and, as such, can be said to be an anti-theology more than a theology. EI is also a preamble – conceptual and methodological – to the rest of the work.

EI is thoroughly polemical. It is, in fact, a systematic undermining of what Spinoza must have considered as the doctrinal core of Christian (and to some extent Jewish) theology and the ideological justification of institutionalized religion in general. Beside full-fledged rejection of some central notions of traditional theological philosophy – teleology, free will and free choice, and good and evil are among the more important ones – Spinoza's anti-theology contains a radical deconstruction of such fundamental concepts as creation, providence, revelation, the freedom of God, and others. Thematically, Spinoza's paradoxical anti-theological onto-theology is built around the discussion of the nature of God, a concept defined mainly as meaning the infinity, unity, uniqueness, and oneness of being. We also have a rejection of all transcendence; an affirmation of the complete homogeneity of nature (i.e., the validity of the same "laws of nature" and of the same norms of rationality throughout all regions of reality); a statement of the absolutely deterministic nature of these laws of nature and of causal relations among all things; and an attempt to show that it is within strict determinism alone that the concept of "freedom" makes sense.

A second main polemical strain of EI is directed at Descartes. Especially important from the present perspective is the rejection of the Cartesian ontology of the Cogito: man, like any other conceivable entity, is a "mode," not a substance. Hence the "Cogito" – the experience of the certainty of the "I think, I exist" – is not the discovery of a substantial, absolute, or primordial mode of being. Substantiality, real thing-ness or ontological and conceptual independence and self-sufficiency, belong, strictly speaking, only to the one infinite being. This becomes yet clearer in the first part of EII, which implicitly, but quite unmistakably, also argues with Descartes, and receives there a concrete meaning. These two polemics constitute an essential element of the thematic background of the first thirteen propositions of EII.

EIIp7 is usually considered the core of Spinoza's solution to the mind-body question. The view offered in the present study is different. EIIp7 states that "the order and connection of Ideas is the same as the order and connection of things," which seems to suggest indeed that the relation between thought and extension in general, and between the human mind and body in particular, is a relation between relations – an isomorphism between the ways things, or modes, as conceived "under" the different attributes, are arranged. This is the *locus classicus* of what gives rise to the exegetic thesis of parallelism: thought and extension, it is said, do not interact causally but are "parallel" different manifestations of one and the same (inaccessible?) reality and, consequently, mutual expressions of each other. The same applies, with the necessary adjustments, to mind and body.

The general considerations presented in Chapters 2 and 3 amount to a partial refutation of the parallelism thesis. A full refutation, however, derives its force from the cogency of an alternative interpretation. What follows is an attempt at such an alternative. Its main contention is that EIIp7 can be understood properly only when it is considered as a step toward what constitutes the real key to Spinoza's mind-body theory: the complex claim that (1) the soul is an idea (prop. 11), and (2) it is the idea of the body (prop. 13). EIIp7 is, sure enough, a crucial step in the development of the doctrine, but it cannot stand by itself. Reading it in isolation from the entire thematic context of the beginning of EII is bound to lead to misunderstandings.

The second axiom of EII – *Homo cogitat* – is a statement of fact. As we have already remarked, for Spinoza the recognition of an original rationality of man is a prerequisite of philosophy. Even if this is not altogether explicit, the source of the certainty in the truth of this axiom cannot be but experience. It is, sure enough, a very special kind of experience, but the experience of thinking – or, more accurately, experiencing oneself as thinking – is also an experience. The Latin text says it in an almost nonchalant manner: "man thinks"; it should perhaps be read as: "obviously, man thinks." The NS adds: "to put it differently, we know that we think." Evidently not conceptual or a priori, there is nevertheless no need to demonstrate this piece of knowledge. We already know it to be true. But, as will soon become clear, this knowledge is far from trivial. The knowledge that we think is the "reflective idea" or the "idea's idea"; it is also nothing but "consciousness" and – most amazingly of all – "method."

The first proposition of EII states "Thought is an attribute of God." This is a statement about the metaphysical nature, or origin, of what we call "thinking." We suggested above that "thought" as an attribute should be understood as a *principle* rather than as an entity; the "principle" underlying all mental activity is explicitly affirmed now to have positive ontological, or "divine," significance; differently put, it is not just a subjectively human perspective on reality. An attribute, as a principle, is a fundamental, irreducible *possibility* (Spinoza

4.1. The Centrality of Propositions 11 and 13

speaks of "essence") of being. Thought, then, is one of these possibilities; and thinking (the characteristic activity of intellects) is a concrete manifestation of one of being's fundamental possibilities.[4] Consequently, what we conceive as the activity of thinking is not reducible to psychological, or psychologistic, categories, and it is not exhaustible by epistemological considerations. Thinking, insofar as it is a manifestation of an ontological principle and of an irreducible facet of being, should not be regarded as a *given* (as an accidental result of evolution, for instance, as "emergent" properties of highly complex nervous systems, and so on), opaque and arbitrary by its very givenness. The radical non-accidentality of the experience of thought, one's awareness that one thinks, is what makes this experience a very special kind of experience. What we experience as the self-transparency of consciousness is a concrete manifestation of an ontological reality, irreducible to its facticity. Thinking – and being conscious of thinking – is not just a *fact*.

A major element of Spinoza's necessitarism is a rejection of the *metaphysical* appropriateness of the concept of the *given* or of pure *facticity*. As we shall see later on (Chapter 7), this is basic to his ethical conception of human existence.  It is also a founding moment of the doctrine of the soul, as well as one of the main links between EII and EI. The concepts of "given" and "facticity" imply contingency, opaqueness, or arbitrariness – all of which mean existence outside the jurisdiction of the principle of reason. Although it has become customary to use this Leibnizian concept as if Spinoza, too, held it, and although there is some fundamental affinity between Spinoza and Leibniz on this matter, there are also deep differences between the two. The most important one, in this context, is that while Leibniz distinguished between the principle of reason and the principle of identity-contradiction, Spinoza collapsed the two into one overall principle of rationality and of the necessity of the world. Where Leibniz attempted, as he described it, to salvage contingency, Spinoza rejected its pertinence and tried to establish a radical necessitarism.

What is common, however, to their respective rationalisms is not so much an opposition to empiricism on the role experience plays in acquiring knowledge as a similar rejection of the ontological and moral pertinence of sheer factuality and givenness. Experience is a necessary moment of the enterprise of philosophy for Spinoza too.[5] Yet for him experience has to be metaphysically grounded. This means not so much its validation as a source of true or rational knowledge, but precisely a *theoretical* overcoming of its alleged opaqueness and contingency. This does not mean that Spinoza ever thought that the aim of science, for example, or even of philosophy, is to actually decipher the origin of being of all existent things. Most of these things remain, of course, opaque and only very partially understood. But it does mean that one can

---

[4] "Possibility" does not have to be understood here in its modal sense (as that which can either exist or not exist), but as an *ontological* concept.
[5] Cf. Moreau (1994).

acquire understanding of the metaphysically non-accidental nature of being as such and, more significantly, that in one privileged case – self-knowledge – this understanding can become concrete and, indeed, redemptory. Over and above its obvious deterministic implications, Spinoza's necessitarism signifies a refusal to let the movement of thought stop at the surface of things or at what is seen from the point of view of experience as an irreducible opacity, givenness, and contingency.

Necessitarism – and this is what distinguishes it from sheer determinism – is a theory of the full intelligibility and rationality of being. This should not be understood as one kind or another of naïve epistemological optimism. For even the Spinozistic philosopher is not supposed to know everything; and a Spinozistic omniscient God, I would dare say, is more a philosophical fable than a real concept. What the Spinozistic philosopher does fully understand, however, is that intelligibility is an original and fundamental *ontological* trait of reality and, in particular, of his own personal existence *hic et nunc*. Spinoza's most daring– also paradoxical – gesture is the identification of the *hic et nunc* with bodily existence. What is explicated at the beginning of EII is how this applies specifically to human reality. That the life of the intellect is a fundamental mode of human being is a metaphysical theme; so is the definition of the soul as the idea of the body. Both are necessary and not just given.

But EIIp1 states more than that. It says that thought is an attribute of God, and that this means that God is a thinking thing.[6] The use of *res cogitans* here has polemical, anti-Cartesian undertones. Man thinks, states the second axiom of EII. But strictly speaking, it is God that is a thinking thing. In EIIdef3, the definition of the concept "idea," the soul (*Mens*) is said to be a "thinking thing," but here too there is no *cogito*, and the *res* in question is not a substance of which thinking is an attribute. The soul can be said to be *res cogitans* in a derivative sense only: strictly speaking, thought is not its attribute; it is *res cogitans* insofar as it is a mode conceived as a (certain, "singular," or "particular") thought. A critical dialogue with Descartes passes through the whole text as a semi-implicit leitmotif. It is, in fact, quite clear that Spinoza is trying here to evade Descartes: strictly speaking, only God is a "thinking thing"; man is ultimately a particular thought. The same use of *res cogitans* as a formula applying to God appears, as we have just seen, in EIIp1; it is repeated in the demonstration of this proposition as equivalent to saying that thought is an attribute of God; and then again in the scholium that follows, where it appears as "ens cogitans infinitum" – "an infinite thinking being." All this seems as an attempt to put the theory of the soul, or of man as a thinking thing, in a general metaphysical context and to circumvent Descartes's *res cogitans*.

The proposition is doubly demonstrated – there is, of course, a proper demonstration, but the scholium that follows is also a demonstration, an alternative and complementary one. The first states that thought is an attribute of God

---

[6] Cogitatio attributum Dei est, sive Deus est res cogitans.

4.1. The Centrality of Propositions 11 and 13

since "singular thoughts, i.e. this or that thought, are modes, which express the nature of God in a specific [certo] and determinate way." This argument has an implicit *a posteriori* element in it. *Prima facie*, it is formulated as a semantic explication of the concept of "singular thoughts" (*singulares cogitationes*). In its center is the claim that this concept *involves*,[7] presupposes, or implicitly contains the concept of an infinite attribute of thought, that is, what we called above "principle" or an irreducible or non-analyzable possibility of being and, specifically, of being thought. The latter is thus understood to be a (necessary) condition of the conceivability or semantic and ontological possibility of (the concept of) any particular thinking. The validity of this demonstration depends, however, on what we possess prior to reflection. We know that we think; but in order to "know" that we think, it is not enough that we think. We have to be able to say "we think"; but in order to do so, we have to understand the concept of "to think," and this is undoubtedly the most non-trivial kind of understanding.

The second demonstration of EIIp1, the one formulated in the scholium, is an a priori demonstration, implicitly hypothetical, at least in its form. It is based on the possibility of conceiving, or thinking, a concept – specifically, the concept of an infinite thinking being or of an infinite thought.[8] Its main move is to draw the inevitable conclusion from such a possibility, namely that *thought* is one of God's infinite attributes: if, or insofar as we can formulate a coherent concept of an infinite thinking being, *Thought* is an infinite, and primordial, possibility of being. The very possibility, or coherence, then, of a concept of "infinite thought" is enough to prove that *thought* is one of the basic facets of reality.

The beginning of EII can thus be read as a hermeneutic gesture of transformation: the immediate experience of oneself as thinking and, hence, of what might have been looked at otherwise as sheer facticity or givenness, is transformed into a fundamental ontological reflection. More specifically and more significantly (and iconoclastically), the developments at the beginning of EII will now gradually make it clear that the mind-body relations too cannot be understood as mere facticity. From the point of view of Cartesian dualism, the relations between mind and body cannot be but a *fact*. It is a fact unaccounted for on the basis of the concept of *thought*, and indeed unintelligible from the point of view of the *Cogito* and, in an even stronger way, from the point of view of the body. Spinoza's mind-body monism, as it is often called, is from the very outset – at least if one takes the propositions at the beginning of EII seriously – an attempt to circumvent the alleged facticity, givenness, and

---

[7] "Competit ergo Deo attributum, cujus conceptum singulares omnes cogitaiones involvit, per quod etiam concipiuntur."
[8] The wording of the scholium should not mislead us: When it is said that "*nos possumus ens cognitans infinitum concipere*," it does not refer to an experience of thought, but to the very possibility – the logical possibility, the possibility-as-a-thought – of a certain concept (or a *noem*).

original unintelligibility of the immediacy of the presence of the body implied in Cartesian dualism.

The second proposition of EII states, in full accordance with the first proposition, that "extension is an attribute of God, or God is an extended thing." The demonstration – and this is also a kind of anomaly – simply states that God's being an extended thing is demonstrated like the preceding proposition. This might seem to readily pave the way for the parallelism doctrine. Yet, it is noteworthy that there is nothing parallel to axiom 2 concerning the body. Nowhere is it said, simply and straightforwardly, that "man extends." Instead, we have axiom 4, which says: "We feel that a certain body [NS: our body] is affected in many ways." This, as we shall shortly see, is highly significant. But what is more significant here is, of course, the "parallelism," or rather equivalence, in ontological status between thought and extension – if my interpretative suggestions in the previous pages are sound, then one must conclude that extension enjoys the same kind of non-arbitrariness and rational transparency as thought.

The next three propositions do not play a direct role in the deduction of EIIp7, but they do provide the context within which it has to be read and understood. The parallelism proposition is preceded by the corollary to EIIp6 and is followed immediately by another corollary. Proposition 6 states that God is a cause of modes of a certain attribute only insofar as he is considered under this same attribute. The corollary adds that

> the formal being of things which are not modes of thinking does not follow from the divine nature because [God] has first known the things; rather the things ideated [or: ideated things; *res ideatae*] follow and are inferred from their attributes in the same way and with the same necessity as that with which we have shown ideas to follow from the attribute of thought" (Curley's translation, slightly altered).

The corollary to the EIIp7, its direct consequence, is the complementary of the previous corollary. It states that

> God's potency [*potentia*][9] of thought equals his actual potency to act. That is, all that which follows formally from God's infinite nature, follows objectively from God's Idea in the same order and the same connection.[10]

Without delving deeper into these difficult texts, they seem to justify the following observation: the fact that they appear at this particular juncture – no accident, of course – permits assessing the general philosophical questioning of which the parallelism proposition is part. Both have very clear ontological significance. The first amounts to a rejection of idealism or of the ontological

---

[9] I follow here Hallett's translation and endorse much of his explanation for his choice. Cf. Hallett (1962), passim.
[10] Chantal Jaquet in her (2004) discusses in some length the meaning of the *aequalis* used here by Spinoza to designate the relation between the potency of thinking and of acting. In this little book Jaquet rightly tries to overcome the habitual use of the notion of parallelism, although her interpretation is still quite different from the one proposed here.

4.1. The Centrality of Propositions 11 and 13

precedence of thought over being. Saying that God is the cause of modes considered under a certain attribute only insofar as he is considered under this attribute means that things do not exist, nor are they what they are, because of God's thought of them or because of their *ideas* as they are in God's intellect. In other words, the being of things is not preceded by their ideas or by their being thinkable; the essence of things is not their concepts but, as Spinoza makes clear in EIII, their *conatus* or actual being as a dynamic effort of self-perseverance. The second corollary affirms the coextension of thought and existence: the potency of thought and the potency to act – which is the same, in Spinoza's dynamic metaphysics, as existence – are equal. This amounts to a rejection of the priority of existence over thought, symmetric to the rejection of the priority of thought over being in the previous corollary. There is nothing in physical reality that is, in principle, not intelligible, conceptualizable, or understandable; conversely, thought has no jurisdiction beyond what there actually is.

There is nothing in what both precedes and follows the parallelism proposition that suggests a "two stuffs" reading of Spinoza's thought-extension monism, or a denial of mind and body causal "interactionism." The parallelism thesis is part of a systematic and symmetrical rejection of two ontologies, which are also two reductionist strategies: Platonist idealism (intellectualism or even "perceptualism") and materialism ("physicalism" or even "existentialism").

EIIp7 itself, which seems at first reading to follow directly from the previous corollary, is not only surprisingly short, but also curiously demonstrated on the basis of one axiom only – EIa4: this proposition, says the demonstration, "is clear from EIa4. For the idea of whatever is caused depends on the knowledge of the cause of which it is the effect" (Curley's translation, slightly altered). Notwithstanding the exact meaning of this axiom, a first observation seems to impose itself here: A proposition demonstrated in such a way, namely as a direct consequence of an axiom, obviously does not add much – it is not, as is sometimes said, positively informative – relative to the self-evident and hopefully transparent axiom. At best it only explicates it or draws consequences in a way that cannot be much more than rendering explicit what was contained implicitly and originally in it.

EIa4 states: "The knowledge [*cognitio*] of the effect depends on, and involves, the knowledge of its cause" (Curley's translation, slightly altered). As it stands, the axiom articulates the idea of the centrality of causal explanations or, more generally, of causation, for the theory of rational knowledge. It is the idea that Spinoza would later in the *Ethics* express by repeating Descartes's famous formula *causa sive ratio*. If the formula itself appears only in Descartes, the idea, of course, is much older and, indeed, a commonplace.[11] Already Aristotle made

---

[11] Cf. Carraud (2002), passim. Carraud traces the history of this idea from Suarez to Leibniz, a period in which, he maintains, "cause" comes to mean mainly "efficient cause." Spinoza uses this formula in EIp11, second demonstration, or EIV, preface.

it clear that science is based on the knowledge of causes. Demonstrated as it is, proposition 7 is not supposed to be much more than an explication or a direct consequence of this principle. It is noteworthy, however, that EIIp7 does not talk of "knowledge" and "causes" but of "ideas" and "the order and connection of things." Having an idea amounts thus to knowing, and Spinoza indeed often equated the two terms, as, for instance, in EIIp20, which says that there is in God "*idea, sive cognitio*" of the human soul.

This *idea sive cognitio* is not as innocent as may appear from the almost offhand way in which it appears here. It expresses Spinoza's peculiar identification of gnoseology with ontology. From the very beginning of the *Ethics*, and all along, there is a constant back-and-forth movement between being and thought,[12] which is also a movement between existence and its intelligibility, and which is explicated and justified by – or, inversely, leads to – Spinoza's thought-extension monism. Rather than an affirmation of matter-consciousness monism, EIIp7 is in an essential step toward giving concrete meaning to the idea that being is one with its intelligibility.

Proposition 7 is immediately followed by parallelist pronouncements such as "the thinking substance and the extended substance are one and the same substance, which is now comprehended under this attribute, now under that" and "a mode of extension and the idea of that mode are one and the same thing, but expressed in two ways" (EIIp7s). These are obviously still part of the Cartesian debate and should not be taken out of the context of Spinoza's radical anti-Cartesian doctrine. With some effort (although, I admit, awkwardly), such pronouncements can be interpreted according to the soul-idea and body-object unity of propositions 11 and 13. The latter, of course, can also be incorporated – as is often done – into a parallelist reading of Spinoza. In this case, however, one risks missing the radical originality of the doctrine contained in the first part of EII. The indeterminacy and ambiguity of the text imposes on the commentator the need to make a strategic decision. Rather than forcing the text into one overall allegedly coherent scheme, I decided to concentrate on one hermeneutical possibility the text offers and more or less ignore what seems to contradict it, assuming, as it would not be too hard to guess, that even if this is not what Spinoza had in mind – and who can know what this was – it is the more intriguing, original, and interesting option.

But even if EIIp7 is read according to a parallelist paradigm, the identity of order stated by proposition 7 is more than isomorphism or grounds for a reciprocal "mapping" of two independent series of events or things. *Causa sive ratio* and *idea sive cognitio* mean that causality is coextensive and, indeed, identical, with intelligibility. That causality and explicability are intimately connected

---

[12] The very first definition of EI states that *causa sui* is "that whose essence involves existence, *sive* that whose nature cannot be conceived except as existing." It is remarkable that already at this point Spinoza uses the never-defined concept of "involving," but also that it is said here about a thing's *essentia* (see *infra*).

4.1. The Centrality of Propositions 11 and 13

is a philosophical commonplace. The traditional identification of causes with reasons goes, however, beyond the more habitual idea that causes are the main instrument in the search for explanations or that explanation are fundamentally causal explanations. The semantic equivalence implied in *causa sive ratio* means that through the knowledge of causes, one does not just explain, but also understands or renders what stands before him intelligible.

Spinoza's parallelism is a parallelism between the order of things and the order of reasons. Thought – the attribute of thought – is not another stuff or a different kind of matter, but the principle of understanding and intelligibility. The metaphor of "the same order and connection" of proposition 7 generalizes axiom 4 of EI, which means that the order in question has an identifiable structure. EIa4 implies an equivalence between *dependence* and *involving*. While "dependence" is rather vague, the verb *involvere* seems to point to something more specific: by this term Spinoza designates the kind of dependence more easily conceived as epistemic or conceptual (or, actually, semantic). The demonstration of EIIp7 retains the kind of epistemic sense of dependence that is what the axiom was about,[13] but the generalization contained in the proposition itself introduces some ambiguity. By ignoring the more precise sense of "dependence" of the demonstration, it thus has become possible not just to talk of two kinds of "causality – physical or material on one side, psychic, psychological, mental, and so on on the other – but also to take the physical causality as a model of the relation of dependence of reasons. When the order of ideas is understood not as an order of reasons but as psychological or, more ambiguously, "mental" order, it becomes easier to verbalize it as a "causal order." Quite often, this obscure mental causality is imagined as, or at least tacitly assumed to be, a kind of mechanical causality. Although this is not always perfectly clear, Spinoza apparently thought the precise opposite: the model after which causal relations have to be construed is the model of relations of thoughts or, in more precise terms, as order of reasons or intelligibility.

The mechanical causal relation – presupposing the exteriority of cause and effect – cannot serve as a paradigm, or model, for the kinds of relation conceivably designated by the verb *involvere*. The equivalence between "cause" and "reason" – implied in the famous *causa sive ratio* – should be understood more from the perspective of reasons than of causes. For Spinoza, it seems, the structure of reality, or the one and the same order that holds between ideas and between things, looks more like an order of intelligibility than like an order of (mechanical) causes. The *conceptual* (or semantic and semi-formal) relation depicted by the Latin *involvere* is where the figure of the structure, or order, of reality has to be looked for. Rather than causality in its habitual sense – assuming that there is such a thing – what constitutes "the cement of reality" has the shape of a semantic relation among concepts. It is this relation that has to be understood as *sui generis*, and it is the one that should serve as a basis or,

---

[13] EIIp7dem: "cujuscunque causati idea a cognitione causae, cujus est effectus, dependent."

indeed, model, for a theory of causality in general. Spinoza does not say this in so many words, but what in the last analysis lends coherence to the discussion at the beginning of EII is the underlying – and tacit – conception of "order" as an order of concepts; this kind of order or relation is best rendered by the term of "involving."

4.2. *Ordo* and *Connectio* of Ideas

The discussion of the perfect definition in the TIE may shed some more light on Spinoza's conception of what he calls "the nature of the order and connection of ideas" (or of what we would prefer call "concepts"). Generally put, the doctrine of the perfect definition can be described as an attempt to elaborate and make sense of a notion of "immanent" or "intrinsic" truth. Spinoza underpins the special nature of this kind of truth by using "adequacy" instead of "truth." He defines "truth" as an external relation, and "adequacy" as an intrinsic property of ideas and, by implication, of propositions and even theories (see Chapter 6). The discussion of the "genetic" (§§ 71–72), "good," and "perfect" definitions (§§ 94–98) is one of the main places where Spinoza was trying to make sense of this central idea.

The discussion in the TIE is still determined by the contention that an object (such as a circle) and its idea are distinct, so that Spinoza develops his doctrine that the true idea's truth is intrinsic on the assumption – intuitively convenient to assume – that it is distinct from its object or *ideatum*. The "idealistic temptation" is here indeed very clear, and it will be overcome completely only in the *Ethics*.[14] The *Ethics* contains no explicit reference to the question of the nature of definitions or to the art of defining, although much of what had been said in the TIE is apparently assumed in the later work, as is obvious from, among other things, the role definitions play in it. But the nature of definitions is not discussed in the later work, and, more importantly, whereas definitions are presented in the TIE as the accomplishment of the process of acquiring adequate knowledge, in the *Ethics* they constitute its beginnings. As such, they cannot be considered as expressing positive knowledge, but only as stipulating the subsequent use of certain central concepts. Implicitly, however, the definitions of the *Ethics* are also expressions of knowledge. One way or another, the doctrine

---

[14] As Rousset says in his commentary of § 71, "it is difficult to express more clearly and forcefully the totally intrinsic character of the truth of the true idea: rare are the idealistic philosophers who went that far" (p. 325, my translation). The endemic ambiguity of Spinoza's use of the objective being terminology is apparent at the very beginning and end of this paragraph; respectively: "the *form* of the true cognition must be situated in that cognition itself without relation to other [cognitions]"; "one has to look for that which constitutes the *form* of the true cognition in this very cognition, and to deduce it *from the nature of the intellect*" (my translation, italics added). This shows again that the "form" of a cognition, or the "formal essence or being" of an idea, is an aspect of an ideational content and an "act" operated by an agent, a subject, or a consciousness.

4.2. Ordo and Connectio *of Ideas*

of the adequate or "perfect" definition as Spinoza expounds it in the TIE is very illuminating from the point of view of his conception of the nature of reason as immanent to being, which is one of the fundamental and permanent motivations of his philosophical work from the beginning to the end. Although Spinoza seldom uses the notion of *involvere* in the TIE, the logic of this connector tacitly informs this work, and the doctrine of the perfect definition is where this is most conspicuous.

"For a definition to be said 'perfect', it has to explicate the inner essence [*intimam essentiam rei explicare*]" of the thing defined (§ 95). In other words, defining is gaining access to the inner truth of things. Spinoza's use of the concept of *essence* is notoriously complex and sometimes ambiguous and even not entirely consistent.[15] In the context of the doctrine of the perfect definition, as well as on several other occasions, it can be taken to mean, more or less, the real, objectively – or *sub specie aeternitatis* – true concept of a thing. "Concept" and "idea" are more or less equivalent terms, and the third definition in EII actually establishes an explicit synonymy between the two: an idea is "a concept of the mind which the mind forms because it is a thinking thing." In the *explicatio* that follows Spinoza adds that he prefers *concept* to *perception* because the first connotes "an action of soul," while the second seems to express passivity. Although Spinoza's use of terms such as "idea," "concept," "perception," and "sensation" suffers from typical ambiguity, it still can be maintained that what he had in mind is something roughly close to what a modern reader is bound to intuitively understand in the concept of "concept," an act of the intellect.

The doctrine of the perfect definition is a doctrine of the activity of the mind. Insofar as the inner essence of a definiendum is indeed the same as its true concept or adequate idea, and insofar as it belongs to the thing itself and not to an inner space of subjectivity, to what a transcendental subject accomplishes or the like, this "inner essence" is describable as "inner intelligibility."

One way, more operational than ontological, in which Spinoza tries to pinpoint the special nature of the kind of definition he calls perfect is by claiming that it enjoys an epistemological superiority over other kinds of definition: unlike the latter, it permits us to deduce all the properties of the object defined. The kernel, however, of Spinoza's doctrine is that the "perfect definition" is what is called the "genetic definition." The definition of the circle as an object generated by the movement of one extremity of a line of which the other extremity is fixed or immobile is said to be more efficient or fruitful than other possible definitions of the circle, such as the one according to which the circle is a line equally distant from a given point or a figure constructed by the addition of an infinite number of infinitesimally small rectangles.[16] Mathematically, of

---

[15] Rivaud (1906) is an old but still very useful study of the notion of essence (and existence) in Spinoza.

[16] See also letter 60 to Tschirenhaus.

course, and as it has often been remarked, this is not very illuminating. It is, however, very illuminating insofar as Spinoza's conception of rational truth is concerned.

Spinoza does not use the term "genetic definition." What he says though about the epistemological value of imagining the generation of a geometrical object is very similar to, and probably inspired by, what Hobbes had said about definitions and, like him, inspired also by Euclid.[17] The circle generated in such a way can indeed be regarded as an ideal object (Spinoza says here *alicujus rei abstractae*, § 95). Although the idea of this object is true, the ideality of the object is not Platonist. Risking some anachronism, one could still say that there is a certain constructivist aspect to Spinoza's words here: the circle, as we have just seen, is "abstract," and the movement of the semicircle that generates a sphere is imaginary: "in order to form the concept of a sphere I feign at will [*fingo ad libitum*] a cause, a semicircle rotate around its center" (§ 72).

Section 72 contains a particularly interesting discussion of the truthfulness of "feigned" ideas. Spinoza talks here of "concepts," and he expresses in a rarely explicit way the same kind of "intensional" conception of concepts as will be later implicitly expressed by the notion of *involvere*. He does it in the TIE by using the term "containing" in the sense in which a concept "is contained" (*continetur*) in another. What Spinoza says here deserves some comment. To form (a true, adequate, rational, or intelligible) concept of a sphere, we feign a cause – a semicircle turning around its diameter. Although we know that no sphere is born in this way in nature, we also know that the idea, or concept, of the sphere thus formed is true. The non-trivial question Spinoza now addresses is how, or in what sense, can the fictional, or even false, affirmation of the rotation of the semicircle be nevertheless the origin of a true idea or of the circle as a "real" object? The affirmation of the semicircle rotation, explains Spinoza,

would have been false if it had not been linked [associated, *juncta*] to the concept of the sphere, or to [the concept] of the cause determining such a movement, or absolutely, if this affirmation is nude [*nuda*]. For then the soul [*mens*] tends to affirm only the movement of the semicircle, which *is not contained in the concept* of the semicircle, but is born from the concept of the determining cause of the movement. This is why falsity consists solely in that something is affirmed of some other thing [although] *it is not contained* [*continetur*] in the concept [of this other thing] as we have formed it" (§ 72; my translation, italics added).

The text is not altogether clear, but its main intention seems nonetheless to be quite straightforward: the idea of a rotating semicircle is "false" if it is understood to signify an existent rotating semicircle. But if it is said without an accompanying affirmation of existence but just as an intelligible content of thought – the phrase "a rotating semicircle" simply makes sense – it is "true." If it is joined to a concept of a cause – for example, if we positively affirm a causal

---

[17] See Hobbes *De Corpore*, IV, 13; Zarka (1996).

4.2. Ordo and Connectio *of Ideas*   109

origination of the rotation of a semicircle – it is again a coherent thought. Most importantly, if it is "contained" (*continetur*) in the concept of a sphere as the origin or the ground of its generation, it is once again "true," and makes sense as a rational – that is, coherently thinkable and fully transparent – concept.

Spinoza speaks here – and in letter 60 to Tschirnhaus in an even more emphatic way – of the rotation of the semicircle as an "efficient cause." It is quite probable that the fiction of the rotating sphere echoes some image of physical, mechanical causation. But this is clearly not a causal explanation in the physical sense of the word. The "link" of the concept of the sphere and of that of the rotating semicircle is a "containment" of the latter in the first. In this text of the TIE (§ 72), the concept of "containment" is still rather vague. It will become less so in the *Ethics*, and especially in EIIp8s and its corollary and scholium, to be discussed shortly. Yet, Spinoza's main intention is already quite clear in the earlier text. Although imagined as a causal process, the genesis of the sphere does not happen in time. The sphere as a result or effect does not replace, as it were, the rotation of the semicircle or its cause. Usually, or intuitively, causal relations are conceived – Hume was not the first to remark it – as essentially involving temporal structure, which means, notably, that causes vanish into their effects. Obviously, this is not the case with the relation the sphere – as a result – has with the rotation of the semicircle, as its cause. Both exist simultaneously: the thing itself (the sphere), its "cause" (the rotating semicircle), and its genesis (the rotation of the semicircle) coincide. They condition, semantically or conceptually, each other reciprocally, in one gesture producing a "true" content of thought. Spinoza conceivably meant something very similar to this when he said the concept of the rotating semicircle is "contained" in that of the sphere. Since the truth of the one depends on the link to the other, they can, in fact, be said to condition each other reciprocally.

Explaining (§ 95) why he chose to illustrate his doctrine of the perfect definition by an "abstract thing" – to avoid being seen too polemic – Spinoza adds that contrary to such abstract objects, when "physical and real entities" are concerned, it is important that definitions reproduce the actual order and express the priority of essences to properties.[18] But the "abstract definition" may all the same help us to see what may remain opaque when the definitions of real things are discussed. The reciprocal conditioning of the cause (the rotating semicircle), the result (the circle), and the genesis (the rotation) are different sides or aspects of one theoretical whole. Conditioning each other, they in fact confer intelligibility on each other and on the whole. The rotation of the circle is perfectly coherent and justified as a concept, or as a legitimate and transparent thinkable content, only in view of its role in the defining – or making sense of – the concept "sphere"; the latter is formulable, constructible, or rationally thinkable on the basis of the concept of the rotating circle. Through feigning

---

[18] In letter 60, even this reserve will disappear: only the genetic definition of the sphere enables the deduction of its properties.

an ideal emergence of the circle, a particular kind of transparency is obtained, a comprehension of the nature of the circle, that – as will become explicit in letter 60 – is not obtainable by other forms of definition.

Precisely because the genetic definition has, in the real mathematical world, no advantage over other definitions, one may suggest that the alleged extra mathematical fruitfulness of the genetic definition is a somewhat clumsy attempt to give rigor to a philosophical thesis: the utmost purpose, or the most valuable product of the scientific endeavor, is gaining access to the immanent *intelligibility* of things. There are, in fact, different levels of intelligibility, and these levels can be conceived as *more or less*. At stake here is the nature of a certain form of rationality supposedly obtainable in this fictional emergence of a geometrical object. The question is not so much the mathematical soundness of Spinoza's theory of the genetic and perfect definitions as that of why do we feel, why Spinoza thinks we feel, and what does it mean to feel, that we gain a deeper understanding of a thing once we can imagine a mode of its production, than by other modes of considering it.

More than a methodology, or a theory about the way mathematical and rational knowledge in general advances or is acquired, Spinoza's doctrine of the perfect definition is a theory about the *nature* of rational knowledge. As a sort of a phenomenology of knowledge, it is meant to convey the idea that real knowledge is that which permits us to overcome all arbitrariness and make explicit the non-accidental nature of the "belonging" of properties to a thing, as it is supposedly exemplified in a paradigmatic way in mathematical objects. It is a sort of full, or adequate, *understanding* of the inner nature of a thing, and this is something quite different from epistemological efficacy, that which permits man to be the "master and dominator of Nature" that the Cartesian method had been after, or that which can be defined by the predictability or pragmatic fruitfulness of a theory.

How all this is applicable to real science or even to mathematical knowledge is a matter I shall not discuss. Spinoza's error about the alleged mathematical superiority of the genetic definition, as is often the case, is symptomatic; it points to something that looked for rational articulation but that has perhaps not yet found the right means to be fully carried out. What seeks expression here, I believe, is something that goes beyond the phenomenology of understanding or comprehension and that can be considered as a fundamental interrogation about the ontological origins of the fact that there are meanings and that man thinks, intellects, and understands. Most accurately perhaps, Spinoza's theory of the perfect definition is an attempt to make sense of the problematic concept of *intelligibility*.

At this point, however, the unclassifiable nature of Spinoza's thought becomes apparent. Intelligibility is a fundamentally Platonist concept. It applies originally to objects whose mode of existence is in their being exclusively conceivable or thinkable. Their ideality – conceived, usually in a more or less intuitive way, on the model of mathematical ideality – is what defines

4.2. Ordo and Connectio of Ideas

their being. Ideality is thus coextensive with intelligibility. The centrality of the thesis of intelligibility in Spinoza locates him squarely within what is called sometimes the "intellectualist" and sometimes the "idealist" tradition. Within this tradition, however, Spinoza occupies a very peculiar place and, in fact, does not really belong to it. Although certainly subject to a permanent idealist temptation, he does his best not to succumb to it. He does so by giving to the body a particular role in his doctrine of intelligibility. Paradoxically, the kind of reciprocal conditioning that Spinoza attributes to spheres and their causes is supposed to hold, with some adjustments of course, between souls and bodies. In order to see it, however, a few more steps are needed.

4.2.a. The Logic of Involving

The term *involvere* is omnipresent in the *Ethics*, and in the second part more than in the other parts. But Spinoza never tried to systematically explicate it or justify its extensive use.[19] Although it has some other uses, it refers usually to what Spinoza must have conceived as a paradigmatically rational relation among concepts (or "ideas"). One of the main places in the *Ethics* where this is most conspicuous is Proposition 8, its corollary, and the scholium that follows it. The explicit systematic role of this proposition is to prepare the ground for two doctrines that might seem incompatible and that will be discussed only in EV: the soul does not have life after the death of the body; it is nonetheless eternal.

But a lot can be learnt from proposition 8 and its corollary and scholium on other issues. A first remark is of a formal nature. The proposition and its annexes constitute a deductive anomaly: the proposition relates in a problematic way to what precedes it and is practically not referred to until the fifth part of the *Ethics*. The demonstration of EIIp8 contains only one short phrase that curiously states that its content – in fact one of the most enigmatic propositions in the whole *Ethics* – is simply "evident from the preceding one" (that is, it should be remembered, from the parallelism proposition), and that can hardly be considered a demonstration. As if this was not enough, it adds that the proposition "is understood more clearly from the preceding scholium," which is also an unusual procedure in what is supposed to be a rigorous process of deduction.

The explicit theme of EIIp8cor is the difference between the ideas, or the "objective being," of existent and non-existent modes. Its main lesson is that the "actual" existence of singular things has to be part of, or involved in, their ideas (*existentiam ... involvent*). The complex theme of this proposition,

---

[19] In the TIE for example, it appears a few times, but usually without the more theoretic connotation it has in the *Ethics*. When the relation cause-effect is exposed as a major bearer of scientific rationality, paradigmatically in mathematical thinking and only secondarily in science of the physical world, Spinoza uses such terms as *comprehendere* – which is still used in the *Ethics*, but rarely (e.g., EIIp8cor and scholium), while in the cause-effect terminology it becomes in the *Ethics involvere* (EIax4).

corollary, and scholium is the mode of being or, as it were, the whereabouts of truth when it is not actually being thought. The corollary first more or less reiterates proposition 8, then adds to it that as long as the singular things exist only insofar as they are comprehended in God's attributes, their *esse objectivum*, or (*sive*) ideas, exist only insofar as there exists an infinite idea of God. It concludes by stating that when these things exist also in the sense that they last or perdure (*durare*; Curley translates: "have duration"), "their ideas also involve the existence through which they are said to have duration."[20]

The proposition and the corollary discuss the relation between ideas and their objects in the special case of non-existing singular things. The question that arises here is, obviously, how can talking about things that do not exist be more than empty noise devoid of meaning? In Spinoza's language, what kind of being do both non-existent modes and their ideas enjoy? The corollary makes explicit what was not altogether so in the proposition: non-existent modes are beings, and positively so. Since they are not contradictory, they are thus not impossible, which means that they are also not simply non-entities. But they are also not just possible in the sense of being free of contradiction. That non-existent modes are not non-beings entails that the discourse about them is not empty, or that their ideas are not fictitious or senseless. The ideas of non-existent modes have the same kind of being as their objects: they are "comprehended in God's eternal idea" in the same way in which the formal essences of these things are contained (*continentur*) in God's attributes.

A third remark concerns the parallel rejection of physicalism and idealism. That ideas and their objects are similarly, or parallelly, contained or comprehended in God's idea and in God's attribute means that the non-non-entity of modes that do not exist and of their ideas is not a matter of pure thought or of pure possibilities. There is a difference then between existence and non-existence and between these two and non-being or sheer impossibility. This complex relation between being and non-being and existence and non-existence will become highly significant when the question of the eternity of the soul arises in EV. Existent things exist in the sense of having duration, lasting, or enduring, while non-existent things are "just" comprised in God's infinite idea or contained in God's attributes. This will be the basis on which a doctrine of the mode of being of the "eternal part of the human soul" – which is different from existence as duration, but also not a figment of the imagination or sheer nothingness – would be constructed in EV.

Once again, Spinoza tries to elucidate his point with the aid of a geometrical example, and once again it adds more embarrassment (EIIp8s). The example is supposed to illustrate and give some indication as to what is meant by "being

---

[20] Which would mean that there is a real difference between the concept of the hundred Thalers Kant only thinks about and that of the hundred Thalers he actually owns; or, differently put, that "existence" is a real predicate and not just the positing of (the referent of) a concept in space and time.

4.2. Ordo and Connectio *of Ideas*

comprehended in God's idea" or "contained in God's attributes." Ultimately, this has to help make sense of the doctrine of the eternity of the soul. The question the reader has to address here is, thus, what is meant by a geometrical object being "contained" in another geometrical object, or, more specifically, how a property of the circle is "contained" in it. Similarly, or parallelly, in what sense can an idea be said to be "comprised" in another idea? There is a distinction, says Spinoza, between such a property just deducible from, or demonstrable on the basis of, the concept of a circle (and, hence, real or not fictional but not existing in act) on the one hand; and this property, or an exemplification of it, actually existent as, for example, drawn concretely on paper or a blackboard, on the other hand.

The reading together of EIIp7 and 8 strengthens the feeling that rather than parallelism between two orders of causes, construed on a more or less imaginary model of mechanical causation, the *ordo & connexio* that holds both in the realm of ideas and the world of "things" is conceived by Spinoza on the model of rational or intelligible content or thought. As a direct consequence of the parallelism proposition, it is remarkable that it is built entirely on the basis of what can be described as the logic of Spinoza's use of the term *involvere*.

In EIIp8 and its corollary and scholium, three terms appear that apparently designate more or less the same relation: *involvere* (which is used once, at the end of the corollary), *comprehendere*, and *continere.* There seems to be some consistency in the respective uses of especially the last two, but, generally speaking, the three of them mean very similar semantic relations. The example given in the scholium, although insufficient (as Spinoza remarks), merits careful reading. The circle *comprehends* an infinite number of lines having a certain property. In the same – parallel, if one prefers – way, the idea (or concept) of the circle *contains* an infinite number of ideas of such lines. A certain construction can be made in infinitely many versions (or a type can have an infinite number of tokens); all those possible constructions are real, albeit non-existent, until an actual construction is effected and materializes in a concrete representation, like, say, in demonstration in a geometry textbook or a drawing made on a blackboard by a teacher. Until such a construction is actually effected, however, it is just comprised in the circle. More accessibly, it is part of the meaning of the concept of a circle, and as such it can be said to be "comprehended" or "involved" in it.

The infinite number of couples of intersecting lines respecting this rule is, to put it differently, implied by the concept of the circle. The use of terms such a *comprehendere* or *continere* underpins the ontological sense of the whole move.[21] The infinite numbers of possible constructions contained in the circle

---

[21] See Deleuze (1968) and Yakira (1994) for what are perhaps the only full discussions of this matter in the whole interpretative literature. It is not an accident that this occurs in the context of a reading of Spinoza done with a constant reference to Leibniz. Deleuze considered this matter as a certain vision about the reciprocal relation or process of folding and unfolding

are not simply contained there in the way apples are contained in a basket, nor are they "potentially" there, like the oak in the acorn, its actual existence depending upon the happy, but accidental, sprouting of the acorn. They are there, so to speak, in full necessity – and, hence, reality – as immediate constituents of the entity called "circle," or of the full meaning of the concept of the circle or, indeed, as the condition of its meaningfulness, conceivability, or intelligibility.

Notwithstanding all their peculiarity and strangeness, EIIp8 and its corollary and scholium do illuminate one of Spinoza's main argumentative strategies. It also permits us to give rational sense, at least to some extent, to notions such as *principle, possibility of being,* or *condition of intelligibility* that we were using in a rather intuitive way in previous sections of this study. It is here, in fact, that the fullest and most explicit formulation of this strategy appears, which informs, in a rather implicit and never fully developed way – besides the rather short discussion of EIIp8 – the entire *Ethics*. Without, apparently, being fully aware of it, Spinoza was putting to concrete use a kind of "intensional" conception of the apophantic structure of propositions and, in fact, of discourse in general and even of rational thought and rationality. On account of the parallelism thesis, the same holds for the structure of reality.

The distinction between the "extension" and "comprehension" (or "intension") of concepts was, so to speak, in the air. Although known since Aristotle, it was explicitly drawn, perhaps for the first time in a systematic way, in Arnauld and Nicole's *Logique ou l'art de penser*, known commonly as *The Logic of Port Royal*. It has become the epicenter of Leibniz's philosophy of logic, and one can say that on this particular point Spinoza is indeed rather close to Leibniz. What had remained implicit in Spinoza became fully explicit in Leibniz. He too frequently used the concept of *involvere*, and his uses of this term are rather similar to Spinoza's. Leibniz's theory of the principle of sufficient reason, insofar as it is built on the famous *inesse* principle (notably in *Le discours de métaphysique*, §§ 8 and 13; *Generales inquisitiones*, passim, and numerous other writings of the same period, circa 1686), is an attempt to give fuller theoretical – and in the logical tracts, formal and technical – formulation to the same idea, or set of ideas, that Spinoza arguably expresses through the use of terms such as *involvere*. According to its canonical formulation in the DM, in every true proposition,[22] the subject includes, or involves, the predicate. Leibniz's principle was turned in Kant's hands into *analyticity* and ever since remained an important part of the Kantian legacy. In the process, much of Leibniz's own acumen, as

---

as being the ultimate intuition of both Spinoza's and Leibniz's respective visions or images of reality. I think that Deleuze was right in his insistence of the special interest of a Spinoza-Leibniz connection and on the special importance, in this context, of what I called the "logic of involvement." But rather than a vague, more or less plastic image of folding and unfolding, there is here, I believe, a theory of reason – rigorously construed by Leibniz, less so by Spinoza.

[22] Or "idea," for in neither Leibniz nor Spinoza was there an irreducible distinction between propositions and their terms.

4.2. Ordo and Connectio of Ideas

well as of the deeper insights of seventeenth-century rationalistic tradition, has been lost. "Analytic propositions" have come to be conceived as true in virtue of the meaning of their constituents and sometimes as simply tautological or "informationally vacuous"; and "synthetic propositions" are said to be true by reference to what lies outside them.

For both Leibniz and Spinoza the truth of all propositions is "analytic," the Kantian distinction senseless, and the generalized suspicion of analytic truth, absurd. This is, among other things, because Kant psychologized Leibniz's *inesse*, first, by introducing the canonic distinction – completely alien to his predecessors' thinking – between analytic and synthetic propositions; and second, by describing the analytic proposition as that in which the predicate is "thought in" the subject. Thinking, for Kant and for much of his posterity, is exclusively the work of the subject, transcendental or not. Thus, when the "inclusion" of the predicate in the subject is not explicit, it is supposed to be "thought" beneath the surface. Both Spinoza and Leibniz can be said to reject, each in his own way, the psychological or transcendental conceptions of thinking, as they begin to take shape in Descartes's *Cogito* and mature in Kant and his posterity. Thought, for Spinoza, is an ontologically fundamental mode of being, not a psychological or transcendental fact.

Another point of encounter between Spinoza and Leibniz is the preference of the intensional attitude over the extensional one. This is an important characteristic of Leibniz's philosophy of logic. The very fact of such a preference is much more important than the technical or semi-technical aspects of the extension-intension distinction. Rather than a stance in a dispute pertaining to the philosophy of logic, this is a metaphysical decision. The attitude shared by Spinoza and Leibniz is probably a general trait of philosophical rationalism in general, but certainly of classical – and in particular the seventeenth and early eighteenth centuries' – rationalisms. Taking such a decision could have been done with an awareness of the stakes involved in it or in a more or less instinctive manner. Leibniz devoted a great deal of time and energy to the technical as well as the philosophical aspects of the matter, while Spinoza did very little and mainly in an oblique way. But for both the adoption of a conception of the nature of rational discourse as fundamentally intensional expresses an essential common orientation: the position of a concept of *intelligibility* as the foundation of a doctrine of reason and of rationality and the idea that intelligibility, in order to be one, has to respect certain formulable conditions.[23]

The logical, semantic relation referred to by terms such as *involvere* becomes the Spinozistic model of the fundamental structure of being. As such, it serves as a sort of conceptual bridge between semantics (or a theory of signification) and ontology. This relation fulfills a fundamental theoretical task both in the theory of being and in the theorization of thought and rationality. Most

---

[23] See Grosholz and Yakira (1998) for a fuller attempt to elucidate Leibniz's doctrine of what was dubbed in this study "conditions of intelligibility."

importantly, it gives content to the abstract affirmation of parallelism: the order and connection, which parallelly holds between ideas and things, is the order most clearly observable as an order of conceptual containment.

4.3. Souls and Bodies

De Natura et Origine Mentis opens, then, with a double affirmation: the *non-priority* of thought over existence and of existence over thought. Possibility, concepts, or ideas; the power of thought, of conceiving, and of conceptualizing, or of perceiving, sensing, or imagining – all these are neither the foundation or origin of existence nor do they exceed it. This is true in the inverse direction as well – there is nothing essentially unthinkable, or unintelligible, in the world as it actually exists, and existence is not the cause or source of thought. What is added in proposition 7 and its corollary is that the fundamental theory of the intellect or of thought has to be elaborated specifically as a theory of *ideas*. Much philosophical thinking in the seventeenth century is carried out using the notion of *idea*. Spinoza's great originality consists in the role he assigns to the *body* in his theory of ideas. This is where he parts way from Descartes, from the occasionalists, and from Leibniz, but also from the empiricists. The doctrine of the metaphysical nature of ideas, as it is expounded in the first part of EII, is supposed to be a detailing and concretization of the general metaphysical principles. As such, it is a first step toward the elaboration of a theory of man as a knowing being; a sensing, feeling, and desiring being capable of wisdom and freedom. At least up to this point there is no indication that Spinoza's fundamental concern is to explain the correspondence between what takes place in our body and what we feel or are conscious of. But it is only in the move that follows the parallelism proposition that the full sense of Spinoza's mind-body theory really comes to light. At its center stand two counterintuitive, perhaps absurd, claims: (1) the soul is not really a *soul* – that is, a *sui generis* kind of being, a first ontological principle, or a substance – but an idea; (2) this idea's object is no other than *the* "body" – that is, this very same "certain" body that one "senses" affected in many ways, and that one conceives as, or knows to be, "one's own body." Here too something that is usually taken to be both *sui generis* and primordial – the *our* (or *my*) – appears as conceptually and ontologically derivative, even fictional: the soul, does not own a body; there is no I who regards the body; there is, at first, a unity of a body and its idea. The full significance of Spinoza's curious ontology of ideas for the mind-body question is thus to be found not in EIIp7 and its alleged parallelism, but in the subsequent discussion and mainly in EIIp11 and 13.

The core of Spinoza's mind-body doctrine are propositions 7, 11, and 13. If the last two – 11 and 13 – are taken seriously; and if proposition 7 is seen, as it should be, as a step toward the doctrine specified only in them, the notion of parallelism should lose its exegetical centrality and eventually even will be discarded. The following discussion is based on the hypothesis that a sound understanding of Spinoza's mind-body theory is based on the following two principal claims: First, the human soul is an idea (prop. 11). Not only is it a mode and not a substance, but it is also not a special, more or less mysterious, kind of entity, such as "consciousness" or "mind" but, specifically, an *idea*. Second, when we call a body "ours,"[24] the real significance of such an appropriation is gnoseological. This particular body is "ours" or "mine" in the way an object is *of* an idea (prop. 13). The idea-soul is the "sensing" of the body as it actually exists (EIIp13cor). But taken seriously, and not just as fruitful metaphor, the claim that the soul is an idea and that the body is its object imposes immediately an obvious question: what is there, if at all, in the relations that conceivably hold between ideas and their objects that can be used in a philosophically fruitful theory of the union, or unity, of mind and body? Thus, one habitual way of saying the *of* relation when ideas and objects are concerned is that ideas are *about* their objects. And indeed, it is not at all clear if, and how, can one say that the soul is about his body.

In my attempt to understand what Spinoza may have been offering as a reply to this question, I shall not be following Spinoza's order of reasons. Instead, I shall begin with a question that is implicitly posed by proposition 13 as a fundamental question and that Spinoza never addresses directly: what is an idea-object relation? He deals in some detail with a close question – the meaning of qualifying ideas as adequate and the nature of adequacy – but what an idea-object relation (or, actually, unity) consists in the "general way," as the scholium after EIIp13 describes the preceding gesture, is never fully explained. But in order to make sense of the claim that the soul is the idea of the body and that the body is the soul's object, we have to try to understand first what being an idea of an object or an object of an idea exactly means.

A few preliminary remarks outline this attempt. First, Spinoza often speaks of the relation of ideas and their objects as a relation of *ideas* and their *ideata*. Although coextensive, the idea-object and idea-*ideatum* couples imply more than just terminological difference. An *ideated* object seems to be less susceptible to being thought as radically other than its idea or as external to it, than just "object." Talking of idea-*ideatum* thus gives a strong sense of unity, like the unity that exists between a concept and its content. Not offering his reader anything like a theory of this unity, Spinoza all the same uses it as a kind of a model for explicating the sort of unity holding between souls and bodies. Second, Spinoza posits the idea-*ideatum* unity as primordial. This means that it has to be thought in itself, without presupposing anything like a thinking subject or pre-given entity such as an intellect, personhood, or consciousness.

These two theses are bold enough. But they become a sort of a conundrum when applied to actually existing things, as Spinoza calls the things of the world, and, in particular, to minds and bodies. In that case, the idea-*ideatum*

---

[24] The NS version on EIIa4 says explicitly what remains somewhat implicit in propositions 11 and 13: the "certain body" that we feel affected in many ways is "our" body.

primordial unity is also exclusive. A particular body's thought, concept, or idea – that idea that is "the first thing which constitutes the actual being of a human Mind" – exists only in an actual and unique idea-*ideatum* unity. It is never fully reproducible by any other mind-idea, and, in particular, there is no "reproduction" of it in God's mind-idea. Understood verbatim, the doctrine formulated here, namely that the mind is an idea and the body its *ideatum*, must strike the attentive reader as very puzzling.

Last, I would add here (without supporting it for the moment by arguments; but see discussion later in the book) that despite appearances, the primordiality of the idea-*ideatum* unity does *not* have to be interpreted as a reductionist theory of subjectivity. It is not an *es dankt* theory, and personhood, individuality, and, in particular, moral agency do not disappear, in the *Ethics* of Spinoza, in a dark night of the universal or of the higher, intellectual functions of reason where all the particular cows are black.

The *ideatum* is the concrete, *hic et nunc* body, and the primordial idea-*ideatum* relation is supposed to give sense to the concrete experience of the union of the soul and the body, which is undoubtedly an unusual and quite counterintuitive thing to say. It should not come as a surprise, then, that many commentators are quite embarrassed by this doctrine. The fact is, many of the available expositions of Spinoza's theory of ideas do one of two wrongs: either they give up the hope of overcoming the strangeness and incoherencies of the text, or they apply too hastily a principle of charity and offer one form or another of verbal reconstitution of the text without tackling its real difficulties and paradoxical nature. Either they claim the theory untenable, or they simply ignore the difficulties by using such tools as quotation marks, as if writing that the mind is the "idea of" the body solves the problem and permits us to go on using our habitual jargon. In fact, however, this is a very problematic matter. Many questions can – and should – be raised here, and it is quite conceivable that not everything that Spinoza says about this and about related issues can be brought together to form a satisfactorily coherent and intelligible whole. Yet, Spinoza's theory does make sense, and it also contains several ideas that, even if he did not always think through their consequences all the way, have not only historical and exegetic importance but also genuine philosophical interest. In any case, the doctrine of the primordial idea-*ideatum* and soul-body unity deserves a close reading.

4.3.a. Ideas and Ideate: Primordiality and Uniqueness

One main reason why this doctrine is puzzling – or should be seen as such – is that Spinoza poses the idea-*ideatum* relation as primordial. Saying that the mind-body union is an idea-object relation is already quite extraordinary, but affirming the primordiality of such a relation is completely counterintuitive. Positing a relation, or a unity, as primordial means that it has to be thought independently of any presuppositions. More specifically, taking the idea-*ideatum* relation as primordial means that it has to be considered independently

4.3. Souls and Bodies

of any epistemological, psychological, or transcendental presuppositions. The idea-object or idea-*ideatum* relation has to be analyzed and understood independently of the concept of a knowing, perceiving, conceiving, or thinking agent, finite or infinite. There is only one presupposition from which the idea-*ideatum* draws its conceivability: that thought is a fundamental metaphysical principle, and that its object, extension, has the same kind of metaphysical status.

This is neither the first nor, for that matter, the last time that there appears, in the history of philosophy, a doctrine about the primordial nature of ideas. Arguably a concept-object relation is studied independently of the concept of a thinking subject in, say, formal logic or in formalized theories of truth. But even in these cases, more often than not a transcendental concept of a knowing subject reappears, more or less implicitly, as essential, if not for the formal theory, then at least for the philosophy of logic. Plato's theory of ideas could be cited as another example. But Spinoza's theory cannot be incorporated into either school. His doctrine of the idea-*ideatum* relation is certainly not a formal theory of the concept. It is also neither "panpsychist" nor Platonist, and not just for the reasons discussed above: for him, very precisely, it is not simply ideas (or intellect) that are primordial, but the idea-*ideatum* complex unity. Ideas have, by definition, contents; and the distinction between idea and content is what the formula of idea-*ideatum* expresses. But because the concept of a thinking agent is not prior to that of idea-*ideatum*, there is a primordial and irreducible unity – or indeed, oneness – of idea and *ideatum*. An immediate consequence of this radical unity is that the idea cannot be said to be "about" its *ideatum*, to "refer" to it, to express or represent it. Spinoza seems sometimes to mean something like one of these more accessible presentations of the concept-object relation, but the logic of his position seems to deny their pertinence.

Closely linked to the positing of the idea-*ideatum* unity as primordial is a second deeply counterintuitive element – its radical uniqueness. That a thing-concept complex is unique is not a difficult thing to say. But that the idea itself is unique is less easy to conceive, especially when the notion of a divine intellect is used or when one thinks, like Spinoza, within the general framework of intellectualism. Truth, adequacy, rationality, and intelligibility are usually considered in the intellectualist tradition as forms of generality. If, in the Aristotelian tradition, the body is a principle of individuality, its "form" would be a principle of generality. Spinoza too defines individuality in the context of a theory of the body (in the little physics after EIIp13); but unlike most rationalist philosophers, thought is for him fundamentally a matter of individuality too. I shall discuss it in more detail later on, but it has to be already emphasized at this point: the individual soul is also, at bottom, the body's true – or adequate – idea, and truth is in God. Spinoza expresses this idea by the use of the customary, if bizarre, notion that the idea of the body, the soul, is in God insofar as it constitutes the soul, *quatenus Mentem constitueret*.

Saying that truth is in God or that God's ideas are the paradigms of true ideas is a typically rationalist way of expressing the absoluteness of truth. But saying, as Spinoza does, that the ultimate truth of a given body, or God's idea of this body, is that which constitutes the foundation of the human soul's actual being is an altogether different matter. The kernel of this thesis is that an idea of a given idea-*ideatum* unity is unique precisely as its *ideatum* is unique.

The radical uniqueness of an individual idea-*ideatum* entity can perhaps be expressed with the aid of a temporal metaphor: a given idea-body unity is a "certain" entity in the sense that it is a fully determined single entity existing, as it were, only "once." It is unrepeatable[25] and strictly one of its kind. Most significant in this Spinozistic version of the principle of the identity of indiscernibles is that this uniqueness applies not only to things, but also to their true ideas. There is no duplicate of the idea part of an individual idea-*ideatum* unity, not even in a divine intellect. To say that there is only one such idea means that the unique, only-once-existing idea, *is* God's idea of the *ideatum* in question, which also exists only once and is unique. The uniqueness of the idea-*ideatum* unity means that the existence of the unique idea fully coincides with the existence of its *ideatum*. This has obvious consequences for the doctrine of afterlife – it makes this doctrine untenable.

Another consequence is that the notion of God's intellect becomes problematic. Spinoza's use of this notion as the place of Truth and as a justification for the use of the concept of "truth" locates him, uncomfortably as it may, within the larger Platonist tradition. Platonic ideal types or (in Christian Platonism) divine thoughts are conceived to be also the ultimately objective or fully adequate truth of things. In the case at hand, the "thing" is the body – that particular, "certain" body – but the truth about it is none other than its idea-soul. That kind of truth – which has been traditionally attributed to God's privileged knowledge of that body, located in a Platonist realm of eternal ideas or essences, in a Platonist-like third world, or conceived as ideal objectivity – not only replicates human knowledge (or *vice versa*) but also functions as the norm of its truth, the measure and criterion of its adequacy. Spinoza does not give up, as other modern (or post-modern) philosophers would do, the notions of God's intellect and of eternal truths, precisely because he retains the full pertinence of the notion of absolute truth, of a *non plus ultra* not indeed of *knowledge*, but of intelligibility. This does not mean, of course, that man can attain such understanding, or become fully rational, but it does mean that intelligibility is taken objectively, that it is conceived as an original constituent of the things themselves. Concepts such as "absolute truth" or "intelligibility" are fully pertinent, indeed indispensable, to an adequate theory of man, not as a transcendent ideal or as indicating an unattainable horizon of an

---

[25] An idea I would express by the use of a term of *one-timeliness*, which is a translation of a typical Hebrew expression חד פעמי – that which happens only once – that has no straightforward equivalent in English.

ever-progressing knowledge, but as a fundamental condition of the possibility to rationally talk of man as a thinking, understanding, and knowing being.

Spinoza reinterprets these notions, however, in a way that radically transforms the significance of the notion of rationality. Instead of an ideality, he turns it into a mode of being of the body. The very unique idea of a particular *ideatum*, or body, the idea the existence of which coincides with the (temporal if not altogether ephemeral) existence of the body, is nonetheless the very same idea by which God thinks this body. As God's idea, it can be said to be the seat of reason or, better, be reason itself. But this idea is the particular human soul of which this body is the *ideatum*, and there seems to be, for Spinoza, no ontological, normative, or evaluational surplus of the one over the other, and, paradoxical as it may seem, the body is the seat of reason, nay, it is reason, not less than the soul.

The upshot of all this seems to be quite straightforward if highly unusual and, of course, subversive: "God's intellect" becomes in Spinoza's hands more of a philosophical metaphor than a concept. The idea (soul) of a certain body is numerically (as the scholastics used to say) one with God's idea of this body,[26] which means that of *this* body/object there is no other fully true or adequate idea/knowledge than its soul. There is no duplicate or ideal-type of the individual idea-soul, neither in other minds, nor, in particular, in God's intellect. That for Spinoza there was no extra-mundane divine intellect needs no special comment. That what he refers to as God's intellect has no being besides the ideas-souls of all natural things is also not a controversial issue. But that God's thought of a given body has no gnoseological surplus over the human thought of this body, or over its idea-soul, is less clear. Spinoza's use of the seemingly traditional "God's intellect" blurs sometimes the radically iconoclastic nature of his position. The logic of the *quatenus Mentem constitueret*, however, is precisely this: there is no ultimate *truth* of the body in question other than its one and only idea-soul, which is also the idea by which God is said to think or know it.

4.3.b. Idea Corposis: *The Text*

I did not seek to present all this as a doctrine that is perfectly coherent and free of difficulties or even contradictions. I do think, however, that it faithfully expresses the deeper significance and the authentic philosophical motivations of Spinoza's endeavor. I also did not try to corroborate my reading of Spinoza's mind-body doctrine by more than some cursory references to the text. I shall now offer a brief textual analysis in order to show that the text does in fact corroborate the presentation I have just offered. There will be not much in the following section over what has been said already, just, mainly, an attempt to interpret the text in its light. There is ample evidence in the *Ethics* – also in Spinoza's other writings – for this reading, but much of it is scattered in

---

[26] Cf., e.g., Della Rocca (1996), p. 119 and passim.

different parts of the text. Here I shall concentrate only on the three propositions of EII – propositions 7, 11, and 13 – which is where the essential elements of Spinoza's mind-body doctrine are formulated. They read as follows:

> Ordo et connexio idearum idem est, ac ordo et connexio rerum (EIIp7).
> Primum, quod actuale Mentis humanae esse constituit, nihil aliud est, quàm idea rei alicujus singularis actu existentis (EIIp11)
> Objectum ideae, humanam Mentem constituentis, est Corpus, sive certus Extensionis modus actu existens, et nihil aliud (EIIp13).[27]

The demonstration of EIIp13 is a curious text. Its first part reads:

For if the body were not the object of the human mind, the ideas of the affections of the body would not be in God [by p9c], insofar as he constituted our mind, but insofar as he constituted the mind of another thing, that is [by p11c], the ideas of the affections of the body would not be in our mind; but [a4] we have ideas of the affections of the body. Therefore, the object of the idea which constitutes the human mind is the body, and it [by p11] actually exists (Curley's translation, altered).

What first needs explanation is the detour this demonstration makes via God. For, *prima facie*, the proposition does not state anything that cannot be derived directly from the parallelism proposition according to its usual reading: if every idea, insofar as it is a mode seen under the attribute of thought, has a corresponding body, which is a mode – the same mode, in fact – seen under the attribute of extension, then all that had to be done is to specify that the body that "corresponds" to this particular idea, which is our soul, is the latter's *object*. Differently put, the abstract mind-body correspondence or parallelism is essentially a relation of an epistemic nature. Implicit throughout Spinoza's use of the term *idea* is that ideas have always, and by virtue of what they are, objects; ideas, as it is sometimes maintained, are "intentionalities"; they are always ideas of objects. The definition of the soul as idea (prop. 11) would make it necessary only to specify its object. The object is the body, says proposition 13. So wherefore God?

Another peculiar feature of the demonstration – especially, once again, in view of the reference to God – is that it is based on experience. That "we have ideas of the affection of the body" follows from axiom 4 of EII, which states that "we *sense* that a certain body is affected in many ways" (italics added). A certain ambiguity may have resulted from the use of the verb *sentire* (see earlier discussion), for it is not altogether clear what is the exact nature of the act it designates. However, the fact that the ideas of the affections of the body, which are nothing but our "sensing" of it, are "in God" indicates that there is

---

[27] In Curley's translation: "The order and connection of ideas is the same as the order and connection of things. The first thing which constitutes the actual being of a human Mind is nothing but the idea of a singular thing which actually exists. The object of the idea constituting the human mind is the body, or a certain mode of extension which actually exists, and nothing else."

4.3. Souls and Bodies

nothing relative about this sensing of the body, that it is fully adequate and, indeed, that it is the ultimate knowledge of the body.

The demonstration of EIIp13, especially its first part – which demonstrates that the object of the idea-soul is *the* (our) body – is based on a curious counterfactual. It can be reconstructed in the following way: if the (my) body had not been the object of the (my) soul, it would have been the object of another idea, which would be (the foundation of) another soul. This other soul would have been the (my) body's idea, which means mine, and the idea-*ideatum*, or the soul-body/object, in question would be me. The logic of this argument is the logic of the necessity of identity – a thing is necessarily what, or actually who, it is. It can be formalized in different ways, for example by using possible worlds language or in terms of a *de re* and not *de dicto* identity. Spinoza, notoriously disliking thinking in formalistic terms, makes nothing of the sort. The constant reference to God is a semi-metaphorical means to convey the sense of necessity otherwise given by formal consideration. This, I suggest, is the first element of making sense of the detour via God in the demonstration of EIIp13.

The essential but implicit element of Spinoza's argumentation in this demonstration is a characteristic reversal of order. It is the facticity of *the existent*, or its concreteness, that is the condition of its identity as an idea-*ideatum* entity. The body is one with its idea or soul (or *haecceitas*, entity, or being) as a primordial and irreducible ontological thesis. The body is a certain body "actually" existing. Its idea, or soul, is its idea no matter what (or in every possible world). And the "I," one may suggest, is the one entity consisting of this body and its idea. One consequence of the necessary identity of the body with its idea is that a certain-idea/certain-body relation is *unique* in a particularly strong sense of the word. God's idea of a certain body is the only idea of this body, and it is one with the soul that senses the body as it exists, this body being the *ideatum* of a given idea-*ideatum* unity. As such, and since what is called "God's idea" of a given object is the ultimate and only full truth or adequacy of this object, the human soul is the only truthful and adequate idea – *sive* knowledge – of the body.

The necessity of the idea-*ideatum* identity leads to more radical consequences. If the idea and its *ideatum* are one – as the counterfactual of the demonstration seems to entail – in the way the morning star and the evening star are one, then, applied to the mind-body context, what had been seen by Descartes as *union* is now conceived by Spinoza to be *unity*, or *onessess*, in the strongest sense of the word. Consequently, the soul does not enjoy an *identity* of its own, independent of its relation to the body.

Since the argument depends on the initial counterfactual, it could be seen as hypothetical. In other words, one could suggest that what remains unaccounted for is a possible resurgence of a Cartesian dream argument: what if all those ideas of bodily affections are merely fictitious, maybe just dreams? If one can envisage, even counterfactually, their migration to other souls, maybe he can similarly envisage that there are no bodies and that we only invent their existence or are driven by some other causes to believe that what we feel is an actually existing body?[28] But Spinoza begins the demonstration by saying that if the body was not the object of the soul, the ideas of its affections would be in God anyway, but insofar as God constitutes another soul. This reference to God would be, it might be said, a Spinozistic version of the Cartesian God's veracity argument. The reality of the affections of the body, or the pertinence of their ideas, are thus never in doubt.

The proposition and its demonstration comprise two parts – the second part of the proposition, not quoted above, states that "the" (soul's) body is the *only* object of the idea-soul. This means – which might look strange given what is called Spinoza's "rationalism," or the allegedly "dogmatic" nature of his philosophy – that other people, other bodies, and the world do not count as the "object" of the soul. It is demonstrated on the basis of proposition 12 (stating that of everything that happens in or to the body, there is an idea in the soul) and axiom 5 (which states that we feel or perceive nothing but bodies and thoughts). In a not altogether unusual manner, the propositions and axiom cited do not seem to fully corroborate the conclusion. That we conceive nothing that is not either bodies or thoughts does not entail that we do not perceive other bodies than our body; unless, that is, *percipere* means here the same as *sentire* and designates the special relation a soul entertains with its own and private body. Spinoza draws, however, the conclusion that *the* body is the soul's only object. Spinoza was no solipsist, even if he says a little later that we mostly conceive our own bodies, even when they (actually we) are affected by other bodies. Obviously we do know other things besides our bodies; it is just that this knowledge is always mediated by our body.

Whether the demonstration is valid or not, an important thesis emerges here. The body is the only object of the idea-soul, and the soul is the only idea of the body. The soul-body complex is a unity or oneness; it is also unique and exclusive. Although this is not said explicitly, the counterfactual argument applied to the singularity of the idea's object works in the same way in the other direction: if the idea of my body had been other than my soul, this other idea would have been the soul of my body, and this idea-*ideatum* or body-soul unity would have been me. Identity, in other words, is a symmetric relation.

What is important to emphasize here, and what could dissipate to some degree the bizarreness of the whole discussion and hopefully give a more complete explanation of the recourse to God in the demonstration, is the following: Spinoza's argument entails a double-faced thesis about the absolute exclusiveness and primordiality of the idea-*ideatum* relation. The certain body, which the certain idea-soul feels as actually existent, is the only body it feels, senses, or knows, in the full, metaphysical sense of these terms; and inversely, it is the only soul of this body, its only idea said in a non-derivative way, and

---

[28] Macherey, 1997, II, p. 116–122, notes too the anti-Cartesian turn of this discussion, which is quite obvious, but he does not elaborate.

the only one that constitutes what one may call the "absolute knowledge" of this body. This is so because the very first relation – the very metaphysically fundamental relation, unmediated by consciousness, subject, intellect, or agent, either finite or infinite – is the idea-*ideatum*, or, indeed, the mind-body relation.

The scholium after EIIp7 purports to explicate the unity of intellect and the object of intellection. It gives as an example a circle "existing in nature" and the idea of this circle that is in God. Coming immediately after the parallelism proposition and just before propositions 11–13, it apparently suggests that the relation between a circle existing in nature, whatever this may mean, and God's idea of this circle is supposed to exemplify the mind-body relation. This in fact means that the relation between the circle and its idea and, by implication, between soul and body, is primordial.

There is a disturbing ambiguity in the way Spinoza presents this whole thing, and it concerns notably the parallel use of "nature" and "God": the circle exists in nature; its idea is in God. Insofar as the example of the circle and its idea is meant to illustrate, however insufficiently, the parallelism thesis, it seems from it that the circle in nature stands for the body, and the idea in God, for the soul, and that the parallelism in question is a parallelism between God and nature. But God *is* nature – *Deus sive natura* says one of Spinoza's more famous phrases – and if we replace "God" with "nature" every time the Spinoza says "God," the picture changes considerably. I shall try later on to show that Spinoza's use of the language of God is not gratuitous and that it underpins the normative and evaluative dimension of his philosophy. Here, in any case, if we say, for example, that the idea of a circle that is nature is also in nature, and in the same way, Spinoza's intention becomes less enigmatic.

Contrary to appearances, then, the reference to God emphasizes the primordiality of the idea-*ideatum* unity. Spinoza's God is not an agent or a subject of thinking. The logic of the previous discussion, and in particular the thesis of the uniqueness of the soul-body unity, leads to the conclusion that Spinoza's notion of God is a useful metaphor that besides its polemic functions serves Spinoza to drive home such theses as the one about the primordiality of the idea-*ideatum* relation. The relation of the circle and its idea, or concept, has to be considered in itself and without an essential reference to someone or something thinking or having this idea. Since thought has no priority over existence, and, inversely, existence has no priority over thought, what is primordial is the idea-*ideatum* relation.

In the last analysis, for Spinoza there is no eternal realm of true ideas, or a divine intellect over and above the concrete thought of the/this body that constitutes the individuality of the individual, above the *hic et nunc*, or the idea-*ideatum* radical uniqueness. The idea-*ideatum* relation is primordial, and the concrete idea-*ideatum* entity is unique. Granted that the mind is an idea, and that the mind-body identity is the identity of idea and *ideatum*, one is faced with the full gravity of the question: what could be a faithful Spinozistic rendering of such idioms as "the soul *feels*, or *grasps*, *perceives* or *knows* the body"? How should we construe the relation between soul-idea and body-object in such a way that would not amount to a simple reduction or elimination of the notions of *soul*, *mind*, or *subject*? That is, without abstracting from the fundamental experience of life, of mind, and of body and without giving up the theoretical dividends assured by such terms? I am not sure if all these questions have satisfactory answers in the *Ethics*; in what follows I shall, however, pursue the line of reasoning entailed by the idea of the primordiality of the idea-*ideatum* unity and offer a reconstruction of Spinoza's mind-body doctrine based on it.

If the soul is the idea of the body, and the body is the soul's object, and if the primacy of the subject or the agent of thought is rejected, whether in its Cartesian or any other form, we actually find ourselves facing the fundamental problem of Spinoza's ontology of man. This question concerns the possible meaning of the concept of "thought," referring to the concrete experience of thinking, insofar as it is conditioned by the primordiality of the idea-object or idea-*ideatum* relation. In other words, the question one has to address here is how to conceive the nature of thinking, reasoning, understanding, and the like, prior to or independently of positing a subject as the foundation or substrate of all such acts – that is, prior to physiological, psychological, moral, or political theories, but also prior to a theory of perception or to epistemology. All this – it should never be forgotten – in an *ethics* and in a philosophy that aims at finding the right way of life and the path to real happiness of the individual person. Despite the fact that we have not begun our discussion in *Ethics* I, that is with God or with substance, and in a sense that I hope will become clearer as we proceed, it is in fact here that we confront Spinoza's fundamental metaphysical views.

4.4. Quid sit Idea, Quid sit Corporis

Spinoza often casts his most radical ideas in traditional terms; quite often they are the same terms, of scholastic or late-scholastic origin, that Descartes was already using, adapted to meet his own needs, and then transformed again by Spinoza. An interesting instance of such a double transformation is the terminological and conceptual cluster surrounding the distinction between *esse objectivum* and *esse formale*. Descartes's (and the Cartesians') use of these terms is far from being unequivocal, and it is a constant source of embarrassment for commentators, an embarrassment that is also present in much of the secondary literature on Spinoza, whose uses of this terminology is also not always free of ambiguities.

The *esse objectivum/esse formalis* (sometimes it is *realitas* and not *esse*) distinction does not begin with Descartes.[29] It has a long and interesting history

---

[29] For the sake of brevity, I shall refer to the whole conceptual and terminological complex by simply using *objective being*.

4.4. Quid sit Idea, Quid sit Corporis

that has attracted the attention of a number of commentators and historians of pre- and early modern thought. Its roots reach all the way back to ancient and mediaeval philosophy, and the context within which it emerges can be described, in very general terms, as the ontology of thinking and knowing.[30] The more immediate background of Descartes's doctrine is a tradition that begins, according to many scholars, with Duns Scotus. The terminology itself appears for the first time, at least according to Normore (ibid., p. 233), in the writings of Scotus's disciple William of Alnwick (c. 1275–1333, according to Wikipedia). The debates around a number of questions articulated using this terminology continue through the writings of thinkers such as Peter Auriol, and then Ockham and others, into those of the later scholastics, notably the great masters of Jesuit theology and late scholastics, Suarez and Vasquez, whom Descartes studied extensively at La Flèche.

Although certainly borrowed from Descartes, Spinoza's use of the distinction between objective and formal being is non-Cartesian and even anti-Cartesian. It can be considered, in abstraction from its more immediate textual context, as part of a radical critique of the Cartesian and, anachronistically speaking, potentially of the entire tradition of transcendental theories of the subject, of the subject as the ultimate origin and seat of rationality, and of the concept of the *subject* as a presupposition of a theory of reason. Yet, there seems to be a significant similarity between Spinoza's use of the term *objective being* and that of some pre-Cartesian philosophers. Scholastic theories of knowledge had never really become *epistemology* in the sense that only the Cartesian "invention," as it called sometimes, of the subject made possible; they had always retained a strong sense of the priority of the question of being, even when in some respects they come very close to modern, or post-Cartesian, modes of thinking. The term *objective being* has strong ontological connotations in the writings of the scholastics as it relates to a real aspect of *res*.[31] With Descartes it becomes a modification of a *mens*, or an *idea* as a cognitive content, in a sense in which the connection to the thing, or object, becomes a problem essentially answered by a theory of representation. Spinoza, like the pre-Cartesian thinkers, thinks of *esse objectivum* as a mode of being of the thing itself rather than a representation of an object located in the mind, intellect, or consciousness of a knower.

---

[30] For an outline of this history, see Normore (1986), pp. 231–235. Cf. also Dalbiez (1929) and Cronin (1966), which contains a comprehensive bibliography. For more references, see the next notes.

[31] Cf. Courtine (1990), p. 182: for Suarez, "the objective concept is not the thing itself, with this denomination of 'being known' which remains external to it; it is, if you want, the thing itself, but insofar that it was *cognitively reduced* to its *objectivity*" (my translation; the French reads: "Le concept objectif, ce n'est pas la chose même, avec cette dénomination de 'connue' qui lui demeurerait purement extrinsèque; c'est, si l'on veut, la chose même, mais pour autant qu'elle a été *cogitativement réduite à son objectivité*.")

The use of the *esse objectivum/esse formalis* terminology, with its inherent equivocations, can be seen as a kind of Wittgensteinian ladder – it is used when better and more precise theoretical resources are not available, only to be disposed of once a certain conceptual clarity about what is at stake is achieved. It is noteworthy that it is still present in the immediate post-Cartesian period, but disappears almost completely afterward. Spinoza uses it, of course, and it figures in a few important debates, notably in the controversy about *true and false ideas*, which opposed two of the most prominent Cartesians, Malebranche and Arnauld, and which attracted a lot of attention and became one of the most important controversies of the time.[32] In the Malebranche-Arnauld controversy, however, it is mainly the epistemological question of *representation*, and the sense in which an idea can be said to represent extra mental entities, that are debated. Leibniz practically does not use it anymore, and after him, it seems to have lost its philosophical vitality completely. Without any pretention whatsoever to exhausting the subject, I would still suggest that the disposal of this ladder can be seen as the consummation of a process leading to the ripening of a central aspect of philosophical modernity, bringing forward and giving explicit formulation to many issues adding up to what can be described as the modern problematic of truth and knowledge.[33]

As the very use of the terminology of objective being suggests it was the question of being that determined the thematic horizon within which evolved the different theological and philosophical discussions where it figured and

---

[32] The stakes of this debate were larger than the question of the nature of ideas that stood at its center (Arnauld, whose *Des varies et des fausses idées* triggered the controversies with a harsh criticism of Malebranche, presents his polemic work as a *préambule*, referring to the fact that its real stakes were theological rather than philosophical), but it is precisely for what there is on this question, rather than that of theodicy or of "nature and grace," that it is remembered. See Denis Moreau (1999). As Moreau justly remarks, the long tradition of English philosophy's interest in the question of *ideas* is one of the main avenues through which the seventeenth century's preoccupation with the "ways of ideas," of which the Malebranche-Arnauld controversy was an important moment, was kept alive. It begins with Locke and his own deep interest notably in Arnauld, and in particular with Reid, who considered the latter as a precursor of his own realism. The English-written literature on the theory of ideas in "early modern philosophy" mainly deals with it in the framework of the debates between realists and idealists. A very partial list of the some recent works on this subject is Jolley (1990), Nadler (1989) and (1992), Watson (1995), and Yolton (1996).

[33] See Courtine, op. cit. p. 169: the doctrine of objective being introduced "a decisive turn [*un virage decisive*] in the essence of truth." Courtine's study concentrates on the changes in the conception of metaphysics that ripen notably in Suarez, on the threshold of modernity. Among many other things, he traces to the later scholastics the emergence of the notion of a human *mens* as the irreducible and *sui generis* "playground" of knowledge. To take just one example, Peter Auriole, after Duns Scotus and still before Ockham, reduces to nothing "the presence of the appearing thing, only in order to highlight more vividly the mind's privilege and the omnipotence of a God who can do without [*se dispenser*] this occasional detour through the *existentia et praesentia rei*"; this is a decisive step on the road that led to the fully explicit position of the problem of subjective knowledge, of its justification and foundation, as it will appear in Descartes.

4.4. Quid sit Idea, Quid sit Corporis

within which emerges gradually a modern concept of epistemology. Such a concept means that inquiry into knowledge and truth becomes primary, independent of the question of being; yet it does indeed emerge in the wake of these late scholastic thinkers who considered knowledge and, even more so, thinking (the thinking of the individual *mens*), as an ontological question. It was fundamentally the *mode of being* of the act of thinking, of ideas, of the intelligible, and of intelligibility that was the conceptual framework of their various discussions. Still, they prepared the way and took some decisive steps toward the later understanding of knowledge. In fact, already for thinkers such as Peter Auriol, the ontological status of thought is relativized to some extent: for this mediaeval (c. 1280–1322) Franciscan theologian, thinking, or knowing, confers on the objects of knowledge, qua objects of knowledge, a type of existence he calls *esse apparent*.[34]

Although the relativization of objective being, as it gradually appears in the later scholastics and then in Descartes, does indeed lead eventually to the positing of skepticism as an essential element or possibility of the theory of knowledge and truth, originally this was not its main concern. The theme that seems to emerge as the most significant aspect of the discussions of the objective being doctrine was how to bridge an "inner," subjective sphere of representation and an "external" or objective world. In retrospect, the discussions about the meaning of the objective being of the things of the world can be described as a long effort of theorizing the differentiating elements of an inner space, more or less closed on itself, of thought. In a sense, the recognition of such inner space is more radical than skepticism. It posits as a fundamental philosophic concern what Descartes and his successors called "thought" and what the pre-modern thinkers call "intellect" or *nous*. The use of the traditional terminology outlines two elements: first, the radically non-reductive, *sui generis* nature of thinking (or intellecting); second, the ontological nature of the traditional concern with thinking, understanding, and knowing.

The objective being ladder, then, reveals a gradual shift, a dialectical movement, toward the position of an inner space of thought conceived as *consciousness* and *subjectivity* (notably, of course, in Descartes). Spinoza would then use the same terminology to problematize Descartes's main moves, and Leibniz,

---

[34] For a general presentation of Peter Auriol, as well as for an up-to-date bibliography, see the online *Stanford Encyclopedia of Philosophy*, as well as the website "Peter Auriol Homepage." Courtine, op. cit., pp. 165–167, says on Auriol: "les actes de connaissance s'adressent directement à l'*esse apparens ou intentionale* que reçoit chaque objet du fait même qu'il est connu et ob-jecté, et indépendamment de son existence réelle ou de sa non-existence […] On peut dire que, quand la *specie* a cessé d'être *ce en grâce de quoi, ce dans quoi* ou *ce par quoi (id quod)* les choses sont connues et se manifestent, pour devenir cela même qui s'objecte (*id quod*) à l'esprit, l'*esse objectivum et apparens* tient lieu de l'*eidos* platonico-aristotélicien, à ceci près que l'être objectif loin de tendre à s'effacer à titre de médiation transparente, fait plutôt obstacle ou écran dans son apparence propre." It is the famous *veil of ideas* that appears here alongside the appearance of a proto-modern conception of the "mental" as a *sui generis* phenomenon.

already giving up the older terminology, would do the same, albeit in a different and less radical way. Finally Kant's transcendental idealism would consummate the de-ontologization of thinking (as well as of moral duty). The history of the objective being doctrine can thus indeed be said to be the history, or pre-history, of the appearance of *epistemology* in its modern, Kantian, and post-Kantian senses. Spinoza is absent from most of the recent studies of this history. Still, he does occupy a place in it, which is important to consider, if not in order to get a more accurate and nuanced picture of it, then at least in order to add to our understanding of his thought. His sources are both scholastic and Cartesian, and in order to appreciate his radical departure from both, a few words should be said here about Descartes's objective being doctrine.

4.4.a. *Objective and Formal Being: The Cartesian Moment*
There has been a great deal of research lately on Descartes's use of the objective/formal being terminology.[35] As has been aptly shown by many scholars – tribute has to be paid here to Gilson's pioneering work – Descartes draws much of his vocabulary, and to some extent his ideas too, from the late scholastics. Nevertheless, and especially under the impact of the new science, in his writings the objective being doctrine undergoes a deep transformation.[36] His use of the traditional distinction between the two beings of a thing – the formal and the objective – is one example for how new theoretical contents are introduced into an older thematic.

Different versions of the *esse objectivum/esse formalis* distinction appear in the Cartesian corpus – already in the *Regulae*, in the *Correspondence*, in the *Meditations* and the *Objections and Replies*, in the Latin version of the *Principia Philosophiae*,[37] and in the conversations with Burman. It is in fact

---

[35] For a comprehensive discussion of this literature, see Noa Naaman-Zauderer, (2010) pp. 19–28. I became acquainted with Naaman-Zauderer's work only after I wrote these things, and I have to pay tribute to her work, in Hebrew and in English. Her perspective is different from mine, but in her writing appear some similar ideas to the ones formulated here. See in particular her (2010). I consulted the manuscript of this book before its publication, and profited from it.

[36] Much of the literature that traces the ways in which the objective being doctrine opens into modernity or simply studies Descartes's uses of it seems to ignore the role of the New Science in this history. The "birth of the modern subject" is portrayed as a movement happening solely within the confines of philosophy and theology. It can, however, be argued (assuming that it happened with Descartes) that it was conditioned upon the emerging New Science – Galileo's in the first place – not less, and perhaps even more, than upon traditional philosophies. The objective being doctrine having been instrumental in articulating a *sui generis* concept of thought and of the ontological closure of consciousness, the New Science symmetrically provided a useful and effective image of the counterpart of thought. What seemed now to be a fully rational theory of the object of thought also posited the latter as wholly different from thought itself.

[37] In the French version, the same idea is explained in simpler terms, giving up the more technical and traditional terminology: there is not much difference among our ideas "en tant que nous les considérons simplement comme les dépendances de notre âme ou de notre pensée," but there are many differences as to what they represent (par. 17; AT, IX, p. 32).

4.4. Quid sit Idea, Quid sit Corporis

very difficult to propose coherent and compact presentation of an allegedly unified Cartesian doctrine on this matter. The complexity of the issues involved in the *esse objectivum/esse formalis* distinction and the deep ambiguity and indeterminacy of the terms used, are undoubtedly part of the explanation for the terminological and thematic hesitations and shifts manifest in the Cartesian texts. The meaning of *objective being* seems to retain a relative stability across the Cartesian corpus, but around it a diversity of terms appears on different occasions, compounding the awkwardness already attaching to the use of the term by Descartess's predecessors.

Probably the most conspicuous occurrence of the objective being terminology is in the first proof of the existence of God in *Meditations III* (in the *Principles of Philosophy* it is the second proof, and it is much less elaborate). Schematically put, the first proof of the existence of God is based, on the one hand, on the "causality axiom," which states that a cause must contain "formally and eminently" as much reality as the effect has (see Chapter 6); and, on the other hand, on the possibility to attribute positive ontological value, status or, as it were, magnitude, to pure ideas, conceived as contents of thought. The core of the proof is the contention that I, or a human mind in general, cannot be the origin of the idea of God. In a certain sense, or seen under a certain perspective, the latter, the idea of an infinite being, of infinite perfection, or, simply, of the *infinite* is an idea like all other ideas that we have or think. The common property of all ideas is precisely this: we (or rather I) think them or "have" them, and qua mode of thought, act of thinking, or as thought by a human mind, the idea of the infinite is no different from other ideas, and has no more reality or perfection than has the mind thinking it. However, it is also an idea of a special kind: insofar as its *objective reality* is concerned it cannot conceivably be "caused" – forged or invented – by a finite intellect such as the human intellect. It has more reality or perfection than a finite intellect, and an effect cannot have more reality or perfection than its cause. We must conclude that the existence an idea of *the infinite* in our thought necessarily points to an infinite cause or source (AT, VII, p. 41; IX, p. 32–33). The double-faced nature of the idea of the infinite is explicated as a difference between two kinds of "reality" that ideas have. The infinite's *formal reality*, or its reality when considered *materially* (as it is put on other occasions), is comparable to that of any other idea of the human mind or to any other thought it thinks; on the other hand, its *objective reality* necessitates an infinite cause.

Notorious for the difficulties involved in this argument, it has not ceased, ever since the Dutch theologian Caterus sent Descartes the *First Objections*, to attract the critical attention of readers, commentators, and critics. Caterus addresses what seems to him a major difficulty: what, he asks, is the meaning of "being objectively in the understanding"? If it means "terminating in the manner of an object the act of the intellect" (i.e., originating in the intellect), then objective being is an "external denomination" (*extrinseca denominatio*), and as such it adds nothing to the being of the thing itself, or is itself nothing.[38] If it is nothing, no principle of causality applies to it and the existence of no real cause can be deduced from the objective reality of an idea. Although Caterus's whole argument is clearly dressed in scholastic, or late scholastic, garb, there is in it an opening toward the Cartesian, nay modern, way of posing the problem of the *origin* of knowledge: it implies a dualism of an inner realm of thought and of knowledge and an external world of effective causality.

Descartes's reply is long and elaborate. He tries to show that ideas are not "pure nothingness," but have reality, in fact double reality, and that being objectively in the intellect, or in thought, is a kind of reality. As such, causal explanations of it are pertinent. True, he says, the sun itself is something different from the idea of the sun that I have, and the fact that I conceive the sun, or think about it, or, precisely, that it *is objectively* in the intellect adds nothing to the sun as it is outside my intellect, but only an external denomination, which means that it "is in the intellect *in the way in which objects are habitually* in it" (AT, VII, p. 102; IX, p. 82; italics added). However, if we consider the ideas themselves, "*being objectively in the intellect* does not mean terminating its operation in the manner of an object, but rather being in the intellect in the manner in which its objects are habitually in it,"[39] which is a kind of reality. Intriguing as it may be, I shall not dwell here on the distinction between "being objectively in the intellect," "terminating its operation in the manner of an object," and "being in the intellect in the manner in which its objects are habitually in it." What is important for us in all this is mainly the following: in order to defend his proof, Descartes has to avoid, strategically, the pitfall of the realism-idealism divide. More accurately put, he has to bypass the conception of *truth* as essentially a relation between what is inside and what is outside thought. The fundamental question he purports to address is that of ideas as such, and the crux of his response is an attempt to say what thought, or ideas, are in themselves. Objective reality and formal reality are two different aspects – or realities – of ideas *per se*, considered at first in abstraction from all relation to what lies outside them. These terms express two different ways of approaching ideas as a theoretical question in itself.

In the proof of the existence of God, the formal reality of the idea of the infinite that one finds in one's thought, or realizes that he had to assume tacitly all along, is the reality it has insofar as it is an idea thought by the intellect.

---

[38] There are slight differences between the Latin (AT, VII, p. 92) and the French (AT, IX, p. 74) versions, but they are immaterial.

[39] My translation; "neque ibi, *objective esse in intellectu*, in intellectu, significabit ejus operationem per modum objecti terminare, sed in intellectu eo modo esse quo solent ejus objecta, adeo ut idea solis fit sol ipse in intellectu existens," AT, VII, p. 103; French version, IX, p. 82. The technical term of *modum objecti terminari* means, roughly, that it is subjective in the sense of belonging to a different realm than the realm of objects. It also refers to the idea that the object is in the intellect as the result of an intentional act – thinking an object is an accomplishment of an operation, intentional in its nature.

4.4. Quid sit Idea, Quid sit Corporis

The understanding of the thinker that he is finite – in the process of doubting, based on the realization that one errs sometimes – presupposes the concept of the infinite (cf. the conversations with Burman, ibid.). Being presupposed – that is, present implicitly in this way – is not nothingness; it *is* a kind of reality. It does not enjoy, however, any ontological advantage, or surplus of perfection, over the reality and perfection the thinker enjoys as the agent who thinks it or implicitly presupposes it when he conceives himself as finite. The objective reality of this very same idea, however, is quite a different thing. In a sense, it *is* infinite; more accurately, its reality or perfection – as an object, or rather content, of thought, or as a concept – is such that its cause cannot be a finite thing (since the finite cannot beget the infinite), which means that it cannot be forged by a finite intellect.

Is there an irremediable equivocation in this superposition of the ontological – effectively caused, containing perfection – with (the power of) thought? Descartes tries to explicate what is inherently and effectively infinite in the idea of the infinite, with the aid of the concept of *complexity* – like the complexity or the inner richness of a thought content – that a very complex plan of a building or a sophisticated mechanism possesses. Such a complexity is "perfection" and the concept of the *infinite* is perfect or contains a complexity that is beyond what any artificial machine or invention can possess.

The *esse objectivum/esse formalis* distinction plays a role in the articulation of another fundamental aspect of the inner duality of thought: its conception as a space of consciousness. In the *more geometrico* exposition at the end of the *Second Replies*,[40] *idea* is defined as "the form of each one of our thoughts, by the immediate perception of which we have knowledge of these very thoughts." The Latin version reads, instead of "knowledge" (*connaissance*), "being conscious of" (*conscious sum*). This should be read with care. Our thoughts assume each a certain "form"; we perceive these forms, which means that apparently we do not "perceive" our thoughts directly; and it is through these perceptions that we gain knowledge, or become conscious, *of our thoughts*. Talking, on the one hand, about "knowledge (or cognition) of thoughts" as if the *object* of knowledge were "our thoughts"; and, on the other, of an equivalence of *knowledge* and *consciousness*, shows that "*thinking*" and "being conscious" are not synonymous. In some unspecified sense thought as such antedates, or is conceptually prior to, the informed thoughts of which we are effectively conscious. One can even go further and suggest that this duality is what gives concrete meaning to the fundamental metaphysical distinction between *substance* and *modes* as it applies to the *res cogitans*: Thought is the condition of the conscious occurrence of acts of thought, acts in which thoughts assume form and become known as objects of consciousness.

---

[40] AT, VII, pp. 160–170 for the Latin version, XI, pp. 124–132 for the French; the definitions in question are on pp. 160–161 and 124, respectively. I translate from the French version.

What had been implicit in the radical personalization of the intellect and of thought effected in the very act of doubting, and what was only semi-explicit in the position of a principle of causality as essential for the theory of ideas and in the emergent concept of *consciousness*, becomes fully explicit in the sequel: the primordiality of the question of *truth* on the one hand and conceiving truth as a relation between what is interior to thought and what is external to it on the other. In a letter to an unknown correspondent, Descartes tries to give sense to the old distinction between *essence* and *existence* in the framework of his own philosophy. The main source of difficulties in this matter, he explains, is that "we do not sufficiently distinguish between things existing outside our thought [*nostra cogitatione*] and the things' ideas which are in our thought." He then explains his intention with the aid of two examples. The first is mathematical: the essence of a triangle and its existence, if they are "taken objectively," are distinct "modally." But insofar as we consider the triangle's existence *extra-cogitationem*, existence and essence are not distinct. "The same is the case with all universals. Thus when I say 'Peter is [a] man', the thought by which I think of Peter differs modally from the one by which I think 'man', but in Peter himself being man is no other than being Peter.... So again, if by 'essence' we understand a thing as it is objectively in the intellect, and by 'existence' the same thing in so far as it is outside the intellect, it is manifest that the two are really distinct."[41]

I have quoted somewhat extensively from this letter, which is of a relatively late date, because it manifests quite clearly the sense of the "Cartesian moment" insofar as the *esse objectivum/esse formalis* thematic is concerned and illustrates the kind of shift towards modern epistemology that is effected with its aid. "Essence" becomes objective being and, in fact, concept; "existence" is fundamentally understood now as external, or rather *independent-of-thought*, existence. This also means that "thought" is conceived as exclusively a subjective affair and "truth" a relation between the inner and the external or between the subjective and what lies outside it. We can watch here in the making, as it were, how a context in which the question of being is prior, is transformed into one that is organized around the primordiality of *truth* and *knowledge* conceived as belonging to a space defined indeed by its *interiority* (immediacy of self-presence, ontological closure, privacy, intimacy, etc.). Moreover, the two questions, that of truth and that of knowledge, become interwoven, and both are understood as relations between the inter-mental and the extra-mental, between an *immaterial* inner realm of thought and an external *material* being. The fact that Descartes gives a geometric example is highly significant: a triangle is not a material object, of course, but it is, as an existent, an extended

---

[41] Partially cited by N. Naaman-Zaudrer, op. cit., which gives a comprehensive account of the matter in the Cartesian corpus (the editors of AT esteem that the addressee was either Father Mesland or Father Vatier, AT, IV, pp. 348–350). English translation, very slightly altered, in Cottingham (1991), pp. 280–281.

4.4. Quid sit Idea, Quid sit Corporis

object or, as it were, a piece of extension.[42] If one bears in mind the reduction Descartes effects of matter to extension – incomprehensible outside the context of the Galilean-Cartesian scientific revolution – the transformation occurring here becomes apparent: the object of thought would become paradigmatically material, and as such, indeed wholly other than the non-material thinking. *Objective reality* as an aspect of thinking becomes an oxymoron. With more than a grain of historical irony, object and objectivity will not be understood anymore as a mode of being of objects-of-thought, the kind of being that contents of thought or concepts have, but as that which exists outside thought, which is independent of it, and which is governed by laws other than the laws of thought – specifically, by the mechanical laws of material nature. Thought would not be referred to any more with the aid of notions such as objective being; it is now conceived as subjective and as subjectivity.

In the *Praefatio ad Lectorem* of the Latin edition of the *Meditations* (AT, VII, p. 8), the double-faced nature of ideas is again addressed, although with partially different terminology. This text is certainly posterior to the exchanges of the objection and replies, and it apparently expresses the result of further reflection on many issues discussed in them. *Idea*, writes Descartes, is an equivocal term: it can be understood "materially" – that is, as "an action of my mind" – and it can be taken "objectively" – as that which is *represented by this act*. Taking ideas "materially" seems to replace *the formal being* of ideas, and it is sometimes thought that Descartes introduces here a new element. The use of the term "act" leads some readers to see it as a second-order concept, abstracting from the strictly ideational meaning of *idea*. This, however, is probably not the case, at least not unequivocally, and it can be suggested that the two terms – formal being or reality and materiality – retain the meaning of *ideas* as concrete or actually conceived contents of thought.

What is stated here in greater explicitness is that those acts or "forms" of our thought, or ideas taken "materially," *represent* the objective being of these same ideas, or the ideas taken "objectively." "Ideas taken objectively" means here for Descartes the *things represented* and not, as some tend to think, *representations of things*. The material being of an idea, or the form thought assumes through an act of thinking, *represents* its objective being. This may sound bizarre, but if its strategic function is considered, it is obvious that this indeed is Descartes's intention. As he emphasizes immediately, preparing the way for his proof of the existence of God, although we do not consider the represented thing as existing outside the intellect, or soul, it can nonetheless be said that, according to its essence (*ratione suae essentiae*), it is more perfect than the thinking agent who thinks it. The strategic role of this claim seems indeed quite straightforward: in the case of the idea of the infinite, which gives us knowledge of the existence of an infinite entity but not knowledge, or full understanding, of the infinite

---

[42] This aspect of Descartes's thought would lead to its fuller development in Malebranche's notion of the *intelligible extension*.

(or of its nature or, precisely, its essence), the distinction is fundamental. The idea of the infinite, namely the idea of the infinite as we become aware of its having already implicitly conditioned the idea of the finite, represents its objective being, but not as it actually is. The *essence* of the infinite, or of the infinite object, remains outside the reach of full human understanding. It is present in its idea, however, according to the formulation Descartes repeats on several occasions, "in the way in which objects are present in it." It is there as represented or, in fact, *presented*, by a form – a moment of conscious, a concrete content, a "mental event" – that my thought, or "mind," assumes. Specifically, it is represented by what I understand when I discover that I err sometimes; that, hence, I am finite; and that the concept *finite*'s intelligibility, the possibility to think it, depends on – in the way concepts depend, that is, presuppose – the concept of the *infinite*. I discover, in other words, that I have all along assumed implicitly the infinite; it is in fact coextensive with my intellect. Metaphorically one could say that the idea of the infinite has been previously (and implicitly) present in one's "soul"; that it is, indeed, an "innate idea."

In the above-mentioned exposition *more geometrico*, Descartes defines (third definition) the objective being (or *reality*) of ideas as follows: "By the *objective reality* of an idea I understand the entity of the thing [*entitam rei*] represented by the idea, insofar as it is in the idea"; and then (fourth definition): "The same things are said to be *formally* in the objects of the ideas when they are in themselves as we conceive them" (my translation). According to these definitions, in cases other than that of the idea of the infinite, the form of thought we have of a represented object represents it as it is. Then, and only then, we can say that the "entity" of a thing, or its "essence," is *formally* in the idea.

This, in other words, is what would qualify for the title of "true" idea – distinct and (fully) clear. One last important element comes to the fore in the space opened, so to speak, in between the two "realities" that belong to one and the same idea and, consequently, in what unites them into one entity. The mediating term is what Descartes calls *representation*. The philosophical and scientific or semi-scientific preoccupation with this notion has a very long history, both before and after Descartes. I suggest that it was to a large extent in the wake of Descartes that the notion of *representation* has been transformed into a modern one, and even, in many respects, has become a central theme of the modern problem of knowledge, perception, and truth. This is true for both the so-called continental and the English-speaking traditions. It is a central topic in the famous debate between Malebranche and Arnauld, as well as in Locke's doctrine of the "veil of ideas," in Reid's criticism of Locke's "way of ideas," and later in Kant, only to become even more central in our days, in contemporary philosophy of mind, in phenomenology, and in semi-scientific or scientific younger disciplines such as cognitive science, linguistics, neuroscience, and so on.

That the notion of *representation* is notoriously ambiguous and multifarious is a commonplace; this, however, does not always prevent confusion. Two

4.4. Quid sit Idea, Quid sit Corporis

distinct meanings are distinguishable in the usual uses of this notion; for the sake of brevity, we could refer to them as the *semantic* (or presentational) and the *semiotic* functions of representing. The first term designates that quality of "mental representations" that make them bearers of meaning, but also of truth and error, or of understanding, conceiving, and reasoning, and that is often confounded with *intentionality*, namely with the in-being in consciousness of ideational, conceptual, or, more generally, mental "content." The second meaning, the semiotic, refers to the function of ideas as representing something in the sense of *standing* for it. This second meaning is closer to the more intuitive sense given to *representation* in everyday discourse, which is also what renders it immediately usable in non-linguistic contexts, notably the political.

I shall not try to offer here a coherent interpretation of Descartes, nor shall I elaborate on the complex and often confused history and current uses of the notion of *representation*. I shall return to this question and to Spinoza's unorthodox avoidance of it in the next chapter; here I shall only remark that given the rather amorphous use of this notion by Descartes – as an inter-ideatic relation on one hand, and as an inner-external relation on the other hand – one can say that his writings announce indeed the great centrality the concept of *representation* would have in modern epistemology. What is important to note here, especially in the context of a study of Spinoza's so-called monism, is that whether understood as "blind" correspondence, defined as some kind or another of a function-like or isomorphic relation between "things" or "objects," and particular thoughts, ideas, or, in a more up-to-date jargon, "mental events" (the immediate metaphor, pace Leibniz, being that of "mapping"); or as "intentional" in-presence in consciousness, *representation* is almost always thought of as a relation, bridging an ontological and/or conceptual gap or difference between the subject/consciousness and the intentional object, between the inner and the external, between consciousness and world, between the mental and extra-mental, or between knowledge and object. As I shall try to show in the next chapter, Spinoza's doctrine of the soul implies a radical relativization of the problematic of *representation* on both its aspects. He does it by typically relying on old jargon, notably that of the objective-formal being distinction, practically turning it upside down.

I have dwelt at some length on the doctrine of objective being in Descartes because, first of all, through it one can get a fuller understanding of the real and original sense of the Cartesian extension/thought dualism, the famous mind-body question being parasitic on it. It also delineates the historical and thematic context within which Spinoza's so-called mind-body theory, or his monism, was conceived, only to stand in the end in radical opposition to it.

4.4.b. *Objective and Formal Being in Spinoza*
The terminology of objective/formal being occurs in most of Spinoza's writings. It is absent from the *Cogitata Metaphysica* and the two political treatises and is referred to obliquely once or twice in the letters, but it appears in all the

other writings, and usually in a non-trivial way. There is an interesting development in Spinoza's use of this terminology along his different writings, and it can be seen as one of the avenues his thought takes in its quest for a way of its own.

Although the *Principles of Descartes' Philosophy* was written after the TIE and the CV, when Spinoza was already in possession of much of his mature philosophy, it would be preferable to look first at this work. As Ludwig Meyer explains in his "Letter to the Reader" – undoubtedly in response to Spinoza's request – the author did not subscribe to the philosophy he set out to present. We also know that Spinoza wrote the first part of his exposition of Descartes's *Principles* in some haste, for he was then already busy articulating his own philosophy.[43] This is just one, rather circumstantial reason to consider this neglected text as an essential link between Spinoza and Descartes.[44]

Most significantly for us here is that the *Principles of Descartes' Philosophy* is the only place in the Spinozistic corpus where one can find a definition, or indeed any elucidation, of the concepts of *objective* and *formal reality*. At the beginning of the *more geometrico* reconstruction of Descartes's *Principles of Philosophy* (first part) Spinoza reproduces the ten definitions given by Descartes at the beginning of his own geometrical presentation – what he calls the "synthetic method" – of his position at the end of the second replies. The third and fourth definitions, both in Descartes's "synthetic" exposition and in Spinoza's reproduction of it, are, respectively, the definitions of *objective* and *formal reality*. Since these notions are not defined or explained anywhere else by Spinoza, we may assume that he thought that his readers would understand the meaning of these terms, and we can also assume that the meaning that he attributes to them in the exposition of Descartes is, more or less, the way he continued to understand these terms subsequently. The third definition thus states that "The objective reality of an idea [*realitatem objectivam ideae*] is the being [*entitatem*] of the thing represented by the idea, *insofar as this entity is in the idea*" (italics added). One could similarly say, adds here Spinoza, "objective perfection, objective artifice etc. For everything that we perceive in the objects of [the] ideas is objectively in the ideas themselves." The fourth definition states that "the same things are said to be *formally* in the objects of [the]

---

[43] As Spinoza writes to Ludwig Meier in August 1663 (letter 15), he had written the first part of the *Principles* in two weeks, especially for the publication of his little book. The second part and what there is of the third were written before, for use, among other things, in the instruction given to the young man who "was staying under the same roof" with him (letters 8 and 9). As Meier makes plain in his preface, Spinoza's first part is not an exact reconstruction of Descartes's *Principles* – he leaves some things out and has the *Meditations* as source as well.

[44] The complex relation of this essay and its appendix, the *Cogitata Metaphysica*, to Descartes and the scholastic thinkers Spinoza had read on the one hand, and to his own philosophy on the other, has been the subject of some research, mainly by late nineteenth- and early twentieth-century German-speaking (mainly Jewish) scholars, mainly Joel, Freidlander, and Kuno Fisher. There are a few more recent studies on this topic by Gueroult, Curley, and a few others.

4.4. Quid sit Idea, Quid sit Corporis

ideas when they are in them, in the same way as we perceive them; and *eminently* when they are not there in this way, but so that they can stand for those [things] which would be such." One can detect in these definitions a shift from Descartes's original use of the notions of formal and objective being. Instead of a distinction between two realities pertaining to ideas as such, the definitions in the *more geometrico* exposition seems to imply an essential distinction between ideas and objects. Spinoza will use the traditional distinction to say the exact opposite.

Spinoza continues, in fact, to use rather extensively the objective/formal being distinction, but it is noteworthy that it has completely disappeared from the proof of God's necessary existence in the *Ethics*. Spinoza's proof, as it is gradually constructed in the first eleven propositions (and, in fact, in the first fifteen propositions) of EI, is based neither on a theory of ideas, nor on a principle of causality, but on the concept of the *infinite*. Descartes, of course, also bases his first proof of the existence of God on the concept of the infinite. But unlike him, Spinoza thought that he could formulate a fully positive concept of the infinite, and not just detect its presence as a condition of his philosophical discourse. Spinoza thus thought he could deduce the infinite's necessary existence by relying exclusively on his theory of the infinite and thus without presupposing an independent principle of causality and prior to the theory of ideas.

The disappearance of the traditional distinction, however, is only temporary. Spinoza will use the objective being doctrine mostly for his own, rather non-Cartesian theory of ideas and mind-body doctrine. There is, however, a path, at least partially traceable, leading from the Cartesian use of the formal/objective being distinction to Spinoza's. In letter 40 to Jarig Jelles dated March 1667, Spinoza refers approvingly to Descartes's proof of God's existence and mentions Descartes's fourth axiom in the *more geometrico* exposition, the "causality axiom," which states that a thing's whole reality or perfection is formally or eminently in its first and total cause. Spinoza thinks, however, that the "axiom" is "somewhat ambiguous" and could be better formulated in the following way: "the power of Thought to think is not greater than the power of nature to exist and to act."[45] On the basis of this "clear and true axiom," Spinoza adds, God's existence stems clearly and irrefutably from God's idea. It is not altogether clear how exactly one deduces God's existence from the new formulation of the axiom, and Spinoza in fact does not really use it in his proof of God's existence in the *Ethics*. It will resurface, however, in the corollary to EIIp7, that is, at the heart of the development contained in the first thirteen propositions of EII and precisely in the same place where the objective/formal distinction reappears.

---

[45] Quod cogitandi potentia ad cogitandum non major est, quam naturae potentia ad existendum et operandum.

What prompted the discussion in letter 40 were some comments by Jelles about the attempt of an unnamed author to refute the Cartesian proofs for the existence of God. The refutation was apparently based on the claim that the regression *ad infinitum* of causal explanations contradicts Descartes's causality axiom. Insofar as causal-mechanical explanations of physical motions are concerned, replies Spinoza, the explanatory movement from one cause to another does give the eternal and total cause of the axiom. But, he immediately adds, it is an altogether different matter when "ideational" causality is concerned. The copying of a philosophy book from another copy of the same book, itself copied from yet another copy, and so *ad infinitum*, is not an explanation in the same sense that a mechanical explanation of motion is, for when I ask whence the book, I am not asking about the shape of the letters on the papers, but about the ideas and meanings they express.

All this, concludes Spinoza, is easily seen from the ninth axiom of his *more geometrico* exposition of Descartes's *Principles* (which is different from Descartes's own axiom). This axiom states that "the objective reality of our ideas requires a cause in which the same reality would be contained not only objectively, but [also] formally or eminently." There is an explication after this axiom, which is supported by a very similar example to the one given in the letter to Jelles. This axiom too has not disappeared altogether, and it recurs – not as an axiom – in precisely the same place as the previous axiom, in the corollary to EIIp7.

How should one understand this complex movement from Descartes to Spinoza? Deleuze, for example, found in the improved formulation of the Cartesian axiom in letter 40 the mark of a search with an axiom of "power" (*puissance*), a substitute for Descartes's axiom of "quantity of reality."[46] The thematic centrality of *potentia* in the *Ethics* is obvious, and Deleuze, of course, was not the only commentator to observe this.[47] What Deleuze neglects, however, is a second element of Spinoza's "search." The corollary to EIIp7 expresses a typical gesture of borrowing and transforming. It crystalizes the reworking of both the meaning and the systematic role of two elements of Descartes's proof of God's existence: causality and objective being.

It is noteworthy that Spinoza uses what Deleuze dubbed the "axiom of power" but also the objective/formal-being distinction, not in the context of the general metaphysics of EI, but in the course of formulating the conceptual and ontological foundations of his mind-body theory. *Potentia* is a general metaphysical concept for Spinoza; it is however remarkable, and certainly no accident that its introduction in the letter to Jelles was accompanied by the

---

[46] Cf. Deleuze op. cit., p. 77. In truth, the notion of "perfection," or of the "quantity of reality," plays a very important role in the philosophy of Spinoza. I shall come to it later.
[47] I would mention here in particular, once again, H. F. Hallett's work on Spinoza, especially his (1962).

4.4. Quid sit Idea, Quid sit Corporis

example of a copied book. Alongside the interpretation of the causality principle in terms of potency, comes also a parallel insistence on the specificity of ideational causality/potency.

I suggested above that the corollary to EIIp7 contains a symmetrical rejection of both "idealism" and "materialism." Such a rejection is also a rejection of two classical forms of reductionism. The double polemic, the parallel rejection of idealism and materialism, or physicalism, implied in the axiom and its reproduction in the corollary, have to be read also in view of the emphasis on the specific character of ideational explanations contained in the explanation of axiom 9, in the *Principles*, and in letter 40. Explicit in the letter and less obvious in the *Ethics* – but arguably still there – is the contention that ideational causality, becoming, if we follow Deleuze, power (or potency, as Hallett proposes to call it), has a different structure from that of physical causality. If this is indeed the case, the famous thought-extension parallelism should not be understood as a mere isomorphism.

The two elements – the general metaphysical principle of causality as potency, and the specificity or irreducibility of thought to physical causality – are not easily reconcilable, which probably explains another volte-face. EIIp9 seems indeed to retreat from the claim about the specificity of ideational causality as presented in the letter. In an apparently more parallelist attitude, Spinoza now presents it in a manner similar to that in which the letter had spoken of physical causality:

The idea of a singular thing which actually exists has God for a cause not insofar as he is infinite, but insofar as he is considered to be affected by another idea of a singular thing which actually exists; and of this [idea] God is also the cause, insofar as he is affected by another third [NS: idea], and so on, to infinity.

The specific nature of ideational causality will be conserved, however, a little bit later in EII. I shall return to it in Chapter 6, section 4. The order of reasons – such as the one that stands at the origin of the aforementioned philosophy book – is usually and intuitively conceived as having a very different structure from the structure of physical force. The potential incompatibility of these two themes is particularly acute in the context of the mind-body monism for which Spinoza is arguing in the first part of EII, and proposition 9 is one more illustration of Spinoza's frequent changes of mind and difficulties in resolving this incompatibility. The objective being terminology is one of the main tools in Spinoza's attempts to conceptualize his non-reductionist conception of thought as part of his doctrine of the oneness of soul and body.

There is much to gain by following the development of Spinoza's uses of the objective/formal being distinction in his earlier writings. It gives a strong impression of assisting in philosophical thinking in the making. In the *Short Treatise*, Spinoza uses the objective being language on two main occasions, at the very beginning and at the very end – in the appendix – of the work. The appendix is usually thought to have been written later than the rest of the text,[48] and in fact, there are deep differences in the uses of this terminology in these two parts of the work. The first, in chapter 1 of the first part,[49] is used as the theoretical basis for the proof of God's existence, which is a gesture still completely within the Cartesian legacy. Spinoza opens his book with two such proofs, an *a priori* proof and an *a posteriori* one, as he calls them. The first is a formalized (rather awkwardly, in fact) version of the ontological proof; the second is a reconstruction of Descartes's first proof, quite reminiscent of the proof Spinoza gives in the *Principles*.

In the second section of the appendix, titled "Of the Human Soul," the objective being terminology reappears, but this time the theoretical use it is put to is radically different from the previous ones. There is a deep shift in the basic understanding of the whole matter, and from now on – in the appendix of the CV, in the TIE, and finally in the *Ethics* – Spinoza's objective being doctrine will be coextensive with his mind-body doctrine. It ceases to play any role in the proofs of God's – or nature's – necessary existence, and, more significantly, it is not conceived anymore as the terminological scaffolding of a doctrine about the nature of ideas as the locus of representation (adequate or inadequate) of an independent ("external") reality, but as a vehicle carrying the sense of a doctrine of ideas as souls, and of the nature of the identity (rather than just "union") of mind and body.

The shift is not consummated until the *Ethics*, and even there not all ambiguities are dissipated, but the direction leading to the iconoclastic theory of the soul being the idea of the body is already traceable in the appendix of the CV and in the TIE. The discussion in the appendix begins by stating that the human soul, just like the human body (relative to extension), is a modification of the attribute called "thought." The polemical import is immediately conspicuous: the soul perishes when the modification of thought perishes, while the attribute itself remains without change. Although it is not yet said with the full explicitness in which it will be said in the *Ethics*, one can easily see here how the future proposition 11 of EII, which states that the soul is an idea, is beginning to take shape.

---

[48] There is an old controversy about dating the different parts of the CV and about which of the early writings – the CV and the TIE – antedates the other. Mignini in his comprehensive and authoritative translation and commentary to the CV, as well as Rousset in a similarly comprehensive and authoritative translation and commentary of the TIE, believe, against Gebhardt's earlier hypothesis that the CV was a first version of the *Ethics*, that the TIE was closer than the CV to the *Ethics*. I profited a great deal from the very detailed exposition of the more ancient debates about these question by the late Yosef Ben Shlomo in his long introduction to his edition and commentary to the Hebrew translation of the CV. See the Works Cited.

[49] There are two supplementary occurrences of the *formal being* in the second chapter, which answers the question "What is God?," but they are not much more than a prolongation of the discussion of the first chapter.

4.4. Quid sit Idea, Quid sit Corporis

In the third paragraph of the second part of the appendix appears a statement that is generally thought to betray the relatively early date of its compilation: Spinoza says here that what we call "soul" has its origin in the body and that the changes that it undergoes depend only on the body. It can be argued, however, that in fact this is already almost identical to the doctrine of the *Ethics*: what is important here is that the reality of thought, and even its *sui generis* nature, is not considered as a metaphysical absolute or – in Cartesian idiom – "substantial" anymore, and that the ontological closure of the "mental" is severely infringed. The gradual construction of the whole argument also shows that it is indeed very close to the doctrine of the *Ethics*. Most significant for us in the present context is the explicit identification of *objective being* and *ideas* on the one hand, and of *formal being* and *objects* on the other. Spinoza reiterates here a few times: the idea *is* an objective being, and its object *is* a formal being or a body. He says in § 7: "since for the existence of an idea, or of an objective essence, nothing is needed beside the thinking attribute and the object, or the formal essence …, the idea or the objective essence is the most immediate mode of the attribute"; and in § 9: "the essence of the soul is only in the existence of an idea or objective essence in the thinking attribute"; and, in particular, in § 15: "the objective essence corresponding to this proportion [of movement and rest, i.e., the body], which is in the thinking attribute, is nothing but, we say, the soul of the body." In the *Ethics* it will not be different, besides one important thing – the objective being and the formal being are strictly two beings of one and the same thing.

The language of objective being appears a few times in the TIE. It helps Spinoza to articulate in this unfinished treatise some of his more original and iconoclastic doctrines. The most significant use of this language in the TIE is in paragraphs 33–41. The topic of these paragraphs is the "true idea." After having enumerated the four (in the *Ethics* and three in the CV) degrees, in fact kinds, of knowledge (§§ 19–24) and after asking which of them is most suitable for our philosophical-ethical purposes (§ 25), the next fundamental question is that of the "way or Method by which we shall know the things to be known in this way" (§ 26). But the "method," as knowledge of knowledge, is itself knowledge, and the first thing to do is to thus find the way to avoid falling into the trap of infinite regress. This is done first with the aid of the example, already mentioned, of material instruments (§§ 26–32): we begin with what we naturally already possess and forge better instruments as we go along.

The intellect similarly possesses a "native power" from which it can ascend to an ever-better knowledge and understanding. In order, however, to see what the intellect's native instruments are, we need to discuss the nature of the "true idea," for truth and true ideas are precisely those native instruments the intellect uses in its quest for self-amendment. Paragraphs 33–43 thus propose a theory of the true idea. These barely two pages, dense and sometimes obscure, contain or announce some of Spinoza's boldest doctrines, in particular: truth is *index sui*, and there are no "external signs" that distinguish the true idea from the false; certainty is nothing but the objective essence or the (adequate) idea itself; method is the reflection on the true idea and hence nothing but the reflective or the idea of the idea; and finally – although this is not said explicitly here – the *idea ideae* – is the awareness of what we conceive, or what Leibniz would call "apperception" or, indeed, consciousness.

It is noteworthy that the whole discussion in these eleven paragraphs is supported by the language of objective being (Spinoza uses the formula *essentia objective*).[50] This not-quite-transparent notion mediates the non-intuitive, or even counterintuitive, identifications that Spinoza effects here: idea and objective essence; idea and the idea's idea; and so on. It is also noteworthy, however, that in connection with the use of this terminology appears the single most notable difference between the TIE and the *Ethics*. Paragraph 33–34 read as follows:

§ 33: The true idea (and we have in fact a true idea) is something different from its ideatum. For a circle is one thing and an idea of the circle is another. In fact, the idea of the circle is not something which has a circumference and a center, as the circle, and the idea of the body is not the body itself; and since it is something different from its ideatum, it would be itself something intelligible; that is, the idea, as to its *formal essence*, can be the object of another *objective essence*, and this another *objective essence*, considered in itself, would also be something real and intelligible, and so on indefinitely.

§ 34: Peter, for example, is something real; but Peter's true idea is Peter's objective essence, and something real in itself, and completely distinct from Peter himself. Hence, as Peter's idea is something real having its own particular essence, it would be something intelligible, i.e., the object of another idea which will contain objectively all that is in Peter's idea formally.

In the *Ethics*, on the other hand, we have:

everything that an infinite intellect can perceive as constituting the essence of substance pertains to one substance only, and consequently that the thinking substance and the extended are one and the same substance, which is now comprehended under this attribute, now under that. So also a mode of extension and the idea of that mode are one and the same thing, but expressed in two ways. Some of the Hebrews seem to have seen this, as if through a cloud, when they maintained that God, God's intellect and the things thought by him [*ab ipso intellectas*] are one and the same. E.g. *a circle existing in Nature and the idea of the existing circle, which is also in God, are one and the same thing*, which is explicated [*explicatur*] through different attributes. Therefore, whether we conceive Nature under the attribute of extension, or under the attribute of thought, or under any other attribute, we shall find one and the same order, or one and the same connection of causes, that is, that the same things follow one another. When I said that God is the cause of the idea, say of a circle, only insofar as he is a thinking thing, and [the cause] of the circle only insofar as he is an extended thing, this was for

---

[50] The late Bernard Rousset is probably the only commentator to have seen in Spinoza's use of this language a matter worth serious reflection. He has some very interesting things to say on it, although I don't always follow his interpretation.

4.4. Quid sit Idea, Quid sit Corporis   145

no other reason than because the formal being of the idea of the circle can be perceived only through another mode of thinking, as its proximate cause, and that mode again through another, and so on, to infinity (EIIp7s; Curley's translation, slightly altered; italics added).

A few pages later, in another scholium commenting on some developments that concern the question of the knowledge of the "external" world, the reader is told that he can now

clearly understand what is the difference between the idea of, say, Peter, which constitutes the essence of Peter's mind, and the idea which is in another man, say in Paul. For the former directly explains [*explicat*] the essence of Peter's body and does not involves existence, except so long as Peter exists; but the latter indicates the condition of Paul's body more than Peter's nature, and therefore while that condition of Paul's body lasts, Paul's mind will still regard Peter as present to itself, even though Peter does not exist (EIIp17s).

That Spinoza's thought had undergone significant changes between the early writings and the *Ethics* is common knowledge; but nowhere, it seems, is there such a straightforward reversal of what had been said in the TIE as in these two scholia. What makes the shift here even more eloquent is the fact that Spinoza exemplifies opposite claims with the very same illustrations: in the TIE, the circle and the circle's idea, or Peter and Peter's idea, are different things; in the *Ethics*, "a circle which exists in nature and this existing circle's idea, are one and the same thing" (EIIp7s). Likewise, the idea of Peter's body, which is Peter's soul, constitutes direct knowledge of Peter's body, while Peter's idea in Paul is a different matter.

Besides the fact that Spinoza gives exactly the same examples in the TIE and in the *Ethics* but draws the opposite conclusions from them, it is also noteworthy that what came together in the earlier work as two examples of one and same issue – the (vaguely ontological) difference between ideas and the ideated things – appears in the *Ethics* in two different thematic contexts: the oneness of the circle and its idea in the clearly ontological context of the parallelism proposition; and the privileged relation between Peter's body and the idea constituting a direct knowledge of it, in the specifically gnoseological context of the propositions coming after the little physics.

That in the TIE both examples purport to illustrate the same thing means that the relation between the circle and its idea is somehow the same as the relation between Peter and his soul. The use of the same examples is an indication that Spinoza continued to think of the two relations together. The ontological doctrine of the idea-*ideatum* unity is unequivocally the foundation of the theory of knowledge, and the idea-*ideatum* relation is what brings together the two doctrines – the ontological and the gnoseological – into one coherent theoretical whole. Spinoza apparently has become, between the earlier works and the *Ethics*, more cautious and perhaps more hesitant about this matter, as can be learned from the many warnings scattered in the first part of EII. But he seems to still be thinking that it is appropriate to illustrate the relation – or unity – between a soul and its body with the relation – or unity – between a circle and its "idea." He thus continues to think of his mind-body doctrine – the soul is the idea of the body – with the thematic and terminological aid of what he conceives to be the relation between geometrical objects and their ideas, or between the formal and objective beings of circles and triangles.

This is not the place to attempt to extract a systematic "philosophy of mathematics" from Spinoza's writings. However, it can be said with some certainty that he held some sort of mathematical realism. Yet his doctrine of the genetic definition as what gives the "true" nature of geometrical objects on the one hand and his claim that the generation or construction of mathematical objects involves elements of fiction on the other[51] show that his realism should not be interpreted as sheer Platonism, at least not insofar as one understands the latter to imply the existence of a transcendent region of eternal and immutable ideal or intelligible objects.

If neither an eternal and immutable archetype in a Platonist (or Leibnizian) "region of ideas" or a "third world," nor a "representation" enclosed in a human (or even divine) intellect, what then can the *idea* of a circle be?[52] A circle, imaginatively generated, is an "ideal" object. In what sense, if at all, can it be said to either differ from, or be one with, its idea (or actually its concept)? Spinoza says first that the circle and its idea are two different things – the circle has a circumference and a center, and its idea does not – only to later retract and say that the circle and its idea are one and the same thing. In the *Ethics*, in fact, the circumference and center disappear, and the distinction within the unity of the circle and its concept is construed as a distinction-within-unity of "existence" and "idea" ("a circle *existing in nature and the idea of the existing circle*, which is also in God are one and the same thing").

What had been equivocal in the TIE becomes unequivocal in the *Ethics*. What had been written from the point of view of a still more or less intuitive, perhaps "natural" understanding of the relations between ideas and their objects matures into the doctrine of the soul-idea/body-object unity in the later text. In the TIE the ideas in question – the circle's and Peter's respective ideas – still seem to be contained in, or thought by, some vaguely presupposed intellect,

---

[51] It may be tempting to interpret this as kind of an embryonic constructivist conception, but there is certainly no subjectivism or any other ontological or epistemological relativization of the value of mathematical thinking. On the generic definition, see TIE §§ 94–97; on the imaginary nature of mathematical objects, see TIE § 72; see also the very important Matheron (1986); Yakira (1990). This reminds one of Leibniz's famous and ingenious description of mathematics as "the logic of imagination" (metaphysics being the "logic of reality").

[52] Spinoza does not say whether it is "a" circle or "the" circle. It is not clear if the circle he talks about is the abstract concept of the circle as such, a generic concept of a circle of a determinate kind, or a materially and concretely given circle. His discussion suffers thus from an irresolvable ambiguity. But since the aim of this example is to explicate the nature of the nature of the soul and body unity, one should not insist too much on this point.

4.4. Quid sit Idea, Quid sit Corporis   147

or possessed by an abstract or paradigmatic agent or knower, other in some essential way from the object. The circle or Peter are "ideationized," or idealized, intellected, conceived, or thought, in a way that seems to be the "normal" way in which such things are thought, conceived, perceived, or known – that is, by a thinker, conceiver, perceiver, or a knower – like, say, the way in which a geometrician understands what a circle is, or a physician knows what Peter's body is like.

The kind of knowledge a physician has of Peter's body is a third person's knowledge, and it is radically different from the knowledge, perception, or sensation Peter has of his own body. From the point of view of the theory of knowledge, that our body "exists as we sense it" (EIIp13cor) means, first, that in a very peculiar sense we can be said to have an adequate knowledge – in fact, the only adequate knowledge – of our body. It also means that the idea of Peter that Paul has can never become a fully adequate knowledge of Peter's body. In other terms, there is a clear priority – from the point of view of rational epistemology – of the first-person perspective on one's self and one's own body over the third-person, allegedly objective, or scientific (e.g., medical) point of view of the same "self" or body.[53]

The distinction between the first and third person views is harder to apply to the geometrician's knowledge of the circle; inversely, an idea-*ideatum* oneness is easier to conceive when it is said of the circle and its idea than when ascribed to the body and its soul. I shall not speculate about the possible meanings of Spinoza's reflections, either in the TIE or in the *Ethics*, about the relation between a circle and its idea. His very claim to an analogy between the circle's idea and the human soul, and between the circle and the body, however, is highly significant, if not for the philosophy of mathematics, then for the understanding of his theory of the soul. A quasi-universal presupposition of theories of mathematical truth is that concepts and objects belong to two separate realms. Truth belongs paradigmatically to the realm of thought; but since it depends on thought's relation with the realm of objects, it is necessarily said, implicitly or explicitly, from a point of view that is neither that of the objects nor that of their concepts. Such a point of view can be called meta-language, meta-theory, or the like, but it always posits, in however a minimal way, a space of rationality that transcends both the realm of objects and that of concepts. There are attempts – intuitionism, constructivism, and Husserl's phenomenology, among others – to avoid the positing of a transcendent point of view, but even in these cases the duality of thought and object is retained.

Even if Spinoza's immanentism makes sense as a theory of mathematical rationality, his attempt to overcome the duality of concept and object insofar as the circle and its idea are concerned is hard to make sense of. It is obvious – the repetition of the same examples with opposing lessons shows it – that Spinoza was thinking, maybe even thinking hard, on the question of the nature of the

[53] See Chapter 5, section 5.3.

relation between mathematical objects and their concepts (and I purposely do not use here "representation"), but it is not at all clear what he could have in mind. Things become more interesting, and more pertinent, however, when it is realized that what he was really after was a way to illustrate, through a paradigmatically rational case, his thesis about the unity of idea-*ideatum* as applicable to the unity of mind and body.

In his thoughts about the circle and its idea, Spinoza was trying to overcome ineffectively and even somewhat clumsily the need for a meta-theoretical stance. The latter is arguably analogous, in the context of a theory of man developed around the thesis that the soul is the idea of the body, to what is commonly referred to as the third-person point of view. When the question of self-knowledge is raised – and this is the issue we are discussing here – the third-person view purports to stand for a paradigmatic objectivity. The analogy Spinoza draws between the circle and its idea and the body and its idea-soul amounts to a rejection of the pretention of the third-person view to be the ultimately objective view of the body. It does not mean necessarily an outright rejection, but rather a relativization. The third-person view is derivative and secondary. Most importantly, the reason for the at least partial inadequacy of attributing to the third-person view on someone else's body full objectivity is that this conception of objectivity is based on an erroneous conception of ontological closure of thought and the exteriority of its object. It is the presupposed thought-object duality that is Spinoza's target in his claim about the oneness of the circle and its idea.

I quoted above at some length the two scholia in which there appear – separately this time – the examples of the circle and its idea and Peter and the idea that is the direct knowledge of Peter's body. The first example, that of the circle and its idea, comes after the alleged position of the mind-body or thought-extension parallelism in EIIp7, and after the immediate conclusion formulated in the corollary to this proposition. The corollary, as we have just seen, reproduces the improved formulation of the Cartesian axiom, as it appears in letter 40, as well as a reformulation of the second axiom mentioned by Spinoza in letter 40:

God's power of thinking is equal to his actual power of acting. That is, whatever follows formally from God's infinite nature follows objectively in God from his ideas in the same order and with the same connection.

The corollary thus combines two theses, conceived by Descartes as two separate, self-evident first truths.[54] Something of this remains in the Spinozistic text. Although they appear as corollaries, they are not demonstrated – again an unusual procedure. Apparently, they are supposed to be accepted as a direct consequence of EIIp7. The latter too is not properly demonstrated, but said to

---

[54] As we remarked above, the second axiom is not an exact reproduction of Descartes's axiom.

4.4. Quid sit Idea, Quid sit Corporis

follow directly from axiom 4 of EI, which, let us recall, states that the knowledge of the effect depends on and involves the knowledge of the cause. The corollary, however, does not just juxtapose the two axioms; it also presents them as fully equivalent formulations of the same thesis. It affirms that the equality of the power to think and the power to act amounts to saying that what follows formally from the nature of God follows from it objectively with the same order.

Proposition 9 adds another clarification to the parallelism doctrine:

> The idea of a singular thing which actually exists has God for a cause not insofar as he is infinite, but insofar as he is considered to be affected by another idea of a singular thing which actually exists; and this [idea] God is also the cause, insofar as he is affected by another third [NS: idea], and so on, to infinity.

This proposition seems also to communicate with letter 40: the order of ideas, or of the thoughts and conceptions, is also – contrary to what had seemed to be said in the letter – an order given to infinite regression. Just as in the case of the mechanical order of causes, the infinite series of causes and effects *is* the "infinite cause": God *quatenus rei singularis affectus*.

On the face of it, there is nothing in all this that goes beyond the general idea of parallelism: the same order of ideas and things, equality of power of thinking and acting, the necessity in which a thing "follows" (*sequitur*) another, the *causal* nature of "order," whether it applies to things or to their ideas. The question thus arises – why keep using the objective being vocabulary? Does it add anything not said already in other ways? For in this dense and difficult part of the *Ethics*, which stretches from the corollary to EIIp7 to the corollary of EIIp8, one finds the *Ethics*' most systematic use of the objective being vocabulary. This is true especially of EIIp8 and its corollary and scholium, where the enigmatic "ideas of singular things, or modes, that do not exist" are discussed (though from a different perspective to the one from which it is discussed in the scholium of EIIp17 just quoted).

I would add to what has already been said concerning EIIp8 and its corollary and scholium the following observation. The issue of non-existent objects has a long history, and like many ontological-semantic questions, it has been resuscitated in modern times. In its long history the objective/formal being distinction had been variously used and, generally put, as a theoretical means of making apparent the *sui generis* nature of thinking within a general theory of being and of the nature of rationality. EIIp8 and its corollary and scholium certainly echo this history. Spinoza, however, reverses the role of non-existent objects. From Plato to Leibniz, to Mainong and onward, the concept of non-existent legitimate objects of thought and of discourse was used to justify the ontological independence of thinking, meanings, intelligibility, or, in the terminology of the seventeenth century, ideas. It also meant that thought has a larger extension than existence. Spinoza, as I have suggested above, refuses to accord to thought greater scope than, or any surplus of being over, existence.

The being of *ideas* of non-existent modes, he says in EIIp8, is the same as that of the non-existent modes themselves:

> The ideas of singular things, or of modes, that do not exist must be comprehended in God's infinite idea in the same way as the formal essences of the singular things, or modes, are contained in God's attributes.
>
> From this it follows that so long as singular things do not exist, except insofar as they are comprehended in God's attributes, their objective being, [*esse objectivum*], or [*sive*] ideas, do not exist except insofar as God's infinite idea exists (respectively, EIIp8 and EIIp8cor).

The multifaceted discussion around the parallelism theme belongs to a long and convoluted work of conceptualization that had begun in the earlier writings and that the fuller and more explicit articulation it received in the *Ethics* did not necessarily put to a definitive end. More profitable than looking for an ever-elusive coherent doctrine, where all the different elements rest peacefully together, may be an attempt to understand the underlying workings of Spinoza's thought; specifically, trying to understand the philosophical reasons and motivations for keeping the old, and imminently obsolete, language of objective being. The use of the traditional terminology – its built-in ambiguity as well – serves Spinoza to keep, within the context of his parallelism, the sense of the *sui generis* nature of thought on the one hand and, more importantly, that of the body and soul's oneness, which, I believe, is the core of his mind-body theory and the real sense of his parallelism.

The history of the traditional distinction was needed in order to offer a reasoned appreciation of the systematic function it plays in Spinoza's philosophy. It can be summed up in the following three points, each of which constitutes a major breach with either the scholastic theory of objective being or Descartes's use of it and, actually, with both:

(1) It effects a full reduction of the objective being to ideas. This is most explicitly and conspicuously spelled out in the corollary to EIIp8, where we read "*esse objectivum, sive idea.*" The Latin *sive* usually designates for Spinoza the full equivalence or synonymy of terms. The formal being becomes the object of the idea.

(2) But the idea does not belong to an inner space of thought, and its object is not part of an external physical world. As is best seen in the case of the circle, the thought, idea, or objective being of a (mathematical, ideal) object, as it is in God (that is, not in the thought of an individual geometrician), is one and the same thing as the object.

(3) But this is not only the case concerning ideal objects (which are to some extent, and insofar as they are constructed, the work of the imagination) but also, indeed first of all and in particular, the case of the concrete body and soul: the soul is an idea (or objective being); it is the idea of the body, which is its object (or formal being, or *ideatum*).

All this prepares the way for the decisive gesture, the one included in propositions 11 and 13, where the oneness of soul and body receives its full sense:

body and soul are one not like two items belonging to two isomorphic series, but in the way in which an idea and its *ideatum*, or objective and formal being, are one.

4.5. The Concept of Immanent Intelligibility

If indeed the thematic framework of the first part of EII is the ontology of thinking; and if its doctrinal core is in propositions 11 and 13, then the history of the doctrine of objective being is relevant to the understanding of the full sense of Spinoza's mind-body theory. To the extent, then, that this traditional doctrine is essentially linked, especially in the series of shifts in the use and meaning occurring between the late scholastics and Descartes, to the investing of the notion of *idea* with representational import; to the extent, furthermore, that the notion of *representation* has become a crucial theoretical instrument for delineating an inner space of thought as the locale of knowledge, truth, and understanding; to the extent, finally, that the position of a *knowing subject* as the foundation of the theory of knowledge, and indeed as the condition of possibility for the construction of the *concepts* of knowledge, truth, intelligibility, thought, consciousness, and so on can be conceived, however schematically, as Descartes's main legacy, then Spinoza's use of the objective being terminology is indeed quite remarkable.

Spinoza rejoins the pre-Cartesian use of the objective/formal being terminology on one important point: both "realities" are supposed to qualify one and the same thing, and not to belong, as it would be for post-Cartesian philosophy, to two separate realms. The synonymy of "ideas" and "objective being," the thesis that the idea of a singular thing is its objective being, means that objective being is not taken here as a property of ideas, or as a mode of their being, some aspect of thought or, in a more modern jargon, of the mental as such. It underlines the sense of the full identity of *idea* and *ideata*, their being two realities of one thing. This has to be emphasized, since many interpreters of Spinoza read this matter as if objective being and formal being are either two perspectives on ideas or the subjective interiority of consciousness and the objective exteriority of things.[55] Spinoza does not use the traditional distinction in order to distinguish between the representational content of ideas and

---

[55] Thus Gueroult (1974), II, p. 64ff, for example, interprets it as a distinction between the *content* and *power* of thought. Another attempt, critical of Geuroult's but not, to my mind, better, is Harris (1993), pp. 42–45, who refers in fact only to one context in which Geuroult discussed it, namely to the question of what kind of relations we can say hold between the infinity of attributes: are there ideas of modes of other attributes than extension? Although the question is discussed often in the secondary literature, it belongs, I believe, to a rather speculative metaphysics with no real bearing on the questions that occupy us here. Spinoza may have not thought differently, although it is mentioned here and there in his writings. His answer (letter 66, probably the shortest) to Tschirnhaus who had raised this question, can be read as an almost impatient dismissal of this matter.

their other aspects, such as, say, their being acts, causes (of other ideas), items of one kind or another, or whatever. Similarly, he does not use it in order to distinguish between representations and the things represented.

The objective and formal beings are different aspects of one and the same thing – indeed of *things* in general. In Spinoza's terms, they are the mode's – all modes' – formal and objective being. The objective being/formal being distinction is thus applicable to the whole range of being, and is equivalent to the distinction between ideas and *ideata*, concepts and objects, and coextensive with the distinction between the attributes. But the similarity ends here between Spinoza's use of the old terminology and its pre-Cartesian, mediaeval, or late-scholastic uses. Unlike the latter – or his contemporaries and successors, for that matter – the most significant equation Spinoza effects here is that between all these more or less familiar and palatable distinctions-within-unities (concepts-objects, ideas-*ideata*, objective-formal being) on the one hand, and souls and bodies on the other. The soul is an idea, says proposition 11. It is the idea, adds proposition 13, of the body, which is the soul's *ideatum* or object. Here Spinoza becomes an iconoclastic Cartesian, dealing with the union of mind-objective being and body-formal being in the framework of the Cartesian revolution, but turning it upside down with the aid of the scholastic use of the distinction between objective and formal being.

Making sense of the series of equivalent, indeed quasi-synonymous, distinctions/unities just enumerated, if taken seriously, requires careful hermeneutical work, for nothing in it fits most mind-body philosophical theories or scientific constructions. It also does not correspond to linguistic habits or to commonsense intuitions. The previous discussion, which lays the foundation for a theory of knowledge, amounts to a suspension – which is not the same as an eliminative reduction – of the idea of a *knower* or a thinking and judging agent. Cartesian subjectivity too is radically problematized. The way Spinoza develops his argument, notably by constructing a concept of individuality only *after* demonstrating that the soul is an idea and that it is the idea of the body, illustrates the radical priority he accords, ontologically and conceptually, to the idea-*ideatum*, objective-formal being, or mind-body relation over the being or concept of a knowing and judging subject. This means that the idea-*ideatum* has to be thought independently of any presupposition, in particular, without presupposing a thinking agent.

If suspending, or even relativizing, the idea of a *human* knowing subject is, after Descartes, in itself a radical step, Spinoza goes yet farther and suspends, or actually reverses completely the sense of, the idea of a *divine* knower and of divine intellect. The theological ramifications of such a move aside, its philosophical significance is in itself quite far-reaching. If such suspension is consistently maintained – and I presume that this was what Spinoza was trying to do – the pure idea-*ideatum*, which is nothing other than the *concept-object* or concept-content relation, the apophantic structure, seems actually to be laid down as the foundation on which one is expected to make sense of dualities

4.5. The Concept of Immanent Intelligibility

such as "thought" and "world," "inner" and "external," "representation" and represented object, and, most bizarrely, mind and body. If I am right in my basic reading of Spinoza, then his mind-body theory should be understood, in the first instance, as an attempt to concretize the formal, metaphysical thought-extension monism by showing it to be an apophantic or "semantic" unity. The mind-body unity is just like the unity of the objective being and formal being of a thing, which is the unity of what the being of a thing is and its being thought or understood. *Esse*, for Spinoza, is not *percipi*, and being is not reducible to being-thought; but being is also not reducible to being thinkable or perceptible, as it would be in Leibniz's more sophisticated Platonism. It is also not reducible to an extra-ideational "matter." The soul is an idea (EIIp11); it is the idea, or objective being, of the body (EIIp13); the body is the soul's object, or its formal being. They constitute a unity in the way in which a thing is one with what it is insofar as it thinkable or conceptualizable. The authentic being of a thing – of any and every thing – contains in itself, as it were, its idea, a conceptual content or intelligibility. It is essentially that by which it is a content, thinkable or conceptualizable. Most remarkably, the latter is the foundation of its soul (when the thing is a human being). As all this, counterintuitive as it certainly is, might seem to the vigilant reader as not much more than confusing the ontological, logical (or conceptual), and epistemological, maybe I should quote here once again Spinoza: "Here, no doubt, the readers will be embarrassed and think of many things which will cause them to hesitate. For this reason I ask them to continue on with slow steps, and to make no judgment on these matters until they have read them all" (EIIp11; Curley's translation, altered). I believe from such a philosophical patience may emerge, in the end, the view of a philosophically interesting attempt, although perhaps only partially carried out, to seriously think through a possible concrete and effective meaning of non-theological monism.

The conclusion of this unusual development is, first, that the human body exists as "we sense it" (EIIp13cor); and, second, that from all this "we understand not only that the human mind is united to the body, but also *what* [quid] should be understood by the union of mind and body" (EIIp13s). The claim that the soul is the idea of the body – especially when *mens* is translated as "mind" – may seem to be a more-or-less accessible metaphor. In fact, often this claim is not taken as much more than a metaphor, and the dualistic otherness of mind and body, or consciousness and brain, is retained in one way or another. That we sense our body and that this sensation has a special status – psychological, perceptual, cognitive in some vague sense, neurological, or phenomenological – is not difficult to conceive and is easily considered to be the meaning of Spinoza's assertion that the soul is the idea of the body. That we sense, think, or know the body as it actually exists; that this sensation or knowledge of the body is truthful or adequate, and even the foundation of rational knowledge and science in general, may become, once the strictly metaphorical reading is overcome, acceptable as both a sound interpretation of

Spinoza and a possible philosophical stance. That this is what is meant by the general ontological principle of the union of soul and body or of the thought-extension monism would thus hopefully not look altogether absurd as well.

But Spinoza goes farther. The soul's sensing, thinking, or knowing of the body is also God's sensing, thinking, or knowing of this particular body. It is the knowing, sensing, or thinking of the body that is in nature just as the body itself is in nature. If this is so, isn't the language of God simply redundant? I do retain, however, this language because Spinoza, of course, does it, but in particular because it has certain theoretical dividends that, however, become apparent only at the end. Thus Peter's soul-idea of his body is no mere duplicate of God's knowledge of Peter's body, nor is God's idea of Peter's body the archetype of Peter's soul. They are the very same thing, just as the morning star and the evening star are one thing. Only that in this case, not only the reference is the same, the "sense," in fact, is the same as well. There is no different content to Peter and to his idea-soul. As such, they contain exactly the same amount of epistemic value or of rationality. This, of course, has many paradoxical consequences, of which the most difficult to accept is that the soul's sensing of the body is the absolute and perfectly valid knowledge of the body, the only adequate idea of it, and also the fount of all forms of rationality and of knowledge in general. Otherwise, there would have been no justification to call the human mind "God's idea of the body."

The most remarkable element of this bizarre mind-body theory is the counterintuitive thesis that the oneness of the idea-*ideatum* is the first and presupposition-free principle of the ontology of man, of human thinking, and of an anthropological ethics. There is, of course, EI, but what gives meaning to the abstract notion of the unity of the attributes is the idea-*ideatum* or objective/formal being unity. Unlikely as it may seem, this doctrine is also the key to resolving at least some of the riddles of Spinoza's philosophy. One major consequence of the thesis of idea-*ideatum* oneness is that the theory of meaning, the theory of truth, and the theory of knowledge have all to free themselves of the fundamental dualism of concept and object, consciousness and content, representation and represented, and the like. The idea-*ideatum* primordial unity is, moreover, and in light of propositions 11 and 13 of EII, the real, metaphysical meaning of what is experienced as the union of soul and body.

Idea and *ideatum* are two modes of being of one entity. Thought and its content, a thing and what it is, and existence and quiddity are among the traditional ways to make sense of this distinction within oneness. What has probably never been attempted, however, is to apply it to the *sensation* or experience of the body and of its affections and the body itself. But Spinoza attempted precisely this: "objective being" means the same as "idea"; the soul is the idea of the body; as such, it is the sensing of the body and of its affections; this sensing is actually the knowledge of the body, for since the human soul is, *ipso facto*, God's idea of the body, it would be difficult to say that God just "senses" the body. All this boils down to the following bold thesis: the

4.5. The Concept of Immanent Intelligibility

idea-objective being-soul is united with the body in the way an idea is united with its object, which means that the body is united with its mind in the same sense in which a thing is united with its quiddity. Another way to put it is to say that the soul is something like the inherent and original *sub specie aeternitatis* intelligibility of the body. A human being is an entity consisting of a body and its proper intelligibility.

This seems to be the real import of Spinoza's soul and body theory. The unity – and not just "union" – of body and soul assimilated to a semantic idea-*ideatum* unity; the radical "bracketing" of the *cogito* implied by the thesis about the primordiality of the idea-*ideatum* unity and by the doctrine of the numerical identity of the human idea-soul of the body and God's idea of this same body; the objective being as the intelligibility of the body. Bizarre as they may look, the first thirteen propositions of EII, if read attentively, lead to these conclusions almost "as if by the hand."

4.5.a. The Body

From the first thirteen propositions of the second part of the *Ethics* emerges an urgent theoretical need. In order to be able to proceed to anthropology, or to the theory of man, which is what will occupy Spinoza in the rest of the *Ethics*, a theory of the body has to be offered. The little physics purports to fulfill this task. From the previous discussion, says Spinoza in the scholium after EIIp13, one could learn not only *that* the human soul is united with its body, but also *what* this unity means; yet,

> no one will be able to understand it adequately, or [*sive*] distinctly, unless he first knows the nature of our body. For the things we have shown so far are completely general and do not pertain more to man than to other individuals, all of which, though in different degrees, are nevertheless animate. For of each thing there is necessarily an idea in God, of which God is the cause in the same way he is the cause of the human body.

The body will be from now on omnipresent in the *Ethics*, sometimes more explicitly, sometimes less. The general tenet of the theory of the body is a rather simplistic mechanistic, corpuscularian, or physicalist conception of corporeality.[56] But the main theoretical purpose of the little physics is to formulate a rational concept of corporeal individuality. A body is the object of the soul, the only *ideatum* of a unique idea. It is the formal being of the one entity that is a "thing" and whose objective being is its soul. Not very illuminating as a physical theory, it includes all the same a few philosophically interesting and not at all trivial ideas. Two of them need to be mentioned here. Based on the idea that the "simplest bodies" are distinguishable not by their *materiality* but "by

---

[56] The notion of *corpora simplicissima* is a kind of surrogate, allegedly permissible within antiatomistic metaphysics (like Spinoza's), of a practical kind of atomism. The little physics echoes the correspondence with Boyle, in which Spinoza proposes a radical mechanistic interpretation of physical reality.

motion and rest, speed and slowness" (second axiom after EIIp13), the doctrine of bodily individuality culminates in a kind of structuralism. The material or corporeal *principium individuationis*, which define the distinctness of composite bodies, are determinate proportions of motion and rest; and as long as these proportions remain more or less stable, the bodies in question retain their distinctness. The proportion of motion and rest can be interpreted as complexity and organization, or structure and form, and its (relative and temporary) stability as the stability of the individual identity of the living organism and, in particular, of the human body.

Secondly, and more interestingly, the compositeness and stability of bodies in general, and of living bodies in particular, is not a metaphysically original fact but the natural outcome of the play of mechanical causes. According to the first definition after EIIp13, composite individuality emerges "when a number of bodies, whether of the same or different size, are so constrained by other bodies that they lie upon one another" or when different bodies move together in one movement. An individual body exists – as a definite entity – as a result of the ways in which the environing bodies cause a temporary stability of "proportion of motion and rest" holding among a few simpler bodies moving together for a while. This acquired stability is nevertheless real and the origin of real individuality. Simpler individual bodies contrive to create ever more complex ones, so that the whole material universe can be considered an individual as well. It is quite clear that what Spinoza had in mind in elaborating this doctrine is the kind of organization that living organisms manifest. What remains obscure is the relation between the doctrine of "physiological" stability as individuality and the metaphysical principle of *conatus*. Introduced in EIIIp6 and 7, the *conatus* is said to be the very essence, or actual being, of all things, but it is not entirely clear, to say the least, how an individuality resulting from the action of the environing bodies becomes an inner effort of self-preservation.

Corporeal individuality is conceived as a *resultant*, and this can be generalized into a thesis about individuality as such. The important point is that the notions of structure and relative stability resulting from the play of natural causes implicitly permits Spinoza to overcome reductionism. The latter often seems to be the consequence of mechanistic explanations such as Spinoza's, especially when teleological or finalistic considerations are rejected in the way he rejected them. Although, as it has been put, Spinoza's is "the most radical attempt to philosophize without *cogito*," it would be wrong to think of Spinozism as a radical attempt to philosophize without an effective concept of individuality and, more significantly, of subjectivity. The principle that stands behind this non-reductionist theory of individuality and, by implication, of subjectivity as well is that a *resultant* is not necessarily or fully reducible to the causes that generate it. What is remarkable about Spinoza's theory, and what makes it not only non-trivial but also original, is that unlike other theories that do not reduce the resultant to its causes – Aristotle and Hegel come immediately

4.5. The Concept of Immanent Intelligibility

to mind, but so is Leibniz's theory of the organism and other similar theories – is that Spinoza tries to make sense of it within a radically non-teleological ontology. Whether such a theory can work can be judged only in light of EV.

The image of a stability of proportion of movement and rest is a more or less symbolic justification for holding a positive concept of real corporeal individuality. Although the text does not say it in full explicitness, the logic of Spinoza's argumentation and EIIp15 in an almost straightforward way[57] suggest that the *idea* of this resulting stability, the "soul," is real in the same manner. The stable proportion of motion and rest apparently stands for that very *idea* that is the foundation of the soul and of which the body is the object. This is an obscure matter that Spinoza never clarified fully, but the order of reasons leading from propositions 11–13 to the little physics seems to suggest some essential link between the soul that is the sensing of the affections of the body, the idea of which the body is the object, and the "nature" of the body as the little physics explains it. Not only the "completely general" things shown in propositions 11 and 13, but also the less general developments that follow the little physics seem to imply a strong connection between the notions of a "stable proportion of motion and rest" and "soul." Propositions 14 and 15 are the foundation of the theory of knowledge and of truth that occupies the rest of EII. EIIp14 points to the connection between the soul's capacity to conceive and the complexity of the body; and EIIp15 states that "the idea that constitutes the *esse formale* of the human soul is not simple, but composed of great many ideas." All this suggests a direct link between the notion of corporeal complexity and structure, as expounded in the group of definitions, axioms, and lemmas after EIIp13 and that of a "soul."

In his attempt to make Spinoza's doctrine about the link between the soul and the complex body more accessible, Gueroult makes two suggestions that are in fact incompatible. According to the first, the soul-idea-ratio of motion and rest should be interpreted as an Aristotelian-like *form* of the body.[58] According to the second, Spinoza's little physics is *une physique pendulaire*, conceived on the model of Huygens' theory of the pendulum expounded in his major work, *Horologium Oscillatorium* (especially the fourth part, which discusses the center of oscillation).[59] The soul-idea-ratio would be, in this case, not the *form* of the body but the *equation* of its mode of motion (oscillation). But a form and an equation, despite some similarities, are two different things. First of all, because where there is no teleology, not much is left of Aristotelianism; and neither Spinoza's theory of man nor Huygens' theory of the pendulum admit teleology. A structure, even if it is conceived architectonically, does not have the kind of efficacy final causes are supposed to have. Secondly, and more

---

[57] "The idea that constitutes the formal being of the human mind is not simple, but composed of a great many ideas."
[58] Gueroult, op. cit., pp. 176–177.
[59] Ibid., pp. 170–185; see also Parrochia (1985), pp. 79–83.

importantly, Spinoza's conception of extension and of the machine of the body is very different from the Aristotelian concept of matter as the uninformed or as pure potentiality.

Body and soul are one as a circle and its idea or a pendulum and its equation are one. The notion of "circle" does not make sense without an idea of the circle, and the same holds for the pendulum. But if body and soul are like a circle and its idea, then, and notwithstanding the radical irreducibility of thought to extension and vice versa, there must be a reciprocal semantic, or conceptual, dependency of the two. This can be said to be just another way of affirming their oneness: the concept of an *idea* does not make sense without the concept of its *ideatum* just as the concept of *objective being* cannot be thought without the immediate positing of a *formal being*, and just as the act of *defining* is unintelligible without the concept of a *definiendum*. Counterintuitive as this may be, what Spinoza seems to be saying is that in just the same way, the *body* cannot be thought without *soul* and vice versa. Put in yet another way, this means that body cannot be thought without being thought, and this thought, in its original and fully adequate sense, is its idea-soul. Similarly, the concept of "soul" immediately involves that of (its) body. Consequently, there is no excess of possibility or of thought over (bodily) existence;[60] but there is also no excess of being over its immanent intelligibility. The *existence* or *being* of a thing, its being the *ideatum* of a certain idea, does not surpass – say, in the Heideggerian sense – its immanent intelligibility. A thing – a human being, for example – is a coextensiveness, if one may say so, of existence as a body with the latter's proper intelligibility, or soul.

4.5.b. Idea Corporis: *What Does It Sense Like to Be a Body?*

Even if one admits that a proportion of motion and rest can be considered as a *principium individuationis* of a body, it is still quite unclear how it can also be said to be a *soul*. An equation, or mathematical description of physical reality, could stand as a useful metaphor for the intellective act that Spinoza's use of the notion of *objective reality* vaguely conveys. Just as the doctrine of the genetic definition served Spinoza as a means of giving positive and effective content to the rational nature of geometric objects, so the notion of an equation can anchor in a tangible image the abstract idea of a complex body's objective being or idea. It can even symbolize God's idea of the body in question. These are different perspectives on one and the same thing: the primary and indigenous intelligibility of all things. Although he did not use this language, Spinoza tacitly borrowed the notion of *intelligibility* from the realm of ideal objects such as circles – its original field of application – and transposed it to a discourse on the human body. If this is so, a notion like the "idea of the body" can be seen as something like the body's *immanent intelligibility*

---

[60] That there is such a surplus would be the core of Leibniz's opposition to Spinoza.

4.5. The Concept of Immanent Intelligibility

conceived, paradoxically, on the model of the way in which the idea of a circle is its original intelligibility as an object.

But Spinoza wanted more. He used the notion of a body's idea or objective being also as a metaphoric representation of the *soul* in a sense that can be described as phenomenological and even psychological. Spinoza's radical breach with the Cartesian legacy on the one hand and with the Jewish and non-Jewish mediaeval philosophical traditions on the other, or his radical iconoclastic attitude in general, becomes apparent only when to the more easily palatable series of overlapping and supposedly synonymous equivalences and unities – idea-*ideatum*, objective/formal being, existence-intelligibility, extension-thought – one more, in the last analysis the most important one, is added: soul-body.

This, however, is where the beginning of EII is leading: soul and body are one just as idea and *ideatum* are one; this oneness is primordial; both its concept and being are prior to, and independent of, the positing of a subject, an agent, or a substrate of thinking. As its objective being, an idea of a body is its native intelligibility. From this primordial reality emerges what we conceive – but also experience – as the thought, sensing, or feeling of a certain body, namely the soul. This is a deeply counterintuitive and highly implausible vision of what mind and body are. Of the many questions it raises, not all are easily, if at all, answerable. All the same, a philosophical orientation that does make sense emerges here. Anticipating the final moment of his philosophical project, which is also where the ultimate sense and value of his doctrine of the unity of body and soul is revealed, Spinoza adds the following remark to the scholium to EIIp13: we cannot deny

that ideas differ among themselves, as the objects themselves do, and that one is more excellent than the other,[61] and contains more reality, just as the object of the one is more excellent that the other and contains more reality.

But, extraordinary as it might seem, the source of valuation is the body. For in order to determine, continues the scholium,

what is the difference between the human mind and the others, *and how it surpasses them* [in excellence or in value], it is necessary for us, as we have said, to know the nature of its object, that is of the human body (italics added).

No wonder that Spinoza adds immediately after this affirmation that he "cannot explain this here, nor is it necessary for the things I wish to demonstrate." The real point of the doctrine that the soul is the idea of the body is the ethical theory Spinoza apparently believes he can found on it. I turn to this theory in the last two chapters of this study, but there is still room here for one last attempt to shed some more light on this obscure matter.

---

[61] The Latin reads *unamque alia praestantiorem esse*, which is difficult to translate. Less specific than *excellence*, it does convey, however, a vague but undeniable sense of valuation.

4.6. Intelligibility and Episteme

In the corollary to EIIp13, Spinoza formulates what he presents as a conclusion of the preceding discussion: "man consists of a mind and a body, and the human body exists as we sense [*sentimus*] of it." Proposition 24 of EII is the opening of a group of propositions where the nature and causes of the fundamental inadequacy of the knowledge of the proper body as well as of the "external bodies" are expounded. Proposition 24 affirms, in what seems to contradict the corollary to proposition 13, that "the human mind does not involve adequate knowledge [or cognition] of the parts composing the human body." Again without an explicit explanation, an essential distinction is introduced, expressed by the use of *sentimus* in the corollary and *cognitionem* in proposition 24.

Although I referred above to the thesis that the soul is the idea of the body as a claim of a gnoseological nature, it should be by now clear that Spinoza's doctrine of the soul-body unity does not consist in what is commonly conceivable as "knowledge." Once the parallelism exegetical scheme is given up, Spinoza's mind-body union cannot be interpreted anymore as *fundamentally* a kind of city-map union (to use once again Leibniz's famous metaphor), and the soul cannot be said to relate to its body by "expressing" it, by being isomorphic to it, by recording its states, by being *about* it, or anything of the sort. The soul, in other words, is not a representation of the body. When Spinoza says that we sense the body as it actually exists, he apparently means something rather different from what is usually meant when one says that "the soul knows the body." This more accessible sense of the epistemic nature of the mind-body union will be elaborated after the little physics and the axis around which it revolves is proposition 24 and 25. Notwithstanding the ambiguity of *sentire*, what Spinoza had in mind when he affirmed that body *exists* as we sense it is most probably something also very different from what is usually understood in words such as "sentiment," "sensation," "feeling," "perception," or the like.

Epistemologically speaking, without a pre-posited subject, consciousness, or mind, there can be no veil of ideas, barrier of perceptions, or subjectivity of feelings between the idea-soul and the body. The ultimate meaning of what Spinoza conceives to be the oneness of soul-body is not that soul *knows* the body. It is the foundation of knowledge, but there are also deep differences between the foundation and what it founds. There is knowledge, in the exact sense of the word and strictly speaking, when Peter's soul knows Paul's body, or, more generally, when Peter knows Paul. In its original sense, Peter's "sensing" of his own body is something else: this sensing is nothing else than "the idea of Peter which constitutes the essence of Peter mind," and it directly explains [*explicat*] the essence of Peter's body.

Pain can serve as a good illustration of the differences in question. Spinoza hardly mentions pain or pleasure in their immediate and straightforward sense of physical pain and pleasure. He explains what these terms mean in the

4.6. Intelligibility and Episteme

scholium to EIIIp11 and refers to them in the *Affetuum definitiones* he added at the end of EIII. "Pain" is the name of the affect of *tristitia* – the soul passage from greater to smaller perfection – when it applies to soul and body alike. The feeling of pain thus seems to be a simplest case to account for in terms of Spinoza's alleged parallelism. A diminution in the force of existence and amount of being is registered in the body in one or another physiological way, and in the soul in one or another form of awareness (it may be subconscious, but this is besides the point) or by some so-called mental items.

A brief comparison with Descartes on one hand and Leibniz on the other will show that things are not that simple. For Descartes the eye does not see (see discussion later in the book) and the body does not feel; the soul does. In other words, when there is pain, the body does not *know* that there is something wrong with it, and it is the soul that interprets the bodily signs and informs itself that its body is aching. The body is a blind, deaf, and unfeeling machine, and this is why, for one thing, the soulless animals cannot be said to feel pain, at least in the sense that essentially involves some knowledge. Although this has turned Descartes into a disliked symbolic figure in animal-protection circles, philosophically speaking, his doctrine of the body-machine is less absurd and less outrageous than it might look, for the alternatives are not theoretically always better. Saying, as Spinoza does, that the soul senses the body as it actually exists is not an altogether easier way to grasp what pain is all about, for if the soul is one with the body in the way the idea of the circle is one with the circle and the feeling of pain is directly a mode of being of the body in its actual existence, one has to concede that the mental somehow belongs to the body and that it is not just a representation of it. If the mental is not an epiphenomenon, Spinoza's explanation of pain is as strange as Descartes' explanation is.

For Leibniz, sensing and feeling are "confused ideas." Feeling is not a concept, but underneath the surface there is always a concept, and the "truth" of the feeling, as it were, is in the concept. Likewise the perception of a color is a confused idea of what is originally a fully clear and distinct concept describing a mode of motion. Spinoza has a similar vision of the relation of concepts and sense perceptions, feelings, and sensations: since "an affect is an idea of an affection of the body," it necessarily "involves some clear and distinct concept" (EVp4cor). This is the reason why "there is no affect of which we cannot form some clear and distinct concept" (ibid.) and also the source of the healing power of reason. Moreover, this is the only means of enabling holding to the thesis of the "numerical identity" of the soul and God's idea of the body. God certainly has an idea of the pain in the aching body; but there is no sense in attributing to God the pain itself. Only if the "truth" of the pain is a concept lying at its bottom – the affect involves a concept – can one avoid the trap of the God-world dualism.

Leibniz overcame the difficulty by insisting that bodies were well-founded phenomena. Spinoza may have accepted such a thesis insofar as the knowledge of the external world was concerned, but certainly not when the nature of the proper body was at stake. He also opposed idealism, such as the idealism Leibniz advocated or otherwise. The underlying, or involved, concept was, for him, a mode of being – the objective being – of the body itself. The pain is thus the pain that the body itself feels, not an exterior instance called "soul" or "mind." The pain may not be the adequate idea of the body, but it is not very far from it. An idea of pain, as Spinoza's puts it, "involves" the adequate idea of the body; the latter, and insofar as it is adequate, can be said to be one with God's idea of the body; but even as God's idea, it is still a mode of being of the body.

The soul, as the idea of the body, is not *about* the body. The soul is the body's sensing – or thinking – itself. It is the body itself insofar as it is thinkable. This sensing of the body is apparently something other than the impressions the body marks on the soul, or the sensations or feelings it imprints in it. The conscious (or unconscious, for that matter) "sense data" are not representations of what occurs in the body outside the soul, and an emotion is not an expression of the ways the brain maps the states of the organism. Because soul and body constitute a primordial unity, there is no closure of thought within a space of interiority; similarly, the body does not belong to a space of exteriority – this exteriority is necessarily conceivable only in relation to the supposed interiority of the soul. This also means that the body is no "stranger" to the soul, and that the soul does not conceive its body from without. Just as an idea is to its *ideatum*, so the soul is to its body. There is no clear answer in the *Ethics* to the question of the emergence of what Leibniz would call "apperception" or of consciousness, but if we use this terminology, the soul-idea can be thought of as an original auto-transparency of the body to itself. This transparency is a concept rather than knowledge.

That everything has an idea may seem to be not much more than reiterating the famous object-idea parallelism. But since the thing-idea relation is primordial; since, that is, the idea-*ideatum* relation is conceived without presupposing a thinking agent or a thinker who "has" these ideas, without a previously posited subject of thought, a substrate in the form of an ego or personal consciousness, what the parallelism amounts to is that everything has an objective "concept" or an intelligible description (but no "describer") or that everything is thinkable or, rather, inherently intelligible. Thought and intelligibility, which I take to be more or less synonymous, are coextensive with existence in general and are inseparable from it. The concept of "thing" is synonymous with "*ideatum*," which means that it essentially involves the concept of "idea." Thing, body, object, and so on cannot be thought or imagined as existing without their ideas. Other than being itself, other than "substance," this general and, indeed, primordial coextensiveness or equivalence of existence and intelligibility nothing is presupposed. Spinoza inverted the direction of conditionality: an agent of thought, a subject, is posterior to the concept of being and of thought as an essential and irreducible possibility of being; the concept of an ego presupposes

4.6. Intelligibility and Episteme

that of substance and of its attributes. The necessity of the idea-*ideatum* identity, the necessity of the existence of an infinite substance with an infinity of attributes, results in the following conclusion: an unthinkable existent world is a contradiction in terms. We can, of course, envisage a world without some thinking thing to think and know it; but if there is a world, it has an idea or concept. Since the world exists necessarily, its idea, concept, or thought exists necessarily as well.

I suggested interpreting Spinoza's doctrine of the soul and body's oneness with the aid of the notion of "inner intelligibility." What Spinoza could have meant by saying that the soul is the idea of the body is, I believe, more or less this: the soul is the body's immanent concept, which is the sense of what and how it actually is. The objective being doctrine in its Spinozistic version means that the way in which a soul "senses" its body is the "meaning" of the body. The body's thought, or the objective being of the formal being that is the body, is not a predicate of the body, nor is the body its substrate. The body's thought is the idea, or concept, or soul, of the body; it is all this with the full immediacy in which a thing is what it is: thinking the body, or sensing it, is a mode of being of the body. The soul is what it feels like to be a body. Better still, it is what it thinks like to be a body; or, in fact, the soul is what it means to be a body.

PART III

5

Bodies and Ideas

A Few General Remarks

5.1. The "External" World

In the scholium after EIIp13, and after emphasizing that the preceding discussion had shown not only *that* the human mind is united with its body, but also *what* this union means, Spinoza adds that "the things we have shown so far are completely general and do not pertain more to man than to other individuals, all of which, though in different degrees, are nevertheless animate." It is not altogether rare that these words are understood as expressing some kind of animism. If animism is a belief about everything being "alive," or having a "soul" or "spirit" in a sense of "personality," "unconscious feeling," "consciousness," "subjectivity," or anything of this kind, then Spinoza was no animist. In fact, it is precisely the opposite, as we can learn from the explication that follows immediately: "For each thing there is necessarily an idea in God, of which God is the cause in the same way as he is of the idea of the human body." In light of propositions 11–13, the lesson of this affirmation seems to be clear enough: a unity of soul and body is indeed a general ontological principle, but its ultimate meaning is that everything has an *idea*, a concept, or even, if one insists, a name that, however, presupposes no name-giver.

With proposition 14 of EII, a new thematic field is opened: the theory of man. Its first part, which occupies the rest of EII, is a theory of knowledge and truth. Knowledge is a topic with a few specific traits. Although Spinoza does not distinguish in a systematic and explicit way between a noetic and an epistemological meaning of the concept of "idea," it is quite clear that with EIIp14 a new theoretical space is opened. Unlike the primordial status of thinking and of intelligibility, "knowing" presupposes a knower. An idea of a body is simply what it is, but in knowledge there is a less and a more, it is subject to becoming and to corruption, and it invites a distinction between the known and the unknown, between ignorance and acquired knowledge, between the explicitly known and the tacitly assumed, between conscious and subconscious. All these aspects of human knowledge now find their legitimate field of theoretic reflection. In fact, it is the thematic of subjectivity that is now introduced. A few linguistic conventions that had to be explained away or, as it were, deconstructed, in the general and special ontologies of the first part and the beginning of the second part of the *Ethics* are now readmitted into philosophical discourse.

Such admittance of previously "deconstructed" terminology into the legitimate theoretic discourse is, first, mediated by the doctrine of the individuality of the body; it is, second, justified on the grounds of a sound derivation from what has been laid down as "foundations," namely the general and particular ontologies of EI and EIIp11–13. In a sense, the anthropological theory of Spinoza is not unlike Leibniz's doctrine of the *phenomena bene fondata*. What it means, in both cases, is double faced: a *resultant* or a *derivative* is not necessarily *reducible* in the sense of not having a reality of its own or of not justifying a specific theoretic discourse. The fact that there are "deeper" ontological and conceptual layers from which it draws its being and meaning does not mean that it has to be collapsed into it or expunged or that it does not enjoy a positive ontological status and conceptual legitimacy. But, second, the deeper meaning remains operative even in the secondary or derivative discourse. It means, in our case, that although knowledge presupposes a knower, the latter is not conceptually and ontologically primordial. In Spinoza's terminology, it is not a substance. But it is also not a philosophical illusion, pure invention, or gratuitous construction, ideologically motivated or whatever.

The theory of man begins thus with a theory of knowledge. In light of the importance given to the theory of the affects in parts III and IV of the *Ethics* and, in particular, to the overcoming the harmfulness of the affects as the way to wisdom and freedom, the place given to the theory of knowledge is highly significant: man is a thinking and knowing being, and the theory of the affects and of the pathology of human life, as well as that of wisdom and of liberation, is based on the theory of the adequate idea and of true knowledge.

The first "deconstructed" notion to make its reappearance in the theory of knowledge is that of "externality"; it remains, however, to some extent metaphorical even when used legitimately. It also implies the symmetrical metaphor of an "interior" space of knowledge. The doctrine of the soul as the idea of the body signifies, as suggested above, a double rejection of the conception of the "soul" as a space closed in itself and of the body as pure "exteriority," implied by the Cartesian dualism as well as by a Leibnizian-like parallelism. Since the body is part of the world in an immediate way, the theoretical pertinence of considering the world, or other bodies, as "external" is radically relativized as well. The metaphor of the externality of the world becomes nevertheless useful with respect to the oneness and individuality of the body and its idea, which is its soul: it expresses the distinctiveness or discernibility of the (my, the body that is philosophically first to be talked about) individual body/soul or *idea/ideatum* vis-à-vis the surrounding things.

5.1. The "External" World

The use of this double metaphor of the inner mind and external bodies also facilitates a more habitual use of a number of concepts and a number of traditional questions such as, notably, the question of "realism" versus "anti-realism." In Spinoza's case, however, this is not so much a question about whether, or how, perceptions, notions, concepts, propositions, or theories that we have, acquire, or formulate refer or correspond to the world and to its objects; it is rather a question about how the external-interior relation can be conceptualized at all. What positive meaning can be given to the seemingly non-problematic saying that our ideas, or knowledge, "correspond" to real objects or are "about" them.

Presupposing the real individuality of man (relative, certainly, but real all the same), one can now assert that man's being in the world is based on the material homogeneity of the body with other bodies. The mind or soul being the "idea of the body," its "being in the world" is a bodily mediation: the soul is first of all an idea of the body, and the many ideas it is comprised of are the ideas of the affections of the body caused by its communication with other bodies. The first step of Spinoza's gnoseology is thus the analysis of the conditions of possibility of, or the real meaning that should be given to, what is referred to as knowledge of "external bodies." This knowledge is based on – but not exhausted by – what can be called "perception." The latter, the immediate "being in the world," although not fully "adequate," is nevertheless the origin of its rational knowledge. Its concept is formulated in EIIp16 and its corollaries:

EIIp16: Idea cujuscunque modi, quo Corpus humanum à corporibus externis afficitur, involvere debet naturam Corporis humani, & simul naturam corporis externi.

Cor. 1: Hinc sequitur primo Mentem humanam plurimorum corpurum naturam una cum sui corporis natura pericipere.

Cor. 2: Sequitur secundo quod idae, quas corporum externorum habemus, magis nostri corporis constitutionem, quàm corporum externorum naturam indicat; quod in Appendice partis prime multis exemplis explicui.[1]

There is no pure and direct perception, then, of "external" bodies. It is always, and by definition, mediated by what the perceiving body is. In fact, perception and knowledge are always mostly self-knowledge. It is noteworthy that Spinoza's conception of the knowledge of the external world is not strictly "realist"; he is, however, also neither a skeptic nor an idealist. The ideas that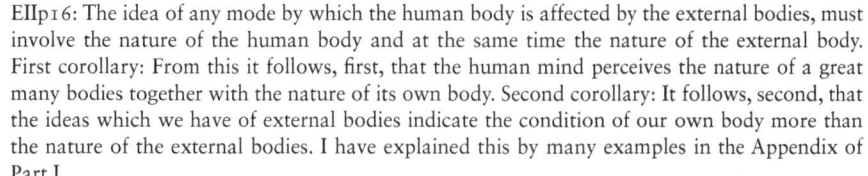

---

[1] EIIp16: The idea of any mode by which the human body is affected by the external bodies, must involve the nature of the human body and at the same time the nature of the external body. First corollary: From this it follows, first, that the human mind perceives the nature of a great many bodies together with the nature of its own body. Second corollary: It follows, second, that the ideas which we have of external bodies indicate the condition of our own body more than the nature of the external bodies. I have explained this by many examples in the Appendix of Part I.

we have of external bodies, says the second corollary just quoted, indicate[2] (or show or express) the nature of our body more than that of the external body that affects our body; by implication, they also indicate, if for a lesser extent, the nature of the external body.

Ideas are the same as knowledge. We know our body (by EIIp13), but we also apparently know other bodies. The soul is the idea of the body, but how can it be also the idea of other bodies? Spinoza's answer has two main parts: first, bodies are part of the world. They are acted upon by other bodies and act on them in turn. The result of this reciprocal action is naturally registered in the bodies that participate in such encounters; Spinoza calls this result *affect*. As any other body or material occurrence, this affect is also "ideated" and, hence, part of the idea of the body or its soul. Second, and more important, the concept of "causal relation" presupposes some commonality. There must be some property shared by things that can be causes and those affected by them. There are common properties and, *ipso facto*, common notions (EIIp37–40). This is the condition of there being a causal relation at all, and also of the possibility of knowledge, by the affected body, of the affecting body.

That the body mediates the perception of the external world presupposes a systematic connection between the two aspects of the knowledge the soul has – that of its own body and that of the external ones. The theoretical mechanism that permits formulating a coherent conception of such mediation again manifests itself by the frequent use of the term *involvere*. The ideas of other bodies are "involved" – implied or presupposed – in the complex idea-soul of the affected body, just as the result of a causal interaction between two bodies depends on – or "involves" – the nature of both bodies.[3]

5.2. The *Idea Ideae*: Consciousness, Evidence, and Method

More than an answer to the idealist, skeptic, or solipsist riddle, Spinoza's theory of perception, and especially of the perception of the external world, undermines the fundamental presuppositions on which the use of notions such as "external world" or "external bodies" is based and, in particular, the

---

[2] *Indicant* – this seems to be one of these terms that lack precise "theoretical" meaning and that Spinoza uses quite often when the point he wants to make permits ambiguity on some inessential aspect of it.

[3] The first axiom of the "little physics" (it comes after the corollary of the third lemma) affirms that "all the manners by which a body is affected by another body follow both from the nature of the body affected and at the same times from the nature of the affecting body" (Curley translation slightly altered). Although seemingly clear, it is in fact rather obscure: among other things, what should we understand by "the nature" of a body? It seems, however, clear that Spinoza had in mind here some consequences of the law of inertia. Spinoza's "physics" should not detain us here. From the point of view of the history of science, it has very little interest, if at all. Its interest lies in the way it expresses a typical philosophical transformation of scientific principles or modes of rationality, or their "interiorization" into philosophical discourse.

5.2. The Idea Ideae: Consciousness, Evidence, and Method

presupposition of the ontological ultimate adequacy of the "external-interior" duality. That he, as we have just seen, still uses this very metaphor does not undermine the metaphysical pertinence of its deconstruction, implied in the *noétique* of the first part of EII. But this means that precisely as the "externality" of the external bodies, and of the external world in general, is problematized, so is the implied "interiority" of self, subject, and consciousness. The restoration of the legitimacy of these and a few more such concepts should not blur the singularity of Spinoza's position on all of them.

One way to underscore this singularity is by widening somewhat the perspective on the question of *ideas*. Generally speaking, Spinoza's way of ideas, like most of his central doctrines, evolves within the Cartesian legacy. It is, however, deeply anti-Cartesian. The concept of *idea* appears in a number of key junctions in Spinoza's argumentation, and it fulfills important theoretical roles. All of its main uses are deeply anti-Cartesian. This is a possible explanation of the very meager presence of Spinoza in most of the recent literature dealing with the seventeenth and early eighteenth centuries' "way of ideas." There are a number of relatively recent studies of, among others, Locke, Reid, Berkeley, Malebranche, and Arnauld and their theories of ideas, and there is also a widespread recognition of the fact that at least some of the questions that are raised by the Cartesian problematic of *ideas* are cognates of themes raised in contemporary philosophy, usually around the question of *perception*.[4]

Spinoza is usually not considered to have contributed anything worth mentioning to this history. There are good reasons for this oversight: Spinoza indeed refused to accept the fundamental premises of the Cartesian "way of ideas" that informed, in one way or another, all the debates about the nature and origin of ideas, even of strongly anti-Cartesian doctrine such as Locke's. What Spinoza refused to accept is the dualisms that are the partially implicit presupposition of practically this whole tradition and that are not limited necessarily to mind-body or thought-extension dualism. These dualisms do not have just metaphysical or anthropological significance, but also important epistemological repercussions, underpinned by such notions as "representation," which has a very important role in the debates around the way of ideas. Spinoza can be said to have tried to circumvent all these dualisms.

Spinoza monism is indeed a much wider matter than just matter-spirit, or even God-world, monism; and the notion of *idea* is very instrumental in theorizing a number of ontological and conceptual continuities or homogeneities that he attributes to things that the Cartesian tradition tends to conceive as non-continuous and heterogeneous. In a sense, all these unities are tributaries or offshoots of one fundamental thesis, namely the reduction of souls to ideas. There is an ontological and conceptual homogeneity – this has already been discussed – between the soul and its thoughts; there is also homogeneity between the idea-soul and the body. The soul is not a substance, a metaphysical

---

[4] See Chapter 3, note 35.

ego, a substrate, or a subject of the ideas it has or thinks; it is an idea itself and a mode just like the ideas it "has," "feels," or "thinks." Likewise, and just as a circle cannot be said to be external to its definition or concept, or an idea to constitute a space of interiority vis-à-vis its *ideatum,* so body and soul are not extraneous to each other. The body is not external to its soul, and the soul is not closed inside itself.

A third remarkable feature of the theory of ideas, of which it has not yet been a question here, is the doctrine of the *idea ideae* or, as it is sometimes called, the "reflexive idea." The doctrine appears in propositions 20–23 of EII and paragraphs 33–39 of the TIE.[5] The thesis of the reflexivity of thought is a very old thesis, of course, and Spinoza's doctrine of the idea's idea belongs to some extent to this tradition.[6] Less usual and less trivial are two identifications that Spinoza effects and that are both thoroughly anti-Cartesian: the first appears mainly in the TIE and partially disappears from the *Ethics,* and it concerns a reduction of the Cartesian concepts of *method* and *evidence* to that of *reflexivity.* More interesting from the point of view of latter-day concerns is the doctrine of *consciousness* implied in Spinoza's concept of the *idea ideae.*

There is no need to elaborate here on the importance of the question of *consciousness* for contemporary philosophy. There is also no way of doing it within reasonable limits. The word itself – *conscientia* in Latin or *conscience* in French – is not new.[7] It is in the seventeenth century that a major shift of meaning occurs, and from a concept with mainly ethical-theological connotations, an inner moral instance, *consciousness* comes to be understood as it is understood nowadays, that is, as a kind of pure interiority, an experience of transparency and absolute intimacy, a special kind of privileged knowledge, or an unusual mode of being of the spirit. It is mainly within the Cartesian substantiation of both thought and extension that this shift happens, and it has certainly to be understood also against the background of the scientific revolution and the emergence of a concept of matter as quality-free, as, indeed, pure exteriority, and as consisting exclusively of what the classics called *partes extra partes.* In this kind of entity there is no room for interiority, and it is what underlies all physical reality and can be considered as the legitimate object of science; as physical science becomes the model of scientificity, the interiority of consciousness may in fact be seen as falling outside scientific rationality or at least as a deep conundrum or as an anomaly.

---

[5] For a detailed comparison of the two texts, see Matheron (1994).
[6] Wolfson, II, pp. 90–97 gives, as usual, a number of useful references.
[7] Latin and French are the main philosophical languages of the period, and it is in the philosophical literature written in these languages – mainly the Cartesian and post-Cartesian literature – that this displacement occurs. Modern English distinguishes between *conscience* and *consciousness,* and the first retains the traditional ethical sense; the French *conscience* connotes both senses. See, e.g., Rodis-Lewis (1971), p. 240; see also the *Robert – Dictionnaire historique de la langue française;* The Shorter Oxford English Dictionary have entries for "conscience," "conscient," "conscientious," "conscious," and "consciousness."

5.2. The Idea Ideae: Consciousness, Evidence, and Method

Spinoza uses the term "conscientia" in this new sense, for example in the appendix of EI or in EIIIp9dem and in the scholium following it.[8] On all these occasions the word refers to a kind of knowledge, specifically self-knowledge or self-awareness, but it does not designate a *thing* (or "entity" or, worse still, "stuff") of any kind. The link with the doctrine of the idea's idea is explicitly made, for instance, in the demonstration of EIIIp9, where a direct reference to EIIp23 is made, and where the *cognoscit* of this latter proposition becomes *conscia*.[9] Moreover, in EIIp20, which opens the discussion of the *idea ideae*, "idea" and "cognition" (or knowledge) are presented as synonymous:

Mentis humanae datur etiam in Deo idea, sive cognitio, quae in Deo eodem modo sequitur, & ad Deum eodem modo referntur, ac idea sive cognitio Corporis humanis.[10]

The reference to God pinpoints two elements of the *idea ideae*: it is as real as the soul, and it is ontologically homogeneous with it. Precisely as the soul is the idea of the body and, hence, its cognition, so the idea of this idea is cognition too. It is knowledge of the idea-soul or, in fact, cognition of cognition. Since the soul contains inadequate ideas, such as images, affects of all sorts, sensations, feelings, emotions, and so on, it is permissible to suggest that the doctrine contained in propositions 20–23, is a doctrine of the kind of knowledge one supposedly has when he knows that, or what, he knows as well as (by a not altogether trivial extension of the meaning of "to know") feels and senses. In other words, the doctrine of the idea's idea is a doctrine of *consciousness*.

It is noteworthy, first, that Spinoza discusses consciousness in terms of *ideas*: whether it is understood as a being, or as an experience, consciousness has for him no special status vis-à-vis ideas in general, which is the generic term with which are theorized all things belonging to thought and to thinking, or to the "mental":

The idea of the mind, I say, and the mind itself follow in God from the same power of thinking and by the same necessity. For the idea of the mind, that is, the idea of the idea, is nothing but the form of the idea [*forma ideae*] insofar as this is considered as a mode of thinking without relation to the object. For as soon as someone knows something, he thereby knows that he knows it, and the same time knows that he knows that he knows, and so on, to infinity (EIIp21s).

Seen from a contemporary perspective, this amounts to a double demystification of consciousness: it is de-substantialized; and it appears to be no more "mysterious" than the fact that there are matter and bodies, ideas in general, or

---

[8] See Macherey (1997), pp. 195–209.
[9] EIIIp9 states that the soul always strives to persevere in its being and "hujus sui conatus est conscia," and the demonstration explains that since "the mind (by EIIp23) is necessarily conscious [*conscia*] of itself."
[10] Of the human soul too there is in God an idea, or [that is] cognition, which follows in God in the same way, and relates to God in the same way, as the idea or [that is] cognition of the human body (author's translation).

concepts in the world. It is, in other words, on an ontological par with bodies and with the bodies' ideas. Just as bodies are thinkable or conceivable – or have ideas – so ideas are thinkable and conceivable, or have ideas as well.[11]

Demystifying consciousness is a major preoccupation nowadays. Contemporary philosophers and men of science – psychologists, neuroscientists, and cognitivists in particular – tend to see consciousness as something "mysterious" or even "anomalous"; some of them see in overcoming this mysteriousness or, precisely, demystifying it, their main mission.[12] What is found to be "mysterious" in consciousness is the experience of being *aware* of experiencing the world, one's own body, and one's own self. Being aware of the perceiving of the world, of the diverse forms of this inner transparency – visual, auditory, olfactory, tactile, and so on – is what Leibniz called "apperception," and although it is the most immediate experience, it seems to defy the attempt to explain it scientifically. It is rare, however, that one finds similarly mysterious the fact that one can use concepts in order to say that consciousness is mysterious, or that one can talk, write, or muse about or otherwise theorize the body, the physiological origin of consciousness, or, for that matter, matter. Using the concept of matter usually does not raise the same puzzlement. Not only matter does not seem mysterious, but it also seems that there is not much mystery in the fact that it is possible to give names to material things or that such things can be conceptualized. Not only atoms, but "atoms" too, are not "mysterious." In other words, that our body has an "idea" – a theoretical description or, by generalizing and abstracting, a theoretical concept or, if one prefers, an equation – does not seem to demand the same kind of explanation the philosophers of consciousness feel they have to give to the experience of "being conscious." Of course, the nature and origin of concepts – mathematical, scientific, or commonsensical – are heavy questions. But usually epistemology is not conceived as an enterprise of the dissipation of a mystery. Just as the physical world, despite its enormous complexity and the difficulty to theorize it, is not said to be "mysterious" in the sense consciousness is, so, for some reason, science – or the knowledge or understanding of the world of bodies or, more precisely, the fact that it is describable, conceptualizable, and potentially known or understood – is not seen as "mysterious" in the sense the transparency or apperception of seeing or smelling is.

[11] The full continuity and homogeneity that unites bodies to their ideas and the bodies' ideas (or souls) to their ideas is spelled out explicitly in EIIp21: "The idea of the soul is united to the Soul in the same way as the Soul is united to the body. Demonstration: We have shown that the Soul is united to the Body from the fact that the Body is the object of the Soul (see P12 & 13); and by the same reasoning the idea of the Soul must be united with its own object, i.e., with the Soul itself, in the same way as the Soul is united with the Body" (Curley's translation slightly altered).

[12] "Consciousness is the biggest mystery. It may be the largest outstanding obstacle in our quest for scientific understanding of the universe." These are the very first phrases in a relatively recent book that seeks to "explain" consciousness: Chalmers (1996), p. xi. Among the very numerous studies of consciousness appearing lately, one could mention Dennet (1991) or the more recent Flanagan (2002).

Spinoza's demystifying enterprise seems to be rather different. By the reduction of consciousness to an idea – to the idea's idea – he circumscribes the naturalization of consciousness. By incorporating the doctrine of consciousness in the theory of knowledge, he avoids the need to look for a satisfactory "scientific" explanation – ending, more often than not, in one form of reductionism or another – of it. Either scientific or rational knowledge needs to be scientifically explained, or consciousness has to be understood in the way knowledge is. Ideas, or thinking – and, hence the derivative consciousness as well – are just like bodies: either both are mysterious, or neither is; either both are supernatural or both are natural.

If many demystifications of consciousness presuppose, often tacitly, the priority of experiencing, of the mental or the psychological over the rational, Spinoza's main gesture follows the opposite path. For him the neurological, psychological, or phenomenological concept of "consciousness," as well as reporting the experience of "being conscious of" can be accounted for and rendered intelligible on the basis of the ontology of the intellect as it is elaborated at the beginning of EII and of the concept of "reason" insofar as it emerges from this ontology of the intellect. The first step after this *noétique*, as we have seen, is a derivation of a doctrine of the perception of the "external" world; after this come explanations of the origin and nature of a few psychological and gnoseological mechanisms that are supposed to constitute a full-fledged theory of knowledge in all its degrees. The doctrine of the idea's idea, which is part of this gnoseology, is in fact a reduction of an eventual theory of consciousness to a theory of ideas, to a theory of reason, and to a theory of knowledge.

5.3. The Body as Being in the World

Rather than another solution to a more or less local mind-body question, Spinoza's doctrine about the soul as the idea of the body stands at the center of a vast and diversified thematic field. The theorization of the ways in which soul and body are related is the foundation of a comprehensive theory of man, or anthropology, and, in particular, of a secular ethics. But its full significance transcends its strategic, or inter-systematic, function; opens theoretic possibilities that lie beyond the confines of Spinoza's system of thought; and points to sometimes unexpected affinities with latter-day thought. Later, in the second part of this study, I return to Spinoza's ontology of thought, this time in order to track its role in the elaboration of the final moment of the *Ethics*, or of what Spinoza describes as the doctrine of salvation, beatitude, and freedom. In the rest of this chapter I wish to examine Spinoza's doctrine of thought in light of some more general and a few more recent philosophical problematics. If, then, the previous three chapters were a looking-backward contextualization of Spinoza, what follows can be seen as an attempt to outline a looking-forward one.

Spinoza is often regarded, read, and written about as a valid participant in contemporary theoretical or ideological discussions. His figure is present in literature, theatre, and even plastic arts like few other philosophical figures. If this literary presence is more symbolic than strictly philosophical, it is even more noteworthy that many philosophers, commentators on his philosophy, and, in particular, men of science find in his ideas a source of inspiration for their own thinking. A few cases are better known than others: Einstein is one, Freud another. In more recent times, and with less spectacular celebrity, neurologist Damasio wrote the interesting – but problematic – *Looking for Spinoza*, and there are many more. There are a few Spinozistic themes, real or imagined, that are used more than others in these writings. His alleged "parallelism" is, of course, one, as his "monism," "immanentism," and a few more. But there are a few other paths, less frequently traveled, that may prove not less profitable, at least for the attempt to weigh the philosophical sense of Spinoza's philosophy in general and of his doctrine of thought in particular. Spinoza's problematic relation to the phenomenological tradition may be one such path.

Some commentators have, in fact, noticed a possibly not altogether trivial fact: Spinoza's relative absence from the phenomenological literature. The late French philosopher Jean-Toussaint Desanti, for example, himself a part-time phenomenologist, formulated "quelques réflexions" on the fact that Spinoza has been "hors jeu" (out of bounds) for the masters of phenomenology. He did it in an intriguing little article in which he told how Merleau-Ponty – at the time (1936) his instructor at the *Ecole normale supérieure* – had refused to accept as intelligible the allegedly Spinozistic idea that to the extent that I can be said to think like God (*Deus quatenus*), "I coincide with the intrinsic connection and productivity of ideas in me." Merleau-Ponty had found it hard to believe that anyone could seriously think that such a phrase might be invested with meaning.[13] The question, implies Desanti, expresses the typically phenomenological refusal to take Spinoza's as a philosophical position with which to reckon; in order to probe into the reasons why the masters of phenomenology have generally been silent about Spinoza, he proposes to perform a little phenomenological exercise and check whether, and in what way, significance can be effectuated into the parenthetical phrase in § 33 of the TIE – *habemus ideam veram* – "we have a true idea."[14] For the phenomenologist he purports to impersonate, the question of "truth" is always a question of the "accès d'un

---

[13] Desanti (1993), p. 114. The masters of the so-called analytic philosophy have also been quite indifferent in regard to Spinoza.

[14] The text reads: "A true idea (and, in fact [*enim*] we have a true idea) ..." Desanti does not mention it – he probably assumed his listeners and readers knew it – but Merleau-Ponty, in fact, cites this very phrase a number of times and in a number of his own writings. Pietersma (1988) is an attempt to show that there is a real affinity between Spinoza and Merleau-Ponty. He lists the references to Spinoza (there are not too many of those) in Merleau-Ponty's writings, but gives them more importance than they apparently had for Merleau-Ponty himself. For most students of philosophy in France between the wars, Spinoza was inescapable.

5.3. The Body as Being in the World

sujet au sens de l'expérience, de soi muetté" (p. 127).[15] Only philosophers who pose this question, in one way or another, can be of interest for him (as a phenomenologist, that is), and Spinoza, precisely because he assumes, as a matter of initial evidence, that *habemus ideam veram* is not just opposed to transcendental phenomenology, but also "*lui échappe*" (he eludes it, remains outside its reach).

If Spinoza is absent from the writings of the phenomenologist philosophers, the latter, including Merleau-Ponty, are more or less absent from the secondary literature on Spinoza as well.[16] Despite all this there are important points on which Spinoza and phenomenology in general, Merleau-Ponty in particular, meet. The following brief remarks about a few such points of convergence are not meant to make a claim about an alleged thematic-historical "influence" or continuity, but to throw some more light on Spinoza's doctrines discussed above, highlight their distinctiveness, and, in particular, point to possible philosophical openings they contain.

Insofar as Merleau-Ponty is concerned, a possible rapprochement with Spinoza would involve above all the role of the body in their respective, deeply secular conceptions of the nature of man's being in the world. Merleau-Ponty's theory of perception means, among other things, that the first person perspective on the world is primordial. In an older article, rarely referred to nowadays, the English scholar H. F. Hallett addressed some critical remarks concerning Spinoza's theory of perception formulated by F. Pollock and H. Barker. According to this criticism, which is just another way to point to an alleged incommensurability between an "objective," or scientific, and philosophical views of the person, Spinoza confused two different meanings of *idea*: the idea as a representation of an object and (according to EIIp13) as a physiological state of the body or the brain. Hallett rejects this critique of Spinoza as itself confusion. It fails to distinguish, he says, between "two perspectives: that of the percipient himself, and that of *another* percipient" (p. 170). According to a view of perception "derived from current post-Spinozistic empiricism," perception of an "external object" is "a causal physical and physiological process followed by a psycho-physical 'fact' or miracle – according as mind is regarded as epiphenomenal or 'substantial'" (ibid.). However, from the point of view of the percipient himself, perception is neither miraculous nor an epiphenomenon of the brain. Spinoza's perspective on perception is the percipient's perspective.

---

[15] Roughly: "the access of a subject to the sense of an experience, in itself muted."

[16] An exception is Lloyd (1996), p. 53, who points to the affinity between what she calls the "perspectivism" of the two, meaning by it that we are in the world in the ways our bodies are in the world. I believe there is a lot of truth in what she says. It is noteworthy that Merleau-Ponty has always tried to locate himself through a complex dialogue with the philosophical tradition and, in particular, the Cartesian legacy. There are important references to Descartes's *Dioptrique* in both his earliest and last works, and he thinks Malebranche's doctrine of the union of mind and body is important enough to devote a whole course to it. Spinoza is rarely mentioned.

Written approximately at the same time as Merleau-Ponty's *Phenomenology of Perception* (which was published in 1945; Hallett's article was published first in 1949–1950), there are some interesting parallels between Hallett's conception of the irreducibility of the perceiver's point of view, which he attributes to Spinoza, and some of Merleau-Ponty's ideas in his theory of perception, both in its earlier, phenomenological, and later versions. More interesting, however, than the more or less conventional first-/third-person debate and the priority given, by both philosophers, to the first-person view over the third-person view of the body and of the world, what reading Spinoza in light of Merleau-Ponty permits us to see is the importance and originality of the much-less-conventional role given to the body.

Spinoza, of course, but also Merleau-Ponty, were not empiricists. This means that the priority given to the first-person's perspective on his own body and on the world has to be understood, with regard to both of them, as a thesis formulated in the context of a rational theory of man. Both Merleau-Ponty and Spinoza – the first directly and the second by implication – defy the pretension of the third person's objectifying, medical, or otherwise scientific perspective, to be the only fully *rational* approach. What Merleau-Ponty says explicitly seems to be implied also by Spinoza: an ultimate rational understanding of human existence has to come to terms with the theoretical irreducibility of the first-person view that implies, more specifically, the immediacy, exclusiveness, and intimacy of the perception of the body.

But there is more to it. The risk of anachronism notwithstanding, one can suggest that both Spinoza and Merleau-Ponty transcend not only empiricism, but also transcendentalism. Both refuse to understand the priority given to the perceiving body according to (in Spinoza's case) Descartes's way or (in Merleau-Ponty's case) Kant's way. Although rejecting both empiricism and what he called "intellectualism," Merleau-Ponty did not question the pertinent adequacy of scientific objectivity; but he purported to found the (partial) rationality of a scientific point of view on the ways the privately owned body is perceived, felt, thought, experienced, or lived. It can be said that Spinoza did something not altogether different. For both, the body constitutes man's being – man's being as such and man's being in the world. It is also the foundation of a philosophically rational knowledge of the world. For Merleau-Ponty human existence is irreducibly *charnel*. In order to emphasize the idea that, from the point of view of the phenomenology of perception, the body is not a physiological machine, Merleau-Ponty chose to refer to it as *chair* (more or less *flesh* in English); Spinoza's doctrine of the soul being the idea of the body and his affirmation that "the human body exists as we feel it" in the corollary of EIIp13 can be seen as opening the way to similar insights.

For Spinoza, the idea-concept of the body and the body, just like any concept and its object, or an idea and its *ideatum*, are the objective and formal beings of one thing. The "one thing," let us recall, has no being besides that of the two realities – formal and objective – that exhaust, so to speak, its being. The

5.3. The Body as Being in the World

"thing" is neither the substrate of these realities nor an agent – an *ego* – of its acts. This is one reason why such a doctrine must seem bizarre for the phenomenologist of perception; reading it from the latter's point of view and, in particular from that of the later work of Merleau-Ponty, may permit all the same to better appreciate the significance of what is implied by it: the primordiality of the idea/object-soul/body unity leads necessarily to a doctrine of the irreducibility of the first-person perspective; this is indeed the perspective of the first person conceived as a body, and as a body engaged in a world of bodies. The metaphysical fact of the radical oneness of the idea-soul and its body/*ideatum* can be thus said to be *experienced* as the immediacy and intimacy of the feeling of the body. The theory of man as an *affected*, or sensing and feeling, body, as it would be developed mainly in EIII, would thus be the concrete theoretical articulation of the general metaphysical fact of the mind-body oneness. It means, for example, that the relation between consciousness and body is not a mapping from one realm of being into another, nor that there is a supereminence of one form of being over the other, but that consciousness is the feeling, perceiving, thinking, and knowing of the body "as it is," which is precisely the conclusion of the special ontology of the first thirteen propositions of EII.

Most significantly, the irreducibility, even primordiality, of one's own perception of oneself as a body, or the sensing-ideation of the body as it is, not only precedes, but is indeed the origin of objectivity, including scientific objectivity. But, as indicated, both doctrines are not kinds of empiricism. Sense impressions do not supply a norm or criteria of the truth of the ideas allegedly abstracted from them, and the adequacy of ideas, in Spinoza's language, is not measured by such extrinsic denomination as their similarity, or otherwise conceived correspondence to extra-ideational objects. Insofar as the first part of EII is indeed taken as a kind of a second beginning of the *Ethics*, it seems that one can say that for both Spinoza and Merleau-Ponty, scientific objectivity – the third and fourth parts of the *Ethics* – is founded on the first-person perspective on one's own body and on the body's being in the world and is not an achievement said and measured from the perspective of independent, ideal criteria of truth. The theory of knowledge, as it is developed in the later parts of EII, is a doctrine of the engagement of the body in the world of bodies and – as such – the foundation of the theory of the perception of the "external" world, of the knowledge of the world, of knowledge in all its forms and degrees from imaginary to objective, of truth, and of scientific rationality.

But a deep divergence between Spinoza and Merleau-Ponty appears here. It turns on what can be called the question of reason. No enemy of scientific rationality, Merleau-Ponty rejected all the same what he called "intellectualism" as a fundamental philosophical position; he rejected "empiricism" as well, but in view of the preceding discussion of Spinoza's *noétique*, his refusal to admit that the "intellect" has a primordial status, either ontologically or transcendentally, has a special significance. Spinoza was indeed one of the "intellectualists" Merleau-Ponty was apparently trying to distance himself from: the "idea" that is the first thing constituting the actual being of the soul (EIIp11) is imagined by Spinoza as a kind of quasi-mathematical equation, a determinate proportion of motion and rest, an "eternal idea" or truth – precisely the kind of thing Merleau-Ponty found incredible that someone could seriously consider. Whatever meaning can be given to such a metaphor, what seems to be ascertainable is precisely the *intellectualist* nature of Spinoza's doctrine of the idea-soul: the "foundation" of the soul is a *concept* or pure intelligibility.

Merleau-Ponty considered his philosophy as a philosophy of the original ambiguity of man's being in the world. Thematized in his later work with the aid of the concept of *the chiasm*, it was seen by him as an irreducible element of the human condition or, more accurately, as the very nature of the perceiving body's being in the world. The ambiguity of man's perception of himself and of the world – his "finitude" if one prefers – is irremediable, even in principle and even *sub specie aeternitatis*, which means that it is also a permanent condition of any attempt, scientific or philosophical, to formulate a rational theory of man. Spinoza thought about man's irreparable finitude in light of a positive concept of the infinite; he even thought, undoubtedly somewhat naïvely, that he had the theoretical means to formulate such a concept in a satisfactory way (notably in the famous letter 12). He thought, in other words, that the philosophical theory of man's finitude is conceivable only on the assumption that a concept of *sub specie aeternitatis* plays an effective and positive role in it and, in particular, that this role is the role it plays in EV. In the last analysis, what separates Spinoza and Merleau-Ponty is not so much their respective theories of knowledge but the possibility to formulate a serious doctrine of beatitude, salvation, and freedom.

5.4. Representation and Intentionality Problematized

On many central themes Spinoza was no Cartesian. He has indeed remained alien to the Cartesian tradition as it evolved far beyond the seventeenth century. His first-person perspective is "ego-less," which is certainly a curious thing to say. Even more curious is that this first-person view, the perspective that for Spinoza is the perspective a body has on itself and on the world, is also a *sub specie aeternitatis* view. I shall attempt to justify this seemingly oxymoronic suggestion in the Part IV of the present study. But first, one more aspect of Spinoza's non-Cartesianism, which is a consequence of his doctrine of the primordiality of the idea/soul-object/body unity, merits some attention.

Spinoza's rejection of the theoretical primordiality of the *ego* and, consequently, of the mutually exclusive substantiality of soul and body, have some rather unusual, iconoclastic, and often counterintuitive consequences. One of them is that the fundamental role given nowadays to the two concepts of *intentionality* and *representation* is circumvented. These two notions have long and mostly separate histories. Not without irony, however, these histories have interlaced in recent times to one, perhaps confused, history. Very briefly, it was

5.4. Representation and Intentionality Problematized

mostly Husserl who turned the mediaeval concept of *intentionality*, revived by Brentano, into a central theme in contemporary philosophical thinking. At least for him, however, it was used in order, precisely, to overcome the omnipresence of representational epistemology in post-Cartesian philosophy. Insofar, then, as the opposing "representation" and "intentionality" express two major theoretical possibilities of modern epistemology, and insofar as one can also show that Spinoza's *noétique* amounts to a parallel problematization or relativization of both, then, indeed, the iconoclastic nature of his thought becomes clearer.

Representation has become omnipresent in modern times. Kant's *vorstellung*, via Wittgenstein's theory of the pictorial nature of language; cognitive science; and theories of artificial intelligence, linguistics, psychology, and so on all seem to be turning around "representations". Descartes and his immediate successors considered "representation" mainly as a semiotic concept. Schematically put, it designated a characteristic relation between the "inner" and the "external"; between thought and knowledge and the world of things; or, in the jargon of the times, between ideas and their objects. A central aspect of the fundamental debates that are provoked by this epistemological dualism and that are prolonged, in one form or another, to modern times, can be described as revolving around the following question: does the concept of "representation" designate a dyadic or a triadic relation? That is, is it a relation between two different "entities," thought and material objects, and if it is, what is its nature? Or is it a relation between material objects, mental "images," and a thinking agent?

As Descartes explains (third objections and replies, fifth reply, AT VII, p. 181), he uses the word *idea* to refer to "all that which is *perceived immediately* by the soul" (italics added). In another place he defines it as "that form of each of our thoughts, by the *immediate perception* of which we know (or aware of – *conscius*) these thoughts" (Replies to second objections, AT pp. vii, 160; italics added). This very general notion of *idea* as the "immediate object" of inner "grasp" is accepted by most Cartesians as well as by Locke and the empiricists. Malebranche's often misconceived doctrine of the "intelligible extension" is a particularly interesting stage in the emergence of the modern, Cartesian problematic of representation; for one thing, with him the equivocacy becomes explicit: this "immediate object" of the soul is the inner – and for him intelligible – representation of the external world, not the external world itself.

Malebranche, in fact, formulates the difficulty in clear terms: how to account for the fact that matter – the inert, blind, and thoughtless radically other-than-thought realm of being – can become *intelligible*, not just an object of thought, but utterly intelligible. The emerging mathematical science added gravity to this question: how can non-thought be known by what was conceived as thought's very essence – mathematics or, as Descartes put it, *mathesis universalis*? More straightforwardly, how can matter be known mathematically? In what sense can nature be said to be a book written in mathematical language? The doctrine of the representational nature of perceiving, thinking, and knowing arguably becomes particularly pertinent in the context of this questioning. Mathematical rationality as representing, expressing, or semiotically referring to the "external" thoughtless reality naturally became a central element of epistemology. One particularly interesting version of the kinds of answers given by Malebranche and his contemporaries is Leibniz's: the relation between the inner representation and external object is a formal relation. The first "stands for" the second, expresses it, and, in particular, can be said to be a rational knowledge of it, to the extent that there is relation of isomorphism between them. As we have already seen, such a relation, thinks Leibniz, can be described as the *mapping* of one realm to the other. This Leibnizian doctrine is interesting not only for itself, but also because his metaphor is still much in use and because Leibniz's doctrine of expression, or "parallelism," appears and makes sense more in the context of epistemology than in that of the mind-body question.

In his correspondence with Dortous de Mairan, when pressed to justify his opposition to Spinoza (who is not explicitly named), Malebranche explains that Spinoza's main error consists in that he

> confuses the world, created extension – which cannot be the immediate object of mind, because it cannot affect the mind, [or] act on it – with the idea of that extension which I call intelligible extension, because it alone affects the mind (Malebranche [1995], p. 85).

Malebranche does not mention "the author's" scandalous theories of the immanence of God, the blasphemous critique of Scripture in the TTP, or any of the doctrines that made Spinoza for his contemporaries, and for a whole century later, the despised atheist. What he considers of importance is, on the contrary, the question of "representation." In a sense, he was right. Spinoza's doctrine of the knowledge of the extended world is founded on a radically non-Cartesian – and secular – conception of the nature of the relation between ideas and their objects, a conception, indeed, that cannot be described with the aid of the concept of "representation."

For the Cartesians – intellectualists such as Malebranche or empiricists such as Locke or Reid – ideas are thus taken to be either "modes" of the thinking thing, representing, by some direct relation – "similarity," "isomorphism," causal efficacy, or so on – the wholly other "object"; or a sort of intermediary entities – sometimes considered as a "veil" – between a "spiritual" perceiving, knowing, and understanding mind, "I," or inner eye, and the "external" world. Spinoza's doctrine of the radical soul-body and body-world unity implies the superfluity of the first, semiotic kind of representation: the soul does not "represent" the body – it neither maps it nor has any other similarity to it. By the same token, it also does not represent the world. The primordial and immediate unity of idea and *ideatum*; the fact that it has to be thought without presupposing any substrate or agent of thought; the positing of this original

5.4. Representation and Intentionality Problematized

unity as the ontological and conceptual foundation of a theory of the charnel individual and its "soul" and, in a perfect continuity, of a doctrine of the bodily being in the world and of the perception and knowledge of the world – all these seem to show that any reconstruction of a Spinozistic theory of meaning and of knowledge has to be done without presupposing any pertinence to the concept of (semiotic) representation. An idea cannot be considered as "representing" its *ideatum*, and this is even clearer when this is said using the terminology of *objective being* – it would not make any sense to say that it represents its own *formal being*.

Although the second kind of representation – the inner content, image, or picture intermediaries between an "inner eye" and an "external" object – adds some complication, it too is superfluous in Spinoza's theory of thought, meaning, and knowledge. The complication results from the proximity between this conception of "representation" and the notion of *intentionality*. Like "representation," "intentionality" has become an omnipresent and highly polyvalent term, and very often its specificity vis-à-vis the notion of "representation" is lost. Without distinguishing, first, between the two, the following observation can be made: according to definition three of EII, an *idea* "is a concept of the mind which the mind forms because it is a thinking thing." In the *Explicatio* immediately following it, Spinoza explains why he prefers to use the term *conceptus* to *perceptionis*: the latter seems to connote the passivity of the soul and its being acted upon by the object (*Mentem ab objecto pati*), while the first expresses an action of the soul. The soul *forms* ideas (or concepts). This seems to be a direct critical allusion to the Cartesian definition of *idea*: ideas are not the *objects* of an inner perception. The mind or soul, precisely because it *forms* ideas, cannot be said to *perceive* them: "ideas are not something mute, like a picture on a tablet," affirms Spinoza in a famous scholium (EIIp43S).

The terminology of *objective being/formal being* leads, historically and thematically, to the concept of *intentionality* in its more specific, phenomenological sense.[17] Confining ourselves to one essential, albeit restricted, use of intentionality, the differences vis-à-vis Spinoza's doctrine of the soul as an idea of the body, can have a real philosophical interest.[18] I shall briefly discuss it in relation to Husserl.

Husserl's famous distinction between *noema* and *noesis* in *Ideen I* is a particularly important discussion of the nature of intentionality. A certain rapprochement between this distinction and Spinoza's *idea/ideatum* or *objective/formal being* can be made on the ground that both express not dissimilar attempts to avoid the trap of the realism-antirealism opposition, which, both seem to think, is devoid of real philosophical pertinence. Another similarity is the critique of dualism. Just before the rather cursory remarks on Spinoza

---

[17] See Courtine (2007); this article recounts the scholastic origins of Brentano's concept of "intentionality" and its links to Duns Scotus's *esse objective*.
[18] For a fuller elaboration of this matter, see Yakira (2001).

in the *Krisis*, Husserl speaks of dualism as the cause of the philosophical incomprehensibility of the question of reason. Just as for Spinoza, Husserl's rejection of dualism is also not as much a contribution to the Cartesian or pseudo-Cartesians debates about the mind-body relations, as it is a refusal to accord them real philosophical interest.

But this is where the similarity ends. Spinoza's idea is not a *noesis* because it is not an *act* but *activity*; and his *ideatum* is not a *noema* because it is not the accomplishment of an act, but an ultimate, irreducible, original, and essential element of the *idea-ideatum* unity and of the action that it is. More importantly, by the reduction of the soul to an *idea*, the concept of transcendental subject, the *non plus ultra* of the phenomenological reduction, loses its main theoretical interest.[19]

The conclusion of this detour into phenomenology is that Spinoza's mind-body theory, which is more than anything else a theory of reason and of thought, is indeed unclassifiable. Completely within the history of Western philosophy, it is also outside it. Radically modern and traditional at one and the same time, Spinoza is indeed neither. This remark is not purely historical. It is also philosophical. Spinoza's iconoclastic and deeply non-conventional theory of the soul as an idea and of its radical, *idea-ideatum* unity with the body, opens many interesting and fertile philosophical perspectives. The challenge of thinking of consciousness, knowledge, and reason outside the framework dictated by either the concept of "representation" or the concept of "intentionality" is one of them. Thinking the body as the ultimate mode of man's being and of man's being in the world, but also as the origin of reason, is another. More than everything else, Spinoza's challenge for contemporary philosophy lies in what was for him the main challenge as well: overcoming the nihilistic temptation of the thought of the body as man's real being in the world and formulating a positive moral theory based entirely on the body's radical here-and-now existence.

Spinoza's unusual attitude toward the two notions of "representation" and "intentionality" sheds a very particular light on his so-called rationalism. The later parts of EII are supposed to give an initial answer to the question of the nature and origin of scientific and philosophical rationality: it is supposed to lead, through a number of systematic steps, from the fundamental doctrine of the soul as an idea, through a construction of the concepts of knowledge and truth, all the way to a doctrine of rational knowledge. But a full answer to the question of what sense can be made of the idea of *immanent*, or *inherent, intelligibility* – which is the intelligibility of the individual bodily existence, or of the first-person perspective – is only hinted to in EII, in the very general and ambiguous mentioning of the notion of the third kind of knowledge. It will be only in the last propositions of the fifth part of the *Ethics* that a full answer to this

---

[19] This is an admittedly very cursory remark. A fuller and more adequate treatment of this matter would need a much longer discussion, which I shall postpone to another occasion.

5.4. Representation and Intentionality Problematized

question is allegedly given. It is discussed in the last chapter of this study. But the fact that what Spinoza calls "a theory of salvation, beatitude and freedom," which is also the ultimate answer to the question of what could a claim that the soul is one's own bodily existence's intelligibility mean, is exposed in the context of the second half of EV and shows that the whole philosophical journey leading to this point is most fundamentally an ethical theory. Everything serves this final conclusion, and only there its philosophical value can be measured.

I mentioned above the double face, polemic and positive, of Spinoza's philosophy in general, and the role of the doctrine of the body in this duality in particular. That the body is not an aggregate of thoughtlessness, an object to be sensed, felt, regarded, studied, mapped and eventually known, and controlled, from without – from the point of view of the "mind," which is other than the body, or from that of the third-person observer – is the main lesson of the non-parallelist monism studied above. But – and this is where the polemic import of this doctrine becomes apparent – as the locus of immanent intelligibility, understanding, and, in fact, reason, and as a foundation of ethical theory, it is the semi-theoretical, semi-symbolic source of what can be described as a *secularization* of reason. Paradoxically perhaps, Spinoza's "intellectualism" – usually considered, justly, as integral rationalism is also, and precisely through the essential role the body plays in the construction of the theory of true knowledge and of human rationality – is a radically *demystified* rationalism.

This notion of *demystification* has become current in contemporary literature on the question of the mind, mental images, consciousness, and thinking, but more rarely reason and rationality. Demystifying in this sense are attempts to show that all these fundamental phenomena of human beings – and probably of other living creatures as well – can be satisfactorily incorporated into what is taken, rightly or wrongly, to be a scientific outlook. The abundance of literature of this kind shows that no decisive result has so far been achieved, which is just another indication that the questions at hand are more, or least are not less, properly philosophical than scientific. To some extent, "looking for Spinoza" from the scientist's laboratory is understandable. Spinoza was a rationalist, and his concept of rationality was based to a large degree on what has been characterized sometimes as the "interiorization" of the principles of rationality of the new science. In the context of the second half of the seventeenth century, this means, very briefly, that on the one hand, the emerging scientific practices were based on characteristic norms of rationality and criteria of scientific and rational acceptability; and, on the other hand, that such criteria and norms inform, sometimes tacitly, the philosophers' (in our case Spinoza's) thought.

Spinoza may have very well had some insights that are not only compatible with all kinds of more recent scientific findings, but that also supply some comfort to scientists who look for philosophical, ideological, or other means to consider their more strictly scientific work within wider horizons. Intellectually or symbolically rewarding as may be such gestures, their theoretical value is usually restricted. On the other hand, they risk blurring the deeper philosophical sense of Spinoza's philosophy. For what is usually alien to present-day scientific philosophy is the kind of non-reductive ontology of thought on which Spinoza's whole theory of man stands. His demystification of reason, tempting as it may look for the contemporary practitioners of the demystification of consciousness, is in truth quite different from what they look for in his writings. Spinoza's mind-body theory as well as a Spinozistic theory of consciousness are based on a fundamental philosophical interrogation – often referred to as "ontological" – on the nature and origin of rational thought, on what is called "reason," and on the meaning of intelligibility. There is a deep demystification of all these in Spinoza, but this means less their theorization in the scientist's way, as their secularization. Science is not necessarily secular, let alone atheist, and the fact that many religious people practice science is just one indication of it. It is harder to be a Spinozist and practice religion. Spinoza's ontology of thought is meant to provide foundation and justification of philosophy's validity as a source of understanding of the world and of one's own condition, as well as, in particular, a special kind of ethical normativity. The validity of reason is moral, and philosophy is ethics. Spinoza's demystification of reason is achieved through giving the body an essential role in philosophizing about it. As a foundation of a doctrine of salvation, beatitude, and freedom, as it is expounded in the fifth part of the *Ethics*, it is indeed an altogether different kind of demystification than the one we find in current scientific or semi-scientific theories of consciousness.

PART IV

6

The Norm of Reason

Adequacy, Truth, Knowledge, and Comprehension

The discussion in Chapter 4 culminated in an account of the Spinozistic doctrine of the unity of soul and body, based on the assumption that the parallelism hermeneutical paradigm had been overcome and on the suggestion that propositions 11 and 13 of EII, instead of proposition 7, should be taken as the core of the doctrine. The inner logic of Spinoza's discussion in the first thirteen propositions of EII leads to a deeply non-Cartesian, and counterintuitive, conception of the ontological grounds of what both common experience and most of its conceptualizations conceive as a union of mind and body. Unsurprisingly, Spinoza himself continues to use the habitual linguistic conventions, even in the context of the first part of EII and elsewhere. In the corollary to EIIp13, for example, it is said that the body exists as "we sense it"; one would think that rather than the more accessible "the soul feels [or senses] the body," the Spinozist philosopher should perhaps say that the "soul *is* the feeling of the body" or that it is the body's feeling of itself. The "we" of this phrase, its grammatical and ontological subject, would not be – as it is presumably usually understood – the presupposition or the condition of possibility of the sensing but its result. The exact meaning of the sensing or feeling (or, if we follow Curley's translation, awareness) of the body by the soul needs to be further clarified; as I shall try to show (and as, in fact, follows from the preceding discussion) this "feeling" is *thinking*. If this is accepted, then the corollary of EIIp13 should be understood as stating that "man consists of a mind and a body, and the body exists *as it is thought*" (this thought being the idea we call its "soul").

A number of commentators have reservations about the parallelistic reading of Spinoza's mind-body doctrine. Some of them regard propositions 11 and 13 as particularly significant. One could cite nineteenth- and early twentieth-century commentators such as Dunin-Borkowski and Joachim; and Yosef Ben Shlomo, Genevieve Lloyd, Chantal Jaquet and a few others in more recent times. Due to the growing general interest in the biological sciences (especially neuroscience and genetics), there is a body of work on a cluster of related topics, including a theory of the emotions, written by Antonio Damasio, Henry Atlan, Emily Rorty, and Martha Nussbaum, among others.[1] While commentators such as Joachim or Ben Shlomo were interested mainly in the metaphysical significance of the doctrine that the soul is the idea of the body, other writers seem more interested in the immediacy and intimacy of the "feeling" of the body by the mind implied by it. Despite the philosophical interest of their work, they usually try to make sense of this feeling by using the vocabulary of "representation" or "intentionality," which indicates that they are thinking about Spinoza in terms of parallelism. Since they are less interested by Spinoza's metaphysical doctrines, they usually do not transcend what I have called the Stoic-medical, or eudaimonic moment of Spinoza's philosophy.

In the later parts of EII, and in EIII and EIV, the precise and radical sense of the soul as the idea of the body practically disappears from the surface of the text. Spinoza's discussion there has the semblance of a more standard epistemology, theory of truth, and psychology due to, for example, the constant use of the term *mens humana* as a name for the locus of affectivity and of knowledge, true or erroneous; the reappearance of a distinction, which had been dismissed in the *noétique* of the first thirteen propositions of EII, between an external object and an internal space of thinking; and the apparent denial of causal interaction between mind and body (see EIIIp2 and its scholium).[2] This part of the *Ethics* thus allows us not only to detect a general Stoic mood, but also to miss the larger sense of Spinoza's theory of man. However, the doctrines that the soul is an idea and that it is the idea of the body continue to play a role throughout, via references to EIIp11 and EIIp13 in numerous demonstrations and in the elaboration of both the theory of knowledge and the theory of the affects. Indeed, the full significance of these two doctrines reappears in the later stages of the *Ethics*, where its importance becomes paramount. The concluding discussion in the second part of *Ethics* V is arguably incomprehensible unless we take the strange doctrine that the soul is an idea and that the body is its object literally and not metaphorically, seriously, and without quotation marks. This explains why many readers who, understandably enough, are not prepared to do so find the end of the *Ethics* enigmatic.

The Stoic-medical moment is not Spinoza's last word; it is superseded by a properly "Spinozistic moment." Unless we understand the final moment of

---

[1] See Works Cited.
[2] Respectively: "The body cannot determine the mind to thinking, and the mind cannot determine the body to motion, to rest, or to anything else"; "the order, or connection, of things is one whether Nature is conceived under this attribute or that." The famous phrase that "experience has not yet taught anyone what the body can do from the laws on Nature alone," by which Spinoza means to undermine the obviousness of the feeling that the soul commands the body to perform complex actions, appears in this scholium. Many writers see in this phrase a premonition of some insights of modern sciences of life.

the *Ethics*, we cannot discern the main *raison d'être* of his entire philosophical enterprise. Principally, we will lose sight of the seriousness and depth of its normative thrust if the medical-Stoic, or eudaimonic, moment is not transcended. There is a normative ambiguity in the very idea of eudaimonic, "medical," or otherwise utilitarian ethical theories. The old Platonic-Stoic idea that there is such a thing as "real happiness," or that what the fool, uninformed, naïve, or even honest and innocent perceives as happiness – as his own happiness – can be considered as "unreal," illusionary, "bondage" (as Spinoza would call it), and even as suffering, is problematic in itself,[3] and becomes a major challenge for an immanentist and radically non-paternalistic position such as Spinoza's.

The "medical" interpretation of Spinoza's ethical philosophy, as articulated, for example, by Deleuze, pinpoints the non-moralist and "utilitarian" dimension of Spinoza's philosophy. It also purports to allow for some objective normative judgments of the kind allegedly pertinent in the medical attitude – health is in some objective sense in the best interest of the patient, and the use of remedies are what objective reason commends.[4] Such rationally assessed self-interest is supposed to determine one's attitude toward oneself and toward one's fellowmen, as well as toward the society in which one lives. Conversely, it is supposed to circumvent the theological illusion and the moralism it imposes on man.

But the question that arises on reading the final part of the *Ethics* is different and more difficult: the immanent normativity of health, happiness, or self-interest does not make sense *sub specie aeternitatis*. The eudaimonic or medical points of view are decisively the individual's point of view. As we have already seen (Chapter 1), from the point of view of "nature," health or sickness makes no sense, and the well-being of this or that individual organism makes no difference. But the "intellectual love of God," as Spinoza explicitly puts it in proposition 36 of EV, is God's – or nature's – love, by which he loves himself. It is then as objective as a thing can ever be, and it does make a difference *sub specie aeternitatis*.

From the ethical point of view, or from the point of view of the phenomenology of happiness, this raises with great acuteness the question of the possibility of ascribing absoluteness to "philosophical happiness": is there such a thing as absolutely and objectively true self-interest? Isn't such a notion self-defeating or even an oxymoron? Differently put: can one differentiate in a fully valid way between real and illusionary kinds of "health," "joy," or "happiness"? On what grounds should one prefer the happiness that wisdom allegedly produces

---

[3] As Martha Nussbaum, among others, rightly claims (2001, passim), eudaimonism is not hedonism and certainly not a license to pursue pleasure no matter what. There is in it, at least in its more classical manifestations, an essential evaluative and normative dimension – there is happiness and there is happiness; not all of them have the same value.

[4] See the discussion of Canguilhem's work on the normal and the pathological in Chapter 1.

to other kinds of happiness? Or ascribe to the blessedness procured by philosophy – by Spinoza's philosophy, of course – more credit and value than to the blessedness of the foolish and the ignorant?[5]

The theory of *salus, seu beatitudo, seu Libertas* radically surpasses the Stoic moment. The normative judgments it contains – which, in fact, constitute it – are supposed to enjoy full "ontological" objectivity and significance. Although affirmed from the point of view of the individual philosopher, it is supposed to be valid *sub specie aeternitatis*. Given the fact that it does not depend on any "revelation," or that Spinoza rejects the coherence of deontological considerations – of the notion of an absolute moral "duty" or of the pertinence of allegedly abstract or ideally existent values – what can be the grounds of the validity of such normativity? If the foundations of Spinoza's ethical theory in all its aspects and states are the concrete interests and needs of the individual, resulting, in the last analysis, from the natural and innate basic endeavor to persevere in existence, what remains unaccounted for is how a philosophical life is more "perfect" and indeed more *valuable* than other forms of life, for it is supposed to be valuable not only from the point of view of the person concerned – which is trivial – but also in some objective sense. The "intellectual love of God" seems to more than one commentator as a nuisance, to be explained away rather than explained. But this difficult concept is the ultimate expression of the seriousness and depth of what can be considered a normative or evaluative dimension of Spinoza's philosophy. It expresses – through its meaning (or undoubtedly intended equivocation) as both the love of God by man and the love by which God loves himself (EVp33 and 35) – the objective, ontologically irreducible *importance* and *value* of a certain kind of existence, conceived around a kernel of an ontological theory of truth and understanding.

On the surface, the notion that the soul is an idea and, specifically, the "idea of the body," does not have normative import. That the body has its own primordial and irreducible "immanent intelligibility" – an "objective being," an idea, or a concept – and that this is somehow "the first thing which constitutes the actual being of the human mind" does not seem to have in itself any particular normative significance or to be a source of value – in whatever way we understand this word. For the modern man of science, psychologist, or philosopher of mind, there is undeniable suggestiveness in formulas such as "the mind is the idea of body." More often than not, however, this is taken as a metaphor. That the epistemological or gnoseological unity of the soul-idea and the body-object is, for Spinoza, an *ontological* fact – or "natural" in a sense that permits

---

[5] In his by now-classic *Le Christ et le salut des ignorants chez Spinoza* (1971), A. Matheron tried to show that Spinoza took seriously the theological principle according to which "*homines vel sola obedientia salvantur*" (TTP, Ch. 15, G, vol. III, p. 185); although I have my doubts about this interpretation, I shall not discuss them here. Suffice it to say that even according to Matheron, philosophical salvation is a completely different thing, and certainly much more valuable, than any real or imagined salvation by obedience.

6.1. Adequacy

us to say *Deus sive natura* – is perhaps less easily digestible for the scientific mind. But if Spinoza's "naturalism" is taken for what it is, namely an ontology, then the normative neutrality of the thesis that the soul is an idea and that its object is the body comes to seem much less obvious.

In order to see how an "inner intelligibility" is also an inner normativity or intrinsic value, a few more steps are needed. Generally speaking, the thematic space opened here, in which the place of norms, of original and irreducible normativity, or of absolute valuation has now to be assured, is the space of "truth": the soul is the "true" idea and, in fact, the knowledge of the body or the body's own intelligibility. Spinoza's first significant move here is to posit the concept of *adequacy* as the axis around which the theory of truth is constructed in both a general sense and a particular sense according to which – bizarrely – the soul is the "true" idea and knowledge of the body.

6.1. Adequacy

EIIdef4: Per ideam adaequatam intelligo ideam, quae, quatenus in se sine ratione ad objectum consideratur, omnes verae ideae proprietates, sive denominationes intrinsecas habet.

Explicatio: Dico intrinsecas, ut illam secludam, quae extrinseca est, nempe convenientiam idea cum suo ideato.[6]

Letter 60 to Walther von Tschirnhaus (January 1675):

Between a true and adequate idea I recognize no difference but this, that the word "true" has regard only to the agreement of the idea with its *ideatum*, whereas the word "adequate" has regard to the nature of the idea in itself. Thus there is no real difference between a true and an adequate idea except for this extrinsic relation.

EIII, def 1:

I call that cause adequate whose effect can be clearly and distinctly perceived through it. But I call it partial, or [*sive*] inadequate, if its effect cannot be understood through it alone.

TIE, § 29:

Solus quartus modus comprehendi essentiam rei adaequatam (only the fourth kind [of knowledge] comprehends the thing's adequate essence; author's translation).

TIE, § 73:

... cogitationes veras, sive adaequtas ... (true knowledge, *sive* adequate).

Spinoza's use of the notion of *adequacy*, employed either as a noun or as an adjective, constitutes an essential stage on the way from what I called the *noétique* to his normative theory of thought. With the aid of this notion the

---

[6] EIIdef4: By adequate idea I understand an idea which, insofar as it is considered in itself, without relation to an object, has all the properties, or [*sive*] intrinsic denominations of a true idea. Exp.: I say intrinsic to exclude what is extrinsic, namely, the agreement of the idea with its object.

reader of the *Ethics* may finally make sense of the fundamental thematic – and normative – distinction between truth and untruth – as well as related distinctions such as knowledge and ignorance, validity and invalidity, coherence and incoherence, consistency and contradiction – by deriving them from the ontological doctrine of the intellect. Spinoza, once again, borrowing from a long philosophical tradition, radically transforms the original sense of the term. Originating in classical and mediaeval philosophy, and then taken over by Descartes, the word "adequacy" in the mid-seventeenth century has more or less established uses: used sometimes in conjunction with the concept of "cause" (see discussion later in the book), it usually occurs in the context of a theory of truth. Although the term has found its way into contemporary epistemology, it does not often occur nowadays in the context of truth theories. The word seems, however, to retain some vague normative connotation it had in its traditional employment and to signify fittingness or suitability assessed according to a (usually implicit) standard. Spinoza invested the term with a new meaning while retaining its vague normative aspect, just enough to link his own use with the tradition. One might say that Spinoza used the concept of adequacy as a bridge between the theory of truth and the ontology of the intellect, allowing the latter to accommodate normative principles.

Wolfson's book on Spinoza contains a long list of the occurrences of "adequacy" in mediaeval philosophy, where it typically appears in definitions of truth. The best-known and most often-quoted instance states that *veritas est adequatio rei et intellectus*.[7] This conception of truth arguably originates in Aristotle's famous dictum, "to say of what is that it is, and of what is not that it is not, is true" (*Metaphysics* IV, 7, 1011b, p. 27). The traditional uses of adequacy usually express a conception of truth based on an alleged "correspondence" relation between knowledge and the known, which means roughly that ideas are first and foremost about extra-cogitative things, or "objects," and that they are true to the extent that they somehow express, depict, represent, or picture what or how these objects are "in themselves." Theories of truth are, moreover, classified as correspondence theories or coherence theories, the latter based on formal and internal relations holding among elements belonging to one system of beliefs or ideas, such as consistency or lack of contradiction or mutual entailment.[8]

---

[7] Cf. Thomas Aquinas, *Questiones Disputatae Veritate*, Qu.1; Wolfson (1961), II, pp. 105ff. See also Gueroult, II (1974) p. 23 n.14. As Gueroult notes here, in order to express the "external" idea-object correspondence that had been traditionally conveyed by *adequacy*, Spinoza uses instead terms such as *convenientia* or *convenire*. From the extremely abundant literature on the concept of truth, I shall mention here only the historical-thematic analysis of the "coherence" theory in Rescher (1973).

[8] The central figure here is Descartes. The question of the adequacy of ideas or of knowledge is raised explicitly in the *Objections and Replies* to the *Meditations*, notably in Descartes's detailed response to Arnauld, where the main issue is the relation among adequate, complete, and

6.1. Adequacy

In the first and second quotes above (EIIdef4 and letter 60), Spinoza draws an explicit distinction between "external" and "internal" characteristics of true ideas or knowledge, the first belonging to "truth," the second to "adequacy." Since, moreover, he seems to be saying that *adequacy* is logically prior to *truth* (when the latter is understood strictly as a relation between an idea and its object and, as such, an "external denomination" – *denominatio extrinseca*),[9] several commentators have claimed that Spinoza actually held a "coherentist" theory of truth. Allegedly dissociating *adequacy* from the context of "correspondence," he is supposed to have transformed it into a principle of the coherence of the system of ideas, of which any single idea is a systematic element. Some think that Spinoza actually held a "realistic" or "correspondence" theory of truth, and yet others believe that Spinoza in fact collapsed the two traditional views into a new theory of truth governed by an original concept he dubbed "adequacy." The problem with much of this exegetic literature is that it often remains within the limits of "truth theories," as it is understood in contemporary, mainly Anglo-American, philosophy.[10] In this context both "correspondence" and "coherence" seem to be more normatively neutral than "adequacy," and the strong normative, or valuational, connotations this notion has in Spinoza's philosophy are often not given enough attention. "Adequacy" seems to imply some *propriety* and some criterion measuring it. In the traditional case of *adequatio rei et intellectus*, the propriety is the propriety of the intellect conceiving of a thing in view of what the "thing" is. It is noteworthy that when Spinoza speaks of this kind of relation between "idea" and its "object," he uses concepts with obvious normative significance, such as *convenire*.[11]

The *coherence-correspondence* dichotomy is unfit for making sense of Spinoza's notions of the true or the adequate idea, for two seemingly opposing reasons: both options are valid, and both are not valid enough. On the one hand Spinoza certainly accepts a certain realist concept of truth: a true

---

true knowledge. Marion (1994) points to the Cartesian context of Spinoza's use of this term. Curiously taking Descartes's side, he however underestimates Spinoza's radical breach with him. Other commentators point to an apparent difficulty in Spinoza's definition of "truth" as a relation of exteriority of the idea and its object, as it seems to contradict the obvious non-exteriority of the idea-*ideatum* relation. Sufficiently discussed in the secondary literature, I shall not address this difficulty directly.

[9] On the important, apparently largely forgotten, role of *denominatio extrinseca* in the scholastic literature, cf. de Libera (2008), chapter 6.

[10] Anglo-American commentators seem to be particularly sensitive to the question of a Spinozist "theory of truth," and they often discuss it in terms of the coherence-correspondence opposition. The "coherentist tradition" apparently descends from the pioneering work (in English) of Harold Joachim in his (1910) and the (1940) posthumous commentary on the TIE. On Joachim himself, his roots in British idealism (or Hegelianism), and his coherentist attitude toward Spinoza, see Parkinson (1993). For a critical discussion of some of Joachim's claims, see Hallett (1962), passim.

[11] Thus EI axiom 6: *Idea vera* debet *cum suo ideato convenire* [usually translated as "agree"].

idea, states axiom 6 of EI, "must agree with its object"; on the other hand, although he does not explicitly formulate a "principle of contradiction," obviously the system of all truths, or the divine intellect as he calls it, is a coherent system of truths, and even coherent in a strong sense. This is almost trivial. Inversely, both theories of truth are based on criteria that are "external" to the "idea" and thus explicitly contradict the definition of "adequacy" as an intrinsic characterization of ideas. The idea-*ideatum* "correspondence" relation is expressly said by Spinoza to be an external relation;[12] and the "coherence" conception is based on evaluating the truthfulness or adequacy of a given idea by its relations to a system of other ideas. One can say, as has indeed been said, that all "singular" ideas are parts of one infinite "idea," and to some extent this is not straightforwardly false. But it makes no sense to attribute to a singular idea, which is apparently something like a simple, pristine thought-content, an "intrinsic coherence." Coherence makes sense only as a relation of a plurality of ideas – Leibniz's famous compossibility – but as Spinoza explains for example in TIE§ 71, the "form" of the true idea is in this idea itself, "without any relation to other ideas," and just as there is a Spinozistic principle for the individuation of bodies (in the little physics after EIIp13; see earlier discussion), so is there arguably a principle of individuation for "souls," or of ideas of the individual bodies. And to say of a single idea that it is "coherent" is trivial to the point of being conceptually vacuous. The question – to put it once again in Leibnizian terms – is what makes an idea, a given content, possible or thinkable. Spinoza tried to give a systematic answer to this question with the onto-gnoseological concept of "adequacy."

Spinoza's doctrine of the "adequate" and "true" ideas or knowledge belongs to the modern, post-Cartesian discussions of the nature of truth and of knowledge in a very roundabout way. The coherence-correspondence dichotomy is not of much help for the attempt to make sense of his concept of "adequate idea." The most important reason for this is that Spinoza, unlike most modern theorists of truth, did not consider the question of truth as independent of ethical theory (and vice versa). Consequently, any discussion of his ideas about truth or, more specifically, about what he took to be the adequacy of ideas, as a theory of purely theoretical or scientific truth as it is understood in modern philosophy, is anachronistic. His ambiguous modernity and heterodox Cartesianism is conspicuous already in the very un-Cartesian manner in which he described the fundamental motivations of philosophical enterprise; his conception of truth is inseparable from his vision of ethical life and of "true" happiness, but there are also more local differences.

---

[12] Which is quite non-trivial and even problematic: if the paradigmatic idea-*ideatum* relation is the one holding between souls and their bodies, and if our previous discussion of this relation makes sense, then of course the last thing that can be said on it is that it is a relation of externality. See more about it in a later discussion here.

6.1. Adequacy

The mediating role "adequacy" plays in the elaboration of Spinoza's doctrine of the nature and origins of normativity comes to the fore when Spinoza uses it as an adjective applicable to causality. The first definition of EIII stipulates that a cause is said to be adequate insofar as the effect can be perceived through it in a clear and distinct way. Spinoza undoubtedly reproduces here a Cartesian formula, itself borrowed from an older and long tradition.[13] The formula "adequate cause" appears in the *more geometrico* appendix added to the Reply to the Second Objections. The fourth axiom reads as follows:

Quidquid est realitatis sive perfectionis is aliqua re, est formaliter vel eminenter in prima et adaequata ejus causa (whatever reality, that is, perfection, there is in a thing, is formally or eminently in its first and adequate cause).

This axiom, dubbed the "adequate cause" axiom, has recently become the subject of a long debate, among mainly English-speaking scholars, about Descartes's mind-body causal interactionism.[14] The notion of "adequate cause" is used by Descartes only in the context of his First Proof of the existence of God as it appears in the Third Meditation, and the difficulties it allegedly raises for his mind-body doctrine are mainly a recent idea. Translating the general metaphysical principle *ex nihilo, nihil fit* into the concrete language of causality, it functions in Descartes's proof as a formal principle of causality, establishing a kind of semi-quantitative relation between cause and effect (and prefiguring, ironically, Leibniz's principle of the equality of the full cause and the entire effect, on which he would base his refutation of Descartes's rules of collision).

Apparently borrowing, then, the notion of *causa adequata* from Descartes, Spinoza however reversed its meaning and function. Descartes had used it in order to make an inference from a given existent (specifically, the idea of the infinite) to its cause, the "causality axiom," enabling him to affirm the (infinite) amount of being necessarily possessed by it. From the definition of "adequate cause" at the beginning of EIII, it might have seemed as if Spinoza was transposing the use of the notion of "adequate cause" to the context of a *propter quid* consideration of the causal relation – explaining and comprehending a thing by proceeding from the cause to the effect; in fact, however, the definition is stated from the perspective of the effect. But this effect, in this case, is nothing else but the active or passive human being.

---

[13] As Theo Verbeek remarks (Verbeek, 2011), the scholastics – he cites John of St. Thomas and Suarez – were using such formulas as *causa proxima et adaequata*, this use being part of long tradition – commencing with Aristotle – of distinguishing between knowledge proceeding from effect to cause (*demonstratio quia* or *per signum*), and the more perfect one that proceeds from cause to effect (*propter quid*).

[14] See, e.g., Radner (1971), Broughton (1986), and Schmaltz (2006), which includes a detailed bibliography of the debate. The issue debated is whether the "causality axiom," or the doctrine of adequate causality, is or is not compatible with mind-body causal interaction.

Noteworthy, firstly, is the fact that the definition appears in the context of the theory of the affects of EIII. More significant is the use of the concept of "adequate cause" in what follows immediately, the second definition of EIII:

> I say that we act when something happens, in us or outside us, of which we are the adequate cause, that is (by def. 1) when something in us or outside us follows from our nature, which can be clearly and distinctly understood through it alone. On the other hand, I say that we are acted on [*pati*; affected or passive] when something happens in us, or something follows from nature, of which we are only a partial cause.

The relation between "our nature" and what follows from it – always necessarily – has two possible modes, that of action and that of passivity. The definition of adequate cause and of activity effectuates a direct link with the definition of freedom (EIdef7). The full significance of this link would become apparent only at the very end of the *Ethics*. But one can affirm already at this point that the complex thematics of adequate causality-action-freedom certainly has an ethical and normative significance.

How the normative dimension is mediated by the concept of "adequacy" can, however, be seen with greater clarity in the ways it is used by Spinoza in his doctrine of the adequate idea. In the TIE "truth" and "adequacy" are distinctly said to be equivalent;[15] but if we expect a more clear-cut differentiation between the two notions in the *Ethics*, we are bound to be deceived. Despite what appears in the axiom of EI and the definition of EII (and in letter 60), as a real distinction, the actual use Spinoza makes of these terms, notably in what is supposed to be the systematic elaboration of the theories of truth and the adequate idea in the latter part of EII, is far from being consistent. Sometimes he seems to respect the distinction, and sometimes he seems to forget it.

In fact, the complexity, ambiguity, and fluidity of Spinoza's use of the term "adequacy" is even greater than just not respecting the distinction between "adequacy" and "truth." Some of the things that he says about knowledge and truth look like a real conundrum. It is hard to see how the following elements can all be held together as parts of one doctrine: First, as Spinoza often says, having an adequate idea is the same as possessing knowledge;[16] second, "adequate ideas" means also "clear and distinct" ideas; knowledge (or having "true" ideas) is *ipso facto* knowledge of this knowledge (EIIp43). It seems thus reasonable and intuitively easy to accept that the human soul "does not involve" either "adequate knowledge of the parts composing the human body" (EIIp24) or "adequate knowledge of an external body" (EIIp25). But then what can the corollary to EIIp13, according to which "the human body exists as we sense it," mean? Propositions 45 and 46 of EII are even harder to accept and also look very counterintuitive: they state, respectively, that "each idea of each

---

[15] E.g., § 73: "si de natura entis cogitatis sit ... cogitationes veras, sive adaequatas formare."
[16] E.g., EIIp43dem: "he who has an adequate idea, or [*sive*] who knows a thing truly."

6.1. Adequacy

body ... necessarily involves an eternal and infinite essence of God" and that "the knowledge of God's eternal and infinite essence which each idea involves is adequate and perfect."

There are many more examples of this kind, and the discussion in EII that follows the physical annex after the scholium of proposition 13 is full of such apparent contradictions and incoherencies. Different attempts to introduce some coherence into this convoluted text may be more or less successful. More interesting and more productive would be to try to understand the reasons for these difficulties. The key to such an understanding may reside in the noetic, or fundamentally ontological – and not epistemological or truth-theoretical – significance of *adequacy*.

Souls and ideas, then, involve or do not involve adequate ideas, or knowledge, of the parts of which the human body is composed. But then why not say simply that we do not know adequately the parts both of our own body and of the external bodies? And why not say simply that we know God adequately? If the first suggestion may seem reasonable, the second is obviously untenable: who can seriously say that we – all of us, whenever we know a body – adequately know the essence of God? I suggest that the answer to this puzzle is to be found in the kind of the universal relation that is ever-present in the discussion in the second half of EII and that is usually designated by the term *involvere*. This relation introduces into the concept of "knowledge" some quite unusual meanings: "knowledge" *involved* in this or that idea or soul is apparently *not*, or at least not always, explicit knowledge. It would not be exact to say, however tempting, that such knowledge is *tacit*. In fact, it is not altogether *knowledge*, if "knowledge" is understood in an epistemic or psychological sense. From a semantic point of view, what is *involved* in an idea, a piece of knowledge, or a thought, is what I referred to as "conditions of intelligibility." More important in the present context is its ontological significance: the conditions of intelligibility, what is "involved" in an idea – a given thinkable or actually thought content – is the underlying *possibility* of its being; that is, of its being as a thought (or of its objective being).

But the ultimate condition of intelligibility and of the being of ideas is being itself, or substance, or what Spinoza calls God. And indeed every idea *involves*, in this sense, the idea of God exactly in the way in which every condition *involves* its condition. I shall not probe deeper into this matter; but I believe that this reading of the matter may make sense of much of Spinoza's use of "adequate (idea)," as well as of much of the theory of true knowledge in EII and in the following parts of the *Ethics*. Assuming it to be valid, I shall instead try to extract from the doctrine of the "adequate idea" its normative import. I propose to do so in three steps: revisiting the doctrine of the "genetic definition" in the TIE; trying to understand the meaning of Spinoza's famous repeated qualification of truth as *index sui*; and, finally, addressing the constant detour via God in the construction of the theory of true knowledge.

6.2. The Genetic Definition

In Chapter 3 I proposed a relatively long analysis of Spinoza's use of the Hobbesian notion of the "genetic definition" in an attempt to make sense of the concept of *intelligibility* that I think informs Spinoza's so-called mind-body theory. There is, however, one element of Spinoza's doctrine of the genetic definition that deserves further attention, namely its normative import. In the reconstruction of this doctrine I suggested that the imagined (or feigned) genesis of a given geometric object – the circle in the example discussed – is the way through which the circle becomes intelligible, or is best *understood*, as a scientific object. It was also mentioned, but not dwelt upon, that Spinoza considered the genetic definition as the "best" or "perfect" definition. This is, of course, a kind of normative statement, and, as we have seen, it expresses the idea that the "perfection" of a definition is evaluated on the basis of how many of the definiendum's properties can be deduced from it.

What is significant in Spinoza's methodological or meta-mathematical ruminations about the "perfection" of the genetic definition is not so much their soundness – which is certainly questionable – but the way in which this notion is used by Spinoza to account for the inherent normativity of rational reasoning. Letter 60 to Tschirnhaus is very revealing in this respect. In letter 59 Tschirnhaus, as usual intelligent and lucid, raises some pertinent questions. He asks Spinoza first to define the true, adequate, false, and dubitable ideas, and then adds a question: what is it that makes one representation (Tschirnhaus says "idea") of a given object – e.g., the circle – preferable to another? Why is it that we can more easily deduce the properties of the circle from one of its adequate ideas than from the others? Spinoza first reiterates the distinction between "truth" and "adequacy" as he formulated it in the *Ethics* (quoted above), and then explains that

> in order that I may know which out of many ideas of a thing will enable all the properties of the object to be deduced, I follow this one rule, that the idea or definition of the thing should express its efficient cause.

The methodological efficacy of the genetic definition seems to be known a priori and independently of any concrete epistemological consideration (or mathematical work concretely carried out): simply, the "good" idea/definition has to involve or express (Spinoza uses both metaphors in this letter) the efficient cause. In the letter to Tschirnhaus Spinoza significantly illustrates his position by another example: the definition of God given in EIdef6. Defining God, he says, as an absolutely perfect being will not enable us to deduce all his properties. We can do so, however, on the basis of the definition given in EI, for, Spinoza adds here in a parenthetical phrase, "I take it that an efficient cause can be internal as well as external."

The whole matter is rather enigmatic. EIdef6 defines God as "a being absolutely infinite, that is, a substance consisting of an infinity of attributes, of

6.2. The Genetic Definition

which each one expresses an eternal and infinite essence." In what way is this definition like the genetic definition of the sphere? In what sense can we deduce from it God's properties in a way that the definition of God as an "absolutely perfect being" does not allow us to do? Or, finally, what has all this to do with the double face, the internal and external, of the "efficient cause"? It is probably impossible to give satisfactory answers to these questions, at least not without a good deal of speculative reconstruction. All the same, a few partial conclusions can be drawn: it seems that for Spinoza, "epistemology," a theory of rational thinking or of mathematical rationality, is not separable from the theory of being in its most fundamental and general sense. The structure of rationality is the same as the structure of being – *causa* is *ratio*. The alleged completeness of knowledge procured by the genetic definition, which is the ground of ascribing to it "perfection," or an epistemological advantage, has its utmost manifestation in the concept of *causa sui*.

This explains Spinoza's peculiar reproduction of the scholastic and Cartesian use of "adequacy" as an adjective qualifying "causes" in EIIIdef1. It is remarkable that this occurs at the beginning of the third part of the *Ethics*, where the theory of the affects is expounded and where the foundations are laid for the doctrines of "bondage" and of "liberation." The displacement effected by Spinoza here, importing a concept belonging to one field of rational discourse – the ontology of causality on the one hand, and gnoseology, epistemology, and theory of truth and of meaning on the other – to a quite different context is the kind of bridging between ontology, a theory of man, and moral theory mentioned above; it is accomplished by characterizing normativity as a doctrine of adequacy.

In the discussion of the genetic definition in the TIE,[17] notably in the attempt to illustrate its epistemological and methodological advantages with the aid of the example of the sphere, Spinoza comes closest to an explicit formulation of the concept of "adequacy" as a normative concept. This happens in the following way: in the rotation of the semicircle, the sphere emerges as a fully determined object; its full determinateness – "all" its properties – is explicated in this way and, as a result, this is also the best definition from a "methodological" point of view. The emergence of the sphere is a process in which a determinate lawfulness is deployed; this "deployment" is not an arbitrary process, or a simple given, but a process that also concretizes a relation of appropriateness or *suitability* of the result to the antecedent and vice versa. This "suitability" we best express, very precisely, by calling it "adequacy."[18]

---

[17] In §§ 71–73; see Chapter 4, section 4.2

[18] Deleuze, in his (1968), comes close to a similar interpretation by trying to explain "adequacy" as a kind of "expression"; since, however, what is expressed according to him is "power" (*puissance; potential*) and not intelligibility, the normative dimension is practically reduced in his presentation of Spinoza, as it is, for that matter, in his own philosophy. A few years before Deleuze, H. F. Hallett (1962) proposed a rather similar reading of this aspect of Spinoza's philosophy, articulated in the concept of "potency-in-act."

We remarked earlier that the two competing customary readings of Spinoza's alleged "theory of truth" – the "coherentist" and the "correspondist" – are, as far as they go, both plausible and insufficient. This is nicely illustrated in letter 60: the idea of the circle certainly "corresponds" to its "object," namely the circle. This "correspondence" is independent of its being thought by an intellect, which means that it is absolute, but also trivial and epistemologically uninteresting. This absolute idea of circle contains all the circle's properties, which means that, ideally and once an epistemological concept of "intellect" is introduced into the theoretical discourse, all the circle's properties are deducible from it. On the other hand, "adequacy" is said to refer to the intrinsic nature of the idea itself, and in this sense the "parts" of a complex object such as the circle cohere. The idea of the circle is, moreover, part of the infinite idea of being in general, or of the system of all ideas (supposing that such a notion makes sense) and can be said to "cohere" with the other ideas that are part of it too. But in both cases the (ideal) "emergence," as implied by the doctrine of the genetic definition, is unaccounted for; consequently, and in particular, the normative dimension of the concept of "adequacy" remains hidden. The crucial element in all this is that, first, the internal property of "adequacy" is not just "coherence" existing among the different parts, or constituents, of a given idea, but a certain order, or direction of movement, in which the result faithfully respects, so to speak, its origin. Second, this "result" is a full transparency or explicitness of the "properties" of the object thus engendered; and finally "engendering" here does not mean coming into existence but is indeed a metaphor, and the causal relation Spinoza is talking about should apparently be understood as a picture of the ontological-semantic relation of condition and conditioned, which is the mode of being of ineligibility.

6.3. *Index sui*: The Norm of Truth

The notion of "norm" appears a number of times in Spinoza's writings, not surprisingly mainly in the TIE. But the doctrine of which it is a part appears in practically all of Spinoza's writings, and in a more or less constant form. Its most compact and famous formulation is found in letter 76 to Alfred Burgh: truth, writes Spinoza to his former friend and present adversary, is *index sui et falsi*. That truth is the sign or mark of truth and of non-truth means that there can be no other criterion of the truthfulness of a given idea than that very true idea's truth itself. There is also no other criterion on the basis of which it is possible to distinguish between truth and non-truth other than truth itself.

Spinoza's thinking on the question of truth is visibly embedded in the philosophical tradition, and different elements of this tradition are present in all his writings. Descartes is apparently the main point of reference, but not the only one. Spinoza's own original positions on the nature of truth are also

6.3. Index sui: *The Norm of Truth*

present all along, although the cohabitation of the traditional and the new is not altogether free of difficulties. From the beginning, "truth" is understood as having a double meaning. The *Short Treatise* (II, 15, 1) as well as the CM (I, VI) already contain the same distinction between truth as "external denomination" and the "internal properties" of the "true idea," the latter to be called only in the *Ethics* "adequacy." The first meaning of "truth" in both works echoes the Aristotelian definition of truth and prefigures EIax6. In the CM there is even an etymological rumination about what might have been the intuitive origin of the philosophical concept of truth: an examination of the meaning of "the true" and "the false" show that these words designate "only the extrinsic marks of things." Since the philosophical use of these words originates with the "common people," it is important to look for their origin: "The first meaning of true and false seems to have had its origin in storytelling, and the tale was said to be true if it was of something that had occurred in actuality and false if it was of something that had nowhere occurred."

The doctrine of the "internality" of the essential properties of truth has as a consequence the principle that truth is *index sui et falsi*. It appears all over. In the *Short Treatise*, for example, it is said that "the clearest things of all make known both themselves and also what is false," and in the *Ethics* (Second part, proposition 43) "He who has a true idea at the same time knows that he has a true idea, and cannot doubt the truth of the thing." The reasoning behind the doctrine that extraneous criteria are not what constitute the essence of truth can only be understood against its polemic background. It is the Cartesian idea of criteria of truth and, more generally, of method that are the target of Spinoza's polemics.

Spinoza nevertheless retains much of the Cartesian terminology: "method," "evidence," the "clear and distinct," consciousness (as the thought of thought or, in his language, the idea of the idea), of course "adequacy," and a few other terms all play central roles in his theory of the true idea. As usual, though, the borrowing is also a transforming, and sometimes the transformation is indeed radical. Thus, the frequent identification of "method," evidence," the *idea ideae*, and "truth" is a typical gesture of borrowing and transforming. The Cartesian themes are thus used by Spinoza to undermine and refute one of Descartes's most important doctrines, that of locating the truth of thinking in *judgment*. He does it from within the Cartesian terminology, as it were, by collapsing judgment into content. Spinoza holds some kind of a rudimentary theory of the redundancy of an independent T operator (to use a contemporary term); more generally, he collapses meta-truth into truth. Thus the scholium of EIIp43 states that no one who has a true idea does not know (Curley and Shirley both translate "unaware"; the Latin says:... *nemo, qui veram habet ideam, ignorat veram ideam...*):

> that a true idea involves the highest certainty. For to have a true idea means nothing other than knowing a thing perfectly or [*sive*] in the best way. And of course no one can

doubt this unless he thinks that an idea is something mute, like a picture on a tablet, and not a mode of thinking, namely understanding itself [*ipsum intelligere*].

The same depiction of the characteristic error concerning the nature of ideas reappears in the final scholium of EII, after proposition 49. Here, however, the nature of the error is more fully explicated: it consists in confusing, or not distinguishing between, ideas or concepts of the soul and images of the things that we imagine, as well as ideas and words by which we designate the things. This seems to be an allusion to Descartes's *Dioptrique*.[19] In the fifth (*Des images qui se forment sur le fond de l'oeil* – "On the Images which are Formed on the Back of the Eye") and sixth (*De la vision* – "On Sight") discourses (or chapters) of this essay, Descartes speaks a number of times of *peinture* (painting) or *tableaux* (pictures). This notion fulfills in this text two connected but distinguishable strategic functions, polemic and explicative.

The polemic is directed, in a general way, against theories of (visual) perception, mainly scholastic, based on the contention that perceiving an object is having an image *resembling* the perceived object. Descartes sees in the way people think of the relations allegedly existing between paintings and the painted objects the origin of this erroneous doctrine about the nature of visual perception. This seems to be the source of what Spinoza says in EII49schol:

> Indeed, those who think that ideas consist in images which are formed in us from encounters with [NS: external] bodies, are convinced that those ideas of things of which we can form no similar image [NS: in our brain] are not ideas, but only fictions which we feign from a free choice of the will. They look on ideas, therefore, as mute pictures on a panel, and preoccupied with this prejudice, do not see that an idea, insofar as it is an idea, involves an affirmation or negation.

Spinoza obviously shares Descartes's rejection of the similitude-based theories of perception. But at the same time, he also rejects Descartes's own theory. There are good reasons to say that the *Dioptrique* (and the parallel *Le monde ou Traité de la lumière*) is the birthplace of the modern mind-body question. The physiological and anatomical researches – fully empirical – that form the basis of the *Dioptrique* are not only extremely interesting in themselves, or from the point of view of the history of science, but also illuminating from the point of view of the history of the philosophical interrogation accompanying the emerging new science of the human body.

Descartes, then, rejects the "similitude" theory of perception. More importantly, his whole discussion of visual perception is based on the assumption that the mind, not the eye, sees.

---

[19] P. Macherey points to a similarity between Spinoza's words here and Aristotle's *Topics*, VI, 2, but the similarity to Descartes is too straightforward to be accidental. See Macherey (1997), vol. II, p. 332, n 1.

6.3. Index sui: *The Norm of Truth*

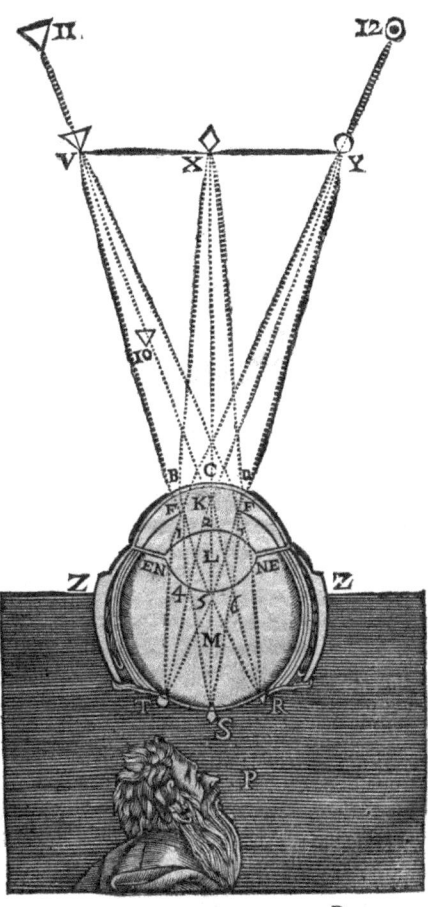

Thus the fourth discourse – "On the Sense in General" – opens with the following statement: "As we know already well enough, it is the soul [*âme*] that senses, not the body." However, the "image" still plays an important role in the theory of sight. Descartes next describes an ingenious experiment: he takes an eye of a recently dead man or a cow, puts it in an "obscure chamber" with a small hole in it, places himself inside, and watches the images appearing on the back of this eye (see drawing). He then surmises that the same image is transmitted through the ocular nerve into the brain, reaching the pineal gland. However, it is not by means of the resemblance of the image and the object seen that "we sense it, as if there were again eyes in our brain," but rather by means of movements that this resemblance is made – just as the movements of a blind man's stick that make him sense what is in front of him – "which act directly on our soul insofar as it is united to our body."[20]

The discussion in the sixth discourse, which is the philosophically most interesting chapter of the *Dioptrique*, is based on the rejection of the resemblance thesis and its replacement by a doctrine of representation and the active role of the "soul" not only in thinking the intelligibles, but also in perception. The engraving reproduced here is equivocal in a very illuminating way. It depicts the experiment described above and is supposed to reconstruct the geometry of the production of the images that can be seen by the figure standing inside the dark room and behind the eye put in the hole – the experimenter – as "painted" on the back of the eye. A few such drawings are given in this chapter of the *Dioptrique*, each of them analyzing a different optical phenomenon. Implicitly, however, this figure also symbolizes the soul: like the spectator in the drawing, the soul is presented with some data, or information, that it has to interpret and conclude for what it stands. More than "sensing," the soul in fact thinks; rather than "soul" in an unspecified sense, it is an "intellect." I suggest that it is here (and in *Le monde*) that Cartesian dualism was invented, and that it was an epistemological doctrine before it became a doctrine of mind-body interactionism. And it is here, in the birthplace of the modern mind-body question and its characteristic dualism, that modern "intellectualism" (or "rationalism") is also born. Spinoza, by following Descartes in his refusal to consider thinking as "imagining," is an "intellectualist"; precisely, however, because of the role the body plays in it, his intellectualism is a rare breed.

Thinking in Descartes is twofold: the more or less passive inner perception – rather understanding – of an intelligible content, and its affirmation or denial by what Descartes calls "will." The act in which a given content is affirmed or denied is free, active, and not passive and, as such, it is not the specific activity of the intellect. The overtly psychologistic metaphor of "will" can be interpreted as prefiguring a doctrine of *judgment*, and if this is accepted, then for Descartes, thinking, insofar as it is the locus of truth or the context in which the question of truth is systematically raised, is *judging*. But judging presupposes a judge or an agent performing the act of judging, metaphysically interpreted as the "substrate" of thought, as a thinking substance, as *res cogitans* or, transcendentally, as a *subject*. In the *Dioptrique*, Descartes's central doctrine receives a first and partial, but significant, expression. Typically, this is done in the context of the "vision of distance" (AT, VI, pp. 137–139): the distance of a certain point relative to other points is known by a "natural geometry." "We" – the paradigmatic agent of thinking qua judging (or, here, interpreting data) – watch what is "seen" and calculate its objective meaning. Spinoza chooses to add here, significantly at the end of EII, to his Cartesian rejection of the "imagist" conception of ideas, that affirmation and negation are intrinsic to ideas. The ideas as "pictures on a table" thus can be said to refer not only to Descartes's

---

[20] AT VI, p. 130; see Descartes (1985), I, p. 167.

6.3. Index sui: *The Norm of Truth*

adversaries, but also to Descartes himself: the dark chamber in the engraving reproduced here may be said to represent, from a Spinozistic point of view, the inner space of the intellect, and the figure in it is the inner watcher, the "inner eyes," as the oft-repeated Cartesian metaphor of the "natural light" implies, by which the judging ego watches the "content" presented to it by the (receptive and passive part of the) intellect. For Spinoza the separation of the soul into two disparate faculties is inconceivable; more interestingly, he denies that there is an inner space of thought, a dark chamber of a soul, or an inner theater. The image of inner eyes, or a watcher, who allegedly examines a content presented to them as a picture or even as a play, is false; these inner eyes of the soul, says an amazing text, "with which the soul sees and observes the things, are the demonstrations themselves" (EVp23s; see discussion later in the book). There are no eyes to see the demonstrations, for demonstrating *is* "seeing."

Leibniz was well aware – and sharply critical – of the psychologistic implications of the Cartesian theory of truth and knowledge. Spinoza can be said to oppose Cartesian psychologism as well. Leibniz opposed Descartes's "intuitionistic"[21] approach, so to speak, from the "left": he did it from the point of view of his own formalistic conception of logic and of the nature of thinking. Spinoza, who was much less inclined and less sensitive than he to the technical aspects of the theory of meaning, truth, and knowledge, did it from "the right." Like Descartes, he rejected the formalistic approach that both attributed to the scholastic philosophers. But he criticized Descartes as well. Made from the noetic point of view, his criticism of Descartes amounts to a rejection of the project of epistemology and a refusal to acknowledge the independence of the question of *knowledge* from the question of *being*. Thinking is a mode of being, and thought is an ontological concept. This, in the last analysis, is why a theory of method cannot precede the theory of being and of man.

The import of the Descartes-Spinoza-Leibniz triad of oppositions and partial agreements – and in particular that of Spinoza's position – can be appreciated in light of the Cartesian doctrine of "evidence" and of the "clear and distinct." Descartes himself does not always make precise whether these terms designate "criteria of truth" or define the essence of truth; in other words, the pure theory of truth and the pragmatics of truth are not always clearly distinguished. Leibniz rejected both as psychologistic (or subjectivistic), and offered instead a comprehensive theory based on his two "great principles": the principle of contradiction and the principle of sufficient reason. The exact nature of the relations between the two principles is a matter of some controversy,

---

[21] Belaval (1960) is the most comprehensive study of Leibniz's attitude towards Descartes. He emphasizes the deep differences between the two by referring to Descartes's theory of reasoning by the term "intuitionism." In much of the secondary literature on Descartes in French, it was customary to do the same. This risks seeming anachronistic, as "intuitionism" is usually understood as referring more or less exclusively to a well-defined approach to the nature of mathematical truth, linked to the Dutch mathematician Brouwer. I keep to this use, however, because it is more neutral than "psychologism" and because I do not see a comfortable alternative.

and I shall not enter into it here. Schematically put, the principle of contradiction is the principle that determines the minimum condition of truth – lack of contradiction; it is, according to Michel Serres's happy metaphor, a kind of "filter" separating the thinkable from the unthinkable or the impossible, letting only that which can be judged "true" or "false" into the realm of thought. The principle of reason, on the other hand, is the principle of the universal demonstrability of truth.[22]

Spinoza embraces "evidence" as a universal trait of the "true idea." Again, this doctrine is explicitly formulated in all his writings, from the CM (I, 6) through the *Short Treatise* (II, 15, 3), the TIE (§ 35) up to the *Ethics*, where it is first said "He who has a true idea at the same time knows that he has a true idea, and cannot doubt the truth of the thing" (EIIp43) and then, in the scholium of this proposition after the lines just quoted, Spinoza poses the following question to the reader:

> who can know that he understands some thing unless he first understands it? That is, who can know that he is certain about some thing unless he is first certain about it? What can there be which is clearer and more certain than a true idea, to serve as a standard [*norma*] of truth? As the light makes both itself and the darkness plain, so truth is the standard [*norma*] both of itself and of the false.

As in Descartes, then, evidence is an immediate characteristic of truth. No less important, however, is Spinoza's stepping away from Descartes, in particular from Descartes' psychologism. Thus, just like Leibniz and for not altogether different reasons, Spinoza does not accept hyperbolic doubt as a helpful methodological stratagem. Doubting is sometimes an empty play of words, and the Cartesian "hyperbolical doubt" is a matter for "an inquiry into obstinacy," not method (TIE § 77). Otherwise, it is only a matter of insufficient knowledge. In any case, there is no "will" to freely accept or affirm a given content or perception, refuse or reject it (which is also a kind of affirmation), or suspend any kind of positive judgment. One cannot seriously doubt a theorem demonstrated *more geometrico*. Likewise, disagreement is also not a matter of different "decisions" taken freely by differing agents. If neither obstinacy nor insufficient knowledge is the issue, there is usually a disagreement on the meaning of words (e.g., TIE § 54).

---

[22] For a more elaborate discussion of the relation between Leibniz's two principles, as well as the differences between him and Spinoza on this matter, see Yakira (1989), pp. 153–196 and Grosholz and Yakira (1998), passim. Cf. Serres (1968), vol. 1, pp. 117–142. Della Rocca (2008) constructs his interpretation of Spinoza on what he presents as the centrality of the principle of sufficient reason (PSR) in Spinoza's philosophy. This is evidently true although, first, the fact that Leibniz distinguishes between this principle and the principle of contradiction is important – at least Leibniz himself thought that the discovery of this distinction was one of his greatest achievements; secondly, Della Rocca sees in the PSR a principle of universal explicability, while I suggest that we regard it rather as a principle of universal demonstrability.

6.4. Explaining Error and Truth

The upshot of all this is a radical relativization of the role of the subject in the theory of truth and of the true idea. The primordiality of the idea of *idea* and of the *idea-ideatum* unity receives thus concrete expression in the doctrine of man as a being of reason, which is *ipso facto* the foundation of a theory of true knowledge. As in Descartes, an important element in the elaboration of this theory is the explanation of error; but Spinoza's explanation is profoundly non-Cartesian.

6.4. Explaining Error and Truth

Spinoza affirms an *advantage* of truth over error.[23] The concept of such an advantage is construed in a theoretical discourse that turns around the difference between the "external" and "internal" properties of the true idea, between truth as the idea-object relation and adequacy as the "inner" characteristic of the true idea. The normative dimension of Spinoza's philosophy begins to take concrete shape, not just as a theory of truth, but also as a technique of the emendation of the intellect. This is, however, a very curious kind of technique. For it is supposed to amend not a machine – of the body or of the mind – so that it may function better than it usually does, but, in an important way, being itself. It silently informs the anthropological parts of the *Ethics* and Spinoza's whole venture.

Paragraph 69 of the TIE implicitly opens the way to such a technic. The *forma veri*, the "form of truth," it says, is not the "extrinsic" relation to what is referred to by the true idea, but is "something real" that is to be found in true thought itself (TIE, §§ 70–71), that is, independent of its relations with other ideas or its object. Spinoza illustrates the distinction between the "external" and the "intrinsic" with the aid of two examples. The design of a building or a machine can be "true" without referring to anything existent, that is, even if the building or the machine drawn in it do not exist. The "truth" of such a design is its intrinsic qualities as a "good" – or executable – plan: if actually constructed, the building would stand and the machine work. Conversely, the fact that an idea corresponds to a real object is not a sufficient condition for it to be "true." If Paul thinks, for the wrong reason, that Peter is there, or perhaps lies about it, and Peter is by chance indeed there, Paul's thought is not made "true" by the mere fact of "corresponding" to an actual situation.[24]

---

[23] If truth is just the "agreement" of the affirmation (or denial) with the thing denied (or affirmed), "it may appear that there is no difference between the false and the true Idea ... and if this should be so, one may justly ask, what advantage has the one from his Truth, and what harm does the other incur through his falsity?" *Short Treatise*, II, p. 15.

[24] These kinds of situation are abundant in contemporary truth-theoretical discussions. Unlike his modern day successors, Spinoza does not try to resolve the apparent paradoxes involved in them by relying on purely semantic or epistemological considerations, but rather by turning the question immediately into an ontological one.

Proposition 36 of EII is an "orphan" proposition; not altogether part of the immediate context in which it appears, it does not serve any explicit or direct role in the subsequent discussion. It states that "inadequate and confused ideas follow with the same necessity as adequate or clear and distinct ideas," which may seem paradoxical[25] or incompatible with the claim about the inherent advantage of truth over error and, more importantly, with the possibility of holding a positive doctrine of freedom. If adequate ideas are necessary, then "fatalism" seems to be the immediate and inevitable conclusion. If writing the *Ethics* is as necessary as the writing of, say, some stupid theological tract, how to account for its advantage? Why, indeed, bother writing – or, better still, reading – it at all?

Proposition 36 appears in this particular place – the doctrine of error – because it apparently constitutes a refutation of Descartes's doctrine of the origin of error as a free decision of the will. By the use of "*same* necessity," it can also be considered as directed against Descartes's alleged breach of the symmetry of free will: prior to affirming or rejecting a given content, the free will is supposed to stand in a state of "indifference." But Descartes seems on a few occasions to imply that the "clear and distinct" determines the will with a greater force over the will than the unclear and confused.[26]

EIIp36, however, is interesting for yet another reason. Read in conjunction with the aporia of TIE § 69 – a non-true truth – it implies a double-faced doctrine of the universal explicability of ideas. Both true and false ideas are explicable. But while errors, false, or non-adequate ideas are explicable by causes that lie outside themselves as "cognitive" contents, true ideas are "explained" by what they are and by what they contain in themselves as true thought-contents or, precisely, as truths. There are many possible answers to the question "why does Paul think Peter is there?" Many of them involve all kinds of causes: Paul was dreaming, had hallucinations, saw something he erroneously thought was Peter's, and so on. But one explanation is different: if Paul had a true idea about Peter's presence, the explanation of him having this idea is Peter's presence, or the truth of the idea that Peter is there. Unlike the first kind of explanation, the second kind is not trivial. Truth is its own explanation, and it is its only explanation; truth, in other words, is *index sui*.

Yet, a question does arise here: in what sense can inadequate and adequate ideas both be said to "follow with the same necessity"? Some commentators

---

[25] As rightly remarks P. Macherey, op. cit., p. 271.
[26] The demonstration is also quite problematic: repeating the conclusion of the previous discussion, according to which inadequacy or confusion exists only in individual human souls, Spinoza simply adds that by EIIp6cor, it results immediately that all ideas follow with the same necessity. This corollary (see Chapter 4) states that the objects of ideas follow from their attributes with the same necessity as ideas follow from the attribute of thought. It is not at all clear why this is needed to prove the necessity of all ideas. The demonstration also contains, in a rather non-habitual way two more propositions, EIIp24 and 28, that are not rigorously part of it, but that are apparently meant only to shed more light on the move effected here.

6.4. Explaining Error and Truth

suggest that the lesson to be drawn from proposition 36 is the "relativity" of the difference between adequacy and inadequacy. But if this is all there is to this proposition, it is redundant and does not do much more than reiterate what has been already proven in propositions 33–35: there is no "ontological" difference between truth and error or between adequacy and inadequacy; error is partial truth, and inadequacy is the privation of adequacy.

Since there are no causal relations between bodies and souls, what explains the truth of Peter's idea in Paul's mind is thus not an "external relation" like the seeing of Peter. The inner quality of a true idea, the *forma veri*, which is the explanation of its truth, is not some casual flow from Peter to Paul's mind. The necessity with which adequate ideas "follow" is thus not causal necessity, and Spinoza's doctrine of the universal explicability of ideas is not a "causal theory of reference" or the like. EIIp36 deduces the "necessity" of the true idea not from the way it is originate in a mind, but from the fact that all "ideas, insofar as they are related to God, are true" (EIIp32). Considered as they are "in God" – that is, considered as what they are as ideas, by their essence or in their original being – all ideas are adequate.

The contention that all ideas, whether adequate or inadequate, are subject to the same necessity is not just another manifestation of Spinoza's alleged "naturalism," but rather belongs to his *noétique*. Human adequate and inadequate ideas emerge by the force of the same universal laws that govern all things in nature. But precisely because adequacy is the original being of ideas, or their essence, the inner necessity of true ideas is not altogether the same as the exteriority of the necessity of inadequate ideas. I would go even farther and suggest that the necessities of truth and error are *radically* distinguishable.

One of Spinoza's most important doctrines – the theory of freedom – is based on a far-from-trivial distinction between two sorts of necessity: that which acts and exists by its own nature and that the seventh definition of EI calls a "free thing"; and that which is determined to act or exist by what does not appertain to its nature, is alien – or exterior – to it, and that the same definition calls "necessary or rather compelled" (*vel potius coacta*: coerced or forced). The two necessities have one and the same source and, more importantly, enjoy equal intensity (for the sake of simplicity, one can call it the "quantity" of necessity). Both are natural, and both do not leave room for indeterminateness or contingency. Qualitatively, however, they differ radically. This is even the most important difference: the one necessity is freedom; the other, bondage (*servituts*). In light of this I suggest reading EIIp36 to imply that equating the adequate and inadequate ideas' necessity is done only from the point of view of the "quantitative" – but not "qualitative" – aspect of necessity.

The subtle play of equivalence and difference between the two necessities may give tangible meaning to the claims that truth is *index sui*, and that it is necessary and still a manifestation of freedom. This doctrine also has interesting ramifications for the view of adequacy as normativity. The universal *explicability* of ideas imposes an ethical *exigency*: if truth is self-explicable, error needs to be explained. Mechanical causal relations are relations of exteriority. They were conceived as relations between *partes extra partes*. The exterior origin of the necessity of inadequate ideas seems to suggest the exteriority of mechanical causes and, consequently, of paradigmatically "scientific" explanations. Error, in other words, has to be scientifically, or even "medically," explained. Truth, or adequate ideas, is not explicable in this way. It is not necessary to understand "explicability" exclusively in causal terms, and, in fact, Spinoza seems to distinguish, parallel to the distinction between two necessities, two forms of explanatory strategies: scientific, causal, or mechanical; and ideational, according to reasons, or rather to the inner meaning or intelligibility of the matter in question. Letter 40 implied the specificity of ideational causality; EIIp9 seems to retract from it; but EIIp36 implicitly reintroduces the thesis of the letter. Apparently Spinoza did not arrive to a satisfactory solution of the tension between the latter and the parallelism thesis (see earlier discussion).

That someone has, or thinks, this or that idea can, and has to be, explained. Insofar as these are adequate ideas – or, seen *sub specie aeternitatis*, ideas *simpliciter* – what defines their being as ideas is their being thought-content, that is, their intelligibility. Spinoza's distinction of two kinds of necessity means that the (causally) explicable should be distinguished from the *intelligible*. Insofar as everything can be explained, the adequacy of adequate ideas, just like any other ideas, can be subject to *why* questions. But there is a great difference between the truth of an idea, the cause of its being an idea, and the fact that it is being thought by a person. One may legitimately ask such questions as "*why* is the proposition 'the sum of the angles of a triangle equals two straight angles' true?" One may also ask "why does Peter think that the sum of angles is 180 degrees?" More awkward, but arguably not altogether impossible, would be to ask a *why* question about the very being of the triangle or its idea. For Spinoza these three questions have one answer, in which geometry, epistemology, and ontology coincide and form together one theme. What explains the necessity of the triangle's "objective being" (the "content" of its idea, the "truth" of a proposition, the validity of a theorem), its true or adequate knowledge, and its "formal being" (the triangularity of the triangle) is one thing: a demonstration. Other explanations – physiological, psychological, or sociological for example – may be true in many ways, but they remain irrelevant as far as adequacy is concerned. The recognition of this irrelevancy is what Spinoza's theory of "adequacy" is all about. A demonstration of a mathematical-like truth is, for Spinoza, inherent to this truth as the conditions of its ineligibility or adequacy. The true idea carries its truth in itself, and its truth and adequacy are hence self-explanatory. They are self-explicable in the most literal sense of the word: they are explicable, but there is no need to look anywhere outside the truth of the true idea for an answer to the question "why is it true."

Inadequate ideas, on the other hand, let alone positively erroneous or false ones, are also explicable. Untruth, moreover, *has* to be explained. Ideas of this kind can – and have to – be explained, or even demonstrated, by some causes or reasons other than themselves. The need to explain inadequacy, and irrationality in general, is imposed by the general hygiene of rational thought. This is precisely what Spinoza does in the propositions in EII that deal with inadequate ideas, and then in the third and fourth parts of the *Ethics*: he formulates guidelines for explaining error, pathology, and irrationality. Such explanations furthermore have a liberating effect – they mitigate the intensity of the affects caused by ignorance of causes and lack of understanding. Insofar as inadequate ideas, unlike adequate ideas, have their origin – or necessity – outside themselves, they can and are to be explained in the "scientific" way, by some kind of causal, "mechanistic" explanation – psychological, sociological, historical, physiological, and so on – in which the "cause" is taken to be external to the effect.

6.5. Adequate Ideas in God and in Man

The ethics of truth – the requirement to explain and emend error – is based on truth-theoretical (if one may so call it) and epistemological considerations. Yet these considerations are not sufficient to account fully for what Spinoza describes as the inner perfection of adequacy because Spinoza's theory of the adequate idea is not really an epistemology but a *noétique*. The strictly epistemological efficacy of the adequate idea – for example, the fact that we can deduce from it all the properties of its object – is a pragmatic advantage; at bottom, it is just a consequence or derivative aspect of what ideas are ontologically.

A remarkable feature of the later parts of EII is the constant reference to God. It is hard to think of many other philosophers whose theories of the *mens humana*, of truth and error, of adequate and inadequate knowledge, and so on, contain such frequent references to God, to God's ideas, or to ideas insofar as they are in God, as does Spinoza in his theory of knowledge. It is also hard to think of theories not only of knowledge but also of truth and of rationality that rely so systematically on a concept of the "body" as Spinoza's; but through the identification of ideas as they are thought by humans and as they are "in God," the ultimate grounding of epistemology in ontology is accomplished.

Spinoza asserts a complete identity – numerical, as it is sometimes called – of the "ideas" as they are thought in or by a human soul, and as they are said to be in God. I would take a further step and suggest that the use of formulas such as "an idea being in God" is metaphoric and, from another perspective, subversive. The metaphor "in God" when applied to ideas and to thinking signifies the essential objectivity and validity of *thinking* that, as a concrete activity – and not as ontological principle – was never for Spinoza anything else but human thinking. For him, the structure of thought is a "surface" as well as beneath-the-surface layers of signification. The range of the significance of an idea is infinitely larger than what is thought on the surface by a given human soul. Insofar as ideas are *knowledge*, what is accessible to a human being at any given moment is always part of a larger context, necessarily partially unknown.

In terms of a phenomenology of knowledge, Spinoza draws a distinction between the *tacit* and the *explicitly* thought or known. But the tacit is fully and actually present underneath the surface and has real efficacy in it. This "actual existence" of the tacit is where the epistemology turns into ontology. What permits talk of this objectivity and efficacy in non-psychologistic terms is Spinoza's use of the verb *involvere*. In Chapter 3 I suggested that we explain Spinoza's extensive use of this term in light of what Leibniz would articulate shortly afterwards as his *inesse* principle, destined to give rational shape to the relations that hold between the surface and the hidden, between the said and the unsaid, between the explicit and the implicit, between what falls within the horizon of awareness and what is beyond it. For Spinoza (just as for Leibniz), this was not conceived as a psychological distinction: if the "surface" is a thought-content, the "underneath" is that which conditions, in the sense of making possible, its being thinkable, understandable, or intelligible.

Reconstructing a possible meaning of the *involvere* operator on the basis of its actual uses in the *Ethics* shows that Spinoza often uses it in a way that completely relativizes the distinction between the explicitly perceived, known, or articulated and the hidden. The unknown or implicit is effectual in "ideas" as conscious thoughts and positively belongs to the same ideas as they are parts of the *mens humana*. Thus, for example, EIIp16 states that

The idea of any mode in which the human body is affected by external bodies must involve the nature of the human body and at the same time the nature of the external body.

The demonstration is based on two simple principles: (1) causal interactions between bodies depend on the nature of the affecting, or causing, bodies as well as on that of the affected ones (first axiom after lemma 3 of the "little physics"); and (2) "The knowledge of the effect depends on, and involves, the knowledge of its cause" (EIax4, which also constitutes the only argument in the demonstration of EIIp7; see Chapter 3). Thus, if the body is "affected" by, say, a sounding or a smelling body or, simply, if one hears or smells something, the "ideas," that is, the hearing or smelling, are said to "involve" the nature of the hearing or smelling body as well as that of the things heard or smelled. The hearing itself, however, is just hearing. In what way can it then be said to involve a nature? That which is "involved" is something like a necessary condition of the possibility of the "hearing." As such, this "nature" and its role in the conscious experience of the hearing strictly reproduces the figure of the *involvere* relation as it constitutes Spinoza's theory of rationality and informs Spinoza's theory all along. More important from the perspective of our present concerns, in the hearing or smelling these "natures" – the natures of the two bodies causally interacting – are necessarily *implicit*. They are not an immediate part of the experience itself.

6.5. Adequate Ideas in God and in Man

The thesis about how perception involves the nature of the exterior body is the foundation of Spinoza's realism and his defense against solipsism. We can truthfully perceive and then conceive the "external" world because the affections of our bodies involve the nature of the bodies that cause them. The rationality, objective and scientific validity, generality, and adequacy of the knowledge of external bodies, or of the external world in general, is based on the doctrine of the *notiones communes* that are also part of what is included, or involved, in the surface content of conscious experience. Knowledge based on "common notions" belongs to what Spinoza calls the "second kind of knowledge" and is usually regarded as referring to scientific, or rational, knowledge in a rather general, palatable sense. Although certainly somewhat naïve, Spinoza's conception of the nature of scientific knowledge contains an interesting and non-trivial semi-nominalistic critique of abstraction and abstract generality. It is, however, insufficient to give a full account of the way the nature of the body is "involved" in experience. As the all-important and non-trivial corollary of EIIp13 states, our body exists "as we sense it"– the experiencing body's nature cannot be reduced to the "objective" scientific theoretician's conception of it. In the final analysis, the nature of our body as a hearing body is what it hears, not that which the audiologist would take it to be.[27]

But a fundamental question arises immediately: how to account for the alleged validity, rationality, intrinsic value, or, indeed, adequacy, of the *privately* unsaid, silent, and implicit. The "common notions" are involved in – and thus condition and justify – the perception of "external" bodies; but the same holds for one's own body, insofar as it is part of the physical world. They are the effective foundations of rational knowledge, which is ultimately a task of rendering explicit the underlying common presuppositions of actual experience. But also "involved" in what appears on the surface, and in a more fundamental way, is the immediate and strictly first-person perception of oneself. This is what Spinoza means by saying that the soul is the idea of the body. This involvement of a particular body's nature in actual experience is the foundation for, or source of, rationality and adequacy that do not belong to science *simpliciter* but to *scientia intuitiva*. Only thus can we make sense of phrases such as "ideas insofar as they are in God," or bold and apparently paradoxical statements such as "The human mind has an adequate knowledge of God's eternal and infinite essence" (EIIp47).

How can one indeed make sense of, let alone justify, such statements? That humans – all of them, always – have "adequate knowledge" of God seems to go against Spinoza's image as a sober rationalist. It invites some comment. The move that leads to this conclusion is not easy to decipher. The reasoning at play here is clarified mainly in the demonstration of EIIp45. Propositions 46

---

[27] This, in fact, was Leibniz's theory – what is hidden in the confused and obscure sense experience, such as the auditory one, is the rational, clear, distinct, and ultimately formalizable and mathematicizable theoretical theory of sound waves.

and 47 and the scholium after proposition 47 spell out some very non-trivial consequences of proposition 45. This proposition states that "Each idea of a body, or of a singular thing, existing in act, necessarily involves God's eternal and infinite essence" (Curley translation modified). Proposition 46 states that "The knowledge of God's eternal and infinite essence which each idea involves is adequate and perfect," and the scholium after proposition 47 opens by inferring from what preceded it that "we see that God's infinite essence and his eternity *are known to all*" (italics added). These affirmations are remarkable: ideas – all ideas of bodies, or all "souls" – involve God's essence; this involving of essence is, in fact, knowledge; it is necessarily adequate and perfect; hence we – all men and all women – have an adequate knowledge of God's essence.

The demonstration of EIIp45, as is often the case in the *Ethics*, is not only a formal justification of the legitimacy of holding the demonstrated proposition to be "true," but is also an explication of its meaning. It leads back, through a number of steps, to the very first and most fundamental principles of Spinoza's metaphysics: EII8cor, EIp15, EIIp6, and all the way to EIax4 and def6. The whole move is very clearly governed by the logic of the *involvere* operator. This term appears in the demonstration twice explicitly and probably one more time implicitly. It is even more clearly apparent in the propositions, axiom, and definition on which it purports to rely. Schematically, the argument proceeds as follows: the concept of "God" (or substance) is the condition of the conceivability of "singular things": "singular things cannot be conceived without God." The ground of this assertion is supplied by the fundamental EIp15: "Whatever is, is in God, and nothing can be or be conceived without God." The ultimate conditionality of everything – specifically of ideas – is now translated into the affirmation that every idea involves God's essence. EIax4 – "The knowledge of the effect depends on, and involves, the knowledge of its cause" – is once again used for effecting a displacement from general metaphysics to the theory of ideas: Spinoza concludes on the basis of the axiom that since God is the cause of all things according to the attribute under which they are considered, the ideas of these things involve the *concept* of their attributes, which is nothing but (by EIdef6) God's infinite and eternal essence. The use of EIdef6, and not of EIdef4 (the definition of "attribute") is noteworthy: it relies not on the *definiendum* of EIdef6 – which is "God" – but on the definiens. What may explain this procedure is the explicit appearance in def. 6 of the notion of "God,"[28] which expresses once again the ontologizing character of this move.

The first phrase of the demonstration is not a part of the actual proving of the proposition; it is a rare reference to the corollary of EIIp8: "The idea of a singular thing existing in act necessarily involves the essence as well as the

---

[28] We skipped one step, where Spinoza claims, on the basis of EIIp6, that the way God is the cause of singular things depends under what attribute the causality relation is examined. I suggested above that we consider "attribute" as a principle and not as an entity; and, more specifically, as a principle of a fundamental and irreducible possibility of being.

6.5. Adequate Ideas in God and in Man

existence of this thing itself (by the cor. of prop. 8 part II)" (author's translation). The formal redundancy of EIIp8cor in the demonstration of proposition 45 is rather obvious; its appearance here nevertheless is not gratuitous. It seems that it is meant to give explicit expression to what was there all along as the still-implicit motivation of Spinoza's *noétique*. The epistemological-semantic doctrine of the objectivity of the tacit and of the epistemological, or conceptual depth of ideas of singular things (that the "essence of God" is "involved" in them), is *ipso facto* a doctrine of their "ontological thickness."

The scholium after EIIp45 clarifies the meaning of the concept of "existence" as it appears in the proposition. The fact that it appears precisely here is no less significant than its content, for it shows that the discussion in this group of propositions (45 to 47) is ontological no less than gnoseological. Differently put, the doctrine of "adequacy" here becomes a vehicle by which the noetic significance of the seemingly gnoseological concept of "adequacy" is brought to the fore. Spinoza distinguishes, in this scholium, between two possible ways in which *existence* can be conceived: "abstractly, and as a certain species of quantity"; and concretely, when "the very nature of existence is attributed to singular things because infinitely many things follow from the eternal necessity of God's nature." Here, he says, it is in the second sense of "existence" "that I am speaking." The concrete sense of "existence" is given by conceiving singular things as modes of the one substance, a mode being defined (in EIdef5) solely by its *dependence*; we know how dependence looks, or what it means to be a mode, when we take a closer look at the semantic-conceptual relation we express by using such terms as *involvere, comprehendere*, or *continere*.

Obviously the "singular things" in question here are human bodies, and the ideas of these singular things, those ideas that "necessarily involve the eternal and infinite essence" or "attribute" of God, are human souls. In two more steps Spinoza arrives at the conclusion already cited: "God's infinite essence and his eternity are known to all [*omnibus esse notam*]" (EIIp47s). However, the syntax of this phrase seems to invite some caution: why not say simply and straightforwardly "we all know God's essence"? That this is not gratuitous pedantry is shown by what the scholium after proposition 47 offers next: turning again to the gnoseological question, Spinoza explains that this adequate knowledge of the essence of God can serve as a means for achieving the third kind of knowledge evoked in EIIp40, second scholium. Now there follows an interesting observation – interesting especially in light of what has just been said about the "universal" knowledge of God's essence. How is it, asks Spinoza here, "that men do not have as clear a knowledge of God as they do of the common notions"? The answer is, because humans cannot imagine God in the way they can imagine, or have images of, bodies. This explanation is no less polemic than it is theoretical, but the main lesson to retain from it is that what we would call "tacit knowledge" – the "common notions" and by extrapolation the essence of God – is considered by Spinoza as valid knowledge; this validity, however, is not a purely epistemological matter but, in the last analysis, ontological: to have adequate ideas is to participate in a specific mode of being.

As Spinoza says in the scholium to proposition 47, because "God's infinite essence and his eternity are known to all" and because all is in God and has to be conceived through God, we can "form that third kind of knowledge of which we spoke in EIIp40, second scholium, and of whose excellence and utility we shall speak in Part V." The *noétique* of the first thirteen propositions of EII, as well as the consequences Spinoza draws from it in propositions 45–47 of EII, are the foundation of the doctrine of the second part of EV, and their full significance can be appreciated only in this context.

7

Man, a Mode of the Substance

7.1. The Eternity of the Soul

The theory of "our salvation, or blessedness, or freedom" is the final step in the long and laborious philosophical itinerary through which Spinoza has been leading his reader "as if by the hand." "All things excellent are as difficult as they are rare," says the famous closing phrase of the *Ethics*. The hard final step of the *Ethics*, contained in the second half of EV, confers its ultimate excellence and value on the entire journey. This is what the long scholium after EVp20 says. It separates EV into two roughly equal parts: the first brings to completion what we referred to in earlier discussions as the stoic-medical (or therapeutic) or eudemonic moment of the theory of liberation. With the preceding discussion, Spinoza writes, "I have covered all the remedies for the affects, or [*sive*] all that the mind, considered only in itself, can do against the affects." And at the end of the scholium, after a condensed summary of the previous discussion, the next, final gesture is introduced: "With this I have completed everything which concerns this present life ... So it is time now to pass to those things which pertain to the mind's duration without relation to the body." It is now time, in other words, to discuss the eternity of the soul. In fact, though, the announcement "without relation to the body" is followed by constant reference to the body in the ensuing discussion.

There is only one straightforward affirmation of the "eternity" of the "human soul": "The human mind cannot be absolutely destroyed with the body, but something of it remains which is eternal" (EVp23). This proposition is undoubtedly one of the most perplexing propositions of the *Ethics* and a major challenge for any attempt to offer a sound and minimally coherent interpretation of Spinoza's philosophy. It is so because through it, or so it seems, Spinoza's alleged religiosity becomes apparent in a way that is hardly reconcilable with Spinoza's secular and naturalistic rationalism. It is, however, also one of the *Ethics*'s most important pronouncements, and dismissing it as is often done, or explaining it away as a mere metaphor, would amount to acknowledge an ultimate defeat, either of the interpreter or of Spinoza – or, indeed, of both.

Common men are "conscious of the eternity of their mind, but confuse it with duration, and attribute it to the imagination, or [*sive*] memory, which they believe remains after death" (EVp34s). The philosopher should know better. The concept of *eternity* is indeed pertinent, but its exact, philosophical meaning is different from that which the common man thinks it is.[1] What Spinoza calls the "eternity of the soul" does not mean that the soul enjoys, or possesses, a surplus of existence, or being, over and above that of the body. Yet, it is not only legitimate, but also necessary, that there exists an idea expressing the human body under the perspective of eternity. The evocation, in the demonstration of EVp23, of EIIp8 means that this eternity of the soul has to be understood along the lines set forth in the discussion of the mode, or nature of being of "modes that do not exist": roughly speaking, the eternity of the soul, or of that "part" of it that remains after the body dies (or that, presumably, pre-exists its birth) has existence that is similar, or even equal, to the existence enjoyed by the semi-semantic implication, or condition, of the "actual" or of the *fact* of the existence of the body.

The last phrase of the demonstration explains how despite the fact that, according to EIIp8cor, "we do not attribute duration [to the soul] except while the body lasts" we, nevertheless, conclude, first, that "since what is conceived with a certain eternal necessity, through God's essence itself" is *something* (or not nothing); and, second, that this "something" is necessarily eternal. The key to this argumentation is the immediate link established here between "necessity" and "being something." With the appearance here of the concept of *necessity*, a significant circle is closed, as the reader is implicitly directed to the very beginning of the *Ethics*. The eighth and last definition of the first part of the *Ethics* is the definition of the concept of *eternity*:

By eternity I understand existence itself, insofar as it is conceived to follow *necessarily* from the definition alone of an eternal thing (Curley translates "*the* eternal thing"; italics added).

And lest it is not clear enough, Spinoza adds to the definition an *explicatio*:

For such existence, like the essence of a thing, is conceived as an *eternal truth*, and on that account cannot be explained by duration or time, even if duration is conceived to be without beginning or end (italics added).

---

[1] It is also arguably different from what most philosophers or theologians think it is and, consequently, also one of the most puzzling notions of Spinoza's philosophy. Besides presentations and paraphrasing it in introductory or general studies of Spinoza's philosophy, I would mention here three studies of a more monographic nature that try to tackle the difficulty head on: Hallett (1930), Rousset (1968), and Jacquet (1997). Nadler (2001) contains also a discussion of this issue, but from a different perspective of the other three studies mentioned here.

7.1. The Eternity of the Soul

Eternity, then, is not a matter of *time* (or duration); it is neither a very long nor even an infinite, or indefinite, time. Not being explained by time conceivably means also that such terms as "timelessness" are vacuous too, as they purport to give a purchase on the meaning of "eternity" by a simple negation of time – which is, after all, a kind of "explanation by time" – and, hence, do not elucidate its positive meaning. From the definition in EI, however, it is clear that rather than being a "very long," and even infinite, or rather indefinite, time, eternity is existence itself seen under a specific perspective: it is existence insofar as it "follows" – is "deduced" or conceived as following – from the definition of an eternal thing. It is existence as necessary or existence conceived *sub specie necessitas*. A central theme of the subsequent discussion of the first part of the *Ethics* is Spinoza's famous "necessitarianism": all existence, or the existence of all things, follows in this way, that is necessarily, from the definition of an "eternal thing."

The adjective *eternal* appears almost always in conjunction with the concept of *attribute*. *Attribute* is that which the intellect conceives as constituting the essence of substance (EIdef4). On the other hand, there seems to be a full equivalence between *eternity* and *necessity*, as it is said explicitly, albeit in a somewhat indirect way, in the scholium to EIp10: "nothing in Nature is clearer than that each being must be conceived under some attribute, and the more reality, or being it has, the more it has attributes which express necessity, or [*sive*] eternity, and infinity." Eternity, then, is existence seen under the perspective of necessity. It is not, however, just any "necessity" but specifically the necessity that rational, *more geometrico* thought, or ratiocination, manifests. It is necessity in the sense "eternity" has in the concept of *eternal truths*. This notion of *eternal truths* is commonly used in the seventeenth century to designate necessary, paradigmatically mathematical truths.[2]

Spinoza's use of the notions of "eternal truth" or "eternity" as a more or less metaphorical way to characterize mathematical, or conceptual, necessity has nothing unusual about it. Yet, although the concepts of *necessity*, *follow necessarily*, and *eternal truth* play a major, indeed constitutive, role in Spinoza's elaboration of the doctrine of "eternity," the latter's meaning is evidently not quite captured by any conception of scientific rationality presumably extractable from it or reconstructed on its basis. As a mode of existence, "necessity" is thus an ontological concept before it is a modal or logical one. I shall not discuss Spinoza's complex ontology of time and of eternity, which has been done by a number of other commentators. Of particular importance of for us here are nevertheless the two following points: *eternity* is indeed for Spinoza an *ontological* concept rather than temporal one; but it is "ontological" in a peculiar sense: it is supposed to capture the meaning of existence as *necessity*. Not of necessary existence, but of existence as necessity. We shall come back to this idea; suffice it to add at this point that, for Spinoza, the meaning

---

[2] See, for example, Rodis-Lewis (1985).

of "necessity" is not reducible to, or exhausted by, either its modal meaning, the formal structure of modality, or by causal "determinism." For more than anything else, Spinoza's necessitarism is a denial of what can be called "the arbitrariness of being."

Another important element, and undoubtedly more original and iconoclastic, is that the theory of eternity as rational necessity, and the doctrine of rational eternity-necessity as denial of the metaphysical arbitrariness of being, are grounded in a radical denial of the idealistic option. Although an "idealist temptation" is constantly present in Spinoza's rationalistic philosophy, it is circumvented; and, once again, it is circumvented in a way that is not only original, rather iconoclastic, and extraordinary, but also paradoxical. Spinoza tries to overcome the "idealist temptation" while retaining the doctrine of eternity as necessity – more precisely: as necessity of the existence of a thing, insofar as it follows its *definition* or *essence* – as the main safeguard against admitting the arbitrariness on being, by introducing into the heart of his ontology of reason and of thought what is usually taken as the paradigmatic locus of arbitrariness: the *body*.

What had been only in preparation in the first part of the *Ethics* becomes clearer in the two complementary moves of the first thirteen propositions of EII and propositions 21–40 of EV. The constant reference to the body has evidently a markedly polemic role, but it also plays a very positive role in Spinoza's theory of beatitude, salvation, and freedom. All these three concepts traditionally appear, like the notion of "eternity" itself, solely in connection to the soul; Spinoza, probably with some subtle irony, announces his doctrine of *salus, beatitude, libertas* as indeed applying solely to the soul and "without relation to the body" (EVp20s), only to continue his discussion by putting the body at its center and with constant reference to it. The semi-ironic, semi-polemic use of the body in EVp21–40 indirectly explicates the "eternity" of the soul as something systematically belonging to the body, the paradigmatic *hic et nunc*. The essential role the body plays in Spinoza's doctrine of the eternity of the soul – of its salvation, beatitude, and freedom – can best be described as a radical demystification of all of these traditional themes and presumably a crucial measure Spinoza uses in his generalized attempt to neutralize the "religious" significance they carry for the non-philosopher. Purged of their non-philosophical meaning, these terms remain nevertheless not only pertinent but indeed of ultimate importance for the philosopher.

Much of what has just been said is given a curious and condensed expression in the scholium after EVp23, which is a fascinating but also very puzzling text. It opens by reiterating the paradoxical, perhaps ironic, contention that, on the one hand, this idea of the body that, as EIIp11 put it, constitutes the actual being of the soul, is a determinate (*certus*) mode of thought (or an idea) and is "necessarily eternal"; yet, on the other hand, we do not recall anything from before the existence of the body. This, however, does not contradict the

7.1. The Eternity of the Soul

supposed eternity of the soul since, as we already know, "eternity can neither be defined by time nor have any relation to time."

Next in the same scholium comes another remarkable affirmation, indeed one of the most remarkable in the whole *Ethics*: even though we do not have recollection of anything that happened before the existence of our body, we still "feel and know *by experience* that we are eternal" (italics added). The experience, however, that Spinoza apparently had in mind when he was writing these lines has very little to do with what is usually understood by this word, although his choice to use this particular term here is very significant. For the "experience" in question is the experience of *comprehending*, or *rationally understanding*:

For the mind feels those things that it *conceives in comprehending* no less than those it has in the memory.[3]

Understanding then, intellecting, thinking, or calling the action by which the *intelligible* is apprehended by whatever name is, therefore, no less vividly and intensely *experienced* by the soul, and is, apparently, no less reliable than what we perceive by the mediation of the body and rely upon as experience. More importantly, intellection is homogeneous with experience in its more habitual sense.

But most remarkable of all is what comes next (which is probably the reason why it is sometimes mistranslated): "For indeed the soul's eyes, by which it sees and observes the things, are the demonstrations themselves" (Curley translation, slightly altered). The seeing itself, the "inner eyes" that are supposed to be seeing inwardly whatever is thought – notably rationally deduced well-formed and valid demonstrations – are nothing but these very same demonstrations. They are the "eyes," not the object seen by the inner eyes and lighted by a natural light. The latter, of course, is the Cartesian (among others) metaphor for "reason" that, as Descartes says in many different ways, like light lightens all objects and is indifferent to the specific objects it lightens at particular occasions. Once again, then, the Cartesian duality – this time, of reason and of its objects – is collapsed into one unique entity: the eyes of the soul are nothing but the demonstrations; there is nothing beyond the act of intellection, and this act is one with the intellect: this is the unity of the intellect as the agent of thought, of the act of thinking, and of the object of thought – the very same unity some Hebrews saw as if through a cloud. Since experience is a *par excellence* affair of *seeing*, it is reasonable to use the ocular metaphor in order to pinpoint the concrete way in which the "intellective experience" is effected. There is no mystical "seeing" here or anything like it, just the banal demonstration – which is

---

[3] Italics added; Curley translates the Latin *intelligendo concipit* as "conceives in understanding." The key word here is *intelligendo*, impossible to translate directly into English. The verb *intelligere* and the adjective *intelligibile* refer, respectively, to the specific action of the intellect and to what is specifically given as an object to the intellect.

not at all banal; indeed, it is the least banal of all things. It is the painstaking toil of the mathematician, geometer, or, in particular, demonstrating metaphysician that constitutes that experience through which one knows that one is eternal.

But then the body, of course, surfaces again. It seems that Spinoza has a special kind of demonstration in mind – not so much the mathematician's demonstration after all, but, as now becomes finally clear, his own philosophical demonstration:

> [T]hough we do not recollect that we existed before the body, we nevertheless feel that our mind, insofar as it involves the essence of the body under the specie of eternity, is eternal.

For this reflexive feeling of thought insofar as it involves the essence of the body *sub specie aeternitatis* is precisely what the demonstrations of Spinoza himself bring about. The way this is done, though, is twofold: by the *content* of the demonstrations on the one hand; and, on the other, reflectively, by their nature as *demonstrations* or by their *being* adequate ideas. In other, more Spinozistic terms, through its both "objective" and "formal" being, the (idea of) the body involving its eternal essence is also a "feeling" of our soul's being eternal.

7.2. The Third Kind of Knowledge

The preceding remarks delineate the space wherein Spinoza's theory of the eternity of the soul is supposed to make sense as an effective concept and as a concrete human option: in the realm of rational knowledge necessity becomes transparent and, as such, the mode of one's own being. But if the rational necessity of mathematical truth – as Spinoza conceived it – can be said to have served him as the model on which he erected his doctrine of the eternity-necessity of the soul, it can hardly fulfill a similar role when the doctrine of "beatitude" is concerned.[4] The main move from the seemingly mathematical model of rational necessity to the concrete rationality of beatitude and freedom of the philosopher is accomplished in the theory of the third kind of knowledge.

The doctrine of the kinds of knowledge appears in all three of Spinoza's main philosophical essays: the *Treatise on the Improvement of the Intellect*, the *Short Treatise on God, Man and his Well-Being*, and the *Ethics*. There are certain differences between the three versions, but the essential doctrine remains more or less the same. Thus in the *Short Treatise* it is a question of "degrees" or "grades"

---

[4] The same does not apply to the doctrine of freedom which, in this sense, can be said to be a mediating step between the mathematical-like concept of necessity on the one hand, and that of human "beatitude" on the other. The necessity that the ideal mathematician espouses in executing a well-formed demonstrating is a paradigmatic case of "free-necessity," and is the opposite of necessity as coercion.

7.2. The Third Kind of Knowledge

of knowledge, in the TIE they are called "modes of perception," and in the *Ethics* "kinds" (*genera*). In the TIE there are four kinds of knowledge, while in the *Short Treatise* and the *Ethics* there are three main kinds of knowledge, but the first is divided into two. The first kind of knowledge is the only source of error, says Spinoza; it is, however, a kind of *knowledge*, and thus not necessarily erroneous in itself. It is the *source* of possible error since, by definition, it is not comprised of *more geometrico* demonstrated truths. The other two kinds are fully rational, or "adequate," and, again by definition, do not involve error. The second kind of knowledge, called by Spinoza "reason," is usually understood to refer to scientific knowledge. More accurately, it is rational or scientific in the traditional sense in which rational knowledge is *general*. There is no indication in Spinoza's discussions of this kind of knowledge if, or how, it can be applied to "science" in the modern sense of the mathematical theorization of physical reality as it begins to take shape within the *république des lettres* of which Spinoza was himself a respected citizen. It is also not at all clear if and how it can inspire in the modern reader some helpful insight into the nature of scientific rationality. All these matters have been abundantly discussed in the secondary literature, and there is no need to do so again here.[5] In what follows we will be concerned only with the third kind of knowledge.

The third kind of knowledge is called by Spinoza *scientia intuitive*, and it is defined by him in more or less the same terms in the three philosophical treatises. It proceeds, it is said in the *Ethics* (in the second scholium of EIIp40), "from an adequate idea of the formal essence of certain attributes of God to the adequate knowledge of the formal essence of things." This is undoubtedly a rather obscure definition, and it is no wonder that it has caused considerable embarrassment and disagreement among readers of the *Ethics*. A main point of contention concerns the religious language in which Spinoza usually speaks about his *scientia intuitiva*. This is the case notably in the *Short Treatise*, so much so that some commentators are ready to take the mystical language of, for example, the "union" of the soul with the object of knowledge and love (II, Ch. 22 and other places), as expressing a real mystical experience. In the TIE the religious language is less conspicuous, and the presentation of the doctrine of the kinds of knowledge on the whole, including the third kind, seems to respond mainly to epistemological worries. In the *Ethics* the religious language reappears, although it is less "mystical" than in the *Short Treatise*. In all three expositions of the doctrine of the kinds of knowledge, however, Spinoza gives the very same illustration, according to which the third kind of knowledge is

---

[5] Gueroult, Rousset, and Macherey in French and Mignini in Italian offer very detailed and useful commentaries; the Hebrew reader has at his disposal the rich commentaries of both the *Short Treatise* and the TIE done by Yosef Ben Shlomo; and in English there are innumerable presentations of this doctrine as well. Among them Wolfson, as usual, proposes a rich, although not necessarily always very relevant, historical background; The *Cambridge Companion to Spinoza* is useful; Hallett has important things to say; and I would add here a reference to Genevieve Lloyd's works on Spinoza.

similar to the way in which, in considering very small numbers – say 1, 2, and 3 – "no one fails to see that the fourth proportional number is 6 – and we see this much more closely because we infer the fourth number from the ratio which, in one glance, we see the first number to have to the second." Without pursuing this particular issue much further, it is possible to say that the "formal essence" from which we are supposed to be proceeding to the knowledge we have when we see a ratio directly is the mathematician's knowledge of the nature of ratio in general, as it is given by the demonstration of the nineteenth theorem of Euclid's book VII and that is, despite possible appearances, a very non-trivial piece of knowledge, which means that behind the apparent simplicity and innocence of the example there is a world of complexity and a very non-trivial kind of reasoning.[6]

The general definition of the third kind of knowledge in the *Ethics* is not only particularly abrupt, but is also presented as not altogether integral to the theory of rational knowledge that is the topic of EIIp40 and the two scholia subsequent to it. The second scholium after EIIp40 opens by announcing that the following presentation of the theory of the kinds of knowledge concerns the ways in which we "perceive many things and form universal notions"; after enumerating the two kinds that give us knowledge in its more common sense, both non-scientific and "scientific," Spinoza adds that in "addition to these two kinds of knowledge, there is (as I shall show in what follows) another, third kind, which we call intuitive knowledge." The purpose of the general – and ambiguous – description given to this other kind of knowledge in EII is apparently not much more than to caution the reader that the theory of knowledge has not yet been fully completed and that the preceding discussion in EII is only part of it. More will come later. This happens in the fifth part of the *Ethics*, where supposedly the nature of the third kind of knowledge is now being explicated and, in fact, is made the pivotal theme toward the elaboration of the final conclusions.

The last paragraph of the scholium following proposition 23 of EV (which, let us recall, states that the human mind cannot be entirely destroyed and that something that is eternal remains) contains a characteristic back-and-forth movement between the elevated "religious" language of eternity and the down-to-earth "naturalistic" language of the actual existence of the body. The convoluted movement of this scholium thus ends with a volte-face: we feel and know by experience, as we have just seen, that we are eternal; we also know that this eternity of ours cannot be defined by time or explicated as duration (*per durationem explicari non posse*); we conclude, then, that our soul cannot be said to perdure (*durare*) but "insofar as it involves the actual existence of the body, and to that extent only does it have the power of determining the existence of things by time, and of conceiving them under duration." This last remark brings us back to duration, to existence, and to the body, but also to knowledge

---

[6] See the remarkable Matheron (1986); Yakira (1990).

7.2. The Third Kind of Knowledge

as the presumably essential activity of the soul in which its "eternity" may be conceived *in concreto* as a mode of existence. It thus clears the way for the next move (more or less propositions 24–33), which is the exposition of the concrete meaning of the third kind of knowledge.

The first step of the exposition of *scientia intuitiva* – EVP24 – is again a paradoxical statement, in its content and in the way it is demonstrated. The proposition says that "The more we understand [or "comprehend," *intelligimus*] singular things, the more we understand God"; and the demonstration simply says that this is evident from the corollary of EIp25. This corollary, which purports to be an evident and immediate consequence of previously demonstrated truths, reads: "Particular things are nothing but affections of God's attributes *sive* modes." Spinoza does not specify here, in EVp24, what exactly he means by understanding singular things, but this apparently happens in what follows.

Proposition 25 of EV is explicitly about the third kind of knowledge, and by implication one can consider proposition 24 as applying to it as well. At first glance, however, the depiction of the third kind of knowledge in proposition 24 might appear to stand in some tension, if not contradiction, with the description of the original philosophical quest as the search for a particular object of knowledge and love (e.g., TIE, §§ 1, 6, 10). It now becomes clear that this knowledge of the "eternal and infinite" object of love, of "entire nature" (TIE, §13), or of God is not an independent kind of knowledge but is conditioned, and apparently identical to, or perhaps contained in, the knowledge of the things of the world, or of these "singular things" mentioned in EVp24. This, however, should presumably not be read as a statement about the knowledge of God as accumulated knowledge of "the things." Although all singular things are, in one way or another, parts, manifestations, or expressions of God, or modes of the one infinite substance, it would be simplistic, if not altogether wrong, to say that according to Spinoza the more we know such things, the more we approach a comprehensive knowledge of nature and God. A less simplistic approach to the understanding of singular things can allegedly be achieved through a certain rapprochement between Spinoza and Kant. This would apparently mean that the "more we know the singular things" amounts to a gesture implicitly positing some "regulative" idea of total knowledge of the whole of nature. Such an interpretation will not do either, and attributing to Spinoza a "progressive" or Kantian-like doctrine, or assimilating the knowledge of *Deus sive natura*, insofar as it depends on the knowledge of "the singular things," to "scientific" knowledge, would arguably miss what was most important to Spinoza.[7]

---

[7] As Richard Mason notes in a remarkable little article (Mason, 2001), many of Spinoza's most important interpreters share the opinion that an assumption of the "intelligibility of nature" or of the world was a fundamental assumption of Spinozism. Mason curiously reaches the conclusion that "Spinoza was not a rationalist," which is a reasonable thing to say only if one

The third kind of knowledge is not altogether "knowledge," at least not "knowledge" in the sense of cumulative, public, and empirical gathering of data, processing it, and reporting about it in a language. It is thus noteworthy that in the subsequent exposition of the nature of the third kind of knowledge itself (EVp26–33) and of its significance for human "beatitude," *intelligere* or *concipio* are used more frequently than is *cognoscendi*. Even if it is true that Spinoza sometimes seems to use these terms interchangeably, it is probably significant that he chooses to refer to the *achievement* of the third kind of *knowledge* as *intelligere*. All these terms are multivalent, their different connotations partially overlapping. But *intelligere*, insofar as it connotes the characteristic act of the intellect, the intellecting itself, or, inversely, the act by which that which is *intelligible* is grasped should be best translated here, I suggest, as "understanding" (also "comprehension" or "apprehension"). In any case, it is noteworthy that while all three kinds of knowledge are kinds of *knowledge*, only in talking about the third kind, *scientia intuitiva*, does Spinoza uses *intelligere* when he describes to what it concretely amounts.

Any attempt to offer here anything resembling a systematic distinction between "knowing" and "comprehending" or "understanding" would be pretentious. Speaking rather informally, one could still suggest, first, that *knowing* and *understanding* (or *comprehending*) are conceptually (and phenomenologically) distinct; second, that they each refer to discernible experiences and cognitive procedures; and, third, that while *knowing* lends itself more readily to an objective construal – epistemologically, but also historically, sociologically, and institutionally – *understanding* too can be understood in non-psychologistic terms, albeit quite different from all these. One could attempt a further step and suggest that although conceivably not altogether intentional, Spinoza's preference of *intelligere* to *cognoscendi* is nevertheless non-accidental and that it underlines what can be more easily surpassed in *understanding* than in *knowing*, namely the presumption of an original duality of the inner realm of knowledge and the external space of its object. This, as we have suggested, is unfit as an adequate interpretation of Spinoza's fundamental doctrine and of what emerges from his *noétique* as the original *idea-ideatum* unity.

The notion of *intelligere* is very frequently used by Spinoza in all his writings, and as has been just said, its appearance is often without any particular purpose. Sometimes, though, its use is not trivial. This is conceivably the case also in propositions 23–28 of part IV. These propositions are part of the relatively long discussion in the middle of part IV (roughly, propositions 19–28) that constitutes the transition from the first part of EIV – in which, as Spinoza says, he believes to "have explained the causes of man's impotence and inconstancy,

---

understands the concept of *rationalism* as referring to some kind of scientism, which, arguably, Spinoza's philosophy was not. But in its Platonic origin intelligibility – and reason, rationality, and so on – are concepts not necessarily reducible to the kind of intelligibility given by modern mechanical or mathematical explanations.

7.2. The Third Kind of Knowledge

and which explains why men do not observe the percepts of reason" (EIVp18s; Curley's translation altered) – to the doctrine of the "wise" or "free man" who has power over the affects and follows the "precepts of reason."

The central theme of these propositions is, on the one hand, the doctrine of virtue as the effort (*conatus*) to persevere in being; and, on the other hand, the doctrine of the rational nature of this *conatus-virtus* insofar as it is directed by reason. It is noteworthy, and perhaps, again, even ironic, that at the center of what might be read – and often *is* read – as a proto-Darwinist theory about the quest for survival as the fundamental texture of (at least living) reality, the reader is confronted with pronouncements such as: it is only as he is determined to act by the fact that he *understands* that man can be said to be acting in the strict sense of the word (EIVp23). Spinoza thus identifies understanding, virtue, and acting; he does the same for living or existing and persevering in one's own being. All these notions are different ways of saying the same thing, namely that the foundation of virtue is "seeking one's own advantage" under the dictate of reason (EIVp24); that "what we strive for from reason is nothing but understanding; nor does the mind, insofar as it uses reason, judge anything else useful to itself except what leads to understanding" (EIVp26); and that "we know nothing to be certainly good or evil, except what really leads to understanding or what prevents us from understanding" (EIVp27).

The same holds for the second part of EV. It seems then that more than "knowledge," the issue at this final stage of the exposition of the Spinozistic philosophical system is a kind of *comprehension* or *understanding* or, precisely, what is achieved through (the Latin) *intelligere*. Again, the *intelligibility* that would be the end product, or indeed the very being, of such an act, is arguably not exactly *knowledge* in an "informational" sense, given, by such locutions as "knowing that": it is not by knowing, say, that the fruit is poisonous and should rather not be eaten that Adam could be "saved" (see later discussion); beatitude or freedom demand some other kind of knowledge. Something that has been more or less implicitly the issue all along becomes explicit through the terminology Spinoza chose to use. Unlike "knowledge" in the sense of either gaining or storing more information, or know-how, or explaining by assigning causes, the concept of "understanding" or "comprehension" in the sense it is given now sits more comfortably in the context of Spinoza's *noétique*. If the second half of EV is to be taken seriously, one can suggest that, on the one hand, this *noétique* is an ontology of that most immediate and apparently banal experience of *understanding*; and, on the other hand, that it is the kind of understanding one experiences in understanding *more geometrico*, that is, when a geometrical concept or a demonstration becomes fully transparent. It is an attempt to give an answer to the question about what one experiences when he "intuits" that 6 is to 3 like 2 is to 1: What is this simplest experience of all? What is "comprehending"? How does one describe it? How does one explain it? What kind of beings are understanding-beings, and what mode of being is an act of comprehending? If philosophy begins in some kind of *wonder*, Spinoza's wonder is wonder aroused by the fact that we intellect, think, and, most amazing of all, understand; or, more precisely, since, as we have suggested above, the soul is the idea of the body and its immanent intelligibility, that (our) bodies are capable of thinking and of understanding, that they are comprehending machines.

The time to show that there is a third kind of knowledge, as had been promised in EIIp40 second scholium, arrives with the first explicit mention of it in proposition 25 of EV. But there is some circularity in Spinoza's detailed discussion of the third kind of knowledge in EV: it seems to presuppose the existence thereof as an established fact. Assuming an alleged definition of the third kind of knowledge in EII, Spinoza first demonstrates that "the more we comprehend [*intelligimus*] the singular things, the more we comprehend God" (EVp24; my translation); and then states, respectively, in EVp25 and EVp26, that "the highest [*summus*] effort [*conatus*] of the mind, and its highest virtue, is comprehending the things by the third kind of knowledge" (my translation),[8] and that "the more the mind is capable of understanding the things by the third kind of knowledge, the more it desires to understand them by this kind of knowledge" (Curley's translation, slightly altered).

What remains not altogether clear here is the exact nature of this knowledge. The definition given in EII is admittedly rather general and even vague, and the first propositions discussing the third kind of knowledge do not explain what exactly is known in that way and what exactly this knowledge looks like. Proposition 25 speaks of it as the soul's supreme effort; proposition 26 explains that the more the soul is capable of understanding things in that manner, the more it desires to actually understand them in this way; proposition 27 speaks of its outcome as the highest "acquiescence,"[9] but nowhere is it described in a more concrete manner.

It is, in fact, not until EVp30 and EVp31 that a better grasp of the nature of the third kind of knowledge and of its relation to the general definition given in EII can be attained. Proposition 31 reads as follows: "The third kind of knowledge depends on the mind, as a formal cause, insofar as the mind itself is eternal." First, it should be remarked that, once again, the positive thesis is

---

[8] Curley translates *summus* by "greatest" and *conatus* by "striving and desire." In the first case this seems to me to blur the normative connotation of the wording (which becomes, however, explicit in the use of *virtus*), and in the second to miss Spinoza's intention in the all-important doctrine and concept of *conatus*. His translation introduces into it, as many other interpreters do as well, an unfortunate teleological connotation. Pautrat translate correctly *effort* (in French), and Shirley cleverly keeps the Latin *conatus*. See also Hallett (1962), who tries astutely to capture the positiveness of, among other things, this Spinozistic concept by his (paradoxical?) concept of "potency-in-act."

[9] The term Spinoza uses is [*Mentis*] *acquiescentia*. This neologism of Spinoza is translated by both Curley and Pautrat, for example, as *satisfaction*. It seems that rather than "satisfaction" Spinoza had in mind some kind of "acceptance," "approval," or "welcoming."

7.2. The Third Kind of Knowledge

inseparably interwoven with a polemic message: that the soul is the (formal) cause of the third kind of knowledge implies that this knowledge, if achieved, and despite the fact that it is as difficult as it is rare, does not have a superhuman or supernatural cause. The human soul is its cause or origin; it has nothing in it that would justify referring to it as "revealed," as "miraculous," or as accessible only to the few privileged ones who are "chosen" by some superhuman authority. Its attainment needs no grace. It also means that "eternity" is not a recompense for good deeds or a virtuous life. The full significance of this last point will become clearer in EVp42, the very last proposition of the *Ethics*, which states, in what might seem a moralistic tone, that "beatitude is not the reward of virtue, but virtue itself." It is certainly significant that this was chosen by Spinoza to be his last word.

Not only is it not supernatural knowledge, but also its object is not supernatural: proposition 30 states that it is in self-knowledge – in the knowledge that the soul has of itself *and of its body* as necessary (that is, *sub specie aeternitatis*) – that we have also knowledge of God, because (so says the demonstration) "eternity is the essence of God insofar as it involves necessary existence." Instead of supernatural revelation, there is knowledge or, indeed, a kind of *understanding*: "To conceive things *sub specie aeternitatis* is to conceive things insofar as they are conceived through God's essence, *as real things*, or [*sive*] insofar as through God's essence they involve existence" (EVp30dem, italics added). Real, necessary, or eternal existence – all are different ways to express one and the same thing: the non-arbitrary, non-simply-given, or non-purely-factual nature of (human) existence.

The main steps of the demonstration of EVp31 are the following: the soul's eternity consists of its cognition of the body and of itself *sub specie aeternitatis*; being eternal means having the knowledge of God (whose very essence is eternity, as stated in EVp30dem); this knowledge is necessarily adequate; and this means that the soul "is capable of knowing all those things which can follow from the given knowledge of God"; according to its definition in EII, knowing things in this way is having intuitive knowledge, or knowing things in the third kind of knowledge.

The key to this rather abstruse argumentation is, I suggest, the "given knowledge of God."[10] The latter formula – certainly non-trivial – probably refers to the knowledge of God as it is "given" – in the sense of having been elaborated, to be found by the reader – in the first part of the *Ethics*. If this indeed is the case, then apprehension of the things "the soul is apt of knowing" as following from the adequate knowledge of God, is exactly what is deduced in the

---

[10] The Latin reads: *Mens, quatenus aeterna est, ad illa Omnia cognoscendum est apta*, quae ex data hac Dei codnitione *consequi possunt* (italics added). Pautrat translates *cette connaissance de Dieu une fois qu'elle est là*, that is – the knowledge of God, *once it is there*. This translation makes sense and avoids the ambiguity of which Curley's translation suffers, although it is not inexact as far as the letter of the phrase is concerned.

Ethics as following from the doctrine of *De Deo*, that is, from the doctrine of God – or substance or nature – as it is expounded in its first part. It is sometimes assumed that the "deduction," or "knowledge," of things as "following from the idea of God" applies to some kind of calculation that yields, in principle at least, knowledge of the "whole," of all existence, or of the "totality" of being. Spinoza's notion of God's idea, or intellect, suggests something of this kind but in a very abstract way. It is important from the point of view of the concrete economy of *scientia intuitiva* and of salvation – otherwise the first and second parts of the *Ethics* turn out to be redundant. Its relevancy, however, should not be understood as implying the legitimacy of a notion of total knowledge. Spinoza never speaks of human knowledge, not even of the third kind, in terms that can be interpreted as envisaging such knowledge from the human point of view, not even as a regulative ideal, let alone as a real human possibility. Progress, even progress of scientific knowledge that was taking shape concretely in front of him, and to which he himself contributed, even if very modestly, was never a major concern of Spinoza's as it was for Descartes, Leibniz, and Kant. The rational effort to gain understanding of the necessity of one's own bodily existence was not for him a historical process occurring on the level of political, cultural, or scientific institutions. For all their importance, these were not party to the "salvation" of the third kind of knowledge.

On several occasions Spinoza stresses the thesis that the third kind of knowledge can be born only from the second kind. This point remains, however, rather obscure, and it is not altogether clear, for example, if, how, and to what extent the direct grasp of an arithmetical proportionality depends on knowledge of Euclid. What is nevertheless quite clear is that while the second kind of knowledge involves a rationality based on some (nominalist or semi-nominalist) conception of generality (the common notions, *notiones communes*), the third kind of knowledge is knowledge of the particular, a direct grasp of the essence of an individual being. However, and despite what appears from its definition and from the arithmetical example given as an illustration, it is not a generic term, but a proper name. Although there is a good deal of ambiguity in Spinoza's dealing with the third kind of knowledge, it seems that the inner logic of this doctrine implies that it is not a kind of knowledge under which many objects can be known, but that it is a knowledge or understanding of one privileged object. The third kind of knowledge is the name of the understanding of one's own body *sub specie aeternitatis*. It means a rational attitude toward one's own existence as metaphysically – and not just causally – necessary, that is, as non-arbitrary, as not simply given.

7.2.a. Perfection I
Proposition 31 and its scholium together constitute a rather complex move. It closes the exposition of the doctrine of *scientia intuitiva* and introduces what will become the topic of the final gesture of EV and, in fact, of Spinoza's whole philosophical enterprise, namely the doctrine of beatitude and freedom.

7.2. The Third Kind of Knowledge

Proposition 31 itself contains, beside its polemic import, a very problematic thesis. To say that "the third kind of knowledge depends on the mind, as a formal cause, *insofar as the mind itself is eternal*" (italics added) means that the eternity of the soul is not an *achievement* but the *condition* of the third kind of knowledge. Yet the third kind of knowledge, the knowledge of God, or the *acquiesecntia* of the soul have all been presented so far, and will be presented in the following propositions as well, as achievements: the more we know the things in the third kind of knowledge, the better we understand God (EVp25dem); from the third kind of knowledge results, or is born, an intellectual love of God (EVp33); the more we know things in the third kind of knowledge, the lesser is the hold death has over us (EVp38 and its scholium); and so on.

Accordingly, the scholium following EVp31 opens with what seems like a direct and unproblematic consequence of the underlying conception of the third kind of knowledge as an achievement: the more one is versed in the third kind of knowledge, "the more he is conscious of himself and of God, that is, *the more perfect and blessed [beatior] he is*" (italics added). This seemingly innocent remark introduces two important and non-trivial notions: "perfection" (which is in fact reintroduced here, after having been used before but in several rather different ways) and "beatitude" (or "blessedness"), which will be at the core of the subsequent discussion. But before getting to this final discussion, a possible objection has to be addressed: if the eternity of the soul is the condition, and not the result, of its conceiving the things *sub specie aeternitatis*, then, obviously, this conceiving of things must have been in it in some sense all along. True, says the scholium, we now understand that what we call "the eternity of the soul" and conceiving the things *sub specie aeternitatis* are one and the same thing. Yet, for the sake of clarity and better understanding, we can keep talking *as if* the soul begins to be and *achieves* a comprehension of things *sub specie aeternitatis*.

The scholium after EVp33 reiterates a similar clarification. EVp32cor states that "From the third kind of knowledge there necessarily arises an intellectual love of God," and proposition 33 states that "The intellectual love God, which arises from the third kind of knowledge, is eternal." The scholium that follows this proposition reads:

Although this love toward God has had no beginning ... it still has all the perfections of love, just *as if it had come to be*, as we have feigned [*finximus*]. There is no difference here, except that the mind has had eternally the same perfections which, as we have feigned it, now come to it, [and it had had them] accompanied by the idea of God as an eternal cause. If joy, then, consists in the passage to a greater perfection, blessedness must surely consist in the fact that the mind is endowed with perfection itself (Curley's translation, altered; italics added).

The eternal soul, the eternity of the soul, or the eternity of that part of it that "remains," is not, however, a condition of this knowledge and of its improvement by being its substrate, its source, or the *locus* of its occurrence, but in a different way. As we have seen, the demonstration that something that is eternal "remains" of the soul (proposition 23) is based on the corollary to EIIp8 that explains the mode of existence of ideas (like that "remaining part" of the soul that is the idea of the body) of modes that do not exist (like the not-as-yet-born or already-dead body). Insofar as it is an *idea*, the soul can thus be said to be the condition of the third kind of knowledge by being, or rather *involving*, a certain kind of intelligible ontological fact that, apparently, is usually tacit but can become explicit as positive understanding.

It is in proposition 32 and its corollary that we "feign" that from the third kind of knowledge arises, is born, or results [*oritur*] pleasure, which is the soul's greatest "satisfaction," and an "intellectual love of God." In fact, the idea that we pass from one state of being to another has accompanied the whole process of elaborating a philosophical theory of man ever since the second part and, in particular, since the positing of the *conatus* as the axis of this theorizing in the third part. Not until the very end of the *Ethics* were there any serious questions about Spinoza's philosophy being a philosophy of the amelioration of human life, of liberation, of self-educating, or of the painstaking acquisition of wisdom and of power over the affects. What the philosophical enterprise has been all about, or so it seemed, is a certain human power, a *potentia*, being deployed, an intellectual aptitude becoming a concrete mode of life necessarily taking place in time. Movement has been at the center of the whole discussion – from relative ignorance to knowledge; from a lesser joy to a greater, more lasting, and stable one; from pathological to sane existence; and so on.

We now discover that this has not been altogether the case. A difficulty resurges here and must be addressed. It "resurges" because, of course, this is not a new difficulty. In differing degrees of explicitness, it has accompanied the development of the argument of the *Ethics* all along. This difficulty is one of the most severe difficulties in Spinoza's philosophy; many of Spinoza's critics raise it, and it assumes many forms. As with other aspects of his thought, it is not until the very end of Spinoza's major work that its significance really comes to light. In one formulation it is the notorious difficulty of "particularization" or of the continuity of the descent in the chain of causes or reasons from the one and infinite "substance" to finite "modes." Now it appears in yet another guise: how should one account for the apparent contradiction between, on one side, the "fact" of the essential "eternity" of the soul and the "innate" knowledge thereof,[11] and, in contrast, the pursuit of happiness and the thesis that the acquisition of higher forms of understanding, beyond being the goal of philosophy, is most crucially the attainment of a higher mode of being. On the one hand, joy, pleasure, and love are conceived as manifestations, results, or the ideational "side" of transitions – obviously in time – from lower to higher forms of knowledge and from lesser to greater well-being or, indeed, being tout court; while, on the other hand, "eternity," which is, so to speak, being par

---

[11] We have already seen: men – all men – "are indeed conscious of the eternity of their mind" (EVp34s).

7.2. The Third Kind of Knowledge

excellence, is not really an achievement but a fundamental ontological fact and a pre-condition of the movement toward "more" being.

As Spinoza repeatedly warns his reader, we have no choice but to continue talking "as if" philosophical comprehension, the kind of human existence accompanying such comprehension and that Spinoza calls "beatitude," and freedom are played out on the field of time. Time, this "aide of the imagination," is in fact unavoidable even at this final moment of the exposition of the rational theory of man. Although often ignored, the problem of reconciling the inevitability of the point of view of temporal existence with a concept of rationality allegedly thought *sub specie aeternitatis* is undoubtedly one of the more difficult questions posed by the Spinozistic philosophical enterprise.[12] More concretely, this question can be formulated as a question about the meaningfulness and relevancy of the point of view of eternity to human life and happiness. Apparently aware of it, Spinoza nevertheless does not address it directly. What he offers his reader instead are the somewhat obscure and cursory clarifications such as the ones referred to above and a number of warnings against remaining within the confines of "the common opinion of men," which do not reach beyond the temporal concepts in which we all necessarily think.

But in effect the entire system of thought of which the *Ethics* is the most exhaustive and authoritative articulation is itself the answer to this question. The nature of Spinoza's enterprise as a whole and of the discussion of the final part of the *Ethics* in particular imposes on the reader the need for a radical hermeneutics. The ambiguity of the language Spinoza uses, its suggestiveness, and the constant back-and-forth movement from the temporal perspective to that of the *sub specie aeternitatis*, as well as the partiality and brevity of the explanations he offers in the last propositions and scholia of the fifth part of the *Ethics*, all help to account for the embarrassment of commentators or for the fact that one can find in the literature on Spinoza reactions as diverse as the complete dismissal of this last part of the *Ethics* by Jonathan Bennett or, at the other pole, a sort of mystical interpretation such as Jon Wetlesen's.[13]

According EVp33s, just quoted, there is a difference between "joy" and "beatitude": if the first consists in the transition, obviously in time, to a greater perfection, the second consists in the fact that "the mind is endowed with perfection itself." The notion of perfection appears also in the demonstration of proposition 27: he who knows the things by the third kind of knowledge "passes to the greatest human perfection." It has appeared quite often in previous parts of the *Ethics*, and its uses by Spinoza are not only diverse but also rather paradoxical. EI speaks a number of times of God's "absolute

---

[12] Not all the commentators, of course, avoid this question. Two examples are Mason (1997), who dedicates a few pages to it; and Macherey discusses it in considerable length in his (1994).

[13] See Wetlesen (1979). Wetlesen is only one of numerous commentators who find in Spinoza's philosophy religiosity or even mysticism. As Moreau (1994), pp. 287–288, rightly remarks, the debates around these interpretative claims are often more verbal than substantive. See Chapter 1.

perfection" (e.g., EIp11s and EIp33 second scholium). EII (def. 6) states: "By reality and perfection I understand the same thing," and later the formula *realitate sive perfectio* appears a number of times. In the theory of the affects of EIII, "perfection" most often refers to the soul undergoing great changes, passing "now to a greater, now to a lesser perfection" (EIIIp11s). If in all these occurrences *perfectio* is used in a categorical way, the preface of EIV seems to offer a *relativist* perspective on the concept of "perfection" – it is just a scheme for comparing among things. This "relativism," however, is more apparent than real, and Spinoza's rather long discussion of the meaning of "perfection" in this preface expresses the extremely problematic nature of the attempt to furnish *non-moralistic normativity* with an ontological foundation.

The preface to the fourth part of the *Ethics* – "On Human Bondage [*Servitude*], *seu* the Power of the Affects" – is an important text. For one thing, it seems to contain a belated and indirect response to Blyenbergh, who had posed a real challenge to Spinoza and had incited him to embark on what has turned out to be his most elaborate (but inconclusive) attempt to explicate the nature of moral normativity and to provide a foundation for normative and evaluative distinctions.[14] As in the letters to Blyenbergh, so in the preface of EIV the notion of "perfection" is the center of the discussion. The preface is also a dense and mazy text; and it is not without significance that here appear two of Spinoza's most famous – and pregnant – idioms: *Deus sive Natura* (twice) and *causa sive ratio*. Both express similar complex and puzzling gestures: Is "God" reduced to nature, and was Spinoza a pantheist? Is it the other way around, and was Spinoza a panentheist or acosmist? Do "reasons" have causal efficacy? Or, maybe causes are the tools of rational explanations? I shall not address these questions here; this has, in fact, been done, either directly or obliquely, in the course of the previous discussion. But I suggest that the fact that they appear in this text is not an accident and that it contains a serious attempt to come to terms with some real difficulties. It thus merits special attention.

Spinoza begins the preface to EIV by presenting the purpose of what the reader would find in this part of the *Ethics*:

Man's impotence to moderate and restrain the affects I call bondage. For the man who is subject to affects is under the power [or, literally, jurisdiction – *juris*] not of himself, but of fortune, in whose power he so greatly is that often, though he sees better for himself, he is still forced to follow the worse. In this part, I have undertaken to demonstrate the cause of this, and what there is of good and evil in the affects. But before I begin, I should say a few words first on perfection and imperfection, good and evil (Curley's translation, somewhat altered).

---

[14] Besides some scattered references here and there, there is next to nothing in English (or in other languages) on the exchange of letters between Spinoza and Blyenbergh. It seems that only Deleuze, in his little *Spinoza: Practical Philosophy*, has dealt seriously with the important exchange with Blyenbergh; see his (1981). Deleuze's discussion of the correspondence with Blyenbergh is admirable in many ways, but it also arguably misses the essential (see infra, section 7.4.).

7.2. The Third Kind of Knowledge

After this general introduction Spinoza first offers what purports to be a nominalistic genealogy of the notions of "perfection and imperfection" and "good and evil." Despite some differences – some highly significant – the critique of both "perfection-imperfection" and "good-evil" is based on one principle: anthropomorphism. More precisely, the fallacy that leads to the fundamental moralistic misconceptions is a typical displacement: terms that are pertinent and even necessary in the context of human life are illegitimately extrapolated into metaphysics and are taken to be applicable to being as such. In both cases it is some form of *comparison* that is the natural context and origin of these terms. In the case of "perfection" and "imperfection," the anthropomorphic fallacy leads to teleological thinking, which is analyzed already in the appendix to EI and is presented there as the more or less ultimate philosophical sin. Its source is diagnosed as man's habitual attitude toward artifacts. Knowing them to be the result of some design or intention of the artisan, people tend to consider them in light of the original plan and to evaluate the extent to which they fulfill their fabricator's intention. When people began thinking with the aid of universals, they forged abstract ideas of such artifacts and, generalizing the natural attitude toward man-made things, took these ideas to be models or standards according to which at first artifacts, and then natural things as well, were assessed by ostensibly absolute standards. This, suggests Spinoza, is the reason "why men also commonly call perfect or imperfect natural things which have not been made by human hand." "Perfection" and "imperfection" are thus forged as teleological notions and give tangible articulation to the prejudice according to which nature acts in view of pre-established ends or that final causes are real and have efficacy outside the realm of man's projections and planning.

In the same way, "perfection" and "imperfection" and "good" and "evil" are *modi cogitandi* or "notions we are accustomed to feign" and on the basis of which we compare the things. If the "perfection-imperfection" couple is a conceptual scheme that permits us to compare things, so to speak, to themselves (or to what they were supposed to be), the "good-evil" distinction is the conceptual space where comparisons are made among different things. Depending on who makes the comparison and what is being compared, "one and the same thing can, at the same time, be good, and bad, and also indifferent." Good and evil, then, are relative denominations.

Spinoza's genealogy of the prejudices expressed by such terms as "perfection," "imperfection," "good," and "evil" is undoubtedly both simplistic and not very original. This, however, attests not so much to a lack of intellectual resourcefulness, but to the fact that the real point of this preface is not the genealogy of teleological thinking. The critique of these terms is the scaffolding for the real message of this text. As was the case in other instances examined here, it is two pronged: polemic and positive. The refutation of the pertinence of the notions in question is part of a complex argument, containing a typical back-and-forth movement of critique, rejection, and partial rehabilitation based on a kind of hermeneutical dialectic. The first, critical step is a heuristics in which the common uses, or misuses, of the terms considered, which are obstacles to a better understanding of the issues involved, are removed or amended. An authentic philosophical concept lies behind the veil of ignorance and prejudice – perhaps also seen as if through the clouds – and it must be made accessible, so that a real theoretical discussion of the questions involved can begin.

Generally speaking, the polemic in the preface is directed against what can be labeled the "moralistic" stance. But there is a significant difference in the ways Spinoza expounds the pernicious outcome of reifying "perfection" and "imperfection" in comparison to "good" and "bad." While the notions of "good" and "evil" do not designate anything positive in things, it is not altogether clear whether the same is true of "perfection" and "imperfection." When Spinoza speaks of "perfection" and "imperfection," it is just one side of the contrast that is mentioned: when men "see something happen in nature which does not agree with the model they have conceived of this kind of thing, they believe that Nature itself has failed or sinned, and left the thing imperfect."

It seems then that the analysis of the conceptual opposition of "perfection" and "imperfection" – but not that of "good and "bad" – reproduces a classical asymmetry. One main argument of classical anti-Manichean and anti-Gnostic theodicies is that evil has no ontologically, or conceptually, *positive* status. The absolutely good God is the only creator, so there is no principle of *evil*, and what God created is necessarily and completely good. What humans perceive, or conceive, as "evil" is the privation of good and neither a positive being nor a real conceptual content. In his dealing with the language of "good" and "bad" Spinoza takes a decisive step beyond tradition and says here about "good" what has been traditionally said of "evil" – that it designates nothing positive in the things. If we consider the things in themselves, they are neither good nor bad nor even morally indifferent. "Good" and "bad" are simply inapplicable to things as they are in themselves.[15]

The same, however, cannot be said of "perfection" and "imperfection." If "good" and "bad" are rejected by Spinoza on similar grounds, as two equally abstract, relative, and metaphysically vacuous notions, it appears that insofar as "perfect" and "imperfect" are concerned, the traditional asymmetry is retained: "imperfection" is nothing but privation of perfection. What is still

---

[15] It is explicitly in order to oppose something such as what Leibniz insists already in the second paragraph of his *Discours de métaphysique*: that there is, in the created things, an intrinsic good, as can be learned from the Biblical story of creation, where it is told that, after each of the six days in which he created the world, God looked back "and saw that it was good." The issue between Leibniz and Spinoza is neither the existence of God nor his goodness. Leibniz's defense of the case (and cause) of God is not directed so much against Spinoza's alleged atheism as against the latter's anti-moralism. What Leibniz tries to defend is the applicability of moral adjectives to being (or to creation).

7.2. The Third Kind of Knowledge 239

implicit in the preface of EIV will become explicit toward the end of the *Ethics*: "perfection," as a term applied to human existence, is a real concept.

The critique of good and perfection is not Spinoza's last word in this preface. Both notions regain their lost dignity, since they are useful for the project of a rational theory of man. Like the use of time in the doctrine of beatitude and freedom, so here too, philosophical reason has to have recourse to some aids of the imagination: "For because we desire to form an idea of man, as a model of human nature which we may look to, it will be useful to us to retain these same words with the meaning I have indicated." "Good" will designate what helps us live a rational life, which we picture to ourselves as the life of a wise and a free man; and "we shall say that men are more perfect or imperfect, insofar as they "approach" this picture or "model."

But, as has just been said, "perfection," unlike "good," is readmitted into philosophical rationality not only as a useful mode of thought, but also as a real *concept*. Immediately after Spinoza presents the prejudicial origin of both notions, "perfection" – but not "imperfection" – is invested with positive content. "Imperfection" remains a prejudicial term, never signifying any positivity: neither the negation of perfection, nor its opposite, but its (always relative) privation. The "perfection-imperfection" mode of thinking originates in the inclination to make comparisons among things belonging to the same specie; and here emerges the equivalence, stated in definition 6 of EII, between the concepts of "perfection" and "reality":

For we are accustomed to refer all individuals in Nature to one genus, which is called the most general, that is, to the notion of being, which pertains absolutely to all individuals in Nature. So insofar as we refer all individuals in Nature to this genus, compare them to one another, and find that some have more being, or reality, than others, we say that some are more perfect than others. And insofar as we attribute something to them which involves negation, like a limit, an end, lack of power, and so on, we call them imperfect, because they do not affect our mind as much as those we call perfect, and not because something is lacking in them which is theirs, or because Nature has sinned. For nothing belongs to the nature of anything except what follows from the necessity of the efficient cause. And whatever follows from the necessity of the nature of the efficient cause happens necessarily.

It first seems that insofar as "being" or "reality" have positive meaning, "perfection" does too. However, the reasons for, and exact nature of, the identification of "perfection" and being are not altogether transparent. It is thus not quite clear why, for example, if "comparison" is a mode of thinking, comparing things insofar as they are "beings," or members of the most comprehensive genus, has a more objective import, or is more theoretically legitimate, than comparing them according to other criteria. One weighty consideration is that Spinoza's words here have to be read against the background of past and contemporary philosophical and theological doctrines defining perfection as a mode, or rather quantity, of being. Once again, the curious dialectic of subversion and traditionalism in Spinoza's stance is unmistakable. Rejecting with one hand a central theoretical motivation for the complex doctrine of "perfection," namely the "teleological prejudice," he with the other hand allows it in as the foundation of his ethical theory. We shall come back to this matter.

7.3. Necessity, Reason, Wisdom, and Philosophy

The paragraph just quoted from the preface of EIV ends with the following statement: "nothing belongs to the nature of anything except what follows from the necessity of the efficient cause. And whatever follows from the necessity of the nature of the efficient cause happens necessarily." This is one more refutation of the teleological prejudice. This time, however, it is not its genealogy or the detection of its psychological sources that serve as the grounds for its refutation but, in a more substantive way, the doctrine of causal, or deterministic, necessity. It is affiliated to the final discussion in the *Ethics* by hinting at the doctrine of human freedom elaborated in the last propositions of EV. The few words Spinoza devotes to causal necessity in the preface to EIV should be read against the background of his entire metaphysics of necessity. The latter constitutes in fact a reversal of the problem of determinism and of its significance for moral theory. Although one has to wait until the very end of the *Ethics* in order to see if and how this reversal can be accomplished, the short text just quoted points to a curious, original, and utterly iconoclastic use of determinism as the grounds of normativity and of the positive value of being.

The alleged incompatibility of determinism, causal or otherwise, with free will is usually considered the obstacle that determinism poses to moral theory. If everything is determined by causes – so goes a very old but still vital claim – and if causes operate according to fixed laws, and if, moreover, humans are part of nature, their actions are completely determined, and there is no room for "free will." Just like any other natural beings, they are subject to natural necessity, and what they do is nothing but the fully determined result of the great chain of causes and effects. What people conceive as their own "choice" and what they call "free will" are chimeras. But without free will and free choice, morality is impossible. What men and women do is perhaps "behaviour," but they do not *act* in the strict sense of the word, and there is thus no room, in the context of a doctrine of human nature, for a positive concept of *agency*. Consequently, and most importantly, humans cannot be held accountable for what they do. Or, in a more theological manner, if the natural or "secondary" causes follow from the First Cause, or God, it is He who is the source of everything that happens, good or bad, for accountability presupposes free choice. From St. Augustine all the way to Kant and many contemporary writers, the same question recurs: are causal determinism on the one hand, or divine foreknowledge, omniscience, and omnipotence on the other, compatible with free will and free choice? If not, then man is not a moral agent; if they are, how so?

To this query Spinoza has a very famous, perhaps notorious, answer: free will and free choice are indeed chimeras. Man's conception of himself as

7.3. Necessity, Reason, Wisdom, and Philosophy

acting out of his free choice is just like what a falling stone, if it was conscious of its fall, would have said to itself – I fall because I freely choose to fall. Taken literally and in its full gravity – as it should be – Spinoza's radical determinism seems to jeopardize any ethical project, including Spinoza's own. If everything is causally determined, or predetermined, so it seems, there is not much point in trying to convince people to act differently from the ways they are determined to behave by natural causes. The fatalistic thesis entailed by this simplistic – but not altogether inaccurate – formulation has been countered by many arguments, among them the many attempts to refute the famous *idle argument* (called by Leibniz the *sophisme paresseux*) that go back to the Stoics, notably Cicero and Chrysippus, and all the way down to Aristotle's *De Interpretatione*.

A particularly interesting version of the refutation of the fatalistic argument from a theological-moral point of view, especially in the context of Spinoza's *Ethics*, is due to Hisdai Crescas's defense of the pertinence of a doctrine of the will within the framework of deterministic philosophical theology.[16] Roughly speaking, Crescas's solution to the difficulty is based on the contention that the will is a necessary presupposition of the determined event. In its classical formulation it states that what is predetermined is not just that the patient is healed or not (and thus, allegedly, either way there is no point in calling the doctor), but also a whole event that includes the calling – or not – of the doctor. The calling – or not – is an integral part of the event of recovery – or not – of the patient; in its turn, the will and decision to consult – or not – the doctor is part of the event of his being consulted (or not) and, hence, of the recovery.

Crescas's work was known to Spinoza, and it was probably more highly esteemed by him than that of other Jewish philosophers he had studied in his youth. Some commentators believe there are significant similarities between Crescas's solution to the question of free will and Spinoza's determinism. In fact, however, Spinoza has a very different argument against the "idle argument" from Crescas's. The challenge of fatalism, the "idle argument," appears sometimes as a disturbing question about the writing itself of the *Ethics*: if everything happens necessarily – if, among other things, discovering the truth and having adequate ideas is itself determined by natural causes – then, like the recovery of Cicero's sick man, it will either happen or not anyway; hence, why bother with writing the *Ethics*? Isn't it futile? Spinoza's answer to this question is not based on an attempt to show that free will and determinism are compatible and is thus very different from Crescas's. Instead of trying to

---

[16] The Hebrew reader can find a concise resume of Crescas's doctrine, as well as some of the affinities to Spinoza, in Zeev Harvey (2010). There are, of course, also many commentaries on and presentations of this important mediaeval Jewish philosopher in other languages. According to some contemporary terminological habits and pseudo-typological categories, Crescas's doctrine would probably be described as "compatibilist" – the notions of free choice and free will are "compatible" with a fully deterministic theory of creation.

circumvent necessitarian determinism, he poses it as the very ground of his answer. Paradoxically, at least from the point of view of the very long – still living – history of this questioning, the doctrine of geometrical necessity, which is usually seen as the source of the difficulty, is the key to his answer to the fatalistic challenge and the condition of the possibility of positive freedom.

In trying to reconstruct a Spinozistic answer to this question or to understand the place of the doctrine of freedom in his determinism, one general remark seems to be necessary here. Crescas's doctrine of free will looks like an example of compatibilism, and Spinoza too is sometimes said to be a kind compatibilist. More often than not, however, what is called compatibilism is a theoretical *deus ex machina* that purports to somehow convince us that the incompatible is, after all, compatible, at least in the one privileged, perhaps "anomalous" case of human will and choice. Seen under this light, compatibilism is usually a kind of *pis aller*, a theoretical "lesser evil" that, in the absence of a better solution, retains two competing but contradictory exigencies (as Kant would put it) of reason, determinism, and freedom. Spinoza's response to this challenge is completely different. For him determinism and free will are indeed incompatible. Reason shows that free choice is an illusion. But freedom is not. Freedom, however, has no sense and is an empty word, *unless* necessitarian determinism is true. There is no need to show how freedom and necessity are compatible – let alone give up one of them – because they are one.

Spinoza's ontology of the necessitarian character of all being is also, if half implicitly, a kind of phenomenology of geometrical thinking. Briefly, this doctrine seems to say that although the geometrician who demonstrates the absolute truth – and necessity – of, say, Pythagoras's theorem, does not choose freely any of its elements and does not *adopt* them as "true" or *reject* them as "untrue," he is nevertheless integrally free in demonstrating the truth of the theorem. His free will does not play any role in demonstrating the theorem, let alone in the structure of the demonstration itself; yet, there is no sense in which the Spinozistic geometrician can be said to act unfreely or, more accurately, to be compelled or coerced by the truth of the theorem. The *Ethics Ordine Geometrico demonstrate* can thus be said to be an attempt to generalize this kind of free necessity into a comprehensive ontology, a theory of man and ethics. As such, it is itself an exercise in freedom.

This, however, is only part of the story. Leibniz, one of Spinoza's keenest readers, understood well that insofar as formal truth is concerned, there is no contradiction between necessity and a certain concept of freedom. But he considered this doctrine wanting from the point of view of moral theory. In his *Theodicy*, and on many other occasions, he uses arguments similar to Crescas's as one element of his strategic, multifaceted struggle to "save contingency," as he called it. The latter, he thought, was a necessary condition for recuperating the coherence and legitimacy of the concepts of choice, accountability, and guilt and, more generally, of a moral point of view. Leibniz, like Spinoza, was no compatibilist, but his life-long search for the Ariadne's thread that would

7.3. Necessity, Reason, Wisdom, and Philosophy

enable our getting out safely from the labyrinth of necessity and freedom was an attempt to counter Spinozism with a complete rationalist philosophy that retains the main tenets of moral theory said to be made untenable by Spinoza.

Leibniz shows that claims about the problematic or even contradictory nature of such notions as free will, moral agency, responsibility, and accountability do not exhaust the threat to moral theory posed by determinism. For even more serious than the putative incompatibilities mentioned is the undermining of the legitimacy of all evaluative thinking, which causal determinism entails. Simply put, the contention that man cannot choose to do things differently from the way he actually does them does not in itself refute the soundness, and objectivity, of applying adjectives such as "good" and "bad" to things in general, and to human behavior in particular. Something else has to be added in order to be able to deny moral language any effective conceptual content in the way Spinoza denies the legitimacy of the language of "good" and "bad." Leibniz indeed understood not only the fact, but also the full significance, of the threat *necessitarism* poses to moral theory. It is even not altogether inconceivable that he became aware of it through his long, in fact incessant, preoccupation with Spinoza's philosophy.[17] Necessitarism means not only that everything is and happens according to natural – usually conceived as causal – fixed laws, but also that what happens cannot be otherwise in the most radical sense, so that the very supposition of an alternative is simply nonsense. This means that no real (unfulfilled) possibilities exist beyond actual existence. The whole point of Leibniz's critique of Spinoza's necessitarism is precisely this: a space of real possibilities has to be found beyond actual existence. This is the *sine qua non* of an effective defense of the coherence and pertinence of the most fundamental moral concepts. If there is no space of real possibilities beyond existence, it seems, there is no room for *any* evaluative thinking.[18] If everything is what it is, if there are no lacunas in reality, if "existence in act" covers the whole scope of being (and of possibility), if things cannot be otherwise than the way they actually are, if thinking cannot open a perspective of possibilities beyond the horizon of existence, then, as Spinoza emphasizes here and on other occasions, nothing can be said to be lacking anything, and no morally evaluative judgments are possible. The issue is deeper than mere critique of teleological thinking or of anthropomorphism, for without being able to envisage a range of unfulfilled, or pure possibilities, nothing seems to be open to thought other than affirmation of sheer *givenness*.

Leibniz put his finger on a real difficulty. In a different way, this is also the sense of Hegel's famous criticism of Spinoza, who had to show indeed

---

[17] Stewart (2006) is an interesting, emphatically non-academic and pro-Spinozist, sometimes simplistic, but overall intelligent and knowledgeable presentation the struggle against Spinoza as Leibniz's main, almost obsessive, motivation. Although certainly an exaggeration, there is perhaps more than grain of truth in this contention.

[18] See Yakira (1989).

some ingenuity in what can be seen as an attempt to avoid the pitfall of pure "affirmatism." This is where the concept of "comparison" comes into play, as enabling a seemingly comfortable use of normative language. The gesture, once again, is complex. The concept of "comparison" or of an act of "comparing" is far from trivial, and Spinoza seems to be aware of this at least to some degree. Comparing, he thinks, presupposes some medium or context within which it can intelligibly be effected. We compare things that belong "to the same genus or specie." In the background of this principle stands the doctrine of "common notions" and "common properties" as well as the concept of *in suo genere* as it appears notably in EIdef2, which defines the concept of "finite in its own kind." The ultimate context of comparing, adds the preface of EIV, is the "one genus, which is called the most general" and that we conceive by the concept of "being" (*entis*). However, and whether he breaches the nominalist confines or not, comparing things, even if conceptually impeccable, cannot in itself transcend pure affirmativeness and open and explain, or ground, evaluation. To judge of a thing that it is greener or bigger than another is not to make a judgment of value or state a normative preference of any kind. Judging a thing stronger or healthier than another cannot be understood purely and simply as attributing to it more perfection, reality, or, of course, value. A healthy and strong criminal cannot be said to have more perfection or value than, say, a frail and ailing Spinozistic philosopher.

Nevertheless, enter evaluation:

insofar as we refer all individuals in Nature to this [most general] genus, compare them to one another, and find that some have more being, or reality, than others, we say that some are more perfect than others. And insofar as we attribute something to them which involves negation, like a limit, an end, lack of power, and so on, we call them imperfect, because they do not *affect our mind as much as those we call perfect*, and not because something is lacking in them which is theirs, or because Nature has sinned (italics added).

It is thus due to the differing degrees of intensity by which the things "affect our mind" that we consider them as possessing more or less reality *sive* perfection. Insofar as this is understood as the basis for the immediately following anti-anthropomorphic polemics – nothing lacks anything that it should have possessed, and nature does not sin – this statement does not raise any particular difficulty. In truth, though, this statement is much less innocent than it may seem at first sight. It implicitly exceeds the pure positiveness and affirmativeness of simple comparing, for initially it is not at all clear how and why things that are conceived to involve a "certain negation, like a limit, an end, impotence, etc." "affect our mind" less than other things; how and why this difference in the ways in which our mind is affected can be conceived as measuring the amount of perfection or reality these things possess; and finally and most importantly, how and why measuring the "quantity of being" can become the foundation of normative, evaluative, and preferential judgments.

7.3. Necessity, Reason, Wisdom, and Philosophy

Criticizing Descartes, Spinoza famously collapses the perception of conceptual content and the "affirming" or judging its truth value into one act of cognizing (more or less) truthful or adequate ideas. But this is a purely intellectual gesture, and to suppose that it essentially contains an evaluative dimension is problematic. Comparing the results of two athletes – to take a somewhat trivial example – cannot in itself be the origin of any *evaluation* of their respective exploits. The mere perception of a difference between them is *not* the same as *judging* them as "higher" or "lesser" achievements, as having more or less reality, and thus being affected more or less by them. Conversely, monstrosity, horrible deeds, or extreme evil may "affect our mind" more than, say, mild goodness, but we still, according to Spinoza at least, judge the former as involving privation and possessing less reality and perfection than the latter.

Evaluating, preferring, and so on express a *sui generis* attitude, act, or intentional structure. This, at least, is what Kant (but also Hume and many others) thought, and on what he based his *Critique of Judgment*. Spinoza's "comparatist" (if one may say so) "modes of thought" may suggest, insofar as they constitute a predisposition not only to compare things, but also to evaluate them, or to invest comparisons with normative import, a kind of proto-transcendental doctrine. Despite these appearances, though, this is not the case. Suffice it to refer back to the discussion above of the eternity of the soul and of the third kind of knowledge in order to realize that the claim about the differing degrees by which less or more perfect real things affect our mind is basically an ontological claim (and not transcendental). "Reality" is real enough for Spinoza, and even doubly so: adequate ideas are modes of being of the soul, but they are also "true," which means that they designate real objects. Mostly, however, they are entities enjoying real perfection and reality, including this ultimate reality that, as we saw, Spinoza called "eternity." One way or another, the psychologism or proto-transcendentalism allegedly implied by Spinoza's doctrine of reality as the ultimate context of comparison is not the real difficulty besetting his ethical theory. The real question is the exact nature of the identification of "perfection" and "reality" – does this mean a reduction of normative and evaluative thought to ontology? Perhaps it is the other way around?

The greatest affect of all, other things equal, is one toward a thing we imagine simply [*simpliciter*], and neither as necessary, nor as possible, nor as contingent (EVp5).

Insofar as the mind understands all things as necessary, it has a greater power over the affects, or is less acted on by them (EVp6).

Let me reiterate: the concept of *necessity* plays a central – and rather unusual – role in Spinoza's ethical theory. Instead of undermining the legitimacy and pertinence of concepts such as *evaluation, value, norms*, and *normativity*, it rather functions as their foundation and justification. As was mentioned above, determinism in all its forms – causal, epistemological, theological, and so on – is usually deemed the main challenge to moral theory or to having a coherent moral point of view. Spinoza stands this common view on its head and renders determinism the ultimate justification of a fundamentally ethical theory of being and of man. This, however, is accomplished through a number of steps, adding up to a rather complex gesture, the consistency of which is not immediately clear.

"Necessity" plays, first, a psychological role. It is, in fact, a double role. In a way that is, once again, reminiscent of the Stoics, necessity is said to have a kind of soothing effect on man's affective life. This has general significance but is arguably of particular importance in the realm of inter-human relations. What we imagine *simpliciter*, that is, as modally neutral (as neither necessary, nor possible, nor contingent), affects us with the greatest intensity (EVp5). This modal neutrality is the way we think of "things" when we lack knowledge of the causes that determine them. This insight can apply to all kinds of wonders or natural "miracles." When men lack knowledge of the causes of such events, and when these events are considered *simpliciter*, they affect men in the strongest way. But the real issue concerns humans. Thus the demonstration begins by evoking the natural attitude toward what is conceived as "free,"[19] and it is after all mainly to humans that we apply the language of freedom. It then explicitly establishes equivalence between the causally decontextualized conception of "things" and the concept of freedom: "imagining a thing as free" is nothing but imagining it *simpliciter*, that is, being ignorant of the causes that determine it. Men appear as "free" in the sense of uncaused by natural causes. This can be described as the negative meaning of being "free" – negative, though, not in the sense given to it by Berlin in his famous article "Two Concepts of Liberty," but in the sense of a privation of knowledge.

Inversely, the more one understands the necessary nature of things, the more one knows that all things are determined by natural causes, the greater is the power one has over the affects (EVp6). What Spinoza has in mind becomes conspicuous in the following scholium: knowing that loosing or lacking something is unavoidable, or necessary, diminishes the sadness caused by the loss or lack. Although cast in general terms and seemingly depicting the affective effect natural events may have on man, this analysis applies more specifically, and more interestingly, to affects caused by human conduct. Attributing free agency and freedom of choice to people confers a particular force to what they do. Considering people to be the source of their deeds, or regarding conscious intentions or free choices as the real causes of actions, leads to attributing responsibility to the actors and to bad affects such as resentment and *ressentiment* or, on the other hand, admiration and veneration.

Propositions 5 and 6 of EV contain two complementary psychological insights: considering man *simpliciter*, which is just a form of ignorance, is transformed into considering him as positively free and, as such, the author of his deeds. This is indeed the origin of the tendency to mystify human existence,

---

[19] As it is described in EIIIp49: "Given an equal cause of love, love toward a thing will be greater if we imagine the thing to be free than if we imagine it to be necessary. And similarly of hate."

7.3. Necessity, Reason, Wisdom, and Philosophy

to ascribe moral responsibility and guilt or, inversely, glory and saintliness to fellow man or to oneself. These are all bad affects and have pernicious consequences. They can, however, be circumvented by understanding where they really come from, the natural necessity of natural causes. Understanding the natural origin of human behavior means that human actors are not regarded anymore *simpliciter*, and the bad effects that result of the ignorance of natural necessity do not accompany anymore the regard we have of other people. When one knows that something that affects him in a negative way is causally determined, he overcomes the bad affects caused by this thing. One can thus be more "stoical" about natural calamities that befall him, but it is clear that the lessons drawn from this analysis concerning human conduct and inter-human relations are more important.

The psychological insights formulated in the propositions at the beginning of EV, interesting as they may be, are only the preliminaries to the more important theme, namely Spinoza's ethical theory. At this stage comes to the fore the negative and polemic dimension of this theory, or Spinoza's radical anti-moralism. The emotive intensity of the attitude toward what is taken *simpliciter* obtains ethical significance when the ignorance of causes is transformed into a positive image of free choice and freedom; and these are notions expressing ethical attitude. It is here that the morality of good and evil imagined as absolutes emerges: human cognitive and emotional apparatus abhors void, and the lack of positive knowledge of causes is filled up by the imaginary and powerful notions of absolute good and bad.

More than on a medical or biological model, Spinoza anti-moralism is based on a theory of truth. More than like sickness, evil doing is like error, not in the traditional-Platonist sense in which evil is interpreted as a kind of ignorance, but more specifically, because like error, evil too is not attributable to a freely acting agent and, hence, is not reproachable as an intentional wrongdoing. Error, of course, is to be avoided, just as are other forms of unwise or harmful behavior. If such forms of behavior occur nevertheless, which is what happens more often than not, they have to be understood for what they really are and explained in the way errors are explained, that is, as the result of natural causes. Inversely, truth, having adequate ideas, or behaving in meritorious ways should not be the source of excessive boasting: "Either very great pride or very great despondency indicates very great weakness of mind" (EIVp56). In this rather negative sense, the necessity of error or of inadequate ideas can indeed be said to be "the same" as that of truth or adequate ideas – both are "natural" in the sense that they do not depend on any morally reproachable or laudable strength or weakness on the part of the human agent.

The insertion of the polemic rejection of moralism in this particular place – at the heart of the exposition of the doctrine of the *Potentia Intellectus* – shows how important it was for Spinoza. The denunciation of moralism is a constant theme of the *Ethics*, and it is expressed in diverse ways, famous among them being his depiction of the moralists as considering the human as forming a kingdom within a kingdom or as being an exception to the natural order, which is only the moralistic excuse to

attribute the cause of human impotence and inconstancy, not to the common power of Nature, but to I know not what vice of human nature, which they therefore bewail, or lough at, or disdain or (as usually happens) curse (EIII, preface).

Propositions 5 and 6 of EV seem to characteristically set irrational affects against reason or rational understanding as the agency for curbing them. In fact, there lurks here a deeper and more complex duality. This duality, or tension, is operative below the surface, as is attested by the following observation: the demonstration of EVp5 refers back to EIIIp49 and to EIVp11 as its two more or less independent sources. As we saw, EIIIp49 affirms that the love (or hate) we feel "towards a thing will be greater if we imagine the thing to be free than if we imagine it to be necessary"; EIVp11 states that the "affect towards a thing we imagine as necessary is more intense, other things being equal, than one toward a thing we imagine as possible, or contingent, or not necessary."

On the face of it, these two propositions are contradictory. The one states that we are affected in the strongest way by what we conceive as free; the second, that when we conceive something as necessary, it affects us more intensely than when we conceive it as not-necessary. But the contradiction here is only apparent. "Free" in the sense given it in the context of EIII – that is, in the context of the theory of the affects – is not a concept, but an image; in EIV, it is a concept, and Spinoza gives this distinction a very explicit expression through the different ways in which he phrases the two propositions – while "free" is assimilated (in EVp5 and in its demonstration) to the modally neutral, in EIVp11 it is no longer about "free" or "unfree" things but about necessary, possible, and contingent ones. "Freedom" is implicitly being used in two different ways: by reason, or rationally, as necessity; and by the imagination, as pure negation and as non-modal. The philosophically legitimate concept of freedom is a kind of necessity – the necessity of being and acting by one's, or a thing's, proper nature. The imaginary and empty notion of freedom is born when we consider things *simpliciter* or outside their causal chain of existences.

The error results from regarding freedom as non-determination. The philosophical truth about it is that, on the contrary, freedom is full determination. What remains common to the philosophical truth and to the error concerning freedom is the psychological power of this notion. Freedom on the one hand and necessity on the other are the sources of what "affect the soul" mostly; when one understands that freedom and necessity are not contradictory but are indeed synonymous, the apparent contradiction dissolves, and the free thing – understood this time as an authentic philosophical concept – can be said to generate the highest possible affect or – which is the same thing – to possess the highest perfection and the greatest amount of reality.

The radical reversal of the role of determinism in ethical theory consists, then, in the following elements: instead of a presupposition of the legitimacy, or condition of the possibility, of the moral point of view, and of fundamental concepts such as responsibility and accountability, free choice is not only a chimera, but its notion is also, and especially, the source of bad affects and, in particular, of the anti-ethics of moralism. From the point of view of moral theory, Spinoza opposes the common view that free will and the freedom implied in this notion are the condition of morality. Not only is this false but, on the contrary, these notions are also the opposite of what can found a real philosophical morality. Second, and metaphysically speaking, there is no room for a concept of free choice because everything is causally determined. But, and again unlike what is taken to be a commonplace, determinism is not a threat to a positive and adequate philosophical ethics. On the contrary, necessitarian determinism – that is, the most radical form of determinism – is the necessary presupposition and condition of ethics. Instead of looking for some imaginary or purely verbal "compatibility" of the incompatible – that is, of free choice or un-caused determination to act, reconciled with rational necessity – one has to understand that what hides behind the affectively or emotionally powerful image of "free agency" is the philosophical concept of freedom as the necessary determination of one's acts according to one's own nature. How this is possible needs now to be explained.

7.4. Perfection II (or: The Mouse and the Angel)

Between December 1664 and June 1665, Spinoza and Willem van Blyenbergh, a merchant from Dordrecht, exchanged eight letters, four on each side, and met once. This is a relatively early date, and what brought van Blyenbergh to write to Spinoza was his reading of the *Principles of Cartesian Philosophy* and the *Cogitata Metaphysica* (1663). He did not have, at that time, a real knowledge of Spinoza's philosophy, and his questions – in fact, objections and criticism – are directed, at least on the face of it, at both Spinoza and Descartes, or at Spinoza's presentation of Descartes. It becomes, however, very soon apparent that there was a deep disaccord between him and Spinoza; the correspondence quickly turned into a bitter polemic and ended in a polite but firm refusal on the part of Spinoza to continue the exchange. Although relatively neglected in the secondary literature on Spinoza, the correspondence with van Blyenbergh is extremely interesting in many ways. It concerns the questions of normativity and valuableness that Spinoza does not address directly, although they may very well be at the heart of his philosophy. It also constitutes the only recorded occasion in which Spinoza was compelled to face squarely an adversary who challenged him with a rather intelligent and principled, if uncompromising and unrelenting, criticism of his ethical theory. Generally put, Blyenbergh forced Spinoza to confront the classical challenge of theodicy. In the context of the Cartesian doctrine of the "continuous creation," in which the exchange purports to unwind, this is formulated in the following way: if to create and to preserve are one and the same thing, it follows "that God is not only the cause of the substance of the mind but also of every striving or motion of the mind, which we call the will." Hence: "either there is no evil in the motion of the will of the soul or ... God himself is the immediate agent of that evil" (letter 18; Shirley translation, p. 806).

It is first of all noteworthy that Spinoza actually engaged in exchange with Blyenbergh, and furthermore, that he continued to write long and elaborate letters even after he understood that his correspondent was not a *bona fide* interlocutor. It would thus seem that Spinoza did indeed consider the challenge as genuine. It appears, at least from the point of view of his correspondent's opening move, that the difficulty Spinoza was trying to overcome was the one free choice and freedom in general poses for determinism. But there is a challenge here for determinism (in its different forms) only if a certain moral point of view is taken for granted as fundamental: if one presupposes the validity of the moral stance, determinism is untenable. The seriousness with which Spinoza takes Blyenbergh's objections is rather revealing. In a certain important sense, Spinoza's and Blyenbergh's respective positions are incommensurable: Spinoza, after all, denies almost everything Blyenbergh believes in, and for him the latter's will to be a Christian philosopher and to follow the revealed word of God (letter 20) is mere superstition, indeed paradigmatically so. The deep gulf between the two is immediately conspicuous. If Adam's will to eat the forbidden fruit, asks Blyenbergh, was determined by God, then this model of sin, Adam's transgression of God's commandment, cannot be said to be "evil" (letter 18).

Spinoza's answer is blunt: the "forbidden" is a metaphor, an image forged for simple men. Philosophically, if the eating of the fruit was a thing not to be done, it was only because the fruit was poisonous and the eating dangerous. Man's deeds are neither rewarded nor punished, and what follows them is the natural result of the natural order, which we describe, again metaphorically, by the use of terms such as "laws." The significance of all this is a radical undermining of the pertinence of the language of morality: duty, the licit or illicit; reward and punishment; good and bad, and so on – all these terms have to be rejected to make room for philosophically valid ones.

Yet Spinoza, the man of the famous *Caute*, chooses not to avoid a debate, and instead of dismissing his correspondent's allegations as unworthy of serious philosophical discussion, engages in just such a discussion. The two positions, Spinoza's and Blyenbergh's, are perhaps after all *not* incommensurable. Although the challenge of theodicy, at least under its classical form, does not present a real difficulty for Spinoza, it does, for him too, bring to the surface a fundamental philosophical question, perhaps the most crucial one.

7.4. Perfection II (or: The Mouse and the Angel)

Behind its more familiar and, from Spinoza's point of view, simplistic and even erroneous form lies a real question: is it possible at all, and if it is how, to show that a fully rationalistic (hence, necessitarian) view of being is not only compatible, but is indeed identical, with a full, comprehensive, and positive moral theory? Blyenbergh, then, raises the classical issue of free will and accountability: if there is no free choice, there is no room for morality. No reproach can be leveled against anyone for anything he might do. Spinoza at first ignores this question and then dismisses it somewhat impatiently: there is no real difficulty here; "free choice" is an empty image; without choosing anything, we are free when we deduce, with absolute necessity, that the sum of the triangle's angles is equal to two straight angles (letter 21; Shirley's translation, p. 825; also see earlier discussion). Spinoza also sees no difficulty in deducing from his determinism the conclusion that to Blyenbergh is scandalous: of course, the notions of guilt and accountability are empty too. What is conceived by Blyenbergh as the core of ethics and religion is for Spinoza altogether nonsensical.

And yet, the challenge is serious. It should be noted that Spinoza, instead of directly answering his correspondent's questions and engaging in a disputation about free choice, immediately transposes Blyenbergh's question. The debate is transformed, and its topic becomes the meaning of "perfection" and the ways in which this concept can legitimately be used within a theory based on a philosophical[20] doctrine of the absolute necessity of God's "action"; how, that is, can radical necessitarism be also an ontology of the objective and positive status of the concepts of *value, normativity,* or, precisely, *perfection*?

Spinoza's argumentation is based on the traditional identification of *perfection* with *reality*. He had dealt with it already in the *Principia philosophiae cartesianae* and in the *Cogitata Metaphysica*, and he returns to it now in his letters to Blyenbergh. The concept of "perfection" and the reality-perfection identification Spinoza is concerned with is based on, and meant to make sense of, a teleological, or finalistic, moral ontology. Linked mainly to the onto-theological Aristotelian tradition, reality-perfection is conceived, roughly put, as the grounds of the objectivity and integral validity of a normativity and a moral point of view based on evaluating or measuring how close a particular thing is to its form, or to the essence of the specie to which it belongs. In Spinoza the systematic function of the perfection-reality identity remains, but its traditional fundamental (conceptual and ontological) meaning, namely teleology, is totally rejected. It grounds a positive concept of normativity and a moral point of view but is emptied from its teleological content. The radical nature of Spinoza's rejection of finalism comes out fully in the interpretation – indeed reduction – he gives to yet another traditional concept: that of *privatio*. The concept of *privation*, he says, does not signify

---

[20] And perhaps even semi-theological – Spinoza agrees to play Blyenbergh's game, so to speak, and accepts using the latter's theological language.

an act of depriving; it is nothing more than simply a state of want, which in itself is nothing. It is only a construct of the mind (*ens rationis*) or a mode of thinking which we form from comparing things with one another. For instance, we say that a blind man is deprived of sight because we readily imagine him as seeing. This imagining may arise from comparing him with those who can see, or from comparing his present state with a past state when he could see. When we consider the man from this perspective, comparing his nature with that of others or with his own past nature, we assert that sight pertains to his nature, and so we say that he is deprived of it. *But when we consider God's decree and God's nature, we can no more assert of that man that he is deprived of sight than we assert it of a stone.* For to say that sight belongs to that man at that time is quite illogical as to say that it belongs to a stone, since nothing more pertains to that man, and is his, than that which God's intellect and will has assigned to him. Therefore God is no more the cause of his not seeing than of a stone's not seeing, this latter being pure negation (letter 21, Shirley's translation, p. 824; italics added).

The polemic, anti-moralistic sense of Spinoza's answers to Blyenbergh is very clear, but it does not suffice to dissolve the difficulty. Blyenbergh was not convinced. If "comparison" is just *ens rationis*, as Spinoza keeps saying, then, in a sense, God does not compare. Each thing is what it is, and this is all we – or rather God – can say of it. If the present blindness cannot be said in any ontologically valid or evaluatively relevant way to be less perfect than the past seeing, then the result is what Deleuze calls *instantanéisme* and what has been referred to above as *affirmativeness*: "real," especially intended morally, is justly said only of existence, eventually of the absolute *hic et nunc*.[21] This means that the only morally legitimate stance one can take is of a neutral observer of what there is or of what actually exists and happens. No judgment can be philosophically justified. Blyenbergh casts his objections in temporal terms, but what is implied in his words goes well beyond temporality and, indeed, presents the gravest difficulty: in a pure, radically non-teleological theory of the positivity of being, all differences between things collapse to mere factuality. If the notion of *perfection* is just *ens rationis*, then "pure affirmativeness" is unavoidable. Not only can no one reproach anybody for anything, but also no objective evaluation or judgment concerning the worth of anything, according to whatever criteria, is possible.

This is the burden of Blyenbergh's last questions, and Spinoza's reaction to them can hardly be considered as providing real answers. In letter 23 of March 1665, his second-to-last letter, one can already detect his growing annoyance. Besides the usual polemics, Spinoza simply states there that everything, the deeds of the wise and the good as well as of the ignorant and malicious, follows necessarily from God's eternal laws and decrees. Yet,

they nevertheless differ the from one another not only in degree but in essence. For although a mouse is as dependent on God as an angel, and sorrow as much as joy, yet a mouse cannot on that account be a kind of angel, not sorrow a kind of joy.

---

[21] Deleuze, op. cit., p 55.

7.4. Perfection II (or: The Mouse and the Angel)

God does not love or hate either the murderers or the righteous; they are, however, not equally perfect. Neither the thief nor the honest man please or displease God; insofar as the respective actions of both are considered in themselves and their reality as *actions*, they are equally perfect. Yet the thief and the honest man are not equally perfect. Spinoza does not go beyond these rather bold affirmations and only adds that how all this is tenable would be duly explained in his *Ethics*, which is still being written.

Spinoza never directly addresses the questions Blyenbergh raises in the *Ethics*. The preface to EIV, discussed earlier, is the only place in which there seems to be an indirect consideration of these questions and apparently contains an implicit reaction to this challenge. The promised explanation appears though, in an oblique way, in the last part of the *Ethics*; and, significantly, it is the concept of *perfection* on which this final discussion turns. Thus:

> The more perfection each thing has, the more it acts and the less it is acted on [*patitur*; suffers or endures]; and conversely, the more it acts, the more perfect it is (EVp40).
>
> From this it follows that the part of the mind that remains, however great it is, is more perfect than the rest.
>
> For the eternal part of the mind is the intellect, through which alone we are said to act. But what we have shown to perish is the imagination, through which alone we are said to be acted on. So the intellect however extensive it is more perfect than the imagination (EVp40cor; references to previous parts omitted).
>
> These are the things I took upon myself to show concerning the mind, insofar as it is considered without relation to the body existence (EVp40s).

This, then, is Spinoza's last word on the human soul: its eternity is also its perfection. *Perfection*, or more precisely its semi-quantitative semantics, functions as the conceptual scaffolding of the last propositions of the *Ethics*. Around it Spinoza weaves together the ultimate conclusions of his ontological ethics (or ethical ontology), and it is this supposedly non-teleological notion of perfection that gives sense to the main concepts that figure in the final discussion of the *Ethics* and to the connections among them: quantity of reality, existence and body, soul, intellect and its power over the affects, activity (and, by implication, freedom), and eternity.

A methodological, indeed strategic, question readers of Spinoza have to constantly face is what to make of the many instances in which he identifies what are usually considered disparate things. God and nature; necessity and freedom; and, of course, mind and body are the most famous examples. Are these reductions of one term to the other? If they are, then in what direction? If not, what exactly does any one of these identifications mean? In the case in hand, does one have to read the identity or equivalence between perfection and reality as a reduction of the evaluative meaning of the first to the sheer affirmativeness of the second? Perhaps it is the other way around? This apparently is not the case, and the nature of the gesture here, as in most other cases, is more complex. Inquiring about the exact meaning of the concept of *perfection* and of the *perfection-reality* identification may very well supply a key to a sound philosophical appraisal of Spinoza's philosophy as a whole. The perfection-reality equivalence appears very early in the *Ethics*: in the scholium after EIp11, which contains Spinoza's version of the proofs of the existence of God, it is explained that whatever *perfectionis, sive realitatis* there is in things that come into being by external causes is due to these causes. Definition six of EII, which stipulates that reality and perfection are synonymous, thus basically justifies or makes explicit what was already assumed before. In the scholium after EIIp1, we find *realitatis, sive perfectionis*, and the idea that reality and perfection are equivalent appears then a few times more in the later parts of EII as well as in EIII. It is abundantly present in EIV and then reappears at the very end of EV. The reality-perfection identification thus informs the discussion of the *Ethics* from beginning to end. It is, however, only toward the very end of the Fifth part of the *Ethics* that the different lines of reasoning converge into one systematic and comprehensive ethical-philosophical set of affirmations where one can finally make sense of the alleged equivalence of being, activity, intelligibility, corporeal prowess, and perfection. The reappearance of the concept of perfection at this final point of the *Ethics* shows that in an important sense it is indeed first of all an ethics.

7.5. The Body and Its Eternal Idea

It is noteworthy that *after* the exposition of the doctrine of the eternity of the soul, of salvation, of happiness, and of freedom (propositions 21–40), in the last two propositions of the *Ethics*, Spinoza returns to speak of a stoic-like wisdom and a more low-key and dispassionate morality. In the scholium after EVp40 he announces that the preceding propositions contain "the things that I have decided to show concerning the mind," implying perhaps that there were things he decided to keep to himself. What has been said, however, he adds, is sufficient to show that "our mind is an eternal mode of thinking" and even one of the constituent elements of "God's eternal and infinite intellect." And as if anticipating the miscomprehension by his future readers, or unwilling to dishearten them by what is apparently accessible to only the few, perhaps embarrassed by the boldness of his own words, he next falls back on the more digestible doctrine of wisdom. He thus states first that "Even if we did not know that our mind is eternal, we would still regard as of the first importance morality [*Piettatem*], religion, and absolutely all the things we have shown (in Part IV) to be related to tenacity [*Animositatem*] and generosity" (EVp41);[22]

---

[22] Curley translates *Generositatem* by "nobility." *Générosité*, however, had been Descartes's main virtue in his *Passions de l'âme*, and Spinoza most probably alludes to Descartes by mentioning *Generositatem* as one of his own main two virtues. It is again noteworthy that Spinoza chooses to evoke here, as a kind of "second-best" morality, the virtues of *Animositatem* and generosity.

7.5. The Body and Its Eternal Idea

and then, in the next and very last proposition of the *Ethics*, that "beatitude is not the reward of virtue, but virtue itself."²³

Propositions 21–40, which contain the doctrine of the eternity of the soul, thus appear as a parenthetical discussion. Eternity is contextualized within the more prosaic theory of wisdom and the non-dramatic doctrine of the rational conduct of life. It looks as if after expounding his rather surprising doctrine of the eternity of the soul, Spinoza had, as it were, second thoughts and decided to take a step backwards and exercise some typical caution, a wise man's *caute*. Whatever the motives behind it were, this move gives the second half of EV an unmistakably ironic aura. Not everything is said fully in the open; some of the most important things are left unsaid, half-said, hinted at, or alluded to. There is an invitation extended to the *erotic* reader, to the one who has the drive and patience, to think seriously about those rare and difficult things that are also the most important ones. Just as Maimonides didn't say, at least according to Strauss's famous "art of writing," everything philosophical he had to say, so Spinoza too, despite the supposed full transparency of the *more geometrico*, remains allusive and ironic at the highest moment of the exposition of his philosophy. But until the ultimate philosophical aim is achieved, or for those who cannot fully achieve it, the last lesson is a lesson of moral wisdom: it is not necessary to know that our soul is eternal in order to live an honest, generous, and courageous life; this also means that one should not – there are philosophical arguments to this effect – make his morality depend on any kind of reward.

Irony is always polemical. This surely comes out in the last two propositions of EV – in a straightforward way in the scholium after proposition 41 (the "multitude" – *vulgi* – are convinced that freedom is license, that moral life is suffering; they live moral life only because of fear of punishment and hope for a reward in an afterlife); and in an implicit and indirect way in proposition 42,

---

Both are the fruits of *Fortitudo*, or the "force of character" (as Curley translates) or, perhaps better, "force of the soul" or spirit (as Pautrat translates; EIIIp59s). These two virtues – (rational) courage and generosity – are practically the only virtues that transcend self-interest, at least in its more simplistic, egoistic understanding. It transcends, in fact, also ancient and stoic *Eudemonist* morality, even in the non-egoistic interpretation of it, as sometimes reason requires that one faces danger and, hence, risks one's life: "The virtue of the free man is seen to be as great in avoiding dangers as overcoming it" (EIVp69; Curley's translation, slightly altered); and "the free man chooses flight with the same tenacity, or [*sive*] presence of mind, as he chooses the battle [*fugam*]" (EIVp69 and cor., respectively; Curley's translation, slightly altered). See Yakira (2004).

²³ Which seems to echo the very famous Hebrew idiom, שכר מצווה מצווה (the recompense of a *mitzvah*, or the fulfillment of a religious duty, is another *mitzvah*). There are many other sayings of this kind in the Jewish tradition, and they all add up to a conception structurally very close to Kant's doctrine of the nature and form of moral motivation as radically non-pragmatist and non-utilitarian, although Kant's concept of duty lacks the irony hidden in this expression of old Jewish wisdom. In view of his theory of *conatus*, self-preservation, and self-perseverance as the origin of virtue, Spinoza's decision to end the *Ethics* with this particular statement is certainly not without significance.

which can be read as attacking the rhetoric of punishment and reward as a moral motivating force.

Spinoza strews along in the discussion contained in proposition 21–40 a few signposts calling for a cautious reading of these propositions. In EVp20 he announced that we were about to embark on a discussion of those "things which pertain to the mind's duration without relation to the body." But the very next proposition, and indeed the subsequent discussion generally, is hardly "without relation to the body": it opens with "The mind can neither imagine anything, nor recollect past things, except while the body endures" (EVp21); and just before its end, it states that "He who has a body capable of a great many things has a mind whose greatest part is eternal" (EVp39).

On the other hand, announcing that now the topic will be what "pertains to the mind's duration" (without relation to the body), propositions 22 and 23 and the important scholium after p23 (see earlier discussion) deal nonetheless with the *eternity* of the soul, which, as we have seen, is something that has to be understood without relation to time and duration. Moreover, into this discussion of the soul's eternity is immediately incorporated a kind of polemical warning: imagination and memory – which, as the demonstration of proposition 21 shows, are functions in which the body plays an essential role – can be envisaged only as long as the body actually exists, that is, only as long as its parts are so related that its individuality or organic being is preserved. The polemic intention is quite clear: there is no "life" or, indeed, existence of the soul beyond the body's "existence in act." The "eternity of soul" is not immortality or afterlife, and metempsychosis, transmigration of souls, or, for that matter, the Hebrew *gilgul* are all nonsensical notions; pervasive as they may be, they are nothing but superstitions.

The implicit, albeit quite clear, polemic import is a constitutive part of Spinoza's doctrine of the eternity of the soul. Steven Nadler has recently suggested that the exceptional harshness of the text of the *herem* imposed on Spinoza may be explained perhaps by the special importance the question of afterlife and of the eternity of the soul had for the Portuguese Jews of Amsterdam. The complex identity crisis of the ex-Marranos made them particularly sensitive, thinks Nadler, to Spinoza's denial of any form of afterlife.[24] Whether this was the case, two things can be affirmed with certainty: the importance of the question of afterlife for the theological and religious traditions is undeniable; the importance and significance of the doctrine of the eternity of the soul in Spinoza's philosophy is both a continuation and a radical transformation of the latter. The resurrection of the dead is one of Maimonides's thirteen principles of faith; he wrote a whole treatise on this subject, and it is part of the Jewish daily prayer. In Christian theology the theme of life after death is not less important. In both cases – in the Judaic as well as in the Christian religious

---

[24] See Nadler (2002), chapter 7.

7.5. The Body and Its Eternal Idea

traditions – the theme of afterlife has, besides its mythic and supra-rational content, also an important symbolic moral import. Afterlife is where all moral accounts are settled, where theodicy receives an ultimate confirmation, and where the scandal of the suffering of the just and the thriving of the wicked is recompensed.

Spinoza's doctrine of eternity is polemic and subversive by its very essence: everything that has been referred to traditionally as the eternity of the soul, afterlife, and resurrection is untrue, superstitious, and nonsensical. However, if Spinoza's dismissal of the mythical sides of the religious traditions is obvious and non-controversial, its significance from the point of view of ethical theory is more complex. On the one hand, eternity plays in his philosophy an analogous role to the one it has for theological ethics, for eternity-as-necessity is Spinoza's way to express the idea that being is absolutely valuable. On the other hand, the constant reference to the body in elaborating his concept of eternity of the soul gives to his ethics a very iconoclastic sense.

Spinoza's message is radical, and it is by its double-edgedness – the positive and the polemic – that this radicalness comes through. The two main components, the polemic and the positive, of the complex move contained in propositions 21–40 of EV are interwoven into a paradoxical, but – to judge by the reactions to Spinozism – efficacious strategy. It is predominantly through the role of the *body* in the architecture of the doctrine that its polemic import is driven home. More perplexing and utterly unconventional, however, is the positive role the body plays in Spinoza's theory. Notwithstanding the content, value and theoretical interest of the doctrine of the body and the soul as its idea, its role in the elaboration of the ultimate consequences of the ethical theory in EV, is certainly different from anything that is usually attributed to it in the context of a psycho-physical theory of the affects, for example, or of a mind-body parallelism in a more general sense. It is indeed hard to see how a more or less mechanistic conception of the body can ground a theory of freedom, or how a mind-body doctrine, usually understood as a doctrine of the union of mind and body, or even as a relation of parallelism in which the one is "mapped" into the other, can make sense of a theory of beatitude.[25] However, this is precisely what Spinoza tries to accomplish.

If the theory of the body and of the soul as its idea is read, in the context of EV, as indeed fundamentally polemical, some of the riddles one encounters in this most enigmatic part of the *Ethics* can be more easily resolved. Proposition 23, which, let us recall, states that something "remains" of the human soul, is in some sense the kernel of the discussion in the second half of EV. It is, however, tightly embedded in a polemic discourse that, arguably, demystifies the notion of an eternity of the soul. The sobering move begins in the previous proposition, of which proposition 23 is presented as an immediate consequence, that states that it is of the soul as an *idea of the body* that we can say that it is

---

[25] And see Damasio's very cautious but avowedly embarrassed words at the end of his (2003).

eternal: "in God there is necessarily an idea that expresses the essence of this or that human body *sub specie aeternitatis*."[26] The demonstration of EVp23 next evokes the *noétique* of EII; specifically, it refers to EIIp13 and EIIp8cor, that is, to the doctrine about the soul being the idea of the *existent* body. This is in order to be able to insist that "we do not attribute to the human mind any duration that can be defined by time, except insofar as it expresses the actual existence of the body ..., that is (by EIIp8cor), we do not attribute duration to it except while the body endures." What reads in proposition 23 as a straightforward affirmation of a privilege of the soul over the body becomes much less clearly so in the demonstration: what "remains" of the soul is nothing else but the "concept or [*sive*] idea which expresses the essence of the human body."

This continues more or less in the same vein in the following propositions, and every positive affirmation of the eternity of the soul is immediately put in perspective: eternity is neither very long nor infinite time. In fact, it is not a question of time at all but something else. It is certainly comprehensible that the non-philosopher confuses eternity and time or duration, for

If we attend to the common opinion of men, we shall see that they are indeed conscious of the eternity of their mind, but that they confuse it with duration, and attribute it to the imagination, or [*sive*] memory, which they believe remains after death" (EVp34s).

The significance of the polemics contained in this final part of the *Ethics* and of the constant reference to the notion of "the body" in a discussion that was promised to be solely about the soul, can perhaps be best appreciated from proposition 39 and the scholium that follows it – that is, from what precedes the closing moment of the theory of beatitude, salvation, and freedom in proposition 40, its corollary, and scholium. Interestingly enough, it is again the body that announces the final step of the *Ethics*. The scholium after EV40 indicates that with it ends the exposition of what was thought to be worth exposing about the soul "without relation to the body's existence," although, of course, the body's existence had been, precisely, the topic of proposition 39 and of its scholium and, in fact, of the whole preceding discussion.

EVp39 and its scholium, although not referred to explicitly in the demonstration of EVp40, mediate the passage to this proposition, which concludes the doctrine of beatitude. They constitute an intermediate stage enabling the transition from the discussion of the third kind of knowledge and of its immediate consequence, the intellectual love of God, to the final conclusion in proposition 40, which is explicitly evaluative and normative. Proposition 39 introduces, without clear continuity with the preceding proposition, the notion of a body "capable of a great many things": he who possesses such a body has

---

[26] The use of "essence" (*essentia*), although opening a complex exegetical interrogation in itself, does not necessarily affect the line of thought suggested here. The essence of the body is sometimes conceived as its *conatus* and on other occasions as the idea of the body or its soul. In EVp22sem, the use of the notion of "essence" gives Spinoza the means to emphasize the *necessity* (or eternity) through which one has to conceive one's own being.

7.5. The Body and Its Eternal Idea

a soul whose greater part is eternal.[27] This is read sometimes as if Spinoza had some kind of preconception of neuroscience: the more complex the brain, the nervous system, or some other imagined machine of the body, the more sophisticated the mental apparatus. Although the text – especially the propositions of EIV referred to in the demonstration of EVp39 (EIVp38 and p30) – may lend itself sometimes to such a reading, Spinoza was, in fact, driving at something quite different.

The scholium following this proposition raises the paradigmatic case of the child whose body is as yet not capable of doing what the adult he will become is. The child's soul, too, knows very little about himself and about God. The concept of "childhood" serves Spinoza, indeed in a paradigmatic way, to drive home his non-teleological notion of perfection: just as in the case of the blind man in the letter to Blyenbergh, so in the case of the child too there is no ground for any kind of reproach and, more importantly, for any regrets or feelings of sorrow, compassion, and so on. Although we know, by comparing the child's present condition with his future adulthood, how limited and less perfect childhood is, thinking about it in counterfactual terms, or imagining that it could – and should – be otherwise is philosophically futile.

If the child is the paradigm of the body that is not capable of a great many things, the adult body is the paradigm of the body that *is* capable of many things. This is so, however, only insofar and to the extent, that he – the adult – "is least troubled by bad affects," which are those affects that are "contrary to our nature" and have thus the power "of bringing it about that all the affections of the body are related to the idea of God." It is indeed hard to see how this relates to any modern conception of the brain or the nervous system, but it is much easier to see how it relates to ethical theory. Rather than opening the way for a philosophical interpretation of neuroscience, of mind-body parallelism, or the like, it gives the doctrine of the body that is capable of great many things, and, in fact, to Spinozism in general, its final shape as a theory of freedom. Proposition 39 itself underlines once again the role of the body in achieving beatitude and prepares the way for a concept of freedom also dependent on the concept of the body and, more specifically, on that of "bodily aptness." The demonstration of EVp39 leads, once again, to the *noétique* of EII and to the doctrine of the soul as the idea of the body, so that the full context in which Spinoza inscribes his last philosophical word is that of the body as the *locus* of freedom and of salvation and of the soul as the idea of the body or – if the reading suggested in previous chapters is correct – as the intrinsic intelligibility of a given individual body.

[27] This proposition echoes the scholium after EIIIp2: "indeed no one has yet determined what the body can do, that is, experience has not yet taught anyone what the body can do from the laws of Nature alone, insofar as Nature is only considered to be corporeal"; but also EIIp13s: "ideas differ among themselves as the objects themselves do, and … one is more excellent than the other, and contains more reality, just as the object of the one is more excellent than the object of the other and contains more reality."

As the scholium of proposition 39 further explains, it is by their aptness, or being "capable of a great many [things]," that human bodies are related (*referantur*) to souls that "have a great knowledge of themselves and of God," that are therefore eternal in their greater part, and that, consequently, "hardly fear death." Fear and hope, as Spinoza often says, are the main sources of bad affects and unhappiness. If happiness consists in overcoming the greatest fear of all, the fear of death, we also have to see, and understand better, how we overcome the delusive hope that, ultimately, is the hope of outlasting life – that is, bodily existence. EVp39 speaks of the eternity of the soul; and it is precisely in this context that the scholium now explains that what we call "happiness" belongs to the down-to-earth and seemingly prosaic vicissitudes or "changes" the body constantly undergoes and, by implication, not to some imagined "spirituality" or immaterial reality. Even in the most radical sense given to the notion of "happiness" – a sense that, precisely, justifies inscribing it in what seems to be religious or semi-religious discourse – it is a matter completely rooted in the body:

> For he who has passed from being an infant or child to being a corpse is called unhappy. On the other hand, if we pass the whole length of our life with a sound mind in a sound body, that is considered happiness. And really, he who, like an infant or a child, has a body capable of very few things, and very heavily dependent on external causes, has a mind which considered solely in itself is conscious almost of nothing of itself, or of God, or of the things. On the other hand, he who has a body capable of a great many things, has a mind which considered only in itself is very much conscious of itself, *and of God*, and of the things. In this life, then, we strive especially that the infant's body may change (as much as its nature allows and assists) into another, capable of a great many things and related to a mind very much conscious of itself, of God and of the things. We strive, that is, that whatever is related to its memory or imagination is of hardly any moment in relation to the intellect (italics added).

Textually (see Part I), there can be no doubt that all the elements that add up to the doctrine of salvation, happiness, and freedom emerge, or are explicated and made sense of, in the *noétique* of the second part of the *Ethics*, namely in the complex move culminating in the assertion that the soul is the idea of the body. Two unusual identities – the two main concrete aspects of Spinoza's monism – condition the ultimate ethical conclusion of the *Ethics*. The first of these identities is the primordial, free of presuppositions oneness of the body and its soul-idea. The second identity, which radicalizes even further the first one, is the identity – numerical identity – of the individual soul and God's adequate idea of the individual body.

Two main ethical consequences, usually considered as opposing each other, give to Spinoza's paradoxical double-faced monism its significance. First, all that is traditionally taken as elevated, important, extraordinary, and valuable is radically implanted in, indeed reduced to, concrete corporeality. Second, concrete corporeality is made into the locus of value and of the seriousness of being. Thought and thinking, intellect, knowledge, understanding, ultimate rationality, personality, or subjectivity are all a matter of the body and do not belong to a transcendent, supernatural, or extra-physical realm of being. However, the body, the machine of the self-experiencing and lived organism, is also the place where agency and freedom, beatitude, and salvation reside. Stripped of their mythological and theological significance and interpreted in line with the doctrine that eternity is a mode of being defined by its inherent necessity, these terms mean mainly value and valuation.

7.6. The Doctrine of Value

The more perfection each thing has, the more it acts and the less it is acted on; and conversely, the more it acts, the more perfect it is (EVp40).

From this it follows that the part of the mind that remains, however great it is, is more perfect than the rest. For the eternal part of the mind is the intellect, through which alone we are said to act (EVp40cor).

EVp40 and its corollary are, as the scholium that follows immediately makes clear, the very last words of the doctrine of the eternity of the soul. In a way that hides below the surface more than what it says *tout haut*, it can be said to explicate the normative import of, indeed, the whole venture. The concept of *perfection* reappears in proposition 40, and it mediates a final explication. The semantic equivalence of "perfection" and "reality" is now shown to include also the concept of *action*. All three are grounds for comparison and support quantitative, or quasi-quantitative, assessments: one can be more active, which means that one is more real or possesses more being, which means that one is more perfect. The corollary adds to it the ultimate concretization: being more active, which is having more being, is also living a more rational life. Since the "eternal part of the soul" is an adequate mode of thought, it is in the first place – ultimately, originally, or ontologically – the adequate idea of the body. An active soul is thus, as affirms the previous scholium, a greater understanding of who and what one is. And all this is enjoying greater perfection.

Implicitly, however, and by implication, this perfection is also freedom. Acting in the exact sense of the term is a mode of being in which a thing is determined according to one's own nature. Acting, explicates the second definition of EIII, means being the adequate cause of whatever happens inside or outside us. This echoes the exact, philosophical meaning of freedom: free is whatever exists and acts by the necessity of its own nature. The demonstration of EVp40 refers to EIIIp3, in which the connection is explicitly made between the concept of action and adequate ideas: the soul's actions originate only from adequate ideas. To have adequate ideas is to be free. The demonstration of proposition 3 of EIII opens with an explicit reference to propositions 11 and 13 of EII: "The first thing which constitutes the essence of the mind is nothing but the idea of an actually existing body." The possibility of adequate knowledge, or of having adequate ideas and, in particular, of interpreting it as ultimate and objective perfection and freedom, is grounded, in the last analysis, in the *noétique* of part II. Without naming it explicitly in the final discussion of EV – except for its title – freedom is the highest philosophical, or indeed moral, moment. It is freedom in the very unusual and counterintuitive way Spinoza conceives it, namely a kind of necessity. Mediated by the ontology of ideas, freedom is seen now not only as a human achievement, but also as a mode of being.

The philosophically adequate concept of freedom, the doctrine that defines freedom as a kind of necessity, is Spinoza's ultimate way to express the irreducible value of existence. We have already discussed the psychological force and semantic complexity of the concepts of necessity and freedom. It is noteworthy that Spinoza's explanation of the psychological power of the notion of free agency transcends the realm of natural causation, indeterminacy, and ignorance of causes and leads into philosophical truth. In a typical move, the likes of which we have already seen on a number of occasions, Spinoza locates the causes of human pathology in a sound and adequate philosophical concept. The psychological forces in question involve – in the Spinozistic sense – an authentic philosophical concept, silently operative underneath the apparent and conscious images. It can go astray and become fallacious and the source of pathology, but amending the imagery of freedom leads to a sound conception to a true freedom.

EIIIp49 gives an important clue for effectuating the move toward a true concept of freedom, which is itself an act of liberation. On the basis of the true definition of freedom, stipulating that "that thing is called free which exists from the necessity of its nature and is determined to act by itself alone" (EIdef7), it now explains the great psychological power of what is conceived as free. EIIIp49 reads as follows:

> A thing we imagine to be free must be perceived through itself, without others (by EIdef7). So if we imagine it to be the cause of joy or sadness, we shall thereby love or hate it (by EIIIp13s), and shall do so with the greatest love or hate that can arise from the given affect (by EIIIp48).

The scholium of EIIIp13 simply defines "love and hate as, respectively, joy and sadness accompanied with the ideas of their causes; and EIIIp48 states that love and hate of a certain object (notably a person) diminishes to the extent that the cause of the joy and sadness involved in them are attributed to other causes. The logic of this reasoning is straightforward and almost intuitive. It seems to go without saying that we shall love or hate what we conceive to be the causes of our joys and sorrows. Why, then, make it dependent on the perfectly counterintuitive definition of freedom in EI that equates freedom and necessity and that is the foundation of one of Spinoza's most notoriously difficult and iconoclastic doctrines?

Paradoxically, the two kinds of freedom, the ultimate source of error and the ultimate philosophical truth, have something in common. Whatever we conceive as free – either by the adequate idea of freedom or by the imaginary

7.6. The Doctrine of Value

one – affects the soul with the greatest intensity. Free agency, the concept and the image, is the source of the strongest affects. Necessity plays here an ambiguous role. On the one hand, it neutralizes or diminishes the intensity of our love and hate of things, mainly other humans. When we understand that they are not free, the intensity of the affects they cause in us is mitigated. On the other hand, necessity underpins the strongest affect of all – the intellectual love of God – which depends on the understanding of God's absolute necessity. The intellectual love of God is born from the third kind of knowledge (EVp32cor), for, as the demonstration of this corollary explains, the third kind of knowledge involves a joy accompanied by the idea of its cause, which is eternal. But "eternity," as we have seen, is not a temporal concept but an ontological one, conveying, above all, the necessary or the absolutely non-arbitrary, nature of the eternal thing. Although half implicit in the propositions dealing with the third kind of knowledge, one can still maintain that it is in these propositions that the strange doctrine of God's – or nature's – necessity-as-freedom of EI becomes intelligible. Calling this necessity – the whole being's necessity – "freedom" induces the most positive affect. Instead of a feeling of helplessness and impotence, as one would expect, Spinoza speaks here of love. As an intellectual love, it is a kind of understanding. Saying of nature that it is absolutely free means that the philosopher's ultimate stance toward it is the understanding of its non-arbitrary nature.

This, however, is still too abstract. The philosophical stance vis-à-vis being is, in fact, an attitude toward existence or, more precisely still, before one's own bodily existence. The last two propositions of the doctrine of *Salus sive Beatitudo sive libertas*, propositions 39 and 40 of EV, bring all the elements of the previous discussions to conclusion: "perfection" and "reality" are equivalent notions. An equivalence emerges here between freedom, perfection, and reality: just as what is conceived as free affects us more, so do perfection and reality. The greater the quantity of reality of a thing, the greater is its perfection and the greater is its power to "affect the soul" (as is said in the preface to EIV). But perfection *cum* quantity of reality is not just an abstraction and a mode of comparing between things. It also refers to a concrete reality: the greater the aptness of a body to do things, the greater is the part of its soul that is eternal (EVp39); this eternal part of the soul is also more perfect than the rest of the soul (EVp40cor); the more perfect a thing is, the more active it is (EVp40); and activity is, by its very definition, equivalent to freedom: both signify existing by the necessity of one's own nature.

The hermeneutic key to this is a concept that Spinoza never uses explicitly. Activity, perfection, adequacy, understanding or intelligibility, and freedom above everything else define the philosopher's stance before his corporeal existence. Philosophical understanding also means the absolute non-indifference or, simply put, *value*, in which the Spinozistic philosopher holds existence, himself, and his body. The two moments of the final discussion of the *Ethics* – the subversive and polemic on the one hand, the positive on the other – sum up as a theory of reason demystified. If the eternal part of the soul is the eternal idea of the essence of the body, not much is left from what the tradition – mainly the Averroist tradition – had called the "active intellect." Since, moreover, God's eternal idea of the essence of the body is identical, or numerically one, with the individual soul, there is nothing in it that surpasses and transcends the idea-soul of the body. What is referred to as God's idea of the eternal essence of the body is nothing but the individual soul, or that which founds its very being. Insofar, however, as this semi-hidden foundation of the soul is also the body's one and only adequate idea, it is also where truth and reason reside or originate. Reason, as the stakes of the philosophical quest and as the utmost achievement of human life, is just the thinking of the body, as it is in itself and as it actually exists. It is grounded in the *hinc et nunc* of the body and has no transcendent source. Such a doctrine can indeed be considered as a radical demystification of reason.

But Spinoza's doctrine of the human soul is also, and precisely by means of the subversion, the polemics, and the demystification, a *positive* theory of the *importance, value, and justification* of reason and of philosophical life. It gives sense to such fundamental and irreducible human experiences as the experiences of understanding and knowledge, it justifies the feeling of freedom, it vindicates life and existence in general, and it pleads the cause of their irreducible importance and seriousness. It does all this by extracting, so to speak, from the experience of bodily life and of the sensing-thinking of one's own body, from the natural affectivity of life as it is grounded in corporeal existence, a thick philosophical meaning. It tries to show that there is no need to mystify all these experiences in order to hold them in the esteem and accord them value. The soul is the idea of the body; it is its thought and a silent understanding of one's own existence "in act," here and now. Like understating mathematical truth, and more significantly than it, the hidden understanding of one's own corporeality can become a concrete mode of life. What is understood in this way is that understanding is simply important or, to put it in other words, that philosophy is a serious matter. Propositions 21–40 thus crown, culminate, and consummate the philosophical journey in an attempt to show that what this journey leads to is the understanding of how this most prosaic and seemingly banal existence – bodily existence – is the origin, source, and justification of *value*, indeed of *absolute value*.

Instead of a Conclusion

Salus sive Beatitudo sive Libertas

Spinoza tried to strip the concept of "perfection" of its teleological and finalistic content. The theological and onto-theological elements traditionally associated with teleology are thus neutralized as well. Spinoza, however, retains one important aspect of the concept of "perfection." It mediates for him, just as it did for many of his mediaeval predecessors, the transformation of the concepts of "being" or "reality" into a source of semi-quantitative and, more importantly, evaluative principles. A thing can have more or less being, different things possess different quantities of reality, and they have, accordingly, different values. The amount of being a thing possesses is its amount of perfection and, most importantly, amount of worth. In a sense, it is the last element – the ethical – that conditions Spinoza's whole venture. Not only ontology is invested with a normative significance, but indeed the order of reasons is reversed, and the ethical motivation conditions the philosophical probing into the meaning of being. Philosophy is the handmaid of ethics, and ontology is fundamentally the theory of the value of being.

Spinoza's philosophy is often described as "materialism." The word "materialism" was, at first, a term of opprobrium, employed for blaming Spinozism of being a kind of moral and theological scandal. It later evolved into an instrument of rehabilitation and appropriation. The French *philosophes* first, and later a number of Russian writers during the communist era, considered Spinoza – albeit, of course, in very different ways – as a "materialist." In the second half of the twentieth century, and under the influence of Marxism (Althusser notably), of the so-called critical school and a few other such intellectual movements, materialistic approaches became again politically and ideologically desirable. Spinoza was extensively studied and written about by philosophers and scholars – notably French, but also German, Italian, and Spanish, among others – belonging to these trends, which, in itself, does not contradict the fact that in these writings on Spinoza remarkable scholarship was often displayed and fresh insights offered. From altogether different ideological perspectives, Spinoza is often considered to be a "naturalist" and his philosophy a kind of "naturalism." No less ambiguous than "materialism," "naturalism" usually refers to some kind of a presumed epistemological advantage of the knowledge gained by the natural sciences over allegedly dogmatic or metaphysical discourses. Naturalism is often understood as implying a mechanistic and materialistic, or rather physicalist, conception of things, suggesting that "matter" and the causal laws governing it have the principal role theoretically, above the "mental," "psychic," and so on, in understanding the structure of reality.

What is common to all these readings of Spinoza may conveniently be presented as an underlying suspiciousness toward "metaphysics," the "great narratives," the potential tyranny of "reason," and so on. There is certainly a strong subversive dimension in Spinoza's writings, and not only in the *Theological-Political Treatise*. It is usually directed against some generic, to some extent symbolic, "religion" conceived as a paradigm of prejudice, superstition, political control, and "bondage" or, more generally put, of irrationality. However, placing Spinoza on the side of systematic "suspicion" would be totally inaccurate. After all, reason and rationality are precisely what Spinoza's philosophy is all about. There is no room in Spinoza for any skepticism or relativism insofar as the pertinence and seriousness of metaphysics or – in the last analysis it amounts to the same thing – the validity of "reason" are concerned. But – and this is where materialism, naturalism, and so on do echo something authentically Spinozistic – reason, he seems to be saying to his readers, is not what you have been thinking, or told, it is. It is a matter of the absolute *hic et nunc*, it has no extra worldly source, and it is not the origin of authority or of a some exigency of obedience. Religion, as Spinoza explains in the TTP, is about obedience; philosophy is about understanding; and the necessity of reason is freedom and not obedience. In fact, the necessity of philosophical truth, which is also truth about how to conduct life and about what is the right thing to do and not to do, is freedom in the real sense of the word, and as such – as necessity – it is the exact opposite of obedience. This aspect of Spinoza's philosophy is, of course, a matter of more or less general agreement, and there is no need to elaborate on it further; what should be emphasized, however, is that the doctrine of the body as the immediate seat of reason is the main theoretical instrument by which Spinoza attempts a radical demystification of reason.

Overcoming the temptation to read Spinoza in light of latter-day ideas, particularly scientific, we see that soul and body play complementary, but symmetrically opposite, theoretic and strategic roles in his philosophy. Taking a step backward from the text and adopting for a moment a more hermeneutical attitude, it can be said that the two concepts, "soul" and "body," are two moments of a complex back-and-forth movement (or, if one prefers, dialectic) in which absolute valuableness, seriousness, and importance on the one hand and demystification and critical sobriety on the other condition and relativize each other. What Spinoza calls the eternity of the soul and the third kind of knowledge are the highest moments of the philosophical quest, and both are discussed by him from the point of view of thought, of the intellect and reason. But the constant reference to the body and its continuous presence in the second half of EV puts it all in perspective and supplies a demystifying thrust to the final moment of the *Ethics*. It is within this complex space that philosophical knowledge, activity, freedom, and perfection, indeed knowledge, activity and freedom *as* perfection, emerge as the crowning theme of the philosophical-ethical venture.

Ironically, Spinoza's *more geometrico* is often ambiguous and opaque. The name "Spinoza" has acquired over the years a symbolic charge whose origin is not always quite clear. These two features are at the origin of the constant temptation to read Spinoza in light of latter-day "materialism," "naturalism," "immanentism," or some other "ism." As far as they go, all these taxonomies are not altogether inaccurate. Spinoza is indeed a philosopher of the essentially *hic et nunc*, of liberation, and of sober rationality. But there are good reasons for deep reservations concerning all general classifications. In the last analysis Spinoza's philosophy is not assimilable to theories of historical, political, or sociological immanence; to critical or liberation theories; or indeed to any other doctrine of a common or intra-human *here and now*. Spinoza's *hic et nunc* is the *hic et nunc* of the individual body, of the private, one's own body. But precisely because of this, it is also irreducible to any naturalistic conception of the body, if by "naturalistic" one understands, as is usually the case, the scientist's general and "objective" – that is, external or third-person – view of the body. Spinoza's *bodily* here and now is the here and now of the corollary of EIIp13 that says, as we have seen more than once, that man is made of soul and body and, in particular, that "*Corpus humanum, prout ipsum sentimus, existere*" – one's own body exists as one senses it, or maybe thinks it,[1] to exist. But it is this immediately sensed, or thought, body that is salvaged, happy, and free. The last propositions of the *Ethics* contain, as Spinoza puts it, a doctrine of *Salus sive Beatitudo sive libertas*. This is Spinoza's final word. As an affair of the idea of the body, this last word is paradoxical to the point of being oxymoronic.

With this gesture a circle is closed. This circle sketches the lines along which the present study of Spinoza's *Ethics* progresses and that brings together two major moments of Spinoza's philosophy: the ontology of ideas and the doctrine of the soul being the idea of the body of the first thirteen propositions of EII; and the theory of *Salus sive Beatitudo sive Libertas* of the second part of EV. I suggested at the outset of this book that we consider Spinoza's philosophy as a philosophy of seriousness. The philosophical quest for understanding is a serious matter – in fact, the most serious matter there is. This seems to be the final word of Spinoza. This is so because the nature of what we call "soul" is to

---

[1] Neither thinks about it, nor feigns, or imagines, but "intellects" it.

understand; and the act of understanding, of intellecting, or of what the Latin calls *intellegere* is what gives sense to what we call "reason." But all this, and the seriousness it involves, stems from corporeal existence, nay, in some bizarre sense *it is* corporeal existence. It is also what constitutes or reveals its irreducible worth. Salvation, beatitude, and freedom is the philosophical understanding, knowledge, or intellecting of the body; or, to say it in a somewhat less dramatic way, it is the foundation of everything that is valuable, truthful, and important and where everything that is valuable, truthful, and important leads. This is, I suggest, the Spinozistic conundrum: is it possible to take seriously the idea that the soul is just an idea and, in particular, that its object is the body in the way in which the circle is the object of the idea of the circle? And can one take seriously Spinoza's doctrine of bodily salvation, beatitude, and freedom? Isn't it all just one big oxymoron? But then again, has anyone ever come closer to the formulation of a fully secular ethics of the absolute value, importance, and seriousness of the *hic et nunc*?

Works Cited

Spinoza'a works: Quotes from the *Ethics* are done according to the by-now standard way of indicating the work itself, then the part, the proposition, and, according to the case, the demonstration, corollary, scholium, and so on; thus EIIp7cor means: *Ethics*, part 2, proposition 7, corollary. The *Tractatus de Intellectus Emendatione* is referred to as TIE and is quoted according to the paragraph numbers as they are given in the Gebhardt edition. The *Short Treatise* is quoted according to part and chapter; the *Tractatus Theologico-Politicus* according to chapter, and page numbers are given according to the Gebhardt edition. Unless otherwise indicated, I used either Curley's or Shirley's translations (with occasional changes, always indicated in the text).

Editions used:

Spinoza Opera, Carl Gebhardt (ed.) 5 vols. Heidelberg: Carl Winters Verlag, 1925.
The Collected Works of Spinoza, 2 vols. translated by Edwin Curley, Princeton: Princeton University Press, vol. I, 1984; vol. II in preparation.
Spinoza. Complete Works, translated by Samuel Shirley, edited by Michael Morgan, Indianapolis: Hackett, 2002.

Amarasingam, Amarnath (ed.), *Religion and the New Atheism. A Critical Appraisal*, Leiden: Brill, 2010.
Arendt, Hannah, "What Is Freedom?" in: *Between Past and Present. Eight Exercises in Political Thought*, New York: Penguin Books, 1977, pp. 141–169.
Atlan, Henri, *The Sparks of Randomness*. Vol. 1, *Spermatic Knowledge*, 2011; vol. 2, *The Atheism of Scripture*, Eng. Tr. L. Schramm, Stanford: Stanford University Press, 2013.
Bayle, Pierre, *Pensées sur l'athéisme*, edited and presented by J. Boch, Paris: Editions Desjonquères, 2004.
Beiser, Frederick C., *The Fate or Reason: German Philosophy from Kant to Fichte*, Cambridge, Mass.: Harvard University Press, 1987.

Beiner, Ronald, *Civil Religion: A Dialogue in the History of Political Philosophy*, Cambridge: Cambridge University Press, 2011.
Belaval, Yvon, *Leibniz critique de Descartes*, Paris: Gallimard, 1960.
Bellah, Robert, and Tipton, Steven (eds.), *The Robert Bellah Reader*, Durham: Duke University Press, 2006.
  Religion in Human Evolution: From the Paleolithic to the Axial Age, Cambridge, Mass.: Harvard University Press, 2011.
Bennett, Jonathan, *A Study of Spinoza's Ethics*, Cambridge: Cambridge University Press, 1984.
Ben Shlomo, Yosef, *Etgar Ha'Spinozism* (in Hebrew: *The Challenge of Spinozism*), Jerusalem: Carmel, 2013.
Bidney, David, *The Psychology and Ethics of Spinoza: A Study in the History and Logic of Ideas*, New Haven: Yale University Press, 1940.
Bitbol-Hespériès, Annie, "La vie et les modèles mécaniques dans la médecine du dix-septième siècle", in: F. Monnoyeur (ed.), *Questions vitales. Vie biologique, vie psychique*, Paris: Kimé, 2009, pp. 47–81.
Blumenberg, H., *The Legitimacy of the Modern Age*, Cambridge, Mass.: MIT Press, 1983.
Bolduc, Carl, *Spinoza et l'approche éthique du problème de la libération: critique du théologico-politique*, Hildesheim: G. Olms, 2009.
Boring, Edwin G., *A History of Experimental Psychology*, New Jersey: Prentice-Hall, 1950.
Bourdin, Bernard, *The Theological-Political Origin of The Modern State: The Controversy between James I of England & Cardinal Bellarmine*. English translation by S. Pickford, Washington, D.C.: The Catholic University of America Press, 2010
Bove, L., Bras, G., Méchoulan, E., *Pascal et Spinoza. Pensées du contraste: de la géométrie du hasard à la nécessité de la liberté*, Paris: Editions Amsterdam, 2007.
Broughton, Janet, "Adequate Causes and Natural Change in Descartes' Philosophy," in: A. Donagan, A. N. Perovich, and M. V. Wedin (eds.), *Human Nature and Natural Knowledge. Essays Presented to Marjorie Grene on the Occasion of Her Seventy-Fifth Birthday*, Dordrecht: Reidel, 1986, 107–127.
Brunschvicg, Léon, *Spinoza et ses contemporains*, Paris: Presses Universitaires de France, 1951.
Canguilhem, George, *Le normal et le pathologique*, Paris: Presses universitaires de France, 1966.
Carraud, Vincent, *Causa sive ratio: La Raison de la cause de Suarez à Leibniz*, Paris: Presses universitaires de France, 2002.
Chalier, Catherine, *Spinoza lecteur de Maimonide: La question theologico-politique*, Paris: Cerf, 2006.
Chalmers, David J., *The Conscious Mind: In Search of a Fundamental Theory*, Oxford: Oxford University Press, 1996.
Charles-Daubert, Françoise, *Les libertins érudits en France au XVIIe siècle*, Paris: Presses Universitaires de France, 1998.
Courtine, J.-F., *Suarez et le système de la métaphysique*, Paris: Presses Universitaires de France, 1990.
  "Histoire et destin phénoménologique de l'*intentio*," in J.-F. Courtine, *La cause de la Phénoménologie*, Paris: Presses Universitaires de France, 2007, pp. 13–36

Cronin, Timothy J., *Objective Being in Descartes and Suarez*, Analecta Gregoriana, vol. 154, Roma: Gregorian University Press, 1966.
Curley, Edwin, "Spinoza's Exchange with Albert Burgh," in Yitzhak Y. Melamed, and Michael A. Rosenthal (eds.), *Spinoza's Theological-Political Treatise. A Critical Guide*, Cambridge: Cambridge University Press, 2010, pp. 11–28.
Cusset, Catherine (ed.), *Libertinage and modernity*, New Haven: Yale University Press, 1999.
Cusset, François, *French Theory: Foucault, Derrida, Deleuze, & Cie et les mutations de la vie intellectuelle aux États-Unis*, Paris: La Découverte, 2003.
Dalbiez, Roland, *Les sources scolastiques de la théorie Cartésienne de l'être objectif*, in: *Revue d'histoire de la philosophie*, 3 (1929), pp. 464–472.
Damasio, Antonio, *Looking for Spinoza: Joy, Sorrow and the Feeling Brain*, London: Vintage, 2003.
Danziger, Kurt, *Constructing the Subject: Historical Origins of Psychological Research*, Cambridge: Cambridge University Press, 1994.
Davidson, Herbert A., *Alfarabi, Avicenna and Averroes on Intellect: Their Cosmologies*, Oxford: Oxford University Press, 1992.
 "Gersonides on the Material and Active Intellect," in: G. Freudenthal (ed.), *Studies on Gersonides: A Fourteenth-Century Jewish Philosopher-Scientist*, Leiden: Brill, 1992, pp. 195–265.
Dawkins, Richard, *The God Delusion*, Boston and New York: The Marine Books, 2008.
Derabander, Firmin, *Spinoza and the Stoics. Power, Politic and the Passions*, New York: Continuum, 2007.
De Caro, M., and Macarthur, D. (eds.), *Naturalism and Normativity*, New York: Columbia University Press, 2010.
De Deugd, C. (ed.), *Spinoza's Political and Theological Thought: International Symposium under the Auspices of the Royal Netherlands Academy of Arts and Sciences. Commemorating the 350th Anniversary of the Birth of Spinoza Amsterdam, 24–27 November 1982*, Amsterdam: North Holland Publishing Company, 1984.
Delbos, Victor, *Le problème moral dans la philosophie de Spinoza et dans l'histoire du Spinozisme*, Hildesheim: Georg Olms, 1988.
Deleuze, Gilles, *Spinoza et le problème de l'expression*, Paris: Les éditions de Minuit, Paris, 1968.
 Spinoza, Philosophie pratique, Paris: Les éditions de Minuit, Paris, 1981.
De Libera, Alain, Thomas D'Aquin, *Contre Averroès. L'unité de l'intellect contre les averroïstes. Suivi des Textes contre Averroès antérieurs à 1270*, translation, introduction, and notes by A. de Libera, Paris: GF-Flammarion, 1994
 L'unité de l'intellect de Thomas d'Aquin. Commentaire du De unitate intellectus contra averroistas, Paris: Vrin, 2004.
 Archéologie du sujet, Vol. 1: *Naissance du sujet* (2007); Vol. 2: *La quête de l'identité* (2008), Paris: Vrin.
Della Rocca, M., *Representation and the Mind-Body Problem in Spinoza*, Oxford: Oxford University Press, 1996.
 Spinoza, London and New York: Routledge, 2008.
Dennet, Daniel C., *Consciousness Explained*, Boston: Little, Brown, 1991.

Darwin's Dangerous Idea – Evolution and the Meaning of Life, New York: Touchstone, 1995.

Desanti, Dominique et Jean-Toussaint, with Roger Paul-Droit, *La liberté nous aime encore*, Paris: Odile Jacob, 2001.

Desanti, Jean-Toussaint T., "Spinoza et la phénomélogie," in O. Bloch (ed.), *Spinoza au XX siècle*, Paris: Presses universitaires de France, 1993, pp. 113–127.

Descartes, René, *The Philosophical Writings of Descartes*, Eng. Tr. By J. Cottingham, R. Stoothhof, and D. Murdoch, 3 vols. Cambridge: Cambridge University Press, 1985.

De Vries, Hent, and Sullivan, Lawrence (eds.), *Political Theologies. Public Religion in a Post-Secular World*, New York: Fordham University Press, 2006.

Dobbs-Weinstein, "Gersonides' Radically Modern Understanding of the Agent Intellect," in: Stephen F. Brown (ed.), *Meeting of the Minds: The Relations Between Medieval and Classical Modern European Philosophy*, Begijnhof, Belgium: Brepols, 1998

"Maimonidean Aspects in Spinoza's Thought," in: *Graduate Faculty Philosophy Journal*, Vol. 17, Nos. 1&2 (1994): 153–174.

Donagan, A., Perovich, A. N., and Wedin, M. V. (eds.), *Human Nature and Natural Knowledge. Essays Presnted to Marjorie Grene on the Occasion of Her Seventy-Fifth Birthday*, Dordrechet: Reidel, 1986.

Donagan, Alan, "Spinoza's Theology," in Garrett (ed.) (1996).

Duff, Robert A., *Spinoza's Political and Ethical Philosophy*, Glasgow: J. Maclehose and Sons, 1903.

Dummett, M., *Origins of Analytical Philosophy*, Cambridge, Mass.: Harvard University Press, 1993.

Dunin-Borkowski, Stanislaus von, *Der junge Spinoza. Leben und Werdegangim im Lichte der Weltphilosophies*, Muenster: Aschendorf, 1912.

Dupéron, Isabelle, *T. Fechner. Le parallélisme psychophysiologique*, Paris: Presses universitaires de France, 2000.

Farrell, Frank B., *Subjectivity, Realism, and Postmodernism – The Recovery of the World*, Cambridge: Cambridge University Press, 1994.

Feldman, Seymor, "Gersonides on the Possibility of Conjunction with the Agent Intellect," in: *Association of Jewish Studies Review*, Vol. 3, No. (1978), pp. 99–120.

Foucault, Michel *Naissance de la Clinique. Une archéologie du regard médical*, Paris: Presses Universitaires de France, 1963.

Histoire de la folie à l'âge classique, Paris: Gallimard, 1972.

Flanagan, Owen, *The Problem of the Soul. Two Visions of Mind and How to Reconcile Them*, New York: Basic Books, 2002.

Frankel, Steven, "Politics and Rhetoric: The Intended Audience of Spinoza's 'Tractatus Theologico-Politicus'," in: *The Review of Metaphysics*, 52, 4 (June 1999), pp. 897–924.

"The Invention of Liberal Theology. Spinoza's Theological-Political Analysis of Moses and Jesus," in: *The Review of Politics*, 63, 2 (2001), pp. 287–315.

Garrett, Don (ed.), *The Cambridge Companion to Spinoza*, Cambridge: Cambridge University Press, 1996.

Gauchet, Marcel, *Le désenchantement du monde*, Paris: Gallimard, 1985).

Goetschel, Willi, *Spinoza's Modernity. Mendelssohn, Lessing, and Heine*, Madison, Wis.: The University of Wisconsin Press, 2004.
Grosholz, Emily R., *Cartesian Method and the Problem of Reduction*, Oxford: Clarendon Press, 1991.
Grosholz, Emily R. and Yakira, Elhanan, *Leibniz's Science of the Rational*, Stuttgart: Franz Steiner Verlag, 1998 (Studia Leibnitiana Sonderheft 26).
Gueroult, Martial, *Spinoza*, Vol.: I – *Dieu*, 1968; Vol. II – *L'âme*, 1974, Paris: Aubier.
  Dianoématique, Book I: *Histoire de l'histoire de la philosophie*; Vol. 1: *En Occident, des origines jusqu'à Condillac*, 1984; Vol. 2: *En Allemagne, de Leibniz à nos jours*, 1988; Vol. 3: *En France, de Condorcet à nos jours*, 1988; Book II: *Philosophie de l'histoire de la philosophie*, 1979, Paris: Aubier.
Gullan-Whur, Margaret, *Within Reason. A Life of Spinoza*, London: Jonathan Cape, 1998.
Halbertal, Moshe, *People of the Book. Canon, Meaning, and Authority*, Cambridge, Mass.: Harvard University Press, 1997.
Hallett, Harold F., *Aeternitas*, Oxford: Clarendon Press, 1930.
  "On a Reputed Equivoque in the Philosophy of Spinoza," in Kasahp (1972) pp. 168–188.
  Creation, Emanation and Salvation, The Hague: Martinus Nijhoff, 1962.
Hammelin, Octave, *La théorie de l'intellect d'après Aristote et ses commentataeurs*, Paris: Vrin, 1953.
Harris, Errol E., *Spinoza's Philosophy. An Outline*, Amherst: Humanity Books, 1993.
Harvey, Warren Zev, "A Portrait of Spinoza as a Maimonidean," in: *Journal of the History of Philosophy*, 19, 2 (1981), pp. 151–171.
  "Maimonidean Aspects in Spinoza's Thought," in: *Graduate Faculty Philosophy Journal*, 17 (1994), pp. 153–174.
  Rabbi Hesdai Kreskas (in Hebrew), Jerusalem: The Jalman Shazar Center, 2010.
  "Spinoza on Ibn Ezra's 'Secret of the Twelve'," in: Melamed and Rosental (eds.) (2010), pp. 41–55.
Hazard, Paul, *La crise de la conscience européenne, 1680–1715*, Paris: Boivin et Cie, 1935).
Heidelberger, M. Michael, *Nature from Within. G. Th. Fecner and his Psychophysical Worldview*, Pittsburgh: University of Pittsburgh Press, 2004.
Hessing, Siegfried, "Prologue with Spinozana – Parallels via East and West," in S. Hessing (ed.), *speculum spinozanum 1677–1977*, London: Routledge & Kegan Paul, 1977, pp. 1–62.
Hight, Marc A., *Idea and Ontology. An Essay in Early Modern Metaphysics of Ideas*, University Park, Penn.: The Pennsylvania State University Press, 2008.
Hitchens, Christopher, *God Is Not Great. How Religion Poisons Everything*, New York: Hachette Book Group, 2007.
Israel, Jonathan, *Radical Enlightenment: Philosophy and the Making of Modernity 1650–1750*, Oxford: Oxford University Press, 2002.
  Enlightenment Contested: Philosophy, Modernity, and the Emancipation of Man 1670–1752, Oxford: Oxford University Press, 2006.
  A Revolution of the Mind: Radical Enlightenment and the Intellectual Origins of Modern Democracy, Princeton: Princeton University Press, 2010.

Jaquet, Chantal, *Sub specie aeternitatis. Etude des concepts de temps, durée, et éternité chez Spinoza*, Paris: Kimé, 1997.
   L'unité du corps et de l'esprit. Affects, actions et passions chez Spinoza, Paris: Presses Universitaires de France, 2004.
James Susan, *Spinoza on Philosophy, Religion and Politics: the Theologico-Political Treatise*, Oxford: Oxford University Press, 2012.
James, William, *The Varieties of Religious Experience. A Study of Human Nature*, Digireads.com, 2004
Joachim, Harold A., *A Study of the Ethics of Spinoza*, Oxford: Oxford University Press, 1901.
   Spinoza's Tractatus de Intellectus Emendatione, Oxford: Clarendon Press, 1940.
Jöel, Manuel, *Spinoza's Theologisch-politischer Traktat auf seine Quellen geprüft*, Breslau: H. Skutech, 1870.
Jolley, Nicholas., *The Light of the Soul. Theories of Ideas in Leibniz, Malberanche, and Descartes*, Oxford: Clarendon Press, 1990.
Jonas, Hans, "Spinoza and the Theory of Organism", in: M. Grene (ed.), *Spinoza. A Collection of Critical Essays*, Notre Dame, Indiana: University of Notre Dame Press, 1973, pp. 259–278.
Kaplan, Yosef, *From Christianity to Judaism: the Story of Isaac Orobio de Castro*, translated from the Hebrew by R. Loewe, Oxford: Oxford University Press, 1989.
Kashap, Paul (ed.), *Studies in Spinoza. Critical and Interpretive Essays*, Berkeley: University of California Press, 1972.
Kojève, Alexandre, *L'athéisme*, translated from the Russian by N. Ivanoff, L. Bibard (ed.), Paris: Gallimard, 1998.
Klassen, Justin D., *The Paradox of Hope. Theology and the Problem of Nihilism*, Eugene, Oregon: Cascade Books, 2011.
Kolakowsky, Leszek, *Chrétiens sans Église: La conscience religieuse et le lien confessionnel au 17e siècle*, translated from the Polish by A. Posner, P aris: Gallimard, 1969.
Koyré, Alexandre, "Le chien, constellation céleste, et le chien, animal aboyant," in: *Revue de Métaphysique et de Morale*, 55, 1 (1950) pp. 50–59.
Kusch, Martin, *Psychologism. A Case Study in the Sociology of Philosophical Knowledge*, London: Routledge, 1995.
Lagrée, Jacqueline and Moreau, Pierre-François, *Louis Meyer, La philosophie interprète de l'écriture Sainte*, traduction, notes et présentation, Paris: Intertextes éditeur, 1988. *Ad captum auditoris loqui: theology and tolerance in Lodewijk Meyer and Spinoza*, Delft: Eburn, 2001.
   Spinoza et le débat religieux. Lectures du Traité théologico-politique, Rennes: Presses Universitaires de Rennes, 2004.
Langermann, Tsvi. Y, "Maimonides and miracles: The growth of a (dis)belief," in: *Jewish History* 18: 2004, pp. 147–172
LeBuffe, Michael, *From Bondage to Freedom. Spinoza on Human Excellence*, Oxford and New York: Oxford University Press, 2010.
Levy, Lia, *L'automate spritiuel. La naissance de la subjectivité moderne d'après l'Ethique de Spinoza*, Assen: Van Gorcum, 2000.
Lila, Mark, *The Stillborn God. Religion, Politics, and the Modern West*, New York: Knopf, 2007.
Livet, Pierre, *Les norms*, Paris: Armand Colin, 2006.

Lloyd, Genevieve, *Spinoza and the Ethics*, London: Routledge, 1996.
Spinoza: Critical Assessments (in four volumes), London: Routledge, 2001.
Macherey, Pierre, *Hegel ou Spinoza*, Paris: Maspero, 1979.
  Avec Spinoza. Etudes sur la doctrine et l'histoire du Spinozisme, Paris: Presses Universitaires de France, 1992.
  Introduction à l'Ethique de Spinoza, Paris: Presses Universitaires de France in five volumes: I. *La nature des choses* (1998); II. *La réalité mentale* (1997); III. *La vie affective* (1995); IV. *La condition humaine* (1997); V. *Les voies de la libération* (1994).
  De Canguilhem à Foucault. La force des normes, Paris: La Fabrique, 2009.
MacIntosh, J. J. (ed.), *Boyle on Atheism*, Toronto: University of Toronto Press, 2005.
Macintyre, Alasdair, "The Debate about God" in Alasdair Macintyre and Paul Ricoeur, *The Religious Significance of Atheism*, New York: Columbia University Press, 1969, pp. 1-55.
Manzini, Frédéric (ed.), *Spinoza et ses scolastiques. Retour aux sources et nouveaux enjeux*, Paris: Presses de l'université Paris-Sorbonne, 2011.
Marion, Jean-Luc, "Aporias and the Origin of Spinoza's Theory of Adequate Ideas," in Segal and Yovel (1994), pp. 129-158.
Martin, Michael (ed.), *The Cambridge Companion to Atheism*, Cambridge: Cambridge University Press, 2007.
Mason, Richard, *The God of Spinoza. A Philosophical Study*, Cambridge: Cambridge University Press, 1997.
  "Intelligibility: The Basic Premise?," in *Iyyun: The Jerusalem Philosophical Quarterly*, 50 (July 2001), pp. 229-244.
Matheron, Alexandre. *Individu et communauté chez Spinoza*, Paris: Minuit, 1969.
  Le Christ et le salut des ignorants chez Spinoza, Paris: Aubier-Montaigne, 1971.
  "Spinoza and the Euclidean Arithmetic: The example of the Fourth proportional," in M. Greene and D. Nails (eds.), *Spinoza and the Sciences*, Berlin: Springer, 1986, pp. 125-149.
  "Le moment stoïcien de l'Ethique de Spinoza," in: P.-F. Moreau (ed.) *Le Stoïcisme aux XVI et XVII siècles. Le retour des philosophies antiques à l'âge classique* vol. I, Paris: Albin Michel, 1999, pp. 302-316.
  "Ideas of Ideas and Certainty in the *Tractatus de Intellectus Emendationes*," in Yovel (ed.) (1994), pp. 83-91.
Méchoulan, Henry, "Hébreux, juifs et phaisiens dans le Traité théologico-politique," in: Emilia Giancotti Boscherini (ed.), *Spinoza nel 350 anniversero della nascita (proceedings of the First Italian International Congress on Spinoza, Urbino, October 4-8, 1982)*, Naples: Bibliopolis, 1985.
  Être Juif à Amsterdam au temps de Spinoza, Paris: Albin Michel, 1991.
  Le droit et le sacré chez Spinoza, Paris: Berg International, 2013.
Meinsma, Karl O., *Spinoza et son cercle: étude critique historique sur les hétérodoxes hollandais*, translated and edited by R. Roosenburg and J.-P. Osier, Paris: Vrin, 1983.
Melamed, Yitzhak Y., and Rosenthal, Michael A. (eds.), *Spinoza's Theological-Political Treatise. A Critical Guide*, Cambridge: Cambridge University Press, 2010.
Merlan, Philip, *Monopsychism, Mysticism, Metaconciousness. Problems of the Soul in the Neoaristotelian and Neoplatonic Tradition*, The Hague: Martinus Nijhof, 1963.

Merleau-Ponty, Maurice, *L'union de l'âme et du corps chez Malberanch, Biran et Bergson*, Paris: Vrin, 1978.
Milner, Jean-Claude, *Le sage trompeur. Libres raisonnements sur Spinoza et les Juifs*, Paris: Verdier, 2013.
Minois, Georges, *Histoire de l'athéisme. Les incroyants dans le monde occidental des origines à nos jours*, Paris: Fayard, 1998.
Montag, Warren, and Stolze, Ted (eds.), *The New Spinoza*, Minneapolis: University of Minnesota Press, 1997.
Montag, Warren, *Bodies, Masses, Power. Spinoza and His Contemporaries*, London and New York: Verso, 1999.
Moreau, Denis, *Deux Cartésians. La polémique Arnauld Malebranche*, Paris: Vrin, 1999.
Moreau, Pierre-Francois, *Spinoza. L'expérience et l'éternité*, Paris: Presses Universitaires de France, 1994.
Spinoza. État et religion, Paris, ENS Éditions, 2005.
Naaman-Zauderer, Noa, *Descartes' Deontological Turn. Reason, Will, and Virtue in the Later Writings*, Cambridge: Cambridge University Press, 2010.
Nadler, Steven M., *Arnauld and the Cartesian Philosophy of Ideas*, Manchester: Manchester University Press, 1989.
Malebranche and Ideas, Oxford: Oxford University Press, 1992.
Spinoza: A Life, Cambridge: Cambridge University Press, 1999.
Spinoza's Heresy. Immortality and the Jewish Mind, Oxford: Oxford University Press, 2002.
"The Jewish Spinoza," in: *The Journal of the History of Ideas*, 70, 3 (July 2009), pp. 491–510.
A Book Forged in Hell. Spinoza's Scandalous Treatise and the Birth of the Secular Age, Princeton: Princeton University Press, 2011.
Negri, Antonio, *The Savage Anomaly. The Power of Spinoza's Metaphysics and Politics*, Eng. Tr. by Michael Hardt, Minneapolis and Oxford: University of Minnesota Press, 1991.
"Reliqua Desiderantur: A Conjecture for a Definition of the Concept of Democracy in the Final Spinoza," in: Montag and Stolze (eds.) (1997), pp. 219–247.
Nelson, Eric, *The Hebrew Republic: Jewish Sources and the Transformation of European Political Thought*, Cambridge, Mass.: Harvard University Press, 2010.
Niewöhner, Friedrich W. "Die Religion Noahs bei Uriel da Costa und Baruch de Spinoza: Eine historische Miniatur zur Genese des Deismus," in: De Deugd (ed.) (1984), pp. 143–149.
Normore, Calvin, 1986, "Meaning and Objective Being: Descartes and His Sources," in: Rorty (ed.) (1986), pp. 223–241.
Nussbaum, Martha C., *Upheavals of Thought. The Intelligence of Emotions*, Cambridge: Cambridge University Press, 1993.
Otto, Rudolf, *The Idea of the Holly. An Inquiry into the Non-Rational Factor in the Idea of the Divine and its Relation to the Rational*, Oxford: Oxford University Press, 1958
Panes, Joshua, *Maimonides and Spinoza. Their Conflicting Views of Human Nature*, Chicago: The University of Chicago Press, 2012.
Parkinson, G. H. R., "Spinoza and British Idealism: The case of H.H. Joachim," in: *The British Journal for the History of Philosophy* 1 (1993), pp. 109–123

Parrochia, Daniel, "Physique pendulaire et modèles de l'ordre dans l'Ethique de Spinoza," in: *Cahiers Spinoza* 5 (1985), pp. 71–92.
Petit, P., and McDowell, J. (eds.), *Subject, Thought, and Context*, Oxford: Clarendon Press, 1986.
Pietersma, Henry, "Merleau-Ponty and Spinoza," in: *International Studies in Philosophy*, 20, 3 (1988), pp. 89–93.
Pines, Shlomo, *Moses Maimonides, The Guide of the Perplexed*, translation and introduction, Chicago: University of Chicago Press, 1968.
  "Spinoza's *Tractatus Theologico-Politicus*, Maimonides and Kant," in: *Scripta Hierosolymitana*, 20, 1998, pp. 3–54.
Pintard, René, *Le libertinage érudit dans la première moitié du XVIIe siècle*, Paris: Boivin, 1943.
Preus, Samuel J., *Spinoza and the Irrelevance of Biblical Authority*, Cambridge: Cambridge University Press, 2001.
Radner, Daisie, "Descartes' Notion of the Union of Mind and Body," in: *The Journal of the History of Philosophy*, 9 (1971), pp. 159–170.
Ravven, H., and Goodman, L. (eds.), *Jewish Themes in Spinoza's Philosophy*, Albany: State University of New York Press, 2002.
Rescher, Nicholas., *The Coherence Theory of Truth*, Oxford: Oxford University Press, 1973.
Ricoeur, Paul., *Soi-même comme un autre*, Paris: Seuil, 1990.
Rivaud, Albert, *Les notions d'essence et d'existence dans la philosophie de Spinoza*, Paris: Alcan, 1906.
Rodis-Lewis, Geneviève, *L'oeuvre de Descartesm* Paris: Vrin, 1971.
  Idées et vérités éternelles chez Descartes et ses successeurs, Paris: Vrin, 1985.
Rorty-Oksenberg, Amelie (ed.), *Essays on Descartes' Meditations*, Berkley, Los Angeles, and London: University of California Press. 1986.
Rosenthal, Michael, "Spinoza's Dogmas of the Universal Faith and the Problem of Religion," in: *Philosophy and Theology*, 13, 1 (2001), pp. 53–82.
Rousset, Bernard, *La perspective finale de l'Ethique et le problème de la cohérence du spinozisme. L'autonomie comme salut*, Paris: Vrin, 1968.
Schmaltz, Ted, "Deflating Descartes' Causal Axiom," in: *Oxford Studies in Early Modern Philosophy*, 3 (2006), pp. 1–31.
Schmidt-Biggermann, W, *Theodizee und Tatsachen – Das philosophische Profil der deutschen Aufklärung*, Frankfurt: Suhrkamp Verlag, 1998.
Schwartz, Daniel B., *The First Modern Jew: Spinoza and the History of an Image*, Princeton: Princeton University Press, 2012.
Schwarzschild, Steven S., "Do Noachites Have to Believe in Revelation? (A Passage in Dispute between Maimonides, Spinoza, Mendelssohn, and H. Cohen). A Contribution to the Jewish View of Natural Law: The Textual Question," in: M. Kelner (ed.), *The Pursuit of the Ideal. Jewish Writings of Steven Schwarzschild*, New York: SUNY Press, 1990, pp. 29–60.
Segal, G., and Yovel, Y. (eds), *Spinoza on Knowledge and the Human Mind (the 2nd Jerusalem Conference – Etica II)*, Leiden: Brill, 1994.
Serres, Michel, *Le système de Leibniz et ses modèles mathématiques* (two volumes), Paris: Presses Universitaires de France, 1968
Smith, Steven B., *Spinoza's Book of Life: Freedom and Redemption in the Ethics*, New Haven: Yale University Press, 2003.

Steenbakkers, Piet, "The Text of Spinoza's *Tractatus Theologico-politicus*", in: Y. Melamed & M. Rosenthal (eds.) 2010, pp. 29–40.

Stewart, Matthew, *The Courtier and the Heretic. Leibniz, Spinoza, and the Fate of God in the Modern World*, New York: W.W. Norton & Company, 2006.

Strauss, Leo, *Spinoza's Critique of Religion*, New York: Schoken Books, 1965.

"How to Read Spinoza's *Theologico-Political Treatise?*," in: *Persecution and the Art of Writing*, Chicago: Chicago University Press, 1988, pp. 142–202.

Taylor, Charles, *Sources of the Self – The Origins of the Modern Identity*, Cambridge: Cambridge University Press, 1993.

A Secular Age, Cambridge, Mass.: Harvard University Press, 2007.

Toulmin, Stephen, *Cosmopolis, The Hidden Agenda of Modenity*, New York: The Free Press, 1990.

Touraine, Alain, *Critique de la modernié*, Paris: Fayard, 1992.

Tugendhat, Ernst, *Self-consciousness and Self-determination*, translated by P. Stern, Cambridge, Mass.: MIT Press, 1986.

Van Bunge, W., Krop, H., Steenbakkers, P., and van de Ven, Jerom (eds.), *The Continuum Companion to Spinoza*, London: Continuum, 2011.

Verbeek, Theo, *Spinoza's Theologico-Political Treatise. Exploring the Will of God*, Hampshire, UK: Ashgate, 2003.

"Spinoza et la tradition scolastique des *Secondes Analytiques*," in: Manzini (ed.) (2011), pp. 115–134.

Vernière, Paul, *Spinoza et la pensée française avant la révolution*, Paris: Presses Universitaires de France, 1954.

Vinciguerra, Lorenzo, *Spinoza et le signe. La genèse de l'imagination*, Paris: Vrin, 2005.

Vyverberg, H., *Historical Pessimism in the French Enlightenment*, Cambridge, Mass.: Harvard University Press, 1958.

Watson, Richard A., *Representational Ideas, from Plato to Patricia Churchland*, Dordrecht: Kluwer Academic Publishers, 1995.

Wetlesen, Jon, *The Sage and the Way*, Assen: Van Gorcum, 1979.

Wolfson, Harry A., *The Philosophy of Spinoza. Unfolding the Latent Proccesses of his Thought*, (2 vols.), New York: Schocken Books, 1969.

Yakira, E., *Contrainte, nécessité, choix. La métaphysique de la liberté chez Spinoza et chez Leibniz*, Zurich: Editions du Grand Midi, 1989.

"What Is a Mathematical Truth?," in E. Curley, A. Heinekamp, and M. Walther (eds.), *Studia Spinozana*, 6 (1990): *Spinoza and Leibniz*, pp. 73–101.

"Ideas of Nonexistent Modes: *Ethics* II Proposition 8, its Corollary and Scholium," in: Yovel (ed.), 1994.

"Leo Strauss and Baruch Spinoza: Remarks in the Margins of Strauss' Timely Reflections," in Nadler, S. Walther, M. and Yakira, E. (eds.), *Studia Spinozan* 13 (1997): *Spinoza and Jewish Identity*, pp. 161–182.

"Spinoza et le problème de l'intentionnalité," in *Philosophiques*, 29, 1 (2001), pp. 139–146.

"Is the Rational Man Free?," in Y. Yovel and G. Segal (eds.), *Spinoza on Reason and the "Free Man,"* New York: Little Room Press, 2004.

Yolton, John W, *Perception and Reality, A History from Descartes to Kant*, Ithaca and London: Cornell University Press, 1996.

Yovel, Yirmiyahu, *Spinoza and Other Heretics* (2 vols.), Princeton: Princeton University Press, 1992.
Yovel, Y. (ed.) *Spinoza on Knowledge and the Human Mind*, Leiden: Brill, 1994.
Zac, Sylvian, *Spinoza et l'interprétation de l'Ecriture*, Paris: Presses Universitaires de France, 1965.
   Philosophie, théologie, politique dans l'œuvre de Spinoza, Paris: Vrin, 1970.
Zarka, Yves-Charles, "First Philosophy and the Foundation of Knowledge," in T. Sorell (ed.), *The Cambridge Companion to Hobbes*, Cambridge: Cambridge University Press, 1996.

Index

affect, 42, 60, 161, 170, 182, 239, 244, 245, 246, 248, 258n27, 262, 263
affirmatism, 244
anthropomorphism, 237, 243
Aquinas, Thomas, 80, 194n7
Arendt, Hannah, 22n36
Aristotle, 30, 36n68, 77, 78, 79n11, 103, 114, 156, 194, 197n13, 204n19, 241
Arnauld and Nicole, 114
Arnauld, Antoine, 114, 128, 128n32, 136, 171, 194n8
Aron, Raymond, 10
Atheism, 7, 8
Atlan, Henri, 64n11, 73n2, 190
authority, 39
Averroes, 5, 75n6, 77n9, 86n21
  Averroism, 78–83
  Averroist, 61, 74, 91

Bayle, Pierre, 5, 11
beatitude, 4, 6, 9, 42, 43, 47n82, 49, 54, 55, 59, 83, 175, 180, 185, 186, 192, 222, 224, 228–235, 239, 255, 257, 258, 259, 261, 268
Beiner, Ronald, 10
Bella, Robert, 10
Ben Shlomo, Yossef, xivn8, 142n48, 189, 190, 225n5
Bennett, Jonathan, 6n7, 61n5, 235
Berkeley, George, 171
Berlin, Isaiah, 246
Blumenberg, Hans, 10n21, 14, 15
Blyenbergh, Willem van, 45, 236, 249–252, 259

Boyle, Robert, 11, 155n56
Brentano, Franz, 80, 81, 181, 183n17
Brunschvicg, Léon, 90
Buldoc, Carl, 73n2
Burgh, Alfred, 202

Canguilhem, George, 45, 46, 191n4
causa sive ratio, 103, 105, 236
Chalier, Catherine, 25n40, 27, 33
Cicero, 241
Cogitata Metaphysica, 137, 138n44, 249, 251
Cogito, 57, 63, 89, 97, 101, 115
Cohen, Herman, 5n3, 30
common notions, 170, 215, 217, 232, 244
compatibilism, 242
conatus, 48, 103, 156, 173n9, 229, 230, 234, 255n24, 258n27
Courtine, Jean François, 127n31, 128n33, 183n17
creation, 39, 238n15
Crescas, Hisdai, 241, 242
Curley, Edwin, 6n7, 24n38, 28n49, 122n27, 138n44, 170n3, 174n11, 254n23

Damasio, Antonio, 53n1, 64n11, 176, 190, 257n26
de Libera, Alain, 79, 80, 82, 86n21
Deleuze, Gilles, 44, 45, 49n84, 58, 61n6, 113n21, 114n21, 140, 141, 191, 201n18, 236n14, 249n20, 252
Della Rocca, Michael, 61n5, 121n26, 208n22
Desanti, Jean-Toussaint, xiiin6, 176

Index

Descartes, ixn1, 4, 11, 47, 55–76, 80, 81n18, 82, 84, 88–90, 97, 100, 103, 115, 116, 123–140, 142, 148, 150–152, 161, 177n16, 178, 181, 194, 197, 202–210, 223, 232, 245, 249, 254n23
  Cartesian, 54, 55, 57, 95
determinism, 85, 97, 100, 222, 240–245, 249, 250, 251
Deus sive Natura, 236
Doobs-Weinstein, Idit, 76n7
Dortous de Mairan, 182
Dunin-Borkowski, Stanislaw, 73n2, 189
Duns Scotus, 128n33

Einstein, Albert, 176
Epicure, 5
eternity, 47, 219–222, 227, 231, 234, 245, 263
eudaimonia, eudamonistic, 191

Fechner, Gustav, 64–71
Foucault, Michel, 45
free will, 31, 85, 97, 210, 240–243, 249, 251
Freud, Sigmund, 176

Galileo Galilei, 11, 81n18, 130n36
Gauchet, Marcel, 10n19
Grosholz, Emily, xiii, 88n25, 89n28, 115n23, 208n22
Gueroult, Martial, ixn1, 58, 79n13, 138n44, 151n55, 157, 157n58, 194n7, 225n5

Hallett, Harold F., 58, 102n9, 140n47, 141, 177, 178, 195n10, 201n18, 220n1, 225n5, 230n8
Harvey, Zeev, 26n45, 32, 33n61, 35, 241n16
Hazard, Paul, 10
Hobbes, Thomas, 3, 5, 8n14, 9–11, 22, 25, 82, 108
Husserl, Edmund, 71n22, 81, 147, 181, 183, 184

idea ideae, 88, 144, 172, 173, 203
idea-ideatum, 117–126, 145, 147, 148, 152, 154, 155, 159, 162, 183–184, 195n8, 196, 209, 228
idle argument, 241
individuality, 54, 80, 94, 118, 119, 125, 152, 155–157, 168, 169, 196, 256
inesse, 214
intentionality, 81, 137, 180, 183, 184, 190
involvere, 105–115, 169, 170, 199, 214, 216, 217

Israel, Jonathan, xivn8, 5, 24n38, 35, 35n66

Jacquet, Chantal, 58, 220n1
James, Susan, 17n28, 23n37, 28n49, 28n50, 32n60, 38n71, 46n82
James, William, 42
Jaquet, Chantal, 49n84, 102n10, 189
Joachim, Harold, A., 189, 190, 195n10
Jonas, Hans, 68n17

Kant, Emmanuel, 36, 43, 88n25, 112n20, 114, 115, 130, 136, 178, 181, 227, 232, 240, 242, 245, 255n24
Kaplan, Yossef, 5n3
Kojève, Alexandre, 7

Lagrée, Jacquline, 5n3, 26n42, 28, 35n66, 46n82
Leibniz, Gottfried Wilhelm, ixn1, xiin3, 11, 22, 36, 56, 58, 61–66, 70n20, 72, 74–76, 80, 82, 99, 103n11, 113–116, 128, 129, 137, 144, 146n51, 149, 153, 156–163, 174, 182, 196, 197, 207–208, 208n22, 214, 215n27, 232, 238n15, 241–243
Levinas, Emanuel, 5n3
Lloyd, Genevieve, 58, 177n16, 189, 225n5
Locke, John, 11, 82, 128n32, 136, 171, 181, 182

Macherey, Pierre, 45, 49n84, 58, 61n6, 124n28, 173n8, 204n19, 210n25, 225n5, 235n12
Machiavelli, Nicolo, 9, 10
Maimonides, 27, 29–36, 73, 74, 77–78, 86n21, 255, 256
Malebranche, Nicolas, 58, 60, 63, 66, 128, 135n42, 136, 171, 177n16, 181, 182
Marion, Jean-Luc, 195n8
Matheron, Alexandre, xiiin4, 28n49, 46n82, 146n51, 172n5, 192n5, 226n6
Méchoulan, Henry, 5n3
Meinsma, 5n3
Mendelssohn, Moses, 30
Merleau-Ponty, Maurice, 60, 63, 63n10, 176–180
Mignini, Filippo, 142n48, 225n5
Milner, Jean-Claude, 5n3
minimal credo, 28, 29
miracles, 24n38, 32–36, 39, 246
Moreau, Pierre-François, xiiin4, 5n3, 12n25, 20n34, 89n27, 99n5, 128n32, 235n13
mysterium tremendum, 41

Index

Naaman-Zauderer, Noa, 130n35
Nadler, Steven, 5n3, 11n23, 26n42, 33n61, 35n66, 128n32, 220n1, 256
necessitarism, 91, 99, 100, 222, 243, 251
Negri, Antonio, 7
Nelson, Eric, 18n30, 26
New Testament, 27
Newton, Isaac, 11
Noachite Commandments, 29
noema and noesis, 183
noetic, noétique, 75–78, 83, 85, 86, 91, 95–97, 167, 171, 175, 179, 181, 190, 193, 199, 207, 211, 213, 217, 218, 228, 229, 258–262
Normativity, 45
numinous, 40
Nussbaum, Martha, 190, 191n3

objective-formal being, objective reality, 106n14, 111, 126–131, 134–144, 149–163, 183, 192, 199, 212
Ockham, William of, 128n33
Oldenburg, 7, 11
Otto, Rudolf, xii, 39–42

pain, 160
panpsychism, 75, 78, 119
Pascal, Blaise, 8, 10, 11, 43, 90
Pascal's wager, 43
Peter Auriole, 128n33
Pines, Shlomo, 33, 73n3, 78n9
Political Treatise, 15, 16, 20, 21, 33, 266
political-theology, 27
Preus, Samuel, 25, 26
principle of reason, 36, 99, 208
Principles of Cartesian Philosophy, 249
prophecy, 39
providence, 39

Reid, Thomas, 128n32, 136, 171, 182
religiosity, xivn8, 4, 5, 16, 39, 235n13
representation, 61, 64, 71, 113, 127–129, 136, 137, 142, 146, 148, 151, 153, 154, 159, 160, 161, 171, 177, 180–184, 190, 200, 206
République des lettres, 3, 11
res cogitans, 100, 133, 206
revelation, 23, 39, 192
Rodis-Lewis, Geneviève, 172n7, 221n2
Rorty, Emily, 190
Rousseau, Jean-Jaques, 10, 21
Rousset, Bernard, 46n82, 106n14, 142n48, 144n50, 220n1, 225n5

salus, sive beatitudo, sive libertas, 4, 49
salvation, 4, 6, 9, 12, 22, 24, 28, 29n53, 35, 42, 43, 49, 59, 83, 175, 180, 185, 186, 192n5, 219, 222, 232, 254, 258, 259, 260, 261, 268
Schmitt, Carl, 14, 18n31
seriousness, 28, 42–48, 191, 192, 250, 260, 264, 266, 267
Serres, Michel, 208
Short Treatise, xivn8, 12, 13, 141, 203, 208, 209n23, 224, 225
Stoicism, Stoic, 19n33, 46n82, 47, 48, 190–192
stoic-medical moment, 46–47, 190, 219
Strauss, Leo, 5, 33, 33n65, 37, 255
sub specie aeternitatis, 47, 107, 155, 180, 191, 192, 212, 224, 231–233, 235, 258
subjectivity, 156

theocracy, 9, 17, 19, 36, 39
theodicy, 242, 250
theology, 4, 12n25, 16, 18n31, 19–29, 33n61, 34, 37, 39, 43, 48, 83, 97, 127, 130n36, 241, 256
Tractatua Politicus, 17–23
Tractatus de Intellectus Emendatione, xivn8, 4n2, 8, 12, 43, 53n1, 54n1, 87–90, 93, 94, 106, 107–111, 138, 142–147, 172, 176, 193, 195n10, 196, 198, 199, 201, 202, 208, 209, 210, 225, 225n5, 227
Tractatus Theologico-Politicus 5, 7, 9, 11, 16–19
Tschirnhaus, 107n16, 109, 151n55, 193, 200

universal religion, 27, 28, 28n49, 31

value, 3, 9, 13, 21, 29, 34, 35, 37, 41, 44, 46, 47, 48, 49n84, 58, 61, 75n6, 131, 146n51, 154, 159, 185, 191n3, 192, 193, 215, 219, 240, 244, 245, 251, 257, 260, 262, 263, 264, 265, 268
Verbeek, Theo, 16n27, 17n28, 28n49, 197n13
Vinciguerra, Lorenzo, 53n1
Voegelin, Eric, 10

way of ideas, 136, 171
Weber, Max, 8n14, 10, 15
Wittgenstein, Ludwig, 181
Wolfson, Harry A., 72, 73, 74, 84, 194

Yovel, Yirmiyahu, xiii, 5n3